# The Whole Learning Catalog

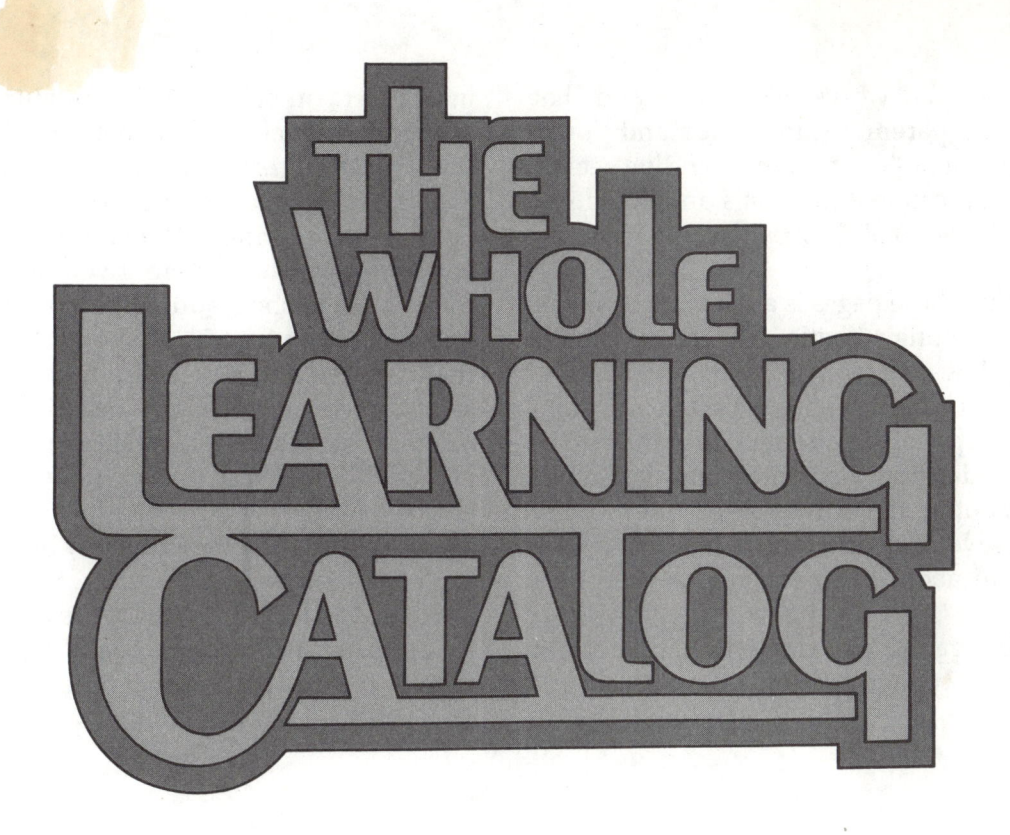

Edited by Bruce Raskin
Designed by Mike Shenon

Education Today Company, Inc.
530 University Avenue
Palo Alto, California 94301

# FOREWORD

Almost everyone who works with kids—and that includes teachers, parents, tutors, aids and youth leaders, among others—is on a never-ending search for top-quality educational materials and activities. It is for them that *The Whole Learning Catalog* has been created.

Included within these pages is a selection of short- and long-term teaching activities (for the classroom and elsewhere), low-cost teaching tools, kids' books, activity resource books and full-color activity posters that promise to capture the attention and interest of children in all grades from elementary through junior high. Complementing the activity ideas and product reviews are essays and opinion pieces written by people who care about kids, for people who care about kids.

In addition to organizing the material in curriculum centered chapters, typographic aids have been built in to assist you in locating information. Rows of stars identify products; free items are boxed under the title *Fabulous Freebee*; and teaching ideas, books and essays are set apart by headline design.

Product ordering information and grade or age-level appropriateness are given at the end of each review. Publisher addresses for children's trade books are on page 151. It should be noted, though, that children's books generally can be purchased or special-ordered through local bookstores—oftentimes saving you considerable shipping and handling charges. Costs for all products have been thoroughly checked and are as current as possible, but prices are always subject to change. Also, be sure to add on a local sales tax when necessary.

Finally, to locate specific types of products—activity cards, teacher resource books, films, workbooks or whatever—see the product index on pages 190–192.

Editorial Assistants: Anne Cory, Kristen Schmidt
Art Assistant: Ann Turnley
Cover design: David Hale
Logotype design: Bob Simmons

Executive Editor: Morton Malkofsky
Design Director: Robert G. Bryant

Copyright © 1976, Education Today Company, Inc., 530 University Avenue, Palo Alto, California 94301. World Rights reserved. No part of this publication may be reproduced by any mechanical, photographic, or electronic process, or in any other form, nor may it be stored in a retrieval system, transmitted, or otherwise copied for public or private use without prior written permission from Education Today Company, Inc.

Library of Congress Number: 76-29238   International Standard Book Number: 0-914092-25-5   Book Code: C01. First Printing August 1976

# CONTENTS

## READING 6

**Activities:** Picture Power; Most Horrible Week in Reading; Egg Carton Match-Ups; Mail-Order Library; Do-It-Yourself Reading Games; VIP Treatment; Looking at Labels

**Materials:** The Monster Books and The More Monster Books; How 2 Gerbils 20 Goldfish 200 Games 2,000 Books and I Taught Them How to Read; Read Around; Pal Paperbacks; Breakthrough Books; We Are Black; Man Literature Series; Adventures in the City; Kookie: The Motorcycle Racing Dog

**Features and Featurettes:** Influential Book Critics; The Reading Teacher's Dilemma; A Workable Approach to Individualized Reading

## ARTS & CRAFTS 16

**Activities:** Giant Jigsaw for Primaries; Ninety-Minute Jewelry; Salvage Sculpture; How to Use Your Noodle

**Materials:** Trash Can Toys and Games; American Folk Toys: How to Make Them; Recycle Notes; Two Hundred Plus Art Ideas for Teachers; Industrial Arts for Elementary Classrooms; Corrugated Carton Crafting; 100 Ways to Have Fun With an Alligator & 100 Other Involving Art Projects; City: A Story of Roman Planning and Construction; Creative Art Tasks Cards; The Little Carpenter; Exploring the Arts With Children; Color Crafts; Steven Caney's Toy Book; A Ball of Clay; Model Cars and Trucks and How to Build Them

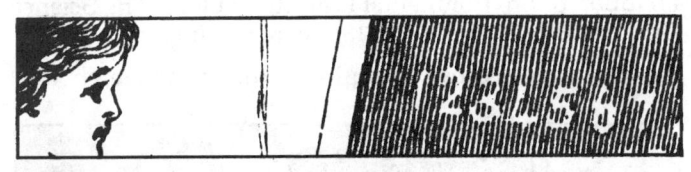

## MATH 24

**Activities:** Perfect Match Math Puzzles; Change Chart; The Price Is Right; Cooperative Pie-Building; Toothpick Technology; Everybody Wins; Station Break; War on Multiplication; Race to the Register; In My Estimation . . .; Blow Up; Bird Feeder Arithmetic; Math Project Days; Fractional Foods; Shuffleboard Math; Meat Market Math; Math House; Mystery Measurements; Taped Computations; Math and the Message; Clip-On Math Cards

**Materials:** Meters, Liters and Grams; Metric Tape; Metricat10n; Magic Squares; Geoboard Activity Cards—Primary and Intermediate; Geoboard Activity Card Kit; Enhance Chance; Teaching Mathematics in the Elementary School; Good Time Mathematics Event Cards; Mancala; String Sculpture; Equations: The Game of Creative Mathematics; Mathematics Spinner Kit; Pacemaker Protractor; Multi-Base Converter; Learning to Think in a Math Lab; Trundle Wheel; I Win; Mathematics in the Making; Count and See; Math Activities for Child Involvement; Tangram Cards; It's a Tangram World; Tangram Tasks; Young Math Books; Aftermath; Circles, Triangles and Squares; Tuf; Foo; Creative Equations; The Aba-Ten Rule; Arithmecubes

**Features:** Specialty of the Day—Mathematical Malnutrition; Selecting a Calculator—Games for the Calculator; The Metric Mystique

**Posters:** Metric—Measuring Up; Shop 'N Solve

## CREATIVITY 52

**Materials:** Developing Creativity in Children; Listening, Looking and Feeling; Becoming Somebody; Put Your Mother on the Ceiling: Children's Imagination Games; New Directions in Creativity

**Feature:** Evaluating and Using Creativity-Development Materials

## SOCIAL STUDIES 56

**Activities:** Shop Talk; West of Cindy Baker Zoo; Neighborhood News; Recycling Stamps; The People's Bank; Assembly Line Simulation; The Good Old Days?; The How and Why of DJI; Want a Job?; The Career Tree; Turning On to the World; Sport Geography; Present-Past

**Materials:** Suggestions for a More Creative Type of Teaching. Subject: American History; The Needs of Man; A Guide to Consumer Education Materials; The Many American Film Series; The Star-Spangled Banner; Jackdaws; Ishi, Last of His Tribe; Your City Has Been Kidnapped; National Gallery of Art Slide Shows; Expression: Black Americans; Along the Niger River: An African Way of Life; Yellow Pages of Learning Resources; John Muir: Father of Our National Parks; A Guide to Games; Maple-Sugar Farmer; Good Cents: Every Kid's Guide to Making Money; Enriched Social Studies Teaching Through the

Use of Games and Activities; The Upstairs Room; Typical Gyps and Frauds; Picture Book of the Revolution's Privateers; Folk Puppet Plays for the Social Studies; Simulation/Gaming/News; Wrapped for Eternity: The Story of the Egyptian Mummy; Economics for Primaries; Five Children and Five Families; Moving People and Things; Railroad Pictures and Map; Life in Rural America; People Who Organize Facts; Trucks and Things You'll Want to Know About Them

**Feature:** Curriculums for One World

**Posters:** Games From Around the World; A Bird's-Eye View

## DO-IT-YOURSELF GAMES & MEDIA 74

**Activities:** Recycling Filmstrips; Learn-Alot-Alopoly; New Ideas for Using Old Films; TV Tactics; Flash Cards on Film; The Convertible Gameboard; Filmstrips in the Making

**Materials:** "U" Film Filmstrip Kit and Slide Kit; Quick Slide; Photography—How It Works Booklet; The Camera Cookbook; Films Kids Like; Children as Film Makers; Movies With a Purpose and Slides With a Purpose; Filmstrip Repair Kit; The Snapshooter

**Features:** Light Writing; The Great Picture Lift

## LANGUAGE ARTS 82

**Activities:** Teaching With the Top Ten; Mystery Writing; Writer's File Box; Weekly News Special; Creative Writing Idea File; Oh Say What You See; Language Blankets; Draw A Rhyme; Five Liners; Practice Patterns; Fill in the Blanks; Living Sentences; The Quilted Story; Encyclopedia Telephonia; Creative Writings Revisited; Vive La Difference!; It's in the Book; Gruesome Garbage, Alias Daily News; The Viewer's Voice; Spelling Survey; B.L.T. is G.O.O.D.; Print It!; To the Best of My Recollection . . .

**Materials:** A Kite Story; Charlotte's Web; Threshold Filmstrips; Sound Filmstrip Sets 37 and 38; Making It Strange; Aha! I'm a Puppet; Puppet Making Through the Grades; Story Starters; Just So Stories; Blend and Build 1; The Selfish Giant; Improvisation for the Theater; Writing for the Fun of It; Daffodils; Turn Not Pale, Beloved Snail; Fog; Aaron Zwieback and His World of Words; Joshua in a Box; Reading/Writing: Success for Children Begins at Home; In Other Words: An Introductory Thesaurus; Consonant Jumble; Tales of the Hopi Indians; Creative Dramatics for the Classroom Teacher; The Writing Center Kit; The Legend of John Henry; An Idea Book for Acting Out and Writing Language; American Folklore; The Writing Bug; Reading Reel and Title Twister; The Mole Film Series; A Story A Story; Write On!; The Marble

**Features and Featurettes:** Modern Poetry, Teacher Style; Joking Around; Comics for Fun and Profit; Science Fiction: Curriculum for the Future; The Language Arts: A Revolution; Spelling Flunks the Test; Simple Word Games and Books to Make

**Posters:** Hink Pink; A Handy Puppet

## CREATIVE MOVEMENT & PLAY 113

**Activities:** King-Size Kickball; The Language of Movement

**Materials:** A Guide to Movement Exploration; Inexpensive Equipment for Games, Play, and Physical Activity; Be a Frog, a Bird, or a Tree

**Feature:** Tips for an Alternative Recess

## SCIENCE 117

**Activities:** Grass on the Half-Shell; An Ecosystem of Your Own; What's in a Label?; Zoo Keepers; Wishbone Connected to the . . .; How Much Noise Annoys?; Waste Watchers; Air Pollution Test; Seedbed in a Bag

**Materials:** Butterfly Garden; Pigs!; City Rocks City Blocks and the Moon; Teaching Science With Garbage; Home-Gro Mushroom Garden; City Leaves City Trees; Microscope; Sockeye Odyssey; Zooming In; Bodies; The Story of Solo; Conservation Education Publications; Pets-'N-Care; Science Experiments You Can Eat; Adventures With a Cardboard Tube; Making Small Things Look Bigger; A Stream Environment; Making Babies; Examining Your Environment; Mirror Cards; Outdoor Classrooms on School Sites; Center for Short-Lived Phenomena Event Reports; Ecology Reprints; The Animals Are Crying; Essence I and II; Observation; Environmental Discovery Units; Punch 'N Gro; River, Where Do You Come From?; Drops, Streams and Containers; The Bug House

**Features:** Selecting an Elementary Science Program; The Pollution of Environmental Education; OBIS: The Science Un-Curriculum; Science 5/13: Economy Import

**Posters:** Take a Close Look; Meet Your Wild Neighbors

## KIDS' LEISURE READING 138

**Books:** The Devil's Storybook; Once Upon a Time: The Fairy-Tale World of Arthur Rackham; George and Martha; The Chick and the Duckling; The Funny Little Woman; Miss Jaster's Garden; The Impossible People: A History

Natural and Unnatural of Beings Terrible and Wonderful; Muffel and Plums; Tomfoolery; How Tom Beat Captain Najork and His Hired Sportsmen; Mom, the Wolf Man and Me; King Grisly-Beard: A Tale From the Brothers Grimm; A Proud Taste for Scarlet and Miniver; The Mushroom Center Disaster; Sing Song Scuppernong; Hurry the Crossing; Omoteji's Baby Brother; Longhouse Winter; The Friends; Jambo Means Hello: Swahili Alphabet Book; Songs and Stories From Uganda; The Truth About Mary Rose; With a Deep Sea Smile; The Girl Who Cried Flowers and Other Tales; The Great Brain Reforms; Dinky Hocker Shoots Smack; Don't Count Your Chickens; Mud Pies and Other Recipes; Bear's Picture; You're the Scaredy-Cat; Mine's the Best; The Wayfarer's Tree; Knee-Knock Rise; The Cool Ride in the Sky; To Market! To Market!; A Magic Eye for Ida; Dreamland Lake; The Best Christmas Pageant Ever; Hildilid's Night; The Underground Cats; The Midnight Adventures of Kelly, Dot and Esmeralda; One Fine Day; The Hundred Dresses; Benjamin and Tulip; Number 24; If I Were a Cricket; A Long Way From Verona; The Borrowers Aloft; Book of Bears; The Easy How-To Book; The Tiger's Bones and Other Plays for Children; The Son of Someone Famous; Julie of the Wolves; The Juniper Tree and Other Tales From Grimm; Leo the Late Bloomer; The Genie of Sutton Place; The Girl Who Loved the Wind; Timothy the Terror; Floating Clouds, Floating Dreams: Favorite Asian Folktales; The Checker Players; The Boy Who Didn't Believe in Spring; Eye Winker, Tom Tinker, Chin Chopper: A Collection of Musical Fingerplays; The Knee-High Man and Other Tales; Alexander and the Terrible, Horrible, No Good, Very Bad Day; Cinderella, or the Little Glass Slipper; Pippen and Robber Crumblecroack's Big Baby; The Wolf Who Had a Wonderful Dream: A French Folktale; The Pooh Party Book

**Magazines:** Cricket; Stone Soup; Ebony Jr!; The Electric Company Magazine

**Feature:** Children & Books: The Eternal Magic

## KIDS HAVE FEELINGS, TOO 152

**Activities:** This Is Me; Improving Student Self-Image; We See!; On the Other Hand . . .; The Giving Tree

**Materials:** A Handbook of Personal Growth Activities for Classroom Use; Greenhouse; After the First; Getting Along; Crossroads; Searching for Values; Clarifying Values Through Subject Matter; People Projects; Kevin; Building Positive Self-Concepts; Preludes to Growth: An Experiential Approach

**Features and Featurettes:** Video and Values; Affective Effluence; Anti-Social; Helping New Kids Feel at Home

## POTPOURRI 164

**Activities:** Calendar Bingo; Travel + A Log = Learning; The Amazing 4-in-1 Cookbook; Summer-to-September Album; Pick A Puzzle; Cereal Box Bonanza; Like Money in the Bank; You Can't Miss It; Reading Roundup—'Rithmetic Rodeo

**Materials:** Connect; An Activities Handbook for Teachers of Young Children; The Mind Benders; Change for Children; Practical Approaches to Individualizing Instruction; EDC News; Workjobs; Individualizing Through Learning Stations; Deal Me In!; Small Voice, Big Voice; Children Are People; American Quarter Horse Booklet and Posters; Learning Games; Survival Kit for Substitutes; A Teacher's Guide to Cognitive Tasks for Preschool; Learning Basic Skills Through Music; You and Me; Veri Tech; Resources for Youth; Concealed Image Process; I Can; Big Rock Candy Mountain

**Features:** Let the Kids Spin Their Own Curriculum; 60 Activities That Develop Student Independence; Self-Instructional Packages; Summer Learning Ideas; The Complete Kite Curriculum

## PRODUCT INDEX 190

Activity Cards, Activity Wheels, Calculating and Measuring Tools, Duplicating Masters, Films, Filmstrips, Games, Kids' Activity Books, Kids' Reference Materials, Media Equipment, Microscope, Multimedia Kits, Plants and Animals, Records, Self-Checking Device, Slides, Supplementary Reading & Enrichment, Teacher Resource Materials, Workbooks

# READING

## PICTURE POWER

Students who suffer battle fatigue in the struggle with reading and 'riting may gain support from another "R" – the rebus. In the ordinary garden variety rebus, pictures take the place of most picturable words. But making a modified rebus, in which pictures take the place of hard-to-spell words, may open up writing experiences for many spelling-shy students. Also suited to the language experience approach to reading, the composing of these special rebuses can be an absorbing activity for the authors and will provide unique reading materials for others.

Suggested resources for rebus writers could include an alphabetized list of service words – the "on," "at," "first," "second," "all," "some" variety – and an ample supply of magazines, catalogs and such. The writers work out their stories, leaving blanks where troublesome spellings come up. The blanks are to be filled – wherever possible – with pictures cut from magazines or with sketches that the students make themselves. (Nouns are easier to find or depict than verbs. And probably some words will need to be asked for and spelled out after all.)

The picture-finding process itself may provide interesting story angles. Pictures that a student just happens upon in a word search may suggest a new twist for the story or might introduce a new character.

Some students might enjoy stockpiling a rebus reservoir. Pictures that look usable – objects, people, obvious actions – can be clipped and collected. These may then be sorted into a set of alphabetized or categorized envelopes ready for future rebus-writing sessions.

Rebus compositions can provide a library of stories for readers who have become disenchanted with "easy reading" materials. And that library can grow as students add picture power to their arsenal of words and become rebus-writing regulars.

Idea by: Jennie J. DeGenaro,
Henrico County, Va.

# THE MONSTER BOOKS and THE MORE MONSTER BOOKS

☆ ☆ ☆ ☆ ☆ ☆ ☆ ☆

A lovable monster named Monster is the hero of two independent sets of early-reading paperbacks. There are 12 full color books in each set. THE MONSTER BOOKS run 32 pages per book; THE MORE MONSTER BOOKS are 40 pages each.

"Monster is not ugly like other monsters. He's kind of tall and his head is skinny." Monster is really the creation of a group of children, aged five to seven, from New York City schools. The language in the stories is their language. And Monster's adventures take place in their environment—the city.

The stories—one in each book—tell how Monster comes to the city, finds a house, cleans it up, finds a friend, has a party and has many other adventures. The stories progress in complexity, vocabulary and length through the 12 books in each set.

Aside from Monster himself, the most intriguing feature of the series is the language. Based on tape recordings of children's commentary and descriptions, the language has a very natural and musical quality and will not jolt the sensibilities of the purist. It derives its vitality from childlike descriptions like "all messed up," "stuff" and "whole bunch of things." Sentence length is another variable. Like an excited child, an excited sentence may rush on for several lines before running up against a period. (Line breaks provide natural resting places, though, so running out of breath is never a real danger.)

The paperbacks are designed for several audiences. They are exciting read-aloud stories for young children. Primaries with a limited sight vocabulary will find satisfying reading, aided by strong plots and visual clues. Older children gain needed reading practice while enjoying Monster's whimsical personality.

The teacher's guide tells about the development of this unique series and gives suggestions about using the books. (There are no guided lessons as such.) The guide also explores reading readiness, offering ideas for aiding children in gaining skills and background. Since the creativity of children was responsible for Monster's existence, it is quite natural that the guide should advocate the use of children's creative writing both as a readiness aid and as a means of extending the interest generated by Monster himself. Monster can become a real ally in the reading program.

Order from: Bowmar, 4563 Colorado Blvd., Los Angeles, CA 90039. Grade level: K–3. Cost: THE MONSTER BOOKS — $12.35 (12 titles and guide); $1.05 for separate titles; $1.05 for separate teacher's guide. THE MORE MONSTER BOOKS — $14.35 (12 titles and guide); $1.25 for separate titles; $1.05 for separate guide. Add 5 percent for postage and handling.

# HOW 2 GERBILS 20 GOLDFISH 200 GAMES 2,000 BOOKS AND I TAUGHT THEM HOW TO READ

☆ ☆ ☆ ☆ ☆ ☆ ☆ ☆

One of the most outlandishly titled of all the books on education, Steven Daniels' HOW 2 GERBILS, is also one of the most down-to-earth and honest accounts of how a teacher can teach the supposedly unteachable.

The book describes how Daniels took an idea from here, put it together with one from there and came up with something new and useful.

Daniels' humorous but helpful chapter on classroom discipline is a classic which has been reprinted several times. "Helpful," in fact, is the best word to describe the book. The implied philosophy is that if Daniels could do it, anyone can (his early disasters are described with bitter-sweet candor). The book's goal is to make his successes as replicable as possible.

Order from: The Cokesbury Co., 201 Eighth Ave., South Nashville, TN 37203. Grade level: Teachers of grades 4–12. Cost: $2.45 paperback, $4.95 hardcover.

## Influential Book Critics...

*"The pages are too thick—this makes them hard to turn without skipping some and you think you're getting more to read than you actually are."*
Review of Tales From India

*"I waited a long time to read this book. I guess it was because I didn't know what zaniest meant and was too lazy to look it up."*
Review of Baseball's Zaniest Stars

*"This was a very funny book. It was a good book, too."*
Review of The Binnies

Fourth and fifth graders in the Jacksboro, Texas, class of Dorothy Prunty write short book reviews like these and send them to the publisher before the books come out. Random House set up the arrangement when Teacher Prunty suggested it, and they've found that it gives editors help "in our evaluation of children's likes and dislikes." (Note: Prunty got there first; the company has no plans to let other teachers do the same.)

# 8 READING

## READ AROUND
☆ ☆ ☆ ☆ ☆ ☆ ☆ ☆

You can read, spell, pronounce, and even compute your way around READ AROUND — a multipurpose board game designed primarily for developing basic language skills. In typical board game fashion, two, three or four primary level players progress around a board by performing tasks — identifying letters, words or whatever.

What makes the game unique is that you decide the material to be identified. With special crayons that come with the game, a different set of words or numbers may be written on the laminated game board, accompanying word cards and score cards each time the game is played. After each game, players erase the words with a piece of cloth or a paper towel.

An instruction booklet describes 11 different games that can be played on the board — in word recognition, contractions, synonyms and math facts, to mention a few. Words or sentences currently being studied in class may be used, or the players may prefer to use the lists of suggested words and sentences provided with the board. And players will probably want to make up other games of their own.

The rule book suggests that players help each other with difficult words so that competition does not become the sole motivation. Rules also recommend that neither penalties nor rewards should be given when mistakes are made or help is offered.

READ AROUND doesn't teach kids to read, but it does provide an enjoyable, nonthreatening atmosphere in which to reinforce basic skills.

Order from: Teaching Concepts, Inc., 230 Park Ave., New York, NY 10017. Grade level: Primary. Cost: $12.95 plus $1.50 postage and handling.

## PAL PAPERBACKS
☆ ☆ ☆ ☆ ☆ ☆ ☆ ☆

If your slower readers are unable to handle regular reading materials, slip them one of the PAL PAPERBACKS published by Xerox Education Publications. Each book, written on an interest level of fifth grade or above and, depending on the book, a reading level of 1.5 to 5.5, has all the necessary components to get the slower reader past the cover and into the text.

Short, simply written, yet mature stories; colorful covers; exciting text illustrations; and titles such as "The Honda Kid," "The Weird Witch's Spell" and "Sports Action" are the ingredients that make these books appealing to older students reading below grade level. The books are packaged in three separate kits with three copies of 18 different titles in each one. Kit A is for reading levels 1.5 to 3.5; Kit A+ is for levels 2.5 to 4.5; and Kit B is for levels 3.5 to 5.5.

As a supplement to the regular reading program or as an addition to the classroom library, these books can fill an important need.

Order from: PAL Paperback Kits, 1250 Fairwood Ave., Box 444, Columbus, OH 43216. Grade level: 5–12. Cost: $39.95 per kit plus $5 postage and handling.

## THE READING TEACHER'S DILEMMA

I know i.t.a.,
I use SRA,
A knowledge of phonics is mine.
I've assigned my troops
To ability groups
I think basal readers are fine.

Linguistics are cool.
My class likes to fool
Around with experience charts.
My kids play Scrabble,
And I often dabble
In reading aloud, with two parts.

My tape recorder,
When not out of order,
Is ready to catch every word.
Earphones on one's head
While stories are read
Means words are seen as they're heard.

Individualize?
I've tried that for size.
I've set up a reading corner.
I let children use
Nasty words that *they* choose,
A la Sylvia Ashton-Warner.

Drill sheets are stellar
(Stored in my cellar
Are all of the Dittos I need).
One problem I find
Drives me out of my mind:
A lot of my students can't read!

— Richard G. Larson, teacher, Milwaukee, Wis.

Reprinted with permission of Richard G. Larson and the International Reading Association.

## MOST HORRIBLE WEEK IN READING

Kids probably would take diabolical delight in a basal series featuring Dick Dracula and Vampire Jane. But lacking that kind of teaching aid, you might try the gore of Poe and the lore of the Twilight Zone to interest your hard-to-motivate readers.

Something in the way of scene setting wouldn't hurt in selling suspense to your class. You might officially proclaim one of these weeks as "The Most Horrible Week in Reading." Then gather up a collection of the finest in spine-tingling classics and science-fiction thrillers that your library or local paperback rack has to offer. (If you're lucky, your Holiday for Horror may coincide with library ordering time, and if you make a good case of it, you may be able to secure the books you want and not be out anything.)

Arrange an area for a book display — if possible, a separate room illuminated with black light for optimum atmosphere. Introduce the students — by small groups — to the books and to the ground rules for The Most Horrible Week in Reading. Each student is to choose a book from the creepy collection. After finishing the books, each student is to capture the essence of the book in some visual form: model, costume, picture, mask, or other such crafts undertaking. These visual displays placed strategically around the school serve as promotion pieces for the books (which at week's end will be available in the library, if that's the way you've worked it out).

A suitable culminating event for The Most Horrible Week might be an all-school program, prefaced by the travels of your monster-clad troupe from room to room, announcing the program and introducing the horror books to their fellow students. A program possibility might be the showing of a horror film (complete with melodrama-style audience participation) or something more creative in the realm of skits and other dramatic presentations. Refreshments? Contests? Prizes? Press coverage? Who knows what evil alternatives lurk in the shadows when The Most Horrible Week in Reading casts its irresistible spell over your class.

Idea by: F. Helena Sturkey,
Copley Junior High School, Copley, Ohio.

## EGG CARTON MATCH-UPS

If you eat four eggs a day on school days and 13 eggs each weekend for the next two weeks, you could get a very high cholesterol level — and the materials for a fine reading game. For one

# 10 READING

complete game you'll need one 30-egg tray and three 12-egg cartons.

Turn the large (empty) tray upside down. On the "bumps" print the lower-case letters "a" through "z". The tray thus becomes a lower-case alphabet board. (There'll be some sections left over and your creativity can take care of those.)

Next, cut out 26 "cup" sections from the smaller egg cartons. Inside each cup print a lower-case letter. Outside, on the bottom of each cup, print the corresponding capital letter. (You might consider using self-sticking labels to avoid the necessity of writing on the uneven carton surfaces.)

A child may choose a capital letter among the separated cups, look for its lower-case form on the alphabet board, and place the cup over the appropriate letter. All the letters may be matched in this way by an individual child or by several children working in a small group. Children may check their work by removing cups and looking inside to see if the form printed in there is identical to the letter on which the cup was sitting.

Other matching games may be devised using cursive and manuscript letter forms, colors and color words, contractions, abbreviations, etc. Egg cartons can also become storage for teacher-made filmstrips and the like — but that's another story.

Idea by: Diane Robinson, Arkport Central School, Arkport, N.Y.

## BREAKTHROUGH BOOKS
☆ ☆ ☆ ☆ ☆ ☆ ☆ ☆ ☆

One difficulty all beginning readers share in common: they must move from reading individual words to reading full and connected sentences. BREAKTHROUGH BOOKS, a set of 45 softcover readers of 16 pages each, are designed to ease that transition. The set is part of a more comprehensive beginning reading program but also can be quite effective used independently.

The books are divided into three color-coded (gold, red, blue) levels of complexity. They are based on simple stories told by children and have titles like "A Rainy Day," "The Loose Tooth" and "Old Houses." These stories of real and imaginary experiences stick close to the language patterns used by children in everyday speech. Punctuation has also been minimized to highlight the free-flowing quality of conversation. And though the books were developed in England, the story situations (except perhaps for "A Cup of Tea") are familiar to American children.

The books are stunningly illustrated by several different artists. The pictures are colorful and full of detail that upon examination often tells as much of a story as the text.

Though youngsters are certain to enjoy these stories, the readers are not without problems. A few of the stories are plagued by what may be interpreted as elements of sexism. "My Mom," for example, has "mom" doing only traditional domestic activities. In another, "Things I Can Do," a little girl and her mother are shown washing and drying dishes while two boys and their father clean the car.

Less substantively but still worth a warning, some of the books are inadequately stapled, a minor fault that can easily be remedied by adding a staple or two of your own.

Order from: Bowmar, 4563 Colorado Blvd., Los Angeles, CA 90039. Grade level: Preschool – 2. Cost: $29.65 per set of 45 readers. Add 5 percent for postage and handling.

## WE ARE BLACK
☆ ☆ ☆ ☆ ☆ ☆ ☆ ☆

Lew Alcindor, Aretha Franklin, Coretta King and little-known Western cowboy Bronco Sam are just a few of the black personalities highlighted in WE ARE BLACK, a supplementary reading kit from SRA. The kit, with its exciting, high-interest "biographies, anecdotes, and essays," has already proved itself both popular and effective in several city classrooms where large numbers of students were reading below grade level. It is designed for use by fourth through eighth graders reading on a 2.0 to 6.0 grade level.

The kit consists of 120 short (two-or three-page) readings printed on durable stock paper with accompanying vocabulary and comprehension skill cards, 40 answer-key booklets, 40 student books with questions and additional readings, and a teacher's guide. The kit is fully individualized with six ability levels. Students progress through the levels of color-coded readings, starting at their own level and proceeding at their own pace. Since students select the readings, check the answers and keep records of what they have read, teachers are completely free to give individual help as needed.

Teachers who have used other SRA reading kits know of their flexibility. WE ARE BLACK is no exception. This high-interest kit can be used for enrichment when regular assignments are completed, as an ongoing supplement to the core program or as a library for recreational reading. Flexibility also extends to the materials within the kit. Some teachers choose to use only the reading booklets and answer cards while others use the entire kit.

If the cost of the kit presents a problem, a solution might be for several teachers to share a kit.

Order from: Science Research Associates, Inc., 259 East Erie St., Chicago, IL 60611. Grade level: 4 – 8. Cost: $77.95 plus $3.90 postage and handling.

# MAIL-ORDER LIBRARY

You know it's going to happen. Each year around the winter holidays you'll be deluged with catalogs from large mail-order houses, department stores, gift shops and food-specialty companies. And all this will culminate in the observance of that most compelling of midwinter rites, the January sale — for which there are also catalogs. (And if your rolling-stone lifestyle has denied you the privilege of being on 103 mailing lists, there are lots of companies eager to send out catalogs; just check magazines, newspapers and colleagues.)

Save those catalogs; they make fine reading-activity materials for students on several different ability levels. "Wish books," with their abundance of colorful photos and tantalizing merchandise, can serve as escape literature for needed fantasy breaks. Readers browsing through may find many appealing items and may find themselves sufficiently motivated to try working out the descriptive text. The pictures provide vocabulary clues — "blue-and-white striped, long sleeved."

Catalogs are reference tools with a definite structure and organization. Children may discover a table of contents or an alphabetized index that can be used to locate items. Other useful discoveries might be the way numbers and letters key the illustrations to their descriptions, or the ways in which items are classified and grouped.

The vocabulary and format of the order blanks may be explored. Filling out an order blank — for a set of fantasy-fulfilling purchases — can be a valuable reading and direction-following activity (not to mention the opportunity for math practice, as kids calculate the cost of seven diamond rings at $869.95 each plus tax).

You may want to structure some activities toward specific skills to get even more mileage out of the catalog-reading experience. Some suggestions follow. (Questions would be keyed to particular pages in a catalog.)

**READING FOR DETAILS.** Does radio D use batteries? How do items A and C differ? How much does item C weigh?

**ABBREVIATIONS.** What do the letters S, M and L stand for? What is HP?

**SKIMMING.** What is the most expensive item on this page? Which items are under $10?

**VOCABULARY.** Which item is called "genuine"? What does "genuine" mean? What is "jade"?

**READING PICTURES.** What wood finish is shown on table M? What shape tablecloth is shown in picture F?

**PHONICS.** Find two words with a vc/cv pattern. Find a word that has a vowel controlled by "r".

**STRUCTURAL ANALYSIS.** Which word has a prefix meaning "half"? Find three compound words.

**UNDERSTANDING GRAPHIC DEVICES.** Which words are printed in italics? Why? What does * in item E mean?

**CRITICAL READING.** Do you think item E is really worth two dollars more than item D? Discuss. Why do people like to have things monogrammed? An item marked "best" may not be best for you. Discuss.

Your mail-order library may have catalogs for a variety of interests from camping equipment to crafts materials. And when you're done reading them, you've got pictures galore for other projects.

Idea from suggestions by:
Mary Jayne Larson, Puunene School, Puunene Maui, Hawaii, and
Isobel L. Livingstone, Rahway, N.J.

## DO-IT-YOURSELF READING GAMES

"I could make one of those," you state emphatically as you examine a reading game — all color and excitement in its bright box. But later you feel your resolve dissolve and you "never get around to it."

If you really decide to do it for sure this time, consider making a game that's flexible enough to be used in many ways. Make your efforts worthwhile.

A very basic and effective kind of game can be created by making or scrounging a spinner or die, designing a game board and developing a deck or two of word cards.

The game board can be made of a piece of tagboard on which you mark a segmented path. Players will travel along this path from "Start" to a goal or destination. Some segments of the path may be designated as bonuses ("Go ahead three spaces"; "Take another turn") or penalties ("Lose a turn"; "Go back a space"), but it's best to keep notations on the game board general to allow for maximum flexibility in using the game. Specific items, tying to particular reading groups, should be reserved for the cards.

Card decks may be developed to reinforce any number of reading areas. One deck might consist of sight vocabulary words for students to recognize and pronounce. Other decks might have words for which synonyms, definitions or rhyming words must be given.

Directions for games will vary in complexity according to the abilities and needs of the players. A simple sight vocabulary game might go like this: The first player — as determined by rolling the highest number, for instance — rolls the die and draws the number of cards indicated. All cards must then be read correctly before the player moves the corresponding number of spaces. Play moves to the left and the player reaching the goal first is the winner.

This game board may be used with different groups simply by changing the card decks or modifying the tasks. Rules may establish bonus value for some words — e.g., compound words win two extra spaces. Children may come up with rule variations of their own, which must be mutually agreed upon, of course. Smaller versions of the game board could be useful at learning stations or for solitaire-type games.

While there'll be no need for Parker Brothers to feel threatened by your gaming efforts, you'll find that your games provide plenty of palatable practice for your reading classes.

Idea by: Karen G. Davis,
Ernest F. Upham School, Wellesley, Mass.

## MAN LITERATURE SERIES

☆ ☆ ☆ ☆ ☆ ☆ ☆ ☆

Becoming acquainted with good literature should be an experience touched with awe, excitement and new realizations that foster an appreciation and understanding of the condition of man. MAN is a literature series that seems to have been planned with such an attitude in mind.

The series comprises four books and a teacher's manual for each of six levels, spanning grades 7 through 12 and up. The books at each level provide separate treatment for each of four literature emphases, indicated by the titles: MAN in the Fictional Mode, MAN in the Poetic Mode, MAN in the Expository Mode, and MAN in the Dramatic Mode. In each book, great care has been taken in selecting both contemporary and older material with real meaning for today's youth.

The books also have special visual appeal, featuring unusually fine art and the work of internationally recognized photographers. The illustrations stimulate thought and feeling and may in themselves provide the basis for discussion and writing efforts.

MAN has a further student appeal in its no-questions, no-exercises format. Teaching suggestions are to be found in a separate teacher's manual.

Books may be purchased as sets — four per student per level — or as individual titles. You may either plan a full literature course around the set, or use titles separately as supplements or as minicourses.

The books are compact — about six-by-eight inches and from 128 to 160 pages. Levels one and two come in soft covers and are printed on high-quality paper that is both attractive and durable.

One warning: Your first look at the cover photos and a sampling of the content is likely to send you to a quiet spot for some enjoyable reading of your own.

Order from: McDougal, Littell & Co., Box 1667, Evanston, IL 60204. Grade level: Level one — 7 – 9; Level two — 8 – 10. Cost: Level one — $2.40 per book; Level two — $2.52 per book; $3.90 for teacher's manual for either level. Add 8 percent to order for postage and handling.

## ADVENTURES IN THE CITY
☆☆☆☆☆☆☆☆☆☆

The setting for this series of six storybooks is home territory for thousands of children. They will readily identify with the young heroes and heroines of these city tales.

Each story is a true incident, and all are made even more real by large "on location" photographs. The models acting out the characters are most appealing and convincing.

Designed for grades two to five, the books have limited vocabulary and easily managed sentence length. The stories are written in a simple, informal style through which both meaning and feeling are well conveyed.

DON'T GIVE UP is the tale of a girl whose fight against pollution leads to a subway ride to city hall with a bag of garbage for the mayor.

BIRD SEED AND LIGHTNING deals with a shy boy and a very special bike.

WALKIE-TALKIE PATROL gives an exciting account of the capture of crooks in an apartment building.

WHO'S THERE? builds spooky adventure around three brothers and their visit to a haunted house.

ROBBY ON ICE tells of a boy's determination to become a great skater.

UNKNOWN AVENUES follows a girl on a frightening tour of strange streets after she takes the wrong bus home.

The books are hardcover with reinforced library bindings.

Order from: Creative Education, Inc., 123 South Broad St., Mankato, MN 56001. Grade level: 2 – 5. Cost $4.95 per book plus $.50 postage and handling.

## KOOKIE: THE MOTORCYCLE RACING DOG
☆☆☆☆☆☆☆☆☆☆

Kookie, a nine-year-old boxer-terrier mongrel that has collected more motorcycle racing trophies than most human competitors, is the subject of this filmstrip and book from Educational Activities, Inc.

A true story — one of a series of "action reading kits" written for students at the third and fourth grade reading level, but of interest even to kindergartners — it tells of Kookie, his master, John McCown, and their experience together as racing partners. The story is warm and interesting and viewers can't help but come away with a certain admiration for this canine competitor.

The filmstrip is available as part of a kit that contains ten softbound copies of the story in book form, a record or cassette, and a teaching guide.

Order from: Educational Activities, Inc., Dept. BW, 1937 Grand Ave., Baldwin, NY 11510. Grade level: Primary – intermediate. Cost: $36, kit with cassette; $35, kit with record. Use catalog number 451 when placing order.

## VIP TREATMENT

If Douglas Jeffers won't touch a story about Cochise, or Coolidge, or Cullen, or Curie, he may warm up to a tale about Douglas Jeffers.

Try writing a story using one of your hard-to-motivate students as the main character. Use your knowledge of the student's likes and dislikes, trademarks and idiosyncrasies to personalize the story. The account should be far-fetched and funny, filled with familiar streets and places that the class — and particularly the protagonist — will recognize and appreciate. And don't forget to fill the tale with data that can provide grist for some follow-up worksheets — for instance, numbers:

Douglas was known as a sharp dresser. He wore $350 suits, $40 patent-leather shoes, $70 custom-made shirts and a diamond pinkie ring worth $3,170.

After some silent preparation, the main attraction gets to read the story aloud. Others may read it aloud too, especially if the content provides a few laughs (it's great to be a comedian for a little while).

You can compose a story that lends itself to work in a variety of subject-matter areas, depending upon the needs of the class. You may want to plan for each student to have a copy of the story to refer to in completing the accompanying worksheets.

The VIP treatment is most effective if used no more than once a week. Kids enjoy seeing their names "in print" and will consider VIP time a huge treat.

Idea by: Alan Klayminc, Brooklyn, N.Y.

## LOOKING AT LABELS

If any household-trash item can be reclaimed as a useful teaching tool, the label from a food can can.

These colorfully illustrated and boldly lettered labels can be cut into uniform sizes and mounted on cards ready for reading games.

Collect identical pairs of labels for Concentration-type games. Pairs also lend themselves to Go Fish games. The skills involved in these games include visual discrimination, visual memory and, in Go Fish, the ability to read the labels or describe the contents pictured with sufficient accuracy that the other players will understand what is being asked for.

Another game may be set up using a deck of label cards and several label boards. Each player receives a label board — a large card on which are pasted four different labels. For each label on the board there should be at least one matching label card in the deck. No two label boards should be exactly alike, although they ought to have some labels in common. Players draw label cards from the deck, covering the labels on their label boards whenever they draw a match. (Bonus turns and other such playing rules may be set up as the players wish.) The first player to completely cover his label board wins.

With a large collection of labels from a wide variety of food classifications, the games devised can be almost as diverse as those for a standard deck of cards. And contributions from the class will cause the collection to grow.

Idea by: Linda L. Daniel,
Thompson School, Charlotte, N.C.

## A Workable Approach To Individualized Reading

BY CHARLOTTE H. BURNS

For years I was a typical junior high school teacher, spending most of my time complaining about my primary grade colleagues who failed to teach the Little Darlings how to read. Then the bomb was dropped. I was given a second grade assignment.

I wandered through the corridors of the dim past trying to remember my second grade practice teaching. There were just two things that came readily to mind. One was the day the supervisor demonstrated that little children can learn big words such as "univalve" and "bivalve," while holding up half a clam shell, then a whole clam shell. The other was that the second grade critic teacher I had in the fall had spent the spring quarter in a mental institution. Somehow none of this seemed too helpful.

Then I remembered the reading groups—those horrid things! But as everyone was saying, "Children are different these days," so perhaps the reading groups had changed as much as the children. But my hopes were short-lived. After six weeks of Susan pinching Johnny under the table, Dave and Sam carrying on a nonstop kicking fight, Sally's concentration darting like a mosquito around the room, Daisy smugly showing off her superior ability to recognize new words on sight, and little Peter's entire group telling every word and being very patronizing about it, I knew kids hadn't changed and reading groups hadn't changed.

I timed my reading groups and to my dismay found that each child was getting approximately *one minute* of individual attention *every other day.* Reading is supposed to be what primaries are all about, and here they were with just one-half minute a day. I am sure more experienced teachers do better, but try timing your children honestly. You may be surprised. And don't fall into the trap of "Today was a bad day. Tomorrow they will get more time."

So in sheer desperation, knowing full well many of the pitfalls that lay ahead, I devised an individualized reading plan. There were just two requirements my understandably hesitant principal insisted upon: One, I had to teach all subjects and not skimp on any. Two, I had to see to it that every child went through the basic series before going on to other books.

All my children had been classified as low or average in ability. You can get both a fair reading-level spread and an unlimited spread in individual needs within that grouping. My goal was to give Dave what he needed to learn with and not waste his time with what Peter needed, to give Sally the challenge she needed, and to help Daisy understand all those words she so smugly called.

My supplies for the project were a huge number of check sheets I devised for my own use, tagboard cut into strips about an inch wide and five inches long, newsprint cut into pieces just large enough to stick out of the library pocket in the back of the reader, and a manila folder for each child's check sheet. I took a small library table, set a chair at one end for me and two alongside for children, and I was ready to open shop.

After the third day, things were moving along smoothly, much sooner than I had any right to expect. The children had become accustomed to the system and no longer unduly anticipated their turn at the table. The order was simple. We just went around the room, up one row and down the next. There was no stigma or prestige about belonging to a particular reading group. Two children were at the table at all times. One was having his reading time; the other was reviewing material in preparation for his turn. When the first one finished, he moved back to his own seat while the second one moved over to the "reading seat." It was, quite simply, using a production-line method for giving individualized help.

The stack of manila folders was on the table beside me in the order the children sat. Each child, while waiting for his turn to read, was welcome to look at his own folder, though after the first time, none did. The folder, containing a stack of my homemade check sheets, was eventually passed on to the next teacher in the hope that it might furnish some background on each child's reading problems.

When a child stumbled over a word, I would write it down on his check sheet and on a separate slip of newsprint. The problem words were reviewed at the end of each session, and the slips were put in the library pocket at the back of the child's book. He had the words at hand to study, and I had them where I could see them the next day. At the next reading time, we went over those words first.

Not every reading session was spent reading, however. Some days were spent exclusively on word drill. Other times we might just sit back and discuss the story the child had just read. When he finished the book, he had to know 90 percent of the words in the list at the back of the book regardless of context. We gave special attention to the words on his list on the check sheet. When he was through with the basic series, he was allowed to pick out a book of his own choice. Sometimes children who had read the same story would work together to dramatize it for the class. Or a child might give an oral book report, being careful not to give the outcome away—possibly motivating some other child to read the book.

When the child was not at the reading table, he was reading by himself. If he had trouble with a word, there were several children in the room who could help him or he could show me the word and I could tell him quietly without interrupting my individual class.

I won't say this program was a panacea. There were many who did not learn as well as I would have liked, but at least I was able to give them all four times as much individual attention and did not waste their time fulfilling somebody else's needs. They were not listening to someone's expressionless reading; they were involved in reading themselves. They were making their own progress without fear of embarrassment or invidious comments from peers.

Charlotte H. Burns is a former second grade teacher at Quartz Hill Elementary School, Quartz Hill, Calif.

# ARTS & CRAFTS

## ARTS & CRAFTS

# GIANT JIGSAW FOR PRIMARIES

The whole is often more than the sum of its parts. This can be especially true of works of art — such as your primary-age children can put together.

For this project you'll need tagboard, scissors, crayons (or paint) and cellophane tape (a lot of it). Tape together large tagboard sheets — taping along the full length of each seam — to form one large sheet that's at least four feet by six feet in size.

Decide which side is to be the back and indicate this in some obvious way — by writing all over it, coloring it, decorating it, or perhaps covering it with pages from a newspaper. On the front, mark jigsaw-like pieces, one for each child and one for yourself. Then cut the pieces apart.

Each person will get a uniquely shaped piece of tagboard on which to draw the funniest face imaginable. (Be sure to have children turn pieces to the front side.) Suggest also that they observe the shapes of the pieces. The contour of the pieces may help children in planning the shapes of the funny faces they'll be drawing.

When all the faces are finished, children try to put the pieces back together again. (If you've put an allover design on the back, children will have another set of clues to help in reassembling the puzzle.) When children find pieces that fit, they come to have them taped together.

Soon the whole puzzle is assembled, much to everyone's delight, and the giant jigsaw is ready to decorate.

Idea by: Rod Windle, Inarajan Elementary School, Inarajan, Guam.

## TRASH CAN TOYS AND GAMES

**by Leonard Todd. Drawings by Chas. B. Slackman. Photographs by Carl Fischer**

Bound in cardboard and printed on recycled paper, this sprightly book by an architectural designer counsels the reader to save such throwaways as scrap paper and tin cans and convert them into Robin Hood caps or a space station. Most of the toys will bring to mind the days when soapbox derby entrants actually used boxes rather than wind-tunnel-tested vehicles.

VIKING, $6.95 (list), $6.26 (school price). Ages 7 – 12. See page 151 for ordering information.

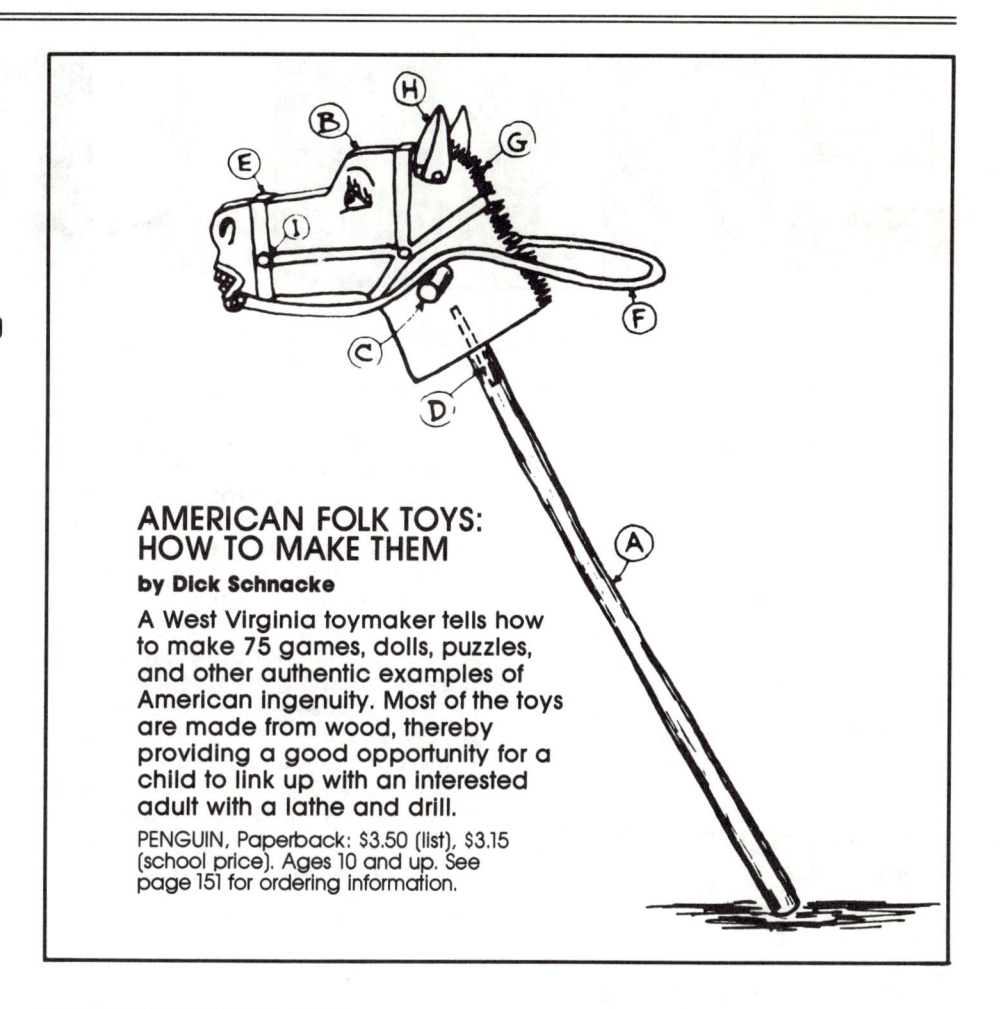

## AMERICAN FOLK TOYS: HOW TO MAKE THEM

**by Dick Schnacke**

A West Virginia toymaker tells how to make 75 games, dolls, puzzles, and other authentic examples of American ingenuity. Most of the toys are made from wood, thereby providing a good opportunity for a child to link up with an interested adult with a lathe and drill.

PENGUIN, Paperback: $3.50 (list), $3.15 (school price). Ages 10 and up. See page 151 for ordering information.

## RECYCLE NOTES: Crafts, Activities, Games

☆ ☆ ☆ ☆ ☆ ☆ ☆ ☆

Among other helpful suggestions, RECYCLE tells how to make lots of "somethings" from practically nothing. This teacher resource is a collection of more than 40 ideas for simple arts-and-crafts projects, games and activities gathered by the Resource Center of the Children's Museum in Boston.

From discarded materials such as cheese cartons, bottle caps and cardboard tubes, RECYCLE suggests making musical instruments. The booklet gives easy directions for creating drums, finger cymbals, shakers, chimes and kazoos out of junk.

RECYCLE describes several useful games — word games, math games and brain-teaser puzzles — based on equipment that is easy to make. Another project is the construction of simple science tools, such as a balance and a water microscope. Directions are clear, brief and are reinforced with drawings.

The booklet is composed of individual handwritten sheets, duplicated and stapled together. While there is no table of contents, most activities are grouped according to categories. If you wish, you will have no difficulty in taking the booklet apart and making separate booklets for the different categories.

Order from: Recycle Notes, The Children's Museum, The Jamaicaway, Boston, MA 02130. Grade level: Teachers of all grades. Cost: $1 plus $.30 postage and handling. Payment must accompany order.

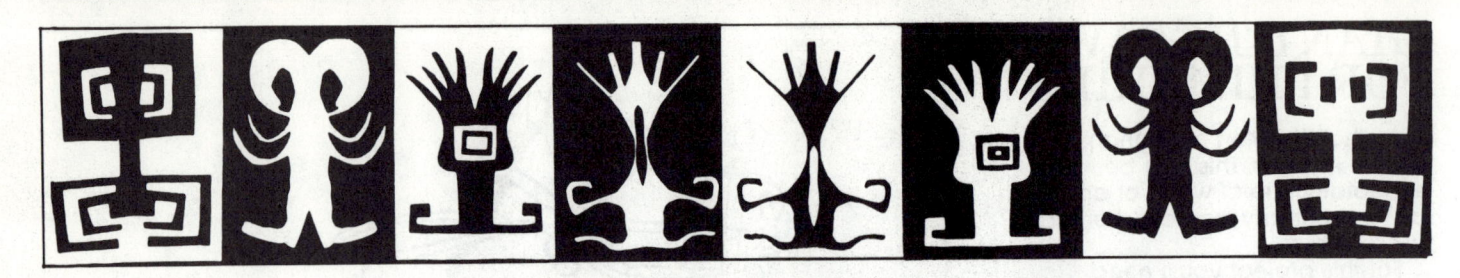

## 18  ARTS & CRAFTS

## TWO HUNDRED PLUS ART IDEAS FOR TEACHERS

☆ ☆ ☆ ☆ ☆ ☆ ☆ ☆

... actually, over 270 art ideas, with 490 photographs of children's work or of children at work. This is a how-to and what-to book that can help channel creative energies in an almost unlimited number of directions.

The book includes suggestions for using a wide variety of materials — tissue paper, water colors, crayons, chalk, cellophane, charcoal, wallpaper, straw, graph paper, sand, wood scraps and many, many more. There are ideas for greeting cards, gift-wrappings, posters, constructions, crafts and ways of complementing children's work in other subject-matter areas using art. Time-honored techniques are given new treatment or used in combination. Ideas abound on every page.

This is not an art manual, but rather a book of ideas. Explanations are brief, often little more than an identification of the project and materials. But since all ideas are accompanied by photos of the finished products, detailed directions are not so necessary. Some techniques that are suggested do require more extensive directions, and in some cases other sources are cited as aids. The intent of the book is to suggest, and perhaps remind you of an art idea you'd had success with before.

At the back of the book are suggestions for management of art classes, handling of materials, and the ever-elusive recipe for crystal gardens.

The book is a fine starter-upper and effective first aid for a creeping case of the what-to-dos. And it might make the sort of gift a busy colleague would appreciate.

Order from: Art Ideas, Box 54A, Yorkville, IL 60560. Grade level: Teachers of all grades. Cost: $4.65. Add $.35 to billed orders.

## INDUSTRIAL ARTS FOR ELEMENTARY CLASSROOMS

☆ ☆ ☆ ☆ ☆ ☆ ☆ ☆

Not a guide to teeny-weeny tools, this book by Marion L. Swierkos and Catherine G. Morse is actually a handbook of handwork.

Designed as a text for in-service or preservice teacher training, the book presents a historical rationale for handwork in the classroom and explores its role in the curriculum. Suggestions are made for the setting up of project areas and even an entire room devoted to handwork.

Part III provides comprehensive tables relating handwork to specific subject-matter areas at various grade levels, keying in these items to the activities described in later chapters of the book.

Perhaps the first parts of the book are of more immediate interest to the crafts specialist than to teachers for whom handwork is a sometime thing. Part IV, however, is the how-to-do-it section, filled with ideas and detailed directions for the following: basketry, ceramics, dioramas and panoramas, food preparation (including some recipes), graphic arts (printing, painting, silk screen), copper enameling, papier mâché, plastics, puppet making (marionettes, too), textiles (weaving, tie dyeing, hooked rugs, stitchery), woodworking, and some miscellaneous crafts such as mosaics, candle making, carving, etc., etc., etc.!

Directions are easy to follow and diagrams are supplied as needed. Photographs throughout show finished articles, and it is reassuring to know that "all examples of finished projects were done by children of the age designated."

This 375-page paperback could become one of the most used references around, since much valuable information is available in one resource.

Order from: Charles A. Bennett Co., Inc., 809 W. Detweiller Dr., Peoria, IL 61614. Grade level: Teachers of all grades. Cost: $6 (list); $4.50 (school). Add $.30 postage and handling.

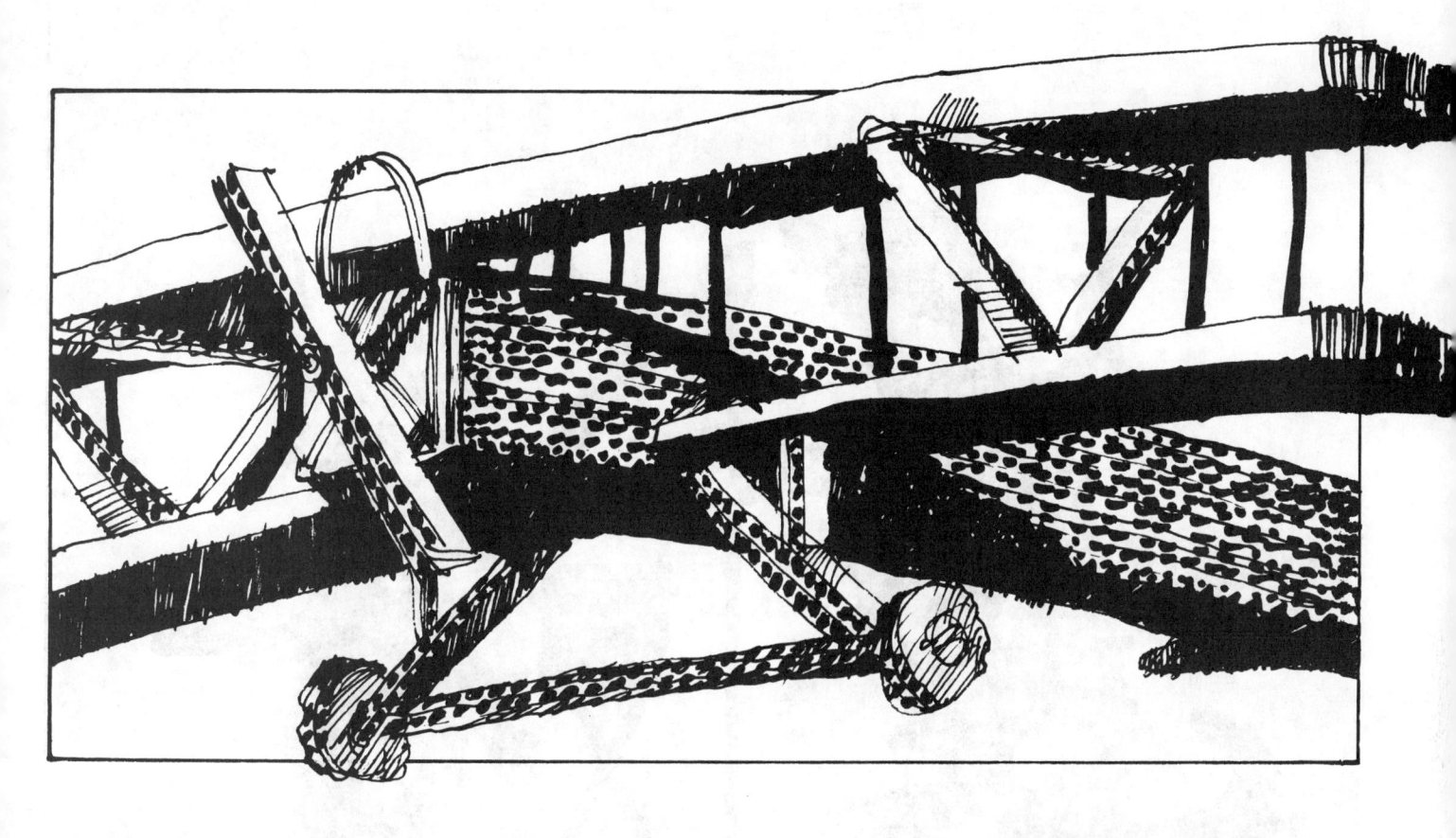

## CORRUGATED CARTON CRAFTING

☆ ☆ ☆ ☆ ☆ ☆ ☆ ☆ ☆
Arched bridges, lampshades, biplanes and simple machines are only a few of the constructions kids can create with corrugated cardboard cartons, a free material readily available from the local grocery or appliance store.

In 48 pages of black-and-white photos, illustrations and brief descriptions, author Dick van Voorst identifies basic single- and double-wall cardboards and suggests different techniques (cutting, layering, bending, folding) for working with them. He then moves into project development, beginning with simple tasks that accustom kids to using the materials and necessary tools. More sophisticated techniques of joining strips of cardboard with match sticks or dowels are also explained.

Corrugated cardboard is a medium of considerable flexibility. Its only drawback is that a mat knife or other sharp-edge blade is needed if the cardboard is to be cut efficiently. Alternatives are for the students to use ordinary scissors (workable but not too neat) or for the teacher to prepare a large assortment of cardboard strips in different lengths and widths for students to use.

Order from: Sterling Publishing Co., Inc., 419 Park Ave. South, New York, NY 10016. Grade level: Teachers of grades 2 – junior high. Cost $3.99 plus $.35 postage and handling. Payment must accompany order.

## NINETY-MINUTE JEWELRY

A jewelry-casting course could cost hundreds of dollars, but you can do about 40 castings for nothing, using rejected materials and equipment from the science department:
- a firebrick (lining material in ceramic kilns)
- large lead sinkers
- scissors or other sharp tool
- pliers for holding sinkers
- asbestos pad to put under brick
- propane torch
- files, emery cloth for finishing
- India ink for patina
- steel wool for burnishing.

Cut the firebrick in half with a bandsaw to provide 12 working surfaces. The brick is soft and cuts easily. With scissor points or any other sharp tool, scratch a grooved design into the brick surface about one-eighth inch deep. Next use the propane torch to melt the large lead sinkers. The drops of melting lead should be directed into the grooves until the design is filled. Reheat the casting to the melting point to strengthen and smooth the outer surface.

After the lead cools (about ten minutes) regroove around the casting with a sharp tool and pry out the cast from the brick. Clean out the remaining brick sand. This inner side is very rough in contrast with the outer surface. Interesting contrasts of rough and smooth texture can be achieved by sanding with an emery cloth or filing.

For a final step, apply India ink to the surface. When it is dry, use steel wool to create a contrast of light and dark shadings.

Idea by: Ernest Neri, Ponus Ridge Middle School, Norwalk, Conn.

## 20 ARTS & CRAFTS

## 100 WAYS TO HAVE FUN WITH AN ALLIGATOR & 100 OTHER INVOLVING ART PROJECTS

☆ ☆ ☆ ☆ ☆ ☆ ☆ ☆ ☆

The projects in this book ask for much more than simply drawing a picture. What they demand is real involvement and self-expression on the part of the student.

One activity asks the "students to create hats which make the wearer look important, silly, dignified, chic." It is followed by an exchange of hats and a discussion of how the hats look when worn by different people.

Another set of activities leads the student through miniaturization drawings and into the task of creating detailed landscapes in an area no larger than a playing card.

In addition to suggesting activities, the book itself is a visual treat. It is cleverly designed and complemented by excellent black-and-white illustrations.

Order from: Art Education, Inc., Blauvelt, NY 10913. Grade level: Teachers of grades 2 – 6. Cost: $3.75. Payment must accompany order.

## CITY: A STORY OF ROMAN PLANNING AND CONSTRUCTION
**by David Macaulay**

The author-illustrator of the Caldecott Honor Book CATHEDRAL turns his master's eye on the imaginary Roman city of Verbonia in order to describe how the ancient Romans built their cities. The drawings are clear and detailed. Another winner.

HOUGHTON, $7.95. Ages 10 and up.
See page 151 for ordering information.

## CREATIVE ART TASKS CARDS

☆ ☆ ☆ ☆ ☆ ☆ ☆ ☆ ☆

This set of art activity cards can help you individualize art experiences without growing several extra pairs of hands. The box contains 72 cards, six-by-nine

## ARTS & CRAFTS

inches in size, with a complete and separate activity on each side. The projects are simple, require few materials and can be finished in short periods of time. The directions are clear and are written with a style and vocabulary suited for children's independent use.

In browsing through the cards, you'll find crayon-on-paper scribble designs, finger painting, printing of several kinds, paper construction projects, mosaics, and 24 tasks called "figures and faces" which include puppets. And that's just part of the package.

The cards can be effectively used in an art center where children may go singly or several at a time and find a wide variety of art activities to choose from, all with little or no guidance.

CREATIVE ART TASKS are also available in a spiral-bound book. The same activities are found in both the book and in the card set.

Order from: Love Publishing Co., 6635 East Villanova Place, Denver, CO 80222. Grade level: 2–6. Cost: $6.50, activity cards; $4.95, book. Add $.50 to order for postage and handling. Payment must accompany order.

### FABULOUS FREEBEE

### THE LITTLE CARPENTER

Any child with even the remotest interest in working with tools will enjoy reading this colorful 24-page booklet from Stanley Tools.

It establishes that there are interestingly different tools for different trades—carpenters, bricklayers, plumbers, blacksmiths, toolmakers—and then goes on to tell more about tools for carpentry. The tools are described simply but never condescendingly. Realistic drawings illustrate all tools mentioned. Large, cheerful lettering that looks hand-printed is used in the descriptions.

In a few instances, the specific functions of the pictured tools aren't made clear. Locating the missing information could make an interesting research project.

Order from: Educational Dept., Stanley Tools, 600 Myrtle St., New Britain, CT 06050. Grade level: 3–6. Teachers may request one free copy; additional copies are 15 cents apiece.

## SALVAGE SCULPTURE

So your kids have decided they're going to save the world through recycling, and they're raiding trash cans for papers and bottles. Well, while they're sorting out recyclables, suggest they contribute to a classroom collection of discards: egg cartons, cardboard tubes, tissue boxes, Styrofoam pieces.

This unlikely assortment can become the inspiration for a cooperative art project. The objective is the creation of a wall-relief sculpture. The foundation material can be a large piece of cardboard—three feet by five feet is a good working area.

Let the group choose discard items and experiment with placement. When they have decided on the design, have them number-code each piece and its location on the cardboard. Tracing around objects can help hold the positions.

Now the artists decorate their materials with usual or unusual media. The students may want to consult with each other about compatible colors or decoration techniques for grouped items.

When items are decorated, students may fasten them in position with white glue. The many shapes, sizes, colors and textures can produce a dramatic effect.

Salvage sculpture won't save the world; but your students will find that it adds a welcome bit of color to their corner of the school.

Idea by: William D. Iaculla, Millbrae School District, Millbrae, Calif.

## EXPLORING THE ARTS WITH CHILDREN
**by Geraldine Dimondstein**

The arts—painting, sculpture, dance and poetry—are discussed in a thorough and stimulating manner by an educator who doesn't believe in easy answers. This book is not a 1-2-3 how-to manual. Instead, Dimondstein provides transcriptions of dialogues between children and their teachers as a model for other teachers. This nongraded curriculum is at once child-centered and content-centered.

Order from: Macmillan Publishing Co., 866 Third Ave., New York, NY 10022. Grade level: Teachers of primary–junior high. Cost: $13.95 plus $.50 postage and handling. Payment must accompany order.

## 22 ARTS & CRAFTS

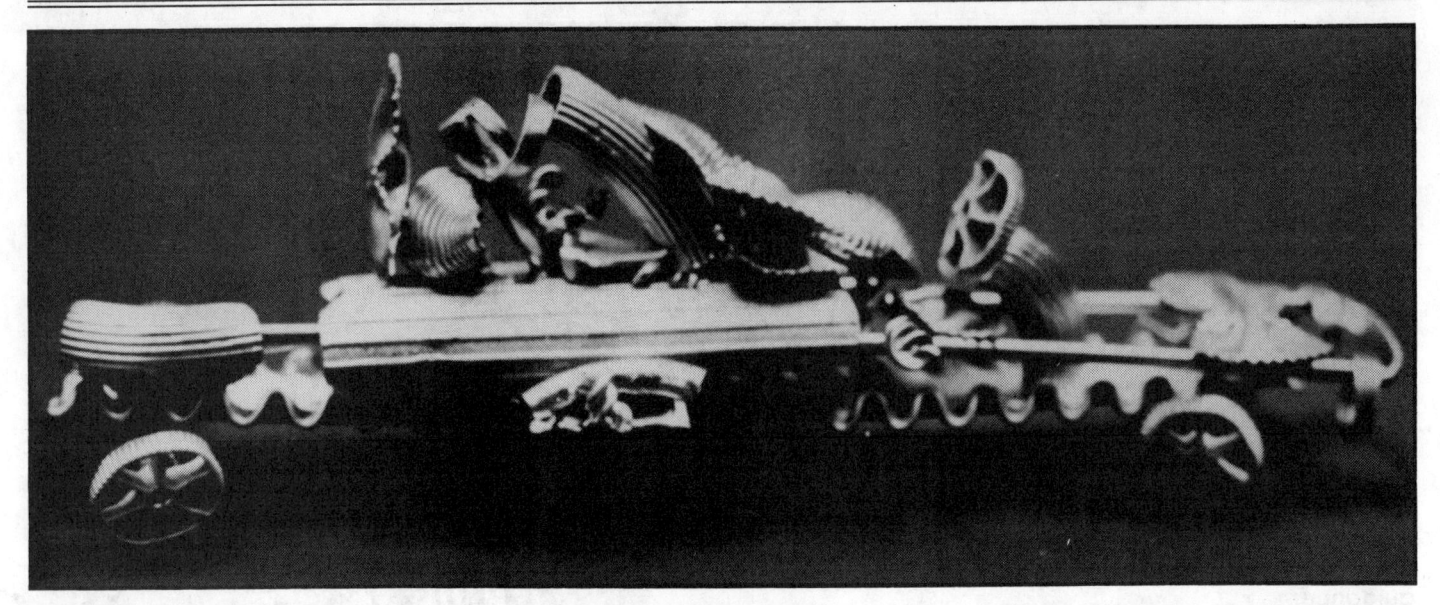

## HOW TO USE YOUR NOODLE

Want a car, motorcycle — or for that matter any kind of vehicle — that's guaranteed not to be a lemon? All you need are some eager youngsters, a large assortment of noodles, some white (school) glue or rubber cement, and for a fancy touch, silver and gold spray enamel.

To get things rolling, set out the noodles — lasagna, manicotti, bows, wide and narrow spaghetti, wheels, curls, shells or other pasta shapes.

Most children will be bubbling over with ideas, but for those who need a little inspiration, you might suggest the usefulness of preliminary sketches or mount a few pictures from hot rod magazines on a bulletin board.

When this project has been done with third through sixth graders, students have worked on their own initiative for up to two or three hours at a stretch.

You can expect both simple and complex designs. All modes of transportation are subject to pastazation — jeeps to boats and trains to rockets. One cautionary note: If the children use white glue, they have to hold the pieces securely until the glue dries. The finished items can stimulate many other activities: auto or transportation shows; contests; stories or poems about the travels and adventures of the pastamobiles, and open-house demonstrations.

The final products make great gifts. And there is no waste. Leftover bits and pieces of pasta can be used to create junk sculptures or collages.

Idea by: Brenda Winston and Barbara Welty, Washington Elementary School, Oakland, Calif.

## COLOR CRAFTS
☆ ☆ ☆ ☆ ☆ ☆ ☆ ☆

The word "color" in the title of this set of three elementary crafts books could refer to the illustrations in the books as well as the projects described. Each of the books averages about 180 pages and there is color on every page.

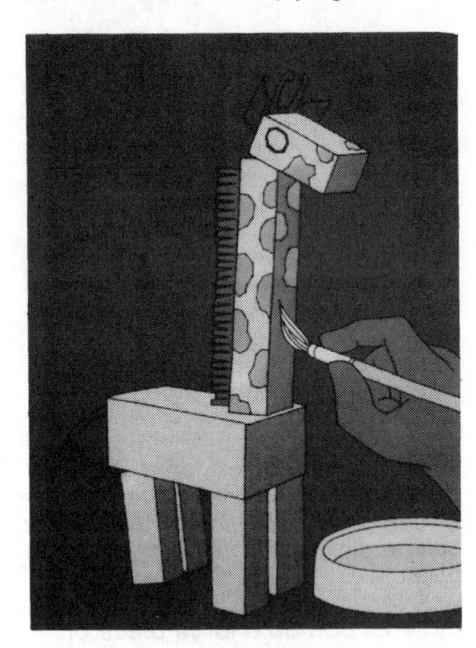

WORKING WITH PAPER, CARD AND CARDBOARD and STRING, RAFFIA AND MATERIAL are the three titles constituting the set. There are at least 60 art ideas in each of these volumes.

Ideas are described in a combination of step-by-step directions and illustrations. Though each project is clearly laid out and fully developed, there is plenty of opportunity for creative youngsters to add personal touches.

The books may be used effectively either directly by students or as resource books for teachers. A color-code system delineates five different levels of difficulty, ranging from very simple activities to advanced projects.

Most teachers should find many new ideas (or variations on old ones) for classroom art activities. Try some of these: a Bugatti sports car or a knight's helmet (from CARD AND CARDBOARD); a hanging paper fish and a fancy paper cockatoo (from WORKING WITH PAPER); bottle covers and raffia lampshades (from STRING, RAFFIA AND MATERIAL). For those unable to obtain raffia (a natural fiber dyed to different colors and often available in crafts shops), yarn constitutes a "reasonable facsimile thereof."

The books are independent of each other and are sold separately.

Order from: Franklin Watts, Inc., 730 Fifth Ave., New York, NY 10019. Grade level: K – 6. Cost: $6.95 per book. Add $.25 postage and handling for first book; $.10 each additional book. Orders under $15 must be accompanied by payment.

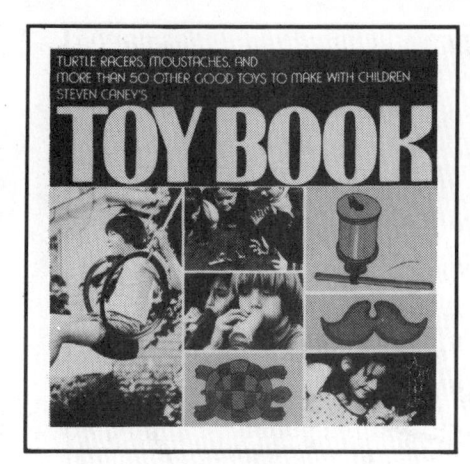

# ARTS & CRAFTS

## STEVEN CANEY'S TOY BOOK

☆ ☆ ☆ ☆ ☆ ☆ ☆ ☆

"Donut Bird Feeders," "Design Boards," "Racing Spools," "Pocket Parachutes" and "Paper Roll Pottery" are just a few of the 51 toy "recipes" described in STEVEN CANEY'S TOY BOOK. Most of the construction tasks are simple enough to be followed by primary-age kids and still hold the interest of older children.

Many of the toys are appropriate for science, math and social studies projects, crafts and leisure-time activities, or gifts. Building directions are in the form of illustrations and simple descriptions. How do you make a "design board"? Just hammer nails randomly into a 10- or 12-inch square board. Then take yarn, string or rubber bands and start designing.

Order from: Workman Publishing Company, Inc., 231 East 51 St., New York, NY 10022. Grade level: Teachers of all grades. Cost: $3.95. Payment must accompany order.

## A BALL OF CLAY
**by John Hawkinson**

Hawkinson proposes some imaginative alternatives to the usual lumpy ashtrays and spindly snakes that kids turn out when they first meet up with clay. The author, who clearly loves the medium ("least expensive, nonpolluting, easy to keep, always ready and the most fun"), uses photographs and drawings to show how to make masks, horses, birds, fishes, dolls, bowls and mugs. All activities are classroom tested.

WHITMAN, $4.50 (list), $3.38 (school price). Ages 7 and up. See page 151 for ordering information.

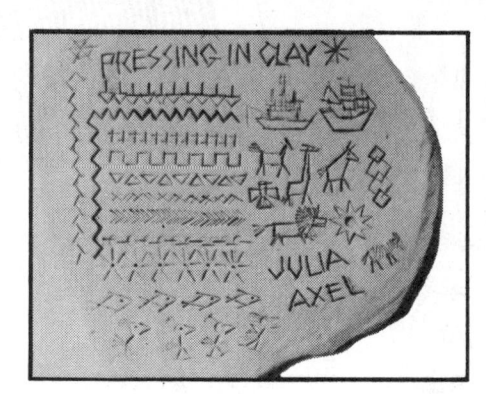

## MODEL CARS AND TRUCKS AND HOW TO BUILD THEM
**by Harvey Weiss**

Detailed photographs, plans and drawings illustrate seven basic models — racing cars, trucks, trailer trucks, tractors, derricks, motor-driven cars and even a car large enough to sit on — in this well-designed and well-written guide. All of the models have clean, simple lines, reminiscent of the work of a New England craftsman — nice to look at and touch and undoubtedly fun to make, too.

CROWELL, $7.50 (list), $5.40 (school price). Ages 9 – 13. See page 151 for ordering information.

# MATH

# OPERATION METRICATION

☆ ☆ ☆ ☆ ☆ ☆ ☆ ☆ ☆

Though metrics conversion is as inevitable as death and taxes, there's no need for gloom. In fact, the prospect of using a measuring system that's logical, precise and easy to compute should come as a welcome relief. But if you still feel someone is threatening you with a meter stick, there are materials that can help build your confidence and provide the experiences your students need.

Students are probably more dispassionate about metrics than the rest of us. For them, "think metric" can mean visualizing a distance in meters or estimating capacity in liters—learning a language by living with it, not by constantly translating. Think metric does have a more positive sound than "think conversion."

▸ **Meters, Liters and Grams** could be a fine way for your class to start in thinking metric. This is a series of six introductory work texts for grades three through eight by Audrey V. Buffington.

No prior knowledge of metrics—on the part of either student or teacher—is necessary. Nor is success dependent on facility with our present measurement system, since conversion computations are not included.

In the grade three book, students work with meters, centimeters, liters, kilograms and grams. Each unit becomes more familiar to the students as they measure, estimate, compute, make models and solve word problems. By grade six, the units of measure have increased to 21.

Each booklet measures about 8-1/2-by-11 inches (actually 21-by-27.5 centimeters) and has 64 pages. The format is open, attractive and designed to facilitate independent student use. Vocabulary is carefully developed, and reading requirements are realistic. Directions are simple, specific and easy to follow. Review is built in. Inclusion of answer keys makes the work self-correcting.

METERS, LITERS AND GRAMS makes the range of metric measures more real.

Order from: Random House, Inc., 400 Hahn Rd., Westminster, MD 21157. Grade level: 3 – 8. Cost $1.50 per book; $1.80 per book for teacher's editions.

▸ **Metric Tape** should be a useful addition to the metric classroom. Pressure-sensitive (that's scientific for "sticky") tape, about one-half inch wide and clearly labeled in centimeters with marks for millimeters, can be applied to strips of tagboard to provide metric measures for each child.

METRIC TAPE is available in 100-centimeter lengths (50 to a roll). Each 100-cm length provides a meter rule.

The tape can also be applied to shelf edges, counters, desk tops and assorted objects as reference rules and reminders to think metric.

Order from: Edmund Scientific Co., 380 Edscorp Bldg., Barrington, NJ 08007. Grade level: Teachers of all grades. Cost: 100-cm tape (#41,376), $3. Payment must accompany order.

▸ **Metricat10n** (yes, that's a 10 in there) is a metrics game that can help break down the mystique of the metric terminology. While students wheel and deal around a Monopoly-style board, they also learn to decipher "deci's" and "deka's."

The game components include seven kinds of metric money. It takes ten milli units to equal one centi, ten centi units for one deci, and so on. Metric terms and money should be a comfortable association for students, since they're already familiar with "ten of this makes one of that" in dealing with pennies, dimes and dollars.

Some elements of the game are unvarnished propaganda against the "enemy" English measurement system. It doesn't mar the game, but it does seem a little unnecessary. Students may want to discuss this.

After a few journeys along Dekameter Boulevard and Hectometer Road, and after collecting a bundle of meters and deci's from the Metric Holding Company, students will begin straightening out the language of metrics. (They may even come up with new activities using the metric money.) METRICATION could be a way to fix those prefixes and have a good time doing it.

Order from: Metrix Corp., P.O. Box 19101, Orlando, FL 32814. Grade level: 5 – adult. Cost: $10.00. Add $.50 for postage and handling. Payment must accompany orders from individuals. School purchase orders will be billed.

# PERFECT MATCH MATH PUZZLES

Number and numeral, fraction and equivalent, problem and answer—all are items for matching activities. Introduce the factor of interlocking halves and you have a matching activity that gives immediate reinforcement.

Sturdy stock that can stand much manipulation is the basic material for these puzzles. Cut the stock into uniform rectangles of a size best suited to the age groups you work with. Plan and mark a free-form center divider line on each and then mark the card with its pair of symbols. Cut along the divider line and you have puzzle pieces ready to use.

If a child is sure of a match, he quickly puts the parts together. If he isn't he may use the contour of the dividing edge as an aid. For older children, make the contour less pronounced to offer more challenge.

If you plan several sets of these matching puzzles to reinforce different number relationships, use different colors of stock for each set so they may be easily sorted out for use or storage.

Idea by: Kevin J. Swick and Dormalee Lindberg, Southern Illinois University, Carbondale, Ill.

# 26 MATH

| 5 | 10 | 15 | 20 | 25 |
|---|---|---|---|---|
| 30 | 35 | 40 | 45 | 50 |
| 55 | 60 | 65 | 70 | 75 |
| 80 | 85 | 90 | 95 | 100 |

## CHANGE CHART

A pocket-sized change chart may be helpful to children learning to make change. Prepare for each child a sheet of paper ruled into 20 one-inch squares (five squares across by four squares deep). Students count by fives across the chart, square by square, writing in the numbers 5 through 100.

Orientation to the change charts involves pointing out that (1) jumps from square to square across each row are "nickel" jumps, (2) jumps down the right-hand side are "quarter" jumps, (3) only those numbers ending in 5 or 0 are on the chart.

Begin using the change chart for easy transactions: "You buy candy for 15 cents and pay with a quarter." (Starting on 15 you make two jumps across to 25; that's two nickels.)

"Something costs 60 cents. You pay with a dollar." (Starting on 60 you make three nickel jumps to the end of the row, and one quarter jump to 100.)

Now try amounts not on the chart. "You buy something for 39 cents and pay with a dollar." (Count by ones—pennies—until you reach a number that is on the chart. In this case one penny will do it. Once on the chart you jump across nickels and down by quarters to get your change: one penny, two nickels, two quarters.)

Counting back change aloud has a nice businesslike sound to it, and the charts help kids keep track of their place until they're really good at it. Then the change charts will go the way of counting sticks and training wheels.

Idea by: Elizabeth Dawson,
Harding School, Hammond, Ind.

## MAGIC SQUARES

☆ ☆ ☆ ☆ ☆ ☆ ☆ ☆

There really is magic in MAGIC SQUARES. It lies in the fact that they can be constructed for use with all levels of ability, are self-correcting in their very makeup, and usually fire up a persistence in the puzzle-solver that's miraculous. They're fun, too.

A Magic Square is a grid of cells, three rows on three rows, or four on four. Numerals are placed in the cells in such a way that the sums worked horizontally, vertically and diagonally are all the same.

Magic Square workbooks use the Magic Square principle to create self-correcting math sheets. The student does a computation sheet reinforcing a particular operation. He puts the answers into specially marked cells of a Magic Square and then adds the rows to check his work.

There are five books, identified by levels A through E. Each book has 40 pages, each a duplicating master. The computation exercises in the series range from basic addition and subtraction of two-digit numbers in level A to multiplication and division with six-digit numbers in level E.

Each master is marked with a skills index, e.g., "Division: two-digit numbers by one-digit numbers, regrouping." This helps in getting the appropriate work to groups or individuals. A complete listing of skills is found on the back cover of each book, along with answers for cases of great "stuckness."

MAGIC SQUARES become a useful activity for math stations, for besides being self-correcting, they can be undertaken without direction once the pattern is established.

Correcting work with an answer key will never bring the same sense of satisfaction that comes with mastering the wizardry of MAGIC SQUARES.

Order from: Charles E. Merrill Publishing Co., 1300 Alum Creek Dr., Columbus, OH 43216. Grade level: Primary—intermediate. Cost: $25.00 for series; $5.50 per book. Add $1 for postage and handling. Payment must accompany orders under $10.

# MATH 27

## GEOBOARD ACTIVITY CARDS

☆ ☆ ☆ ☆ ☆ ☆ ☆ ☆

The geoboard is a math instructor's equivalent of the safety pin. It is an extremely simple classroom tool, yet one with multiple applications. To sit down, though, and dream up dozens of activities for each of the different math operations can be a time-consuming affair. Printing and illustrating them in the form of activity cards would take even longer. Here, then, is a selection of commercially produced activity kits:

▶ Scott Resources, Inc., has two boxes of cards by Alan Barson. GEOBOARD ACTIVITY CARDS — PRIMARY contains more than 100 cards directed toward the primary grades. There are tasks that require one to distinguish "sameness" and "difference," plus activities related to design, counting, coordinates, perimeter and area.

Scott's GEOBOARD ACTIVITY CARDS — INTERMEDIATE is for the upper elementary grades. It includes activities in more than 20 different mathematical areas from general exploration and counting to properties of mathematical systems.

Order from: Scott Resources, Inc., P.O. Box 2121, Fort Collins, CO 80522. Grade level: 1 – 3, primary set; 4 – 6, intermediate set. Cost: $13.95 per set plus 5 percent postage and handling. Payment must accompany orders from individuals.

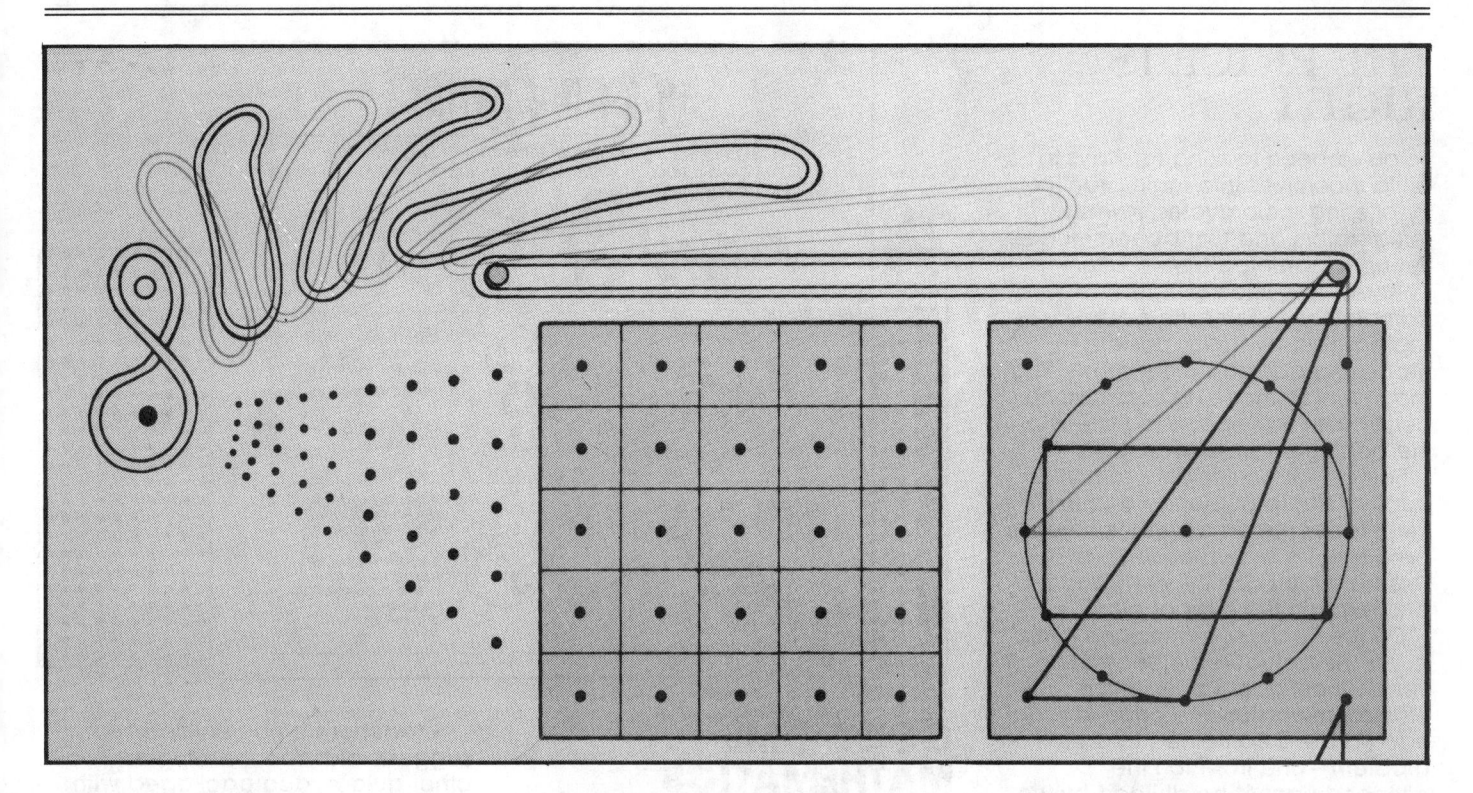

▶ A GEOBOARD ACTIVITY CARD KIT by John Trivett is produced by Cuisenaire. The kit begins with general explorations of the geoboard and advances to work with fractions and other more difficult concepts. The activity cards are directed toward the intermediate and junior high grades.

Order from: Cuisenaire Company of America, Inc., 12 Church St., New Rochelle, NY 10805. Grade level: 3 – 9. Cost: $11.95 plus 5 percent postage and handling.

## ENHANCE CHANCE

☆ ☆ ☆ ☆ ☆ ☆ ☆ ☆

ENHANCE CHANCE is not designed to equip your students to beat the house at its own game. It's a game book that offers ways to use dice to extend and reinforce mathematical concepts — and to have fun. The fun part is important.

To play the games, you'll need more than one pair of dice. You'll also be using unusual dice — with fractions, symbols and such — that you can make with self-stick labels.

Duplication of the playing board pages is suggested. An alternative to copying would be to pull out the playing board pages (they are perforated for easy removal) and place them in plastic sleeves.

Rules for games are stated briefly, which in some cases operates against easy understanding. You'll want to preview rules and fix the play well in mind before trying a game. The play can be carried on without fuss once the procedure is established.

Games include activities such as plotting points on a number line, graphing points on a grid, arranging digits to achieve numbers evenly divisible by a given number from two to nine, and coloring in given percentages of a 100-square box. The book provides for several levels of challenge, both in the variety of games and in the variations within games. Students are encouraged to invent new variations as well.

This is a game book that will enhance the chance of increasing math interest, and the odds are it will boost proficiency, too.

Order from: Activity Resources Co., Inc., P.O. Box 4875, Hayward, CA 94540. Grade level: 1 – 8. Cost: $3.50. No charge for postage or handling if you prepay. ($.50 will be added to billed orders under $10).

## 28 MATH

# THE PRICE IS RIGHT

If you've been looking for ways to build incentives into math practice, try offering motorcycles, jewelry, refrigerators and Caribbean cruises. Set up a game patterned after the TV show "The Price Is Right," complete with fantastic prizes—represented by travel posters, magazine ads and other props. You may want to make up some winners' certificates with space to write in the particular prizes won.

Select four contestants from your captive studio audience and invite them to "come on down." (It helps to be a bit of a showperson yourself.) Describe the prize they're trying for and explain the rules of play.

On the TV show, contestants try to guess the actual retail price of an item without going over. In this classroom version, the price tag for each prize is contained in a division problem—one in which the dividend cannot be divided by the divisor evenly (e.g., 17 ÷ 3). Each player is asked to estimate the "whole number" part of the quotient. (In other words, what number × 3 comes closest to 17 without going over?)

Duplicate prizes will be awarded in case of ties. (Or you may want individuals to try for their own prizes rather than compete.)

After about four or five sets of contestants have had turns, winners try for the "Grand Showcase." This involves several items with "prices" that must be estimated without going over.

For students with active imaginations, winning a matched set of sports cars—even on paper—can bring some welcome diversion to division.

Idea by: Patricia Dubie and William Kane, Christopher Gibson Elementary School, Dorchester, Mass.

# TEACHING MATHEMATICS IN THE ELEMENTARY SCHOOL
**by Lola June May**

Written specifically for education students, this hefty (350-page) book is also useful for practicing teachers dealing with metrics, individualized instruction, math games, sets, number theory, informal geometry and problem solving.

Order from: The Free Press, 866 Third Ave., New York, NY 10022. Grade level: Teachers of primary–intermediate. Cost: $5.95, paperback; $9.95, hardcover.

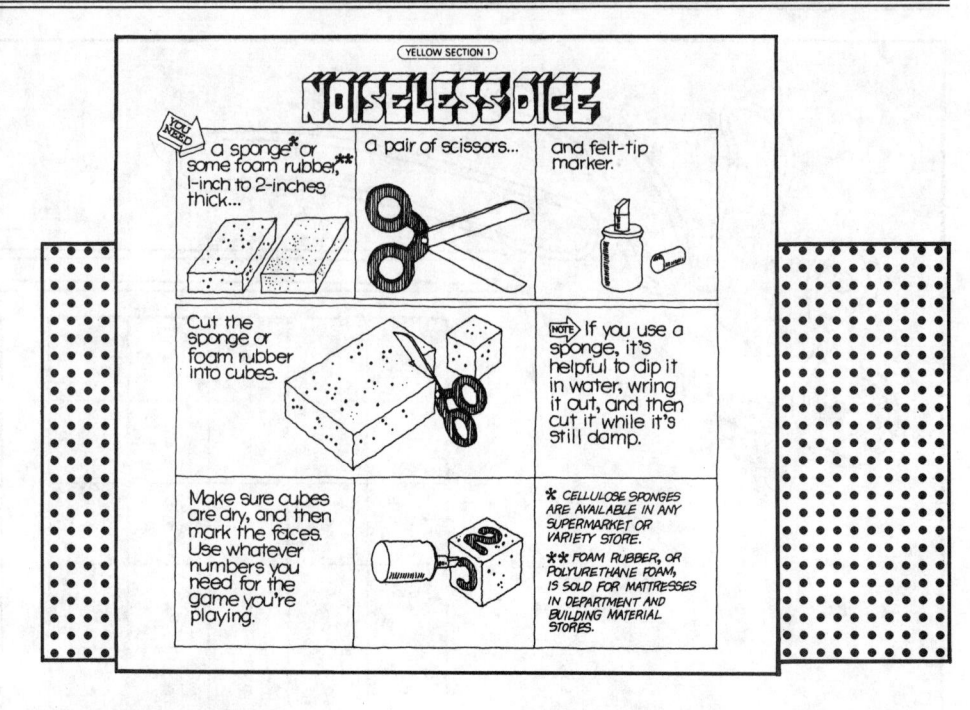

# GOOD TIME MATHEMATICS EVENT CARDS
☆ ☆ ☆ ☆ ☆ ☆ ☆ ☆ ☆

An event implies action, and that's just what is called for in each of the 100 activity cards in this kit of supplementary math materials.

Part of a larger supplementary math program, but available separately, the event cards are organized into five skill areas: "Numbers and Operations," "Measurement," "Geometry," "Statistics and Probability" and "Functions and Graphs." A final "Yellow Section" describes how to make the simple games and tools for use in the other five sections.

Designed for intermediate grade students who already have mastered the basic math facts, the cards offer a lively, enjoyable approach to math. Responses are not limited to computations, but call for other means of expression. Card No. 4 in the "Numbers and Operations" section, for example, calls for manipulative activity (working with toothpicks), estimating (the number of toothpicks in three boxes), and then asks the student to "Explain what you've done with a drawing or story."

Though the set contains 100 cards, the activities number much higher. On the front of each card is a main event and on the reverse side are usually two or three related activities. In addition, the back of each card pulls things together with a brief statement about the activities, a summary of the concept or a definition.

A teacher's guide entitled "Help!" suggests classroom strategies. Two other guides, also packaged with the activity cards, explain how to make and use geoboards and tangrams.

The front of each card is colorfully illustrated and designed for easy readability. The cards are printed on sturdy, laminated cardboard.

Though the cost of the kit runs high for an individual teacher's budget, teachers willing to share the cost and the kit will find this a useful addition to their math lessons or learning centers.

Order from: Learning Resource Center, 10655 S.W. Greenburg Rd., Portland, OR 97223. Grade level: 4–6. Cost: $19.88 plus 10 percent postage and handling. Payment must accompany order. School purchase orders will be billed.

# MANCALA
☆ ☆ ☆ ☆ ☆ ☆ ☆ ☆ ☆

MANCALA, also known as Kalah and the African Stone Game, is an ancient African game that has spread throughout the world. It involves two players each trying to accumulate a larger number of beads than his opponent. In playing this game younger children will develop skills in counting while older children and adults will sharpen their skills in problem solving and reasoning.

Creative Publications has produced an attractive, inexpensive wooden-board version of the game, which is a nice way to introduce the game to kids. But once they have learned how to play, it is simple for them to make their own personal reproductions of the game. The materials necessary for doing so are egg cartons and stones or beans. By simply cutting an egg carton in half and gluing half the top on either end (for Kalah spaces), each student can have his own personal game board.

Order from: Creative Publications, P.O. Box 10328, Palo Alto, CA 94303. Grade level: 3–12. Cost: $11.13. Payment must accompany orders from individuals. School purchase orders will be billed.

## COOPERATIVE PIE-BUILDING

Some fraction slices, a pinch of cooperation and a dash of competition add up to some nice, round, pie-shaped wholes and some high interest. Fractions take on new meaning when children work together to build wholes by combining parts.

Cut 12 identical discs — about six inches in diameter — from tagboard. Six of the discs will be cut into fractions — halves, thirds, fourths, fifths, sixths and eighths — and then labeled with their appropriate number name. Six of the discs remain wholes to build on.

Assign the six whole pieces to students who will serve as fraction collectors. Then distribute the fraction pieces, one to a child. The culminating task is for the children to put together wholes among themselves, using the fraction pieces. The children who were assigned the whole discs will be responsible for collecting just the right fractions to exactly cover their disc. (You'll want to determine the logistics of the collecting process before the chaos sets in.)

With younger children you may want to limit the parts to halves, fourths and eighths. The others may produce the problem of some "almost wholes," since children will be arranging the fractions visually, not mathematically. To prepare for this, work out ahead of time the combinations that make a "legal" whole. (How are you at lowest common denominators?)

Children will soon begin to anticipate what is needed to fill, and the use of equivalents will come into play.

The class may develop new rules and strategies. Putting a pie together may prove almost as much fun as taking a pie apart.

Idea by: Andy Klee, Superior School, Superior, Wyo.

# Specialty of the Day—
# Mathematical Malnutrition

by Leroy G. Callahan

The cereal boxes on our breakfast tables provide daily reminders of the "Minimum Daily Requirements" for good nutrition. In the classroom, there are no cereal boxes to remind us of the intellectual nourishment that should be contained in a 45-minute reading lesson or in a half hour spent at a math interest center. The complexity of the intellectual needs of children does not allow for such quantitative precision. We do, however, have general guidelines for an intellectual diet deemed proper for happy, productive living. Making reference to mathematics fare only, adequate nutrition can be achieved through a proficiency in skills needed in day-to-day interactions with the environment, the ability to apply these skills in appropriate life situations, and a sense of mathematics as a logical system of related ideas.

How have we gone about satisfying the need for these curriculum nutrients? Unfortunately, in much the same manner as we have sought to satisfy the need for food nutrients. In both cases, we have quite consistently moved from periods of complacency and blind neglect to periods of crisis and self-defeating activity. Consider the crash diets, pre-processed foods, energy-charged junk foods and chemical additives that often contribute to nutritional problems. Parallel phenomena exist in education, greatly complicating the quest for a proper balance of experiences.

**Crash Diets.** The water diet. The grapefruit diet. The drinking man's diet. Whatever the variation, most crash diets are so narrowly specialized that serious nutritional imbalances occur. Similar problems may occur in overspecialized mathematical diets. In elementary mathematics, it was popular a decade and a half ago to prescribe crash diets limited to structural and abstract mathematics. The very appropriate objective—to achieve an appreciation for and understanding of the logical structure of mathematics—became a compulsion for the movement's zealots. The immediate consequence for many students and teachers was intellectual indigestion. Later and more general consequences of this dietary imbalance were a drop in student proficiency in some math skills and an inability to apply the skills they did acquire to practical situations.

Another crash diet was offered by those who joined in the hasty retreat from the extremes of "modern math." These "return-to-the-fundamentals" advocates offer steady diets of paper-and-pencil computational exercises. An effort is sometimes made to make the fare more palatable by sprinkling "individualized instruction" over the surface. This usually involves a quasi-scientific "systems" approach to mathematics instruction. Though this diet may produce little violent mathematical indigestion, it tends to be so watered down and bland that few who consume it will ever perceive math as a system of logically related ideas. The result is a stunting of intellectual development. But then, crash diets were never meant to promote "growth and development."

**Pre-processed Foods.** The pressure of limited time can make this approach very appealing. Pre-processed math eliminates the need for lengthy preparation periods—no muss, no fuss; it's in the bag. Behaviors are specified. Math instruction simply becomes a matter of transmitting these abstract and symbolic behaviors to our students.

For example, the pre-processed program may specify—and the teacher may promulgate—that it is important for a primary student to be able to respond to a subtraction situation represented as $13 - 8 = ?$ But if this abstract and symbolic representational statement is to have real meaning, it must be preceded by proper exploratory experiences. Such experiences can range from work with coins and other countables from real-life situations to work with number lines to finding "other names" for 13 on a number balance. And both the amount of such exploration and the preparation needed for it can differ widely among children.

By-passing such experiences and moving directly to the symbolic end-products often results in students turning in acceptable performances on symbolic tests. But test-taking prowess doesn't necessarily indicate understanding. A strict diet of pre-packaged programs precludes real individualization and adds little to a child's intellectual growth.

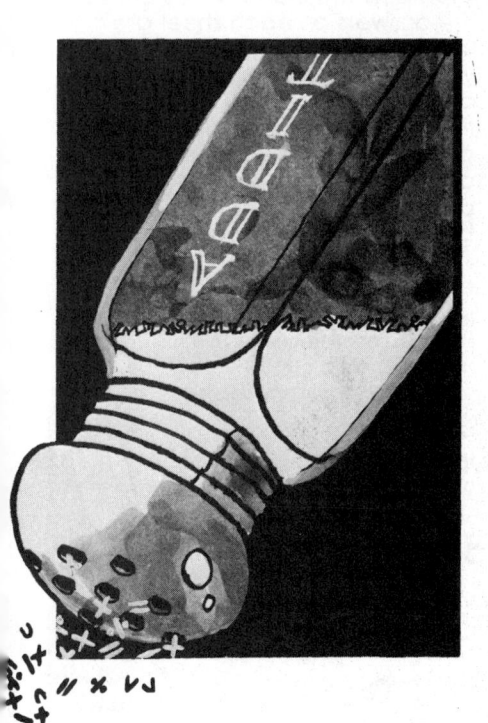

**Additives.** The math curriculum is often loaded with "additives." Some may alter the flavor, some may merely be extenders. Consider these:

∩ { } > <

Sets, functions and relationships can indeed be introduced at an early stage in the mathematics curriculum. But if adding these elements results only in superficial learning, the student is likely to end up memorizing a lot of symbols that do little beyond coloring the mathematics curriculum and certainly add nothing to its substance.

Choosing nutritious intellectual fare for children is a serious responsibility for teachers, just as choosing nutritious food is a serious responsibility for parents. Each should be aware of what constitutes a balanced diet. And when mathematics is the fare, the desired equilibrium can be elusive, because math is a constantly evolving science.

Thus decisions about math curriculum and materials must be based on a clear understanding of what comprises meaningful, practical, significant and intellectually stimulating learning. The teacher should carefully examine and compare programs and materials, and look for flexibility, variety and a balance of the theoretical and the practical. You should also know your children and their needs, read and listen to experts—and provide your own salt. Once you have the basics clearly in mind, you can shop around, vary your menu, add a few sensible snacks when appropriate, and watch the children grow.

*Leroy G. Callahan is associate professor in the Department of Elementary and Remedial Education, State University of New York at Buffalo.*

# TOOTHPICK TECHNOLOGY

Your students don't have to be disciplined architects to create elaborate three-dimensional shapes. Using readily available, inexpensive materials, kids can build models that develop skills and understanding in math, science and art.

By sticking toothpicks into small molded balls of ordinary window putty, Plasticine or clay, or peas soaked in water, they can build a variety of structures: pyramids, cubes, parallelepipeds, or even geodesic domes. And their experimentation with the different shapes can lead them to discover a number of basic principles. Each student-designed structure can have its own line segments, angles, height, length, width, strength factor and aesthetic quality. Comparisons can be made between two- and three-dimensional forms.

To begin, you can challenge your students to make a three-dimensional object that has four sides (a pyramid). Give the students at least six toothpicks and enough material to make the four joints. As they get the knack, discuss the various types of forms they can build. Then add more materials and watch the structures grow.

If you're working with primary grade students, you might want to begin by giving a demonstration of how to construct a simple three-dimensional form. Intermediate and upper grade students can do most of the experimenting for themselves.

*Idea by: Julie Jones, Longfellow Elementary School, Salida, Colo.*

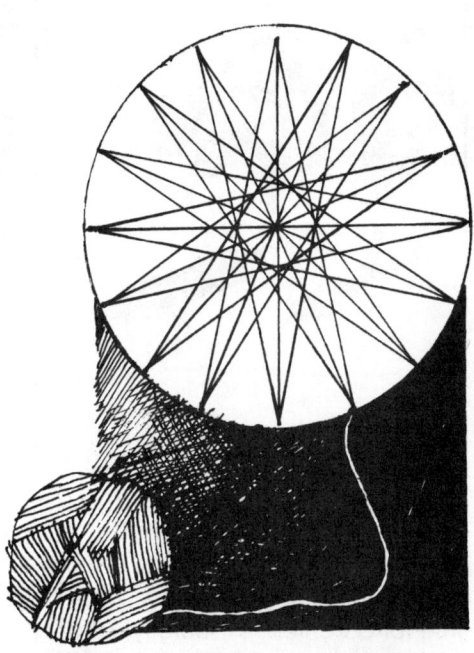

# STRING SCULPTURE

☆ ☆ ☆ ☆ ☆ ☆ ☆ ☆

The connection between string designs and mathematics isn't as slight as it may first appear. "Sculptures" created with string, thread, yarn, monofilament or pencil and paper involve a good many geometry-related skills. And the more complex three-dimensional designs require use of mathematical tools in constructing the necessary circles and ovals, angles, rectangles and triangles.

String sculpture involves stretching straight lengths of thread or drawing straight lines between points. When many points are connected, the intersecting lines form an "envelope" or seemingly curved outer edge. The eventual result is the creation of aesthetically pleasing geometric forms and patterns.

This 64-page book by John Winter gets users off to an easy start by showing how to make basic two-dimensional designs with pencil and paper. It progresses into more complex three-dimensional forms using cardboard and plastic.

Many illustrations and sample patterns, most drawn on graph paper, are provided. The basic forms suggested in the book can be used to create an infinite variety of original sculptures. This book is primarily a teacher resource but can be used independently by older students.

*Order from: Creative Publications, P.O. Box 10328, Palo Alto, CA 94303. Grade level: Teachers of grades 3–high school. Cost: $3.98. Payment must accompany orders by individuals. School purchase orders will be billed.*

## EVERYBODY WINS!

Right about now might be a good time for a contest, especially if that contest gives everybody a good run outdoors. Tell your students a contest is about to begin, appoint a record keeper and move on out to a corner of the building or the playing field.

The activity is this: students run from the corner where they are to the next corner, taking turns so that only two will be running at the same time. Each contestant will report to the record keeper the number of steps taken. And nobody wins yet.

Back inside the room, the record keeper lists the numbers of steps — arranged in sequence from lowest to highest — on the board. The range is noted, the median found and the average computed. Now to find the winners — as many as possible.

Class One winners might be those whose numbers fall nearest the median. Class two might be the prime numbers. Class Three, numbers above the average, or those numbers that can be evenly divided by three, or all even numbers, etc., etc. The students themselves may find other categories, using the data in new ways to get more winners.

After the crazy contest is over, students may deal with some more concrete considerations: (1) measuring the actual distance run and figuring the length of each person's running step; (2) estimating the number of steps required to cover the distance at a walk; (3) pacing off the distance and figuring the length of one's pace to use as a portable measuring tool — a standard all too soon rendered obsolete by lengthening limbs.

Idea by: Pauline Davies, Simmons Elementary School, Aberdeen, S. Dak.

## STATION BREAK

Overheard at a math station: "An ace and a joker! That's 1 and 0. Maybe I'll do better at the beanbag toss."

Imagine five carnival-like math stations, each managed by a child who's armed with a red pencil for noting the numbers each player "wins" — and perhaps an assistant to field those beanbags and shuffle those cards. Each station provides an activity that yields numbers. The numbers available and the operations to be performed with them can be planned to meet the needs of differing grade levels. (Mr. Theismann's kindergartners play for two numbers under 6, to be written on their worksheets in the form of an addition problem by each station manager.)

At one station, children may draw two cards from a deck of jokers, aces, twos, threes, fours and fives. At another station, children throw beanbags through numbered holes in a board. Or sponges may be tossed into half-gallon milk cartons cut in half, bunched in a box and each marked with a number. Two numbers may be collected from dice or dominoes. (Younger children may copy off the dots and count.) One station may have a race track for toy cars. Children take turns sending a car across a paper marked off with numbered lines. The line closest to the place where the car stops is the number collected for that turn.

The children tour the stations with their worksheets, receiving an addition problem at each. The problems are then worked out and the answers on each sheet are totaled — a teacher task with the younger ones, and a chance to check over the work. The child with the largest total wins. (The fact that at one or two stations the numbers are determined by pure luck gives a break to the less accomplished beanbag tossers.) And since math skills are being strengthened, everybody wins.

Idea by: Tom Theismann, Folwell School, Rochester, Minn.

## WAR ON MULTIPLICATION

Since multiplication tables can be a formidable adversary for many in your class, you shouldn't have any conscientious objection to this kind of war.

War is adapted from a card game you may have played as a youngster. The War material is a deck of homemade cards — three-by-five index cards with the multiplication facts. You can begin with a limited range if you wish and add new facts as students progress.

The battle plan is as follows:
1. Shuffle cards thoroughly.
2. Divide the deck equally between two players. (You'll have to alter the rules slightly for more than two.)
3. Players reshuffle their cards but may not look at them.
4. Each player reveals his top card and calls out the value of the face. The higher value wins, and that player picks up both cards. Each player is allowed approximately five seconds to answer. If he doesn't answer, or gives the incorrect response, he loses the card to his opponent.
5. If both players' cards have the same value, e.g., $3 \times 8$ and $4 \times 6$, War is declared. Each player lays three cards face down and then one face up. The player with the highest value on the face-up card wins all the cards for that play.
6. The game goes on until one player cleans out the other. The game could also be a timed event, the winner being the one with the most cards at the end of a specified time.

The losers are winners, too, as they become quicker with the multiplication tables. You'll find too that you'll have enough volunteers for this war that a draft won't be needed.

Idea by: Alan Van Cott, Islip Middle School, Islip, Long Island, N.Y.

# MATH 33

## EQUATIONS
## The Game of Creative Mathematics

☆ ☆ ☆ ☆ ☆ ☆ ☆ ☆ ☆

You say the math wizard down the hall has been setting up Equations tournaments? You say that your class has been bugging you to start one too? And you're too embarrassed to tell them that even the directions look tough? Well, help is on the way.

First, for those who haven't heard of EQUATIONS — and that's all right too — it's a game of mathematical logic. Put out by WFF 'N PROOF, creators of "games for thinkers," EQUATIONS can be quite challenging to both players and leaders.

The basic objective of play is to arrange a balanced equation, using the numbers and symbols on sets of colored cubes. (The ability of the players determines which set of cubes is used.)

The cubes are rolled out. The numbers on top are called "Resources." Out of the Resources the first player picks the number for the right-hand side of the equation. This number is the "Goal." Other players work to match the Goal — in their heads at first. They decide which of the remaining Resources may or may not be used. Players must keep changing ways of matching the Goal as the game goes on.

Need help? To get this useful, fascinating and addictive game going, read the booklet "One Teacher's Guide to Equations." After several pages of introduction and tournament talk, there are lesson plans. The plans offer a logical and painless initiation to EQUATIONS for players and teacher alike.

Suggestions are provided for introducing the game to grades 6 through 12 and for working with earlier grades as well.

With the helpful support of this guide, EQUATIONS can be used in many ways — as math enrichment, math motivation or math instruction.

Perhaps the next class to host an Equations tournament will be yours.

Order from: WFF 'N PROOF, 1490-EQ South Blvd., Ann Arbor, MI 48104. Grade level: Intermediate — high school. Cost: $9 plus $1 postage and handling. Payment must accompany individual orders. School purchase orders will be billed.

## MATHEMATICS SPINNER KIT

☆ ☆ ☆ ☆ ☆ ☆ ☆ ☆ ☆

Colorful and fun, this kit is a kaleidoscope of 22 math activity cards.

A game of sorts, it can be played by a single child or a small group. The player slips one of the cards into a plastic cover, spins the needle attached to the cover and proceeds to solve the problem chance has given him.

Though the kit's contents are grouped roughly for two grade levels — primary and intermediate — a classroom test showed that the activities are best suited for the upper elementary grades.

What is special about the kit is the colorful design of each of the cards and the element of chance introduced by spinning the needle. Combined, they make for an involving learning experience.

The teacher certainly isn't limited to the cards supplied with the kit. Using the provided cards as models, teachers and students can easily make their own cards, creating them out of six-by-six-inch pieces of cardboard and using felt pens, crayons or paint for illustrations.

Order from: Houghton Mifflin Co., Dept. M-L, One Beacon St., Boston, MA 02107. Grade level: 3–7. Cost: $3.39 plus 8 percent postage and handling. Payment must accompany order.

# 34 MATH

## PACEMAKER PROTRACTOR

☆ ☆ ☆ ☆ ☆ ☆ ☆ ☆ ☆

You can make circles with it; construct, measure and bisect angles; find the heights of tall structures; make geometric designs; or chart the route an airplane will cover. And more. The PACEMAKER PROTRACTOR is a unique little tool for serious mathematicians, students of intermediate grade level or above — or just plain doodlers.

The PACEMAKER PROTRACTOR is a square piece of amber-colored plastic with a large open circle in the center. Spanning the circle is a removable rotor that turns 360 degrees and has holes along its perimeter. The rotor is used for drawing circles of varying sizes. The outside edges of the square are marked off into inches and centimeters for measuring. Other parts of the protractor contain fixed, measured round holes for making circles.

An instruction booklet explains how to operate the device, make designs with it and carry out several other procedures. Diagrams of the designs accompany the explanations. Older or faster students can use the guide by themselves; others will need help from the teacher.

The PACEMAKER PROTRACTOR may be used either in place of or supplementary to a standard protractor. Students exploring randomly will find out for themselves many of the protractor's possibilities.

Order from: Frey Educational Research, Inc., 7434 Craigmere Dr., Cleveland, OH 44130. Grade level: Intermediate — high school. Cost: $2.95, protractor and teacher's guide; $1.95 per protractor; $1.25 per teacher's guide. Add $.70 postage and handling to all orders.

## RACE TO THE REGISTER

While shopping is becoming an increasingly grim experience for most of us, your class can recapture some of the old consumer spirit with a "Going Shopping" game. Action centers around a game board that the children can help construct. First they can collect supermarket ads and coupons, clipping out individual items (with prices). The items are then sorted according to supermarket categories — produce, meat, health and beauty aids, etc. These items then become the "stock" for the shelves of your game board.

Using a full-sized piece of poster board, arrange items in rows from a START space to a REGISTER. In the aisles between the rows, draw arrows to indicate the direction that the player-shoppers are to move.

Other equipment for the game: dice, tokens (one for each player), scribble pads and pencils, play money (not absolutely necessary).

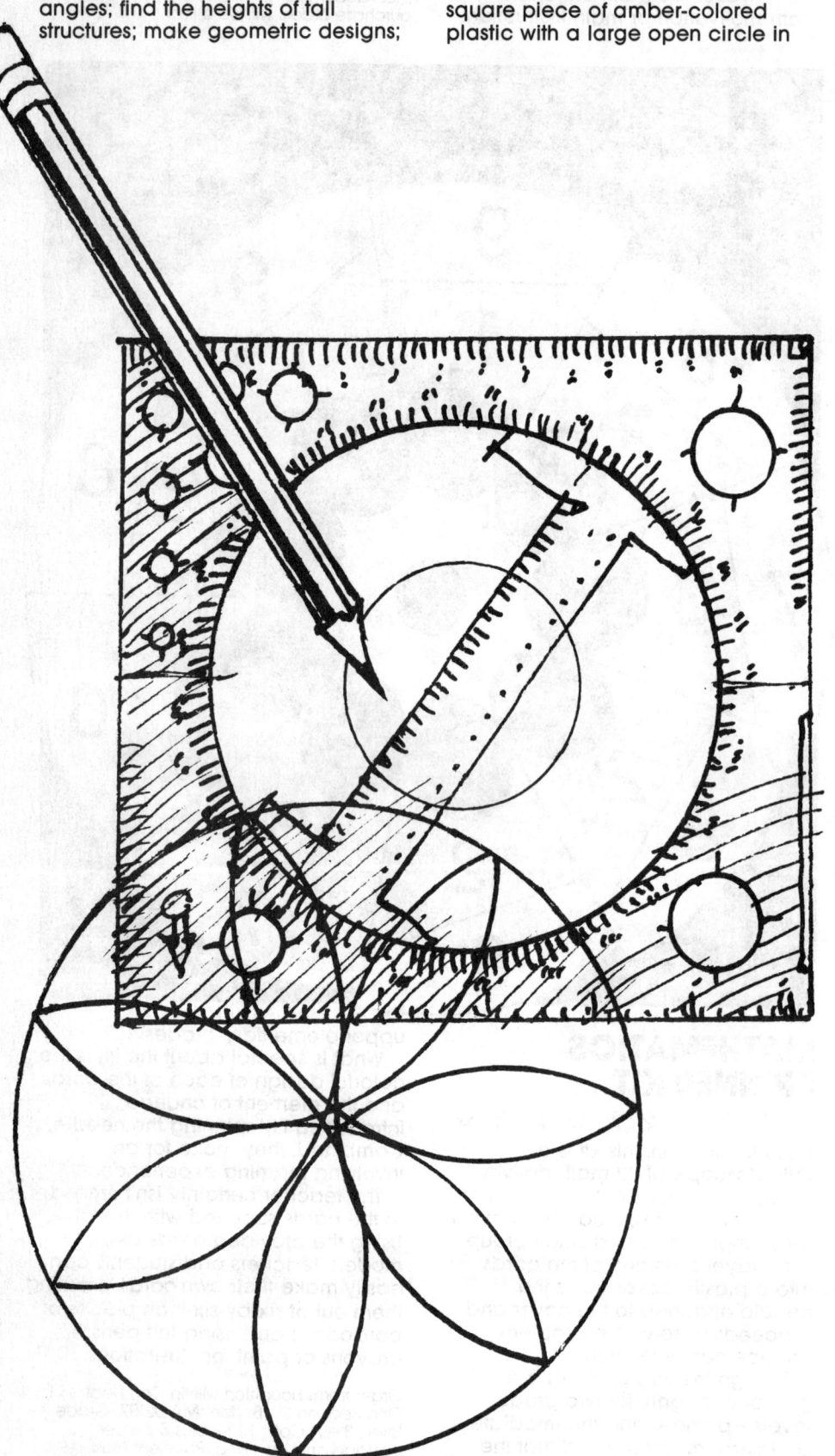

Before the shoppers start out, they're assigned a certain sum of money — somewhat on the skimpy side, such as $7.00. This is their limit. The first player rolls the dice and moves the indicated number of spaces. Whatever the token lands on must be purchased. The player records the price on the pad.

The first player to reach the register stops the game. If this player's total comes in under the limit, the game is over. (A checker at the register will verify the total.) If the total is more, that player is out of the game and play continues. The first player to reach the register and total out within the limit wins.

Other game boards can be assembled to represent the hardware store, toy store, drugstore or sporting goods store. Just look for appropriate items in catalogs and sales circulars. You may also want to scatter some "reward" or "forfeit" type spaces among the merchandise. Rules may call for "pay as you go" or setting a time limit or providing for a number of chances to turn down purchases. Or how about a "50% off" sale on everything — for a maximum of math practice and the fulfillment of a shopper's dream?

Idea by: Irene Butcher,
St. Linus School, Dearborn Heights, Mich.

# IN MY ESTIMATION . . .

Try something new for Monday mornings: the Monday Morning Estimation Contest. Plan tasks that involve quantity, that have elements students can use to qualify their estimates (rather than just guess) and that can be worked out without too much physical hassle (checking the width of your local river at some specific place at a time when the stream is cresting at 12 feet over flood stage could be somewhat tricky).

Here are some challenges just for starters:

▶ If the pieces of licorice in this package were laid end to end, how far would the licorice extend — in centimeters? You may measure one of the pieces. (No taste testing!)

▶ How many grams does this bag of marshmallows weigh? A sample marshmallow is provided for weighing only.

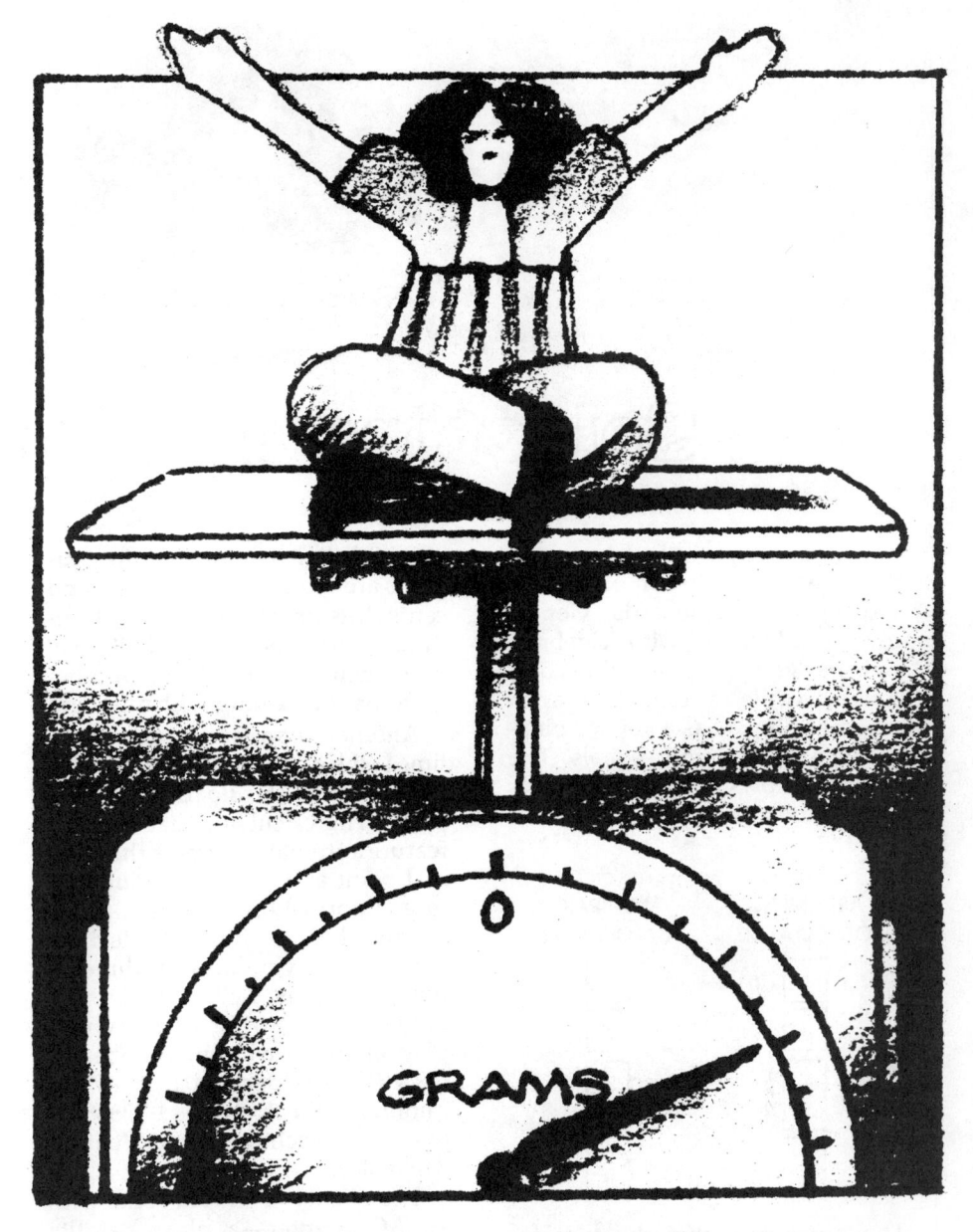

▶ How many millimeters will this plant grow in two weeks? You may take measurements twice during the first week.

▶ How many kilograms will our class weigh altogether? You may weigh one person besides yourself.

▶ How many seconds will it take a Hot Wheels car to travel 10 meters on a ramp that slopes 1 meter? You may test the car at a slope of 25 centimeters and 75 centimeters.

▶ How long will it take you, in seconds, to run around the school building twice? You may measure the distance and try a ten-second test.

▶ Without looking, estimate the number of tile squares that cover the hallway floor between the office and the gym. You may measure one square.

▶ Estimate the capacity of this pan to the level marked. You may take one linear measurement.

▶ Estimate the number of dried beans needed to make a weight that will balance your math book.

Estimating is only the beginning, of course. Graphing the guesses and then going through the various processes for checking out the challenge and getting the correct answer can provide learning along many different lines. You might encourage some sealed-bid challenge contributions from your students, too. The Monday Morning Estimation Contest could become a tradition, yielding — among other benefits — a class of truly educated guessers.

Idea by: Craig Yaker, Mountain Elementary School, Los Alamos, N. Mex.

# Selecting a Calculator

BY WALLACE P. JUDD

When you buy a calculator, your choice will lie between arithmetic and algebraic keyboards. Generally, a calculator with algebraic logic has keys for plus, minus and equals, while a calculator with arithmetic logic has a key for plus-equals and for minus-equals. The diagram shows you what the keys usually look like.

```
   KEYS ON AN           KEYS ON AN
   ARITHMETIC           ALGEBRAIC
   CALCULATOR           CALCULATOR

      ÷                    ÷
      ×                    ×
      −                    −
      =                    +
      +                    =
      =
```

The difference, though, goes far deeper than the keys. To subtract on an arithmetic calculator, you enter the first number as a plus entry, the second number as a minus entry. The sum of a plus entry and a minus entry then shows up on the display. For example, to subtract three from five on an arithmetic calculator, you key in

```
  5  +     3  −
     =        =
```

The displayed answer is two. To do the same problem on an algebraic calculator, you push

```
  5  −     3  =
```

Any calculator you consider for classroom use should have at least an eight-digit readout. If the students are working with dollars and cents, this limits them to the hundred thousands. Fewer digits will limit their exploration of number patterns and dealing with numbers.

Another important feature sometimes missing from inexpensive calculators is the floating decimal point. The calculator that has this feature automatically puts the decimal point at a place providing the most information. To see if a calculator has a floating decimal point, just divide four by three. If the readout is 1.33, the decimal point is not moving to allow display of the maximum number of threes in the decimal part of the number. If the answer is 1.3333333, then the machine has a floating decimal point.

The calculator should come with an AC adapter—a plug that fits into a wall socket. If the calculator doesn't have a plug, you'll have to buy one at an additional cost of five to seven dollars. If the calculator doesn't take an AC adapter, you'll constantly be having to change batteries.

Perhaps the most important feature in the logic of the machine is a constant. Some machines have an automatic constant. Others have a key that allows you to use the constant feature. Either is fine, but no constant means a severe limitation both on using powers of numbers and on exploring number patterns by division and multiplication. For example, if you want to find the product of 24691358 times several different numbers, you can key it into the calculator every time you use it—a lot of work—or you can use the constant feature of your calculator and key in 24691358 once, and then proceed to multiply by your set of numbers. Either type of constant saves a lot of key pushing and allows a student to play with numbers with much more ease.

One other feature, the floating negative sign, is nice to have but certainly shouldn't be thought of as a necessity. On most calculators, an answer of negative three shows on the display like this:

                    3

Because of the blank spaces between the two elements, it's easy for the student to overlook the negative sign. A calculator with the floating negative sign would display the number as −3. It brings the negative sign much more to the attention of the student.

## How Many Calculators Are Needed for A Classroom?

There is no research on this topic yet. But during a summer school program the author observed, one for every four or five students seemed to be reasonable. The best judgment is based on available funds and how much you want each student to use the machine. If you want each one to handle it one third of the class time, then you obviously need one for every three students. Remember, though, that the student should plan what he's going to do with the calculator before he actually uses it. Thus, planning time should not be considered time on the calculator.

# Games for the Calculator

Here are a few calculator games that reinforce computational skills:

**Nim.** This is a variation of an old game that is usually played with straws or beans. The object is to see who can keep from getting to 21 or over. Two players take turns. The first player pushes the 1, 2 or 3 key. He then pushes the plus key. The second player, having the same key options, then takes his turn. The players keep taking turns until somebody goes to 21. The first person to reach 21 or go over *loses*.

With older students this can be played with the keys from 1 to 6, with the player reaching 50 or over being the loser.

**Guess and Check.** If you have two calculators, two students can play this game. If there's only one calculator, the two players first have to write down their guesses on paper, then check them one at a time.

To play, pick a number that's big, say 516. Now pick a smaller number, say 30. The players guess what number can be divided into 516 30 times. They then check it out on the calculator. Their scores are their answer minus 30, and the winner is the person who has the score nearest zero. (It doesn't matter whether it's plus or minus.) In this game, if one person guessed 27, he'd divide 516 by 27 and get 19.111111. His score would be 19.111111 minus 30, or −10.888889. If the other person guessed 25, he would divide 516 by 25 and get 20.64. His score would be 20.64 minus 30, or −9.36. The second player would win.

The game develops estimating skills very quickly because it has immediate feedback. It can also be played as a multiplication game. Pick a big target number and a small number to start with. What do you multiply the small number by to get the target number?

**Reversie.** One person puts in a number that repeats two digits, such as 353535. (The smaller of the two digits has to come first.) The other person then tries to put in a number that can be added to 353535 to get 535353—in this case, 181818. The game can be played with larger or smaller numbers. Older students might be able to figure out how to use the larger digit first, as in 626262.

**Target K.** Pushing only the function keys (+, −, ×, ÷ or =) and the 3 key, how can you get the calculator to read out 11? (It is possible.) The name of the game derives from the fact that the constant key is "K" on many calculators. A single digit is the only constant you can use. And obviously, you are trying to reach a target number with that constant.

The game can be complicated by making the target number bigger, or by making it a negative number. It can also be good practice for pre-algebra students to predict how they'll do it before they ever touch the keys. Younger students have lots of fun with the calculator trying to hit the target number, though they're usually unable to reconstruct how they did it.

Wallace P. Judd is the author of GAMES, TRICKS, AND PUZZLES FOR A HAND CALCULATOR (Dymax, Box 310, Menlo Park, CA 94025).

## MULTI-BASE CONVERTER

☆ ☆ ☆ ☆ ☆ ☆ ☆ ☆ ☆ ☆

If the concepts of regrouping and place value are a bit overwhelming for your kids, bring in a MULTI-BASE CONVERTER, a device that helps move these skills from the abstract to the concrete, from the head to the hands. Because the converter may be used for counting, adding and subtracting in bases 2 through 12, it is useful both for learning new bases and for working in the students' own base-10 or decimal system.

The converter is a simple rectangular pegboard made of durable plastic. Across the top of the board are labels for six place-value columns. Labels for bases 2 through 12 are listed in a column down the right-hand side.

When a base row is being used, it is marked by a narrow, movable slide, oriented horizontally across the board. Peg holes in the slide match peg holes underneath. Both conversion of numbers and calculations with numbers are carried out by manipulating colored pegs. The various colors of the pegs as well as their placement represent number values.

The converter serves the same role as an abacus or calculator, and thus can be used in working with most prepared materials involving addition and subtraction in other bases. Teachers who are already familiar with other bases or the use of an abacus will have no trouble understanding how to use the converter. Others may have to spend some time getting acquainted.

An instruction booklet explains to teachers how to use the converter. The components of the decimal system are described first. Since all bases operate on the same principles, there is a logical transition from the decimal system to other bases.

Order from: The Judy Co., 250 James St., Morristown, NJ 07960. Grade level: 1–6. Cost: $4.25. Add $.65 for shipping and handling on orders up to $10; add 8 percent on orders over $10. Payment must accompany orders from individuals. School purchases orders will be billed.

## LEARNING TO THINK IN A MATH LAB

☆ ☆ ☆ ☆ ☆ ☆ ☆ ☆ ☆ ☆

A resource, a practical aid and an inspiration for tired teachers—these are a few ways of describing Manon Charbonneau's book. Physically, it comprises three parts: (1) suggestions and ideas about setting up and facilitating learning in a math lab, (2) over 120 activity-card ideas, (3) notes on using these activities.

The first part of the book is packed with solid experiences and sound advice. Its format—no chapters, no subheads—rather necessitates the creative use of underlining or note making to help in the recall and retrieval process, but the discursive style rings with sincerity and the joy of helping children learn.

Charbonneau provides suggestions for a wide variety of materials with which to stock a math lab, including such items as macaroni, marbles and matchbox toys. She sets the prospective math lab user at ease with accounts of her own background and experiences. Her philosophy of dealing with learners and the learning process pervades the discussion of math lab operations. Examples of successes and mistakes from her considerable experience bring a sense of reality to the math lab.

The activity cards are, as Charbonneau notes, not to be used as a text — "neither topic nor sequence is that important. Use your own best judgment for your children." Some categories featured in the cards are: the use of number lines, other names for numbers, measuring, using scale, maps, shapes, solids, metrics, kitchen lab. The style of the cards is brief: "Make a 'road map' with good directions to your house. Don't forget the scale of miles." And the first card for each category is intentionally broad and open-ended (for the go-go-go kids!): "Weigh as much as you can each week. Find different ways to record your work."

The book (soft-cover, about 70 pages), its activities and suggestions are aimed at discovery, intensive, independent investigations, and — as the title states — learning to think.

Order from: Creative Publications, P.O. Box 10328, Palo Alto, CA 94303. Grade level: Teachers of intermediate grades. Cost: $3.18. Payment must accompany orders from individuals. School purchase orders will be billed.

## TRUNDLE WHEEL

☆ ☆ ☆ ☆ ☆ ☆ ☆ ☆ ☆

The trundle wheel is one of those "now-why-didn't-I-think-of-that-before?" inventions. It is simply a wheel attached to a handle, and when the contraption is lightly pushed or pulled, it punctuates each meter with a loud click. For students of all ages, it makes a fine measuring device.

Available in either durable plastic or wood, the trundle wheel is especially useful for measuring long or curved distances. It is much easier to manipulate than the "end-over-end" procedure used with a yardstick or ruler, particularly for kindergarten or early grade students. In the upper grades, the trundle wheel can be used to measure circumferences and odd-shaped perimeters.

Order from: Selective Educational Equipment, 3 Bridge St., Newton, MA 02195. Grade level: K – junior high. Cost: $10.75, meter trundle wheel made of wood. Orders under $20 must be prepaid. Only school purchase orders will be billed. Add 5 percent on billed orders.

or

Order from: Creative Publications, P.O. Box 10328, Palo Alto, CA 94303. Grade level: K – junior high. Cost: $10.60, meter trundle wheel made of plastic. Payment must accompany orders from individuals. School purchase orders will be billed.

## BLOW UP

An interesting method for involving students in a discussion of scale and ratio makes use of an eight-by-ten black-and-white photograph — one of the teacher's face works especially well. The students won't know what the subject of the photo is until after they complete the activity.

The teacher should cut the photo into one-inch squares — an eight-by-ten photo will produce 80 pieces.

Number each piece on the back in a way that will make it easy to reassemble the photograph. For instance, the numbers 3-4 can signify the third row down and the fourth column in.

The pieces are then distributed to the members of the class. In addition, each child should have a sheet of paper which can be trimmed to a size — eight inches by eight inches. The student will then attempt to reproduce his small section of the photo on the large sheet of paper. Students can use pencils or a single color of crayon or marking pens. When finished, the students copy the number of their photo pieces onto the back of their drawings.

You are now ready to assemble the students' drawings in a way that will make a composite blow-up of the original photograph. The blow-up will be eight times as large as the original picture.

A slight variation on this procedure will give a different effect. Again, have students use pieces of a photograph cut into squares. But this time have the students copy their pieces of the photo onto eight-by-ten-inch rectangular sheets of paper. The finished composite drawing will stretch out and distort the original image.

Idea by: David Greenberg, Media Specialist, Philadelphia, Pa.

## BIRD FEEDER ARITHMETIC

If you live in a place where it is feasible to have a bird feeder in operation, you have the makings of a fascinating math tool. Your class will have many sets to count: birds on the feeder, birds on the ground, birds on the wing. There are also sets of sizes, colors and kinds.

If the feeder is frequented by small numbers of birds, children won't have much difficulty in keeping tabs on the additions and subtractions of comings and goings. But the fact that birds don't seem to be willing to stand still and be counted may give problems. You may want to take a quick series of photos for children to work with.

Younger children may enjoy showing bird arithmetic problems with felt cut-outs on a flannel board.

Older students can handle more complex calculations growing out of the bird feeding situation:
1. How much bird seed was used today? Keep a record of how much is used each day for two weeks. Find the average amount used each day.
2. What is the weight of a bag of seed? How many days should a bag last?
3. What is the cost of a bag of bird seed? How much is that per ounce? Per daily ration? How much does bird seed cost in larger bags? Is the larger bag a better buy?

Many other problems concerning weight and costs and feeding could be raised and answered. And while you're at it, you will find you can focus on the feeder for science, art and language activities. The birds come out well, too.

Idea by: Earl Hoffmann, Northern Illinois University, De Kalb, Ill.

## I WIN

☆ ☆ ☆ ☆ ☆ ☆ ☆ ☆

Even the losers come out ahead at I WIN — card games in which all the players get in some painless practice with math facts.

There are two kinds of cards in each I WIN deck. On each of 25 cards is an incomplete equation, printed in black. The other 25 cards are answer cards, printed in red.

In the basic game, players try to match algorithms and answers while following rules resembling those of rummy. There are additional instructions for related games.

A player may challenge the matches of another. An answer key is provided to settle such questions.

There are 12 I WIN decks, each using only one mathematical process. The decks are grouped into six sets with two decks to a set. Sets 1 and 2, for grades one and above, each contain one deck in addition and one in subtraction. Sets 3 and 4 are for grades two and up. Set 3 has decks in addition and subtraction, and Set 4 deals with multiplication and division. Sets 5 and 6, for grades three and above, each contain one deck in multiplication and one in division.

Teachers interested in individualizing instruction, especially through use of learning centers, will find the games particularly useful. And since the cards are in no way childish — they have the feel and appearance of ordinary playing cards — they can be effectively used to help junior highs catch up on basic math.

Order from: Scott, Foresman and Co., 1900 E. Lake Ave., Glenview, IL 60025. Attn: Ordering Dept. Grade Level: 1–9. Cost: $4.80 per set. Add $.50 postage and handling on orders under $5; $.75 for orders from $5 to $10; and 8 percent of total cost on orders over $10. Payment must accompany order.

## MATH PROJECT DAYS

Getting out of math class can be an appealing thought. But maybe just "getting out" once in a while can be equally attractive. Plan for an occasional day when math goes outside — at least outside the classroom.

Start collecting outdoor projects:

1. USING BASES. Survey the school and environs for things that can be counted: cars, windows, fence posts, paving blocks, trees. Assign each student several countables and a base to count them in. Later, have the class convert all findings to base ten and see how the totals compare. Recounts may be called for — especially if it's a nice day.

2. AREA AND PERIMETER. Let students choose their own units (meters, yards, jump ropes) to measure and compute perimeters and areas for playing fields, parking lots and game areas, such as the tetherball court. Collect a few estimates ahead of time if you like and start a contest.

3. PERCENTAGES. The basketball court is the site for this activity. Assign each student a certain number of tries at making a basket. Have students record the number of makes and misses and then compute the percentages. Ten is an easy number of tries to start with in teaching the concept.

4. NONVITAL STATISTICS. Borrow a few stopwatches and appoint an equal number of timekeepers. Now stage some "crazy races" with students competing against the clock. Races might involve using a specified step (hopping, baby steps), balancing something (telephone book on head, potato on spoon), or racing in pairs (wheelbarrow race, three-legged race). Students can help think up others — the sillier the better. Have individuals record their times for each "event" and use the data in making bar graphs of their own performances.

Take a look around and see what other sorts of outdoor math projects you come up with. Plan some indoor ones too — for that fifth rainy day in a row.

Idea by: Robert A. Zaske, Circle Pines, Minn.

## MATHEMATICS IN THE MAKING

☆ ☆ ☆ ☆ ☆ ☆ ☆ ☆

Those who find fingers a handy (sorry) calculating device will be happy to know an expert agrees. Book 2 of this 12-book series recommends fingers for converting decimal numerals into binary numerals.

Each of the 32-page, two-color booklets in the series MATHEMATICS IN THE MAKING by Stuart Bell and others takes up a different math topic: "Pattern, Area and Perimeter;"

# MATH

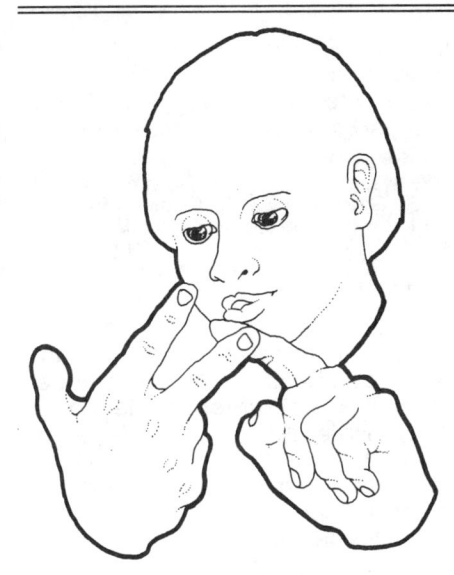

"Binary and Other Numeration Systems;" "Looking at Solids;" "Rotation and Angles;" "Curves;" "Scale Drawing and Surveying;" "Transformation and Symmetry;" "Networks;" "All Sorts of Numbers" (odd, even, factors, prime); "Sets and Relations;" "Graphs;" "Statistics."

Topics are developed by a blend of explanations, questions and activities, and are supported by large figures, diagrams and illustrations. Each topic is introduced by reference to common experiences and items — dominoes, a classroom of children, bike riding, turning a key. Development is orderly and logical but fairly rapid, with little built-in reinforcement. A great deal of material is treated in each of the booklets.

Planned for introduction to advanced third graders and challenging through junior high, the activities require creative thought. Extensive use of the manipulation of objects greatly helps illustration of abstract concepts.

Vocabulary is controlled, but students may be aware of and enjoy such British-isms as "turn it round," "monitor," "petrol" and "favourite."

Booklets come complete with answers, which makes them ideal for independent work. Depending on the age group you teach and individual needs, you may use the booklets for enrichment activities, small group or whole class instruction, or as a teaching resource. The many intriguing activities can easily serve as models for supplementary practice projects, and are bound to trigger discussions and further investigations. They're fascinating.

Order from: Houghton Mifflin Co., Dept. M-L, One Beacon St., Boston, MA 02107. Grade level: 3 – junior high. Cost: $1.59 per book plus 8 percent postage and handling. Payment must accompany order.

## COUNT AND SEE
**by Tana Hoban**

One of the very best of Hoban's series of eye-pleasing photo books on the basics. In this one, the number is printed on the left-hand page with the photo (3 school buses, 30 bottle caps) opposite.

MACMILLAN, $.95, paperback. Ages 3 – 6. See page 151 for ordering information.

## MATH ACTIVITIES FOR CHILD INVOLVEMENT

☆ ☆ ☆ ☆ ☆ ☆ ☆ ☆

Tired of the standard math drills? Looking for some ways to put variety into math activities? This book by Enoch Dumas offers no fewer than 450 ideas to add spice to everyday math lessons. And most of the activities require little preparation.

Don't, however, expect each of the ideas to be brand spanking new. There are simply too many in the book for that to be possible. But even familiar activities can be adapted for use in other ways. And taken as a whole, this extensive collection constitutes a very handy resource indeed.

The book is organized in chapters by concept area: numbers, numerals, sets, addition and subtraction of whole numbers, multiplication and division of whole numbers, geometry, fractional numbers, decimals, percents, measures and measuring, and word problems. The chapters are further broken down by type of idea: activities, materials, bulletin boards, history, games, verses, charts, music, shortcuts, patterns and so on.

The "games" in each chapter may well be the most involving. In "Who Are You?" for grades one to four, between 2 and 19 players use three-by-five-inch cards with numerals from 0 to 18 written on them to gain practice in addition or subtraction facts. "Pin one or more cards on each player. Leader says, 'Who is nine plus five?' Player who has 14 says, 'I am 14.' Leader continues with addition and subtraction facts for which players have sums or differences." The game may also be played using multiplication or division facts.

This 280-page paperback can do a lot to keep math lessons from dragging.

Order from: Allyn and Bacon, Inc., College Division, Link Dr., Rockleigh, NJ 07647. Grade level: Teachers of grades K – 6. Cost: $6.95. No shipping and handling charge if payment accompanies order. Add $.50 on billed orders.

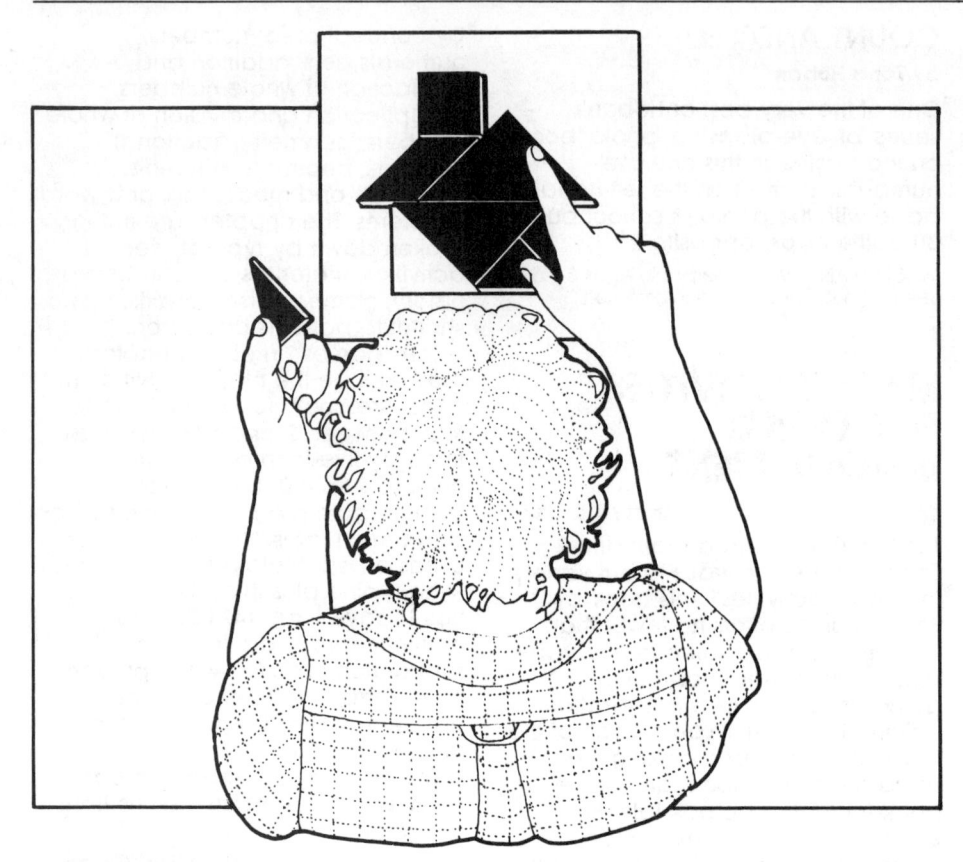

## TANGRAMS

☆ ☆ ☆ ☆ ☆ ☆ ☆ ☆

If you think a tangram is something on wheels or maybe one of those mysterious metric measures, you have one interesting discovery ahead. The tangram looks to be an innocent set of seven geometric shapes — two large triangles, a medium-sized triangle, two small triangles, a square and a rhomboid. And these seven pieces can be fitted together to form a square — after a while.

The tangram is an ancient Chinese puzzle. The story goes that a ceramic tile, the prized possession of a learned Chinese, was dropped on a stone floor. The tile broke into seven pieces, which the scholar spent a lifetime attempting to reassemble.

The tangram puzzle possibilities, beyond the reconstruction of the original square, are myriad. Designing free-form and symmetrical patterns and matching given shapes are the basic classroom operations with tangram pieces. The levels of sophistication range from the touch-and-move system, to visual preplacement, to the purely analytical approach. As pieces are manipulated, the various proportional relationships between and among the pieces become clear. These relationships become the basis for many other activity possibilities.

The tangram is an activity item that requires little guidance and can be used in odd moments without creating space, time or confusion problems. And the learning that grows out of working with tangram pieces goes far beyond the exultation in the solving of a puzzle.

▶ TANGRAM CARDS, a part of the ESS program, are puzzles that progress in difficulty from those doable by preschoolers to some that are fairly tough for adults. There are 121 puzzles on 64 cards divided into three sets according to difficulty. Set I has 17 puzzles using four or less of the seven tangram pieces. Each card shows the child which pieces to use. Work can be done right on the cards, with the child fitting the pieces into the outline of the shape. Set II has 27 puzzles using five tangram pieces. Set III provides students with 77 puzzles using all seven pieces. The final 6 puzzles are shown half-size, so pieces cannot be fitted to outline. This makes solution a visual process.

Though cards are numbered within each set, this does not show relative difficulty among puzzles. Children may wander through and find "easy" ones in among harder ones.

The teacher's guide explains the background of the use of the tangram, and offers suggestions for introducing and using the cards. Related activities are also described.

The cards are 7-1/2-by-9 inches in size and the sets are color coded.

Order from: Webster/McGraw-Hill, 1221 Ave. of the Americas, New York, NY 10020. Grade level: K — 8. Cost: $5.49 (includes all three sets on 64 cards; sets not sold separately); $2.28 for teacher's guide; $2.37 for four sets of plastic tangram pieces.

▶ IT'S A TANGRAM WORLD is a 92-page teacher aid and workbook with an approach to tangrams that includes many areas of subject matter. The book relates the tangram pieces to number concepts, music, part-whole relationships, measurement and other areas.

The first few pages of the book serve as an orientation for the teacher and offer suggestions for using the book. Following this are several ideas for games developed around the tangram pieces. Next come problem pages, exploration pages, and pages that appear to be "pure arithmetic." Further inspection shows these activities to be based on the relationships between the tangram pieces. Students are able to solve arithmetic problems using the tangram pieces themselves.

All pages are perforated, and in most cases each activity is complete on one page. The copyright allows you to make copies of the material for your own class needs.

Though not all pages will be useful for all classes, many of the ideas can be adapted and applied to various elementary levels.

Order from: Educational Science Consultants, P.O. Box 1674, San Leandro, CA 94577. Grade level: Teachers of all grades. Cost: $3.50 plus 10 percent postage and handling. Payment must accompany individual orders. School purchase orders will be billed.

▶ TANGRAM TASKS is a set of 15 cards with 30 tangram puzzles to solve. One side of each card is numbered, and these puzzles use only two to six of the tangram pieces. Children must experiment to discover which of the seven pieces should be used in solving these puzzles.

The unnumbered puzzle on the other side of each card is more difficult, requiring the full seven pieces. Children may fit pieces inside the outlines of the puzzles on either side of each card.

The cards, seven-by-eight inches in size, are printed on heavy paper.

Order from: Teachers Exchange of San Francisco, 600 35th Ave., San Francisco, CA 94121. Grade level: 2 — 6. Cost: $1.75 for task cards; $1.85 for 5 sets of tangram pieces. Both prices include postage and handling. Payment must accompany individual orders.

# FRACTIONAL FOODS

1/16 + 1/16 + 1/16 could add up to a sweet smile if the 16ths are fudge fractions. A Fractional Foods party could be a means of introducing fractions in a way that's concrete — with all due respect to the cooks — and tasteful.

The party begins with plans for preparing food. Group children in twos or threes and have them decide on a dessert that can be easily divided into fractions for serving, e.g., brownies, cake, fudge. Each group is to find and bring in a recipe for the chosen treat and is responsible for copying the recipe on large paper. The class can then read and study the various fractional measures used.

If some of the foods can be prepared at school with class members contributing ingredients, the practical use of fractions will be underscored. Some food preparation might be assigned as homework, with parents' consent and cooperation. Supplemental items may be bought and brought.

When items are assembled, decisions must be made regarding the size and number of parts, and how best to achieve equal-sized fractions. Various cutting plans may be tried on the chalkboard before decisive slices are made.

In setting up for the party, children label each food, indicating the fractional part being featured (Chocolate Fudge . . . Enjoy 1/10.)

Depending upon the supply of Fractional Foods you acquire, you may want to invite faculty members and representatives of other classes to join you — as you subtract fractions, bit by tasty bit.

Idea by: Sister Eileen Waldron, St. Elizabeth School, Richmond, Va.

# SHUFFLEBOARD MATH

It's no secret that learning math through drill can be tedious, boring and counterproductive. Turn it into a game, though, and your kids will shuffle right through the practice session, developing fingertip command along the way.

Find a large sheet of plywood and draw two triangular regions with numbered divisions on it, as in shuffleboard. Sitting on the floor, at opposite ends of the board, two students alternate sliding a numbered wooden disc into the boxed-off numbered areas of the board. The student who slides the disc multiplies the number marked on the disc by the number on the board. If two students are having trouble with the nines tables, they could each be given a disc with a nine on it. If a student slides the disc into the seven region, he multiplies nine times seven. A correct answer earns him 63 points.

The player with the larger cumulative point total at the end of a certain time period wins. An optional third student — let's say one needing practice in addition — could keep track of the scores. The players are thus motivated throughout the game to try to land on and multiply the larger numbers.

Idea by: Sam Kane, Sequoia Intermediate School, Newbury Park, Calif.

## MEAT MARKET MATH

Meat costs can bring some here-and-now relevance to your mathematics teaching. Have students bring in meat ads from market circulars and newspapers. Ads should include the name of the cut, the price per pound, and a picture of the meat, if possible. Label ads by market if you wish. Ads may be mounted on cards or on a chart categorized by kind of meat, by cut or by market.

The mathematics of meat may take several forms. Younger children may practice reading the dollars-and-cents prices. They may also compare prices — more than and less than. The specific differences can be computed as ability allows. Discuss with the children the meaning of pricing "per pound." List other items sold by weight.

Older students might compute the cost of a three-pound pork roast at Ed's Supermarket, or the cost of a four-ounce (before cooking) serving of hamburger at $1.49 a pound.

Students may want to watch the prices of several particular cuts over a period of time, calculating the amount of change and the percentage of change — perhaps graphing the data. Or they may want to compare cuts from market to market. Articles about factors affecting meat prices could be clipped on a regular basis.

Invite the manager of a local meat market to describe various cuts and explain why their prices differ. Considerations such as the proportion of bone or fat in the weight of a cut or the amount of cooking time required for less tender cuts may lead to other math activities.

The class might try cooking meat to test the shrinkage. Or your cost-conscious students may want to seek out recipes and serve up some main dishes that feature alternative protein foods — calculating costs per serving, doubling recipes and other such math tasks. Parents may be interested in these recipes.

Given the meat price picture in recent times, even your youngest students will find in the pages of the supermarket specials some real live experience with higher math.

Idea by: Dolores Allen,
John Russell School, Marine Corps Base,
Quantico, Va.

## YOUNG MATH BOOKS

☆ ☆ ☆ ☆ ☆ ☆ ☆ ☆

Seemingly abstract mathematical topics become activities for learning-by-doing in CIRCLES, WEIGHING

& BALANCING, WHAT IS SYMMETRY? and ESTIMATION — four of the titles in a set of supplementary paperbacks for the primary grades. To a somewhat greater extent than others in the series, these books present a bountiful supply of probing questions and workable activities.

A fine vehicle for activity-centered learning, WEIGHING & BALANCING begins by asking the young reader to make some general weight comparisons between an apple and a book, then between a candle and a stick. The questions lead right into the use of balances by suggesting activities using mobiles and seesaws. Once kids have explored at length on their own, the book helps the conceptualization process by occasionally summing up.

The four books are designed for the lower elementary grades, but early primaries will probably need help in using all but WEIGHING & BALANCING. The other three books suggest good activities for older kids as well.

Order from: Thomas Y. Crowell Co., Inc., Dept. SS, 666 Fifth Ave., New York, NY 10019. Grade level: Primary. Cost: Paperback — $1.45 (list), $1.04 (school price); hardcover — $4.50 (list), $3.24 (school price). Payment must accompany order.

## AFTERMATH

☆ ☆ ☆ ☆ ☆ ☆ ☆ ☆ ☆

After figuring the square feet in a 12-by-14 room, and after regrouping the tens and the hundreds, and after solving for "a", there's AFTERMATH. It's a series of four books for math enrichment that don't look like math books at all. Designed for students in grades five through nine, books one through four have puzzles, problems, codes, games and facts of the widest and wildest variety. The activities are based on math skills, and the solutions require creative thinking. Students will discover that the tasks require both brain time and brain power.

Each book has nearly 100 pages of activities followed by a section giving the solutions — proof that the problems can be solved. The activities increase in difficulty from book one to book four, incorporating some of the higher level skills of the junior highs.

The same activity pages in the AFTERMATH books are also available as duplicating masters. Two 48-page booklets of masters provide the same material as the books at each level. (1A and 1B in duplicating masters equal book one.)

Students who have had the opportunity to work into AFTERMATH will find many ideas that make regular-math more exciting, too.

Order from: Creative Publications, P.O. Box 10328, Palo Alto, CA 94303. Grade level: 5–9. Cost: $4.77 per book; $16.96 for series of four books; $9.01 for each booklet of masters; $63.60 for series of eight booklets of masters. Payment must accompany individual orders. School purchase orders will be billed.

## MATH HOUSE

A teaching aid that looks like a neat brick house and works like a teaching machine may help your class master those pesky arithmetic facts.

Cut a sheet of poster board into the silhouetted shape of a house front with a pointed roof. Draw a number of rectangular "windows" 3-1/4 inches deep by 3-1/2 inches across. Cut slots the full depth of the window on both left and right. Do not cut the top or bottom. Complete the house front by adding details such as bricks, shrubs, flowers.

Now you're ready for the math part. For each math fact you want to reinforce, take a pair of three-by-five cards. Staple or tape the cards together in pairs, one on top of the other, down the left-hand side and in about one inch from the edge. On the top card of each pair (held horizontally) write the number sentence. On the bottom card write the answer. The cards may then be inserted into the window slots, tucking the left-hand stapled edge and the right-hand edge of the bottom card only. Leave the top card free at the right-hand edge so that it may be easily lifted up.

The house is now ready for use by groups, teams or individuals. Children work with the math problems and check their own answers by opening the windows.

You can give the house a new look and provide practice in new areas by making up the appropriate question-and-answer card pairs. You may have a math house one day and a reading house or science house the next. You might even try a joke house or a riddle house and make Peeping Toms out of your entire class.

Idea by: Patricia Miller, Vernridge Elementary School, Pittsburgh, Pa.

## MYSTERY MEASUREMENTS

48" x 12" x 40". That's a bookcase, in case you're wondering. And it could be one of the items on a Mystery Measurements list, if you have a bookcase that size.

To set up a Mystery Measurements contest, first measure assorted objects in your room—boxes, books, game cards, furniture—and record their dimensions. Include some standard-sized items, things 8-1/2-by-11 inches, for instance. Depending upon the level of your class, you may want to use square or cubic units.

From your measuring data, select five objects as the Mystery Measurement items and write the five sets of dimensions on the chalkboard. Tell students that the figures represent five mystery objects in the room. It is their challenge to track down the items, checking them out with the ample supply of measuring tools you have provided. Advise students that more than one item may have the same measurements, and encourage them to list as many objects as they can that measure up.

At the end of the contest period, reveal your answers. Students with alternative answers will be invited to demonstrate their proofs.

Students may want to contribute their own mystery measurements for the next contest and try to baffle their friends. Be prepared for something that measures 21.7-by-28 centimeters showing up on a list.

Idea by: Don Mack, Culver City, Calif.

## CIRCLES, TRIANGLES AND SQUARES
**by Tana Hoban**

Collectors of Hoban's excellent series of books for primary children won't want to miss this one. Black-and-white photographs introduce geometry in a way that's fun to look at.

MACMILLAN, $5.95. Ages 3—6.
See page 151 for ordering information.

## TAPED COMPUTATIONS

Some useful math materials are being tossed into the family trash with great regularity: those cash-register tapes from trips to the market, the drugstore and the variety shop. Start a class-wide campaign to see how many of these instant addition and subtraction practice tools you can salvage.

If you manage to collect a large supply of tapes, you can pick and choose the lengths and the numerical ranges that fit the computational capabilities of your children.

Cut apart each tape between the listed costs and the total. With short tapes you can mount both sections on construction-paper cards, if you wish them to last awhile. Those portions of the cut-up tapes that have the totals go into one shoe box; the upper portions go into another. Students then try to find and match up the pairs of

# MATH 47

separated parts, putting the original tapes back together again. (You may want to code the parts for an answer key or create a pattern-matching device so that the activity will be self-checking.)

Some tapes don't stop with a simple sum; they go on to add in taxes. Some tapes even show the amount of money the customer hands over and registers the change that should be returned. These change-return tapes can be cut apart just above the final total and then cut again to separate off the amount of change to be returned. Students then need to find the difference between the total and the amount given in payment on one portion of the tape before searching for the correct change portion. (Students may need reminding about transposing the total and the amount paid before attempting to subtract — or they'll be coming up with change in minus numbers and will never find a match-up!)

Tapes differ in color, appearance of the figures, etc. — factors that shouldn't be overlooked in setting up the activities for greatest challenge. Also, for young children you might want to stay away from some of those tapes from the weekly grocery-shopping trips — unless the kids are ready to work with astronomical arithmetic.

Idea by: Carolyn Lamoreaux, Caroline Street School, Saratoga Springs, N.Y.

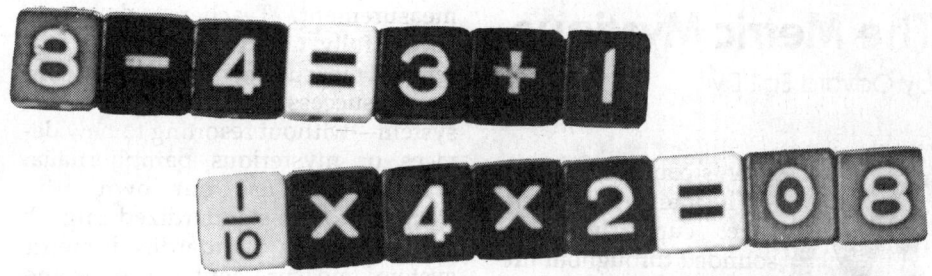

$8 - 4 = 3 + 1$

$\frac{1}{10} \times 4 \times 2 = 08$

## TUF
☆ ☆ ☆ ☆ ☆ ☆ ☆ ☆

Scrabble's math cousin, TUF, is a game based on equations instead of words. In the basic game, players race against time in using dicelike cubes to form two, three or four number equations in addition and/or subtraction. More complex variations on the game introduce multiplication, division, fractions, decimals, exponents and roots.

Unlike most educational games, which ask players to wait their turn while others play, TUF allows players to work individually and simultaneously. It does, however, possess the usual drawbacks of packaged games. There are pieces of equipment to keep track of — 64 dicelike cubes coded in six colors, plus three color-coded timers. But the packaging of TUF is such that it is immediately obvious if any dice are missing when you put away the set. The egg timers are amazingly durable.

TUF proved to be exceptionally popular with 8- to 12-year-olds in an open classroom setting. It is one of the few math activities that can hold the attention of a high-energy group. It also retained its popularity as an indoor game over a long period of time.

Teachers should familiarize themselves with the different versions, since the rules pamphlet is not adequate to move younger students from the simple games to the more challenging ones without a little help from a friendly adult.

Order from: Cuisenaire Company of America, Inc., 12 Church St., New Rochelle, NY 10805. Grade level: 3—12. Cost: $9.95 plus 5 percent postage and handling.

$10 \times 10 + 4 + 1 = 105$

## FOO
☆ ☆ ☆ ☆ ☆ ☆ ☆ ☆

Neither an invective nor the name of some exotic Oriental food, FOO is a math game that reinforces the Fundamental Order of Operations, i.e., the order in which arithmetic operations are carried out in a multioperational equation. In the game, two to four players must make proper sequenced computations in addition, subtraction, multiplication and division.

The game's components are a deck of 78 playing cards and four plastic card racks. Every card has a number from 1 to 9 or an algorithmic symbol printed on it. In the corner of each card is another number which indicates the point value of the card.

Players are dealt seven cards, and as in rummy, draw and discard. The object is to build an equation that yields 12. The first player to make an equation using all seven cards says "FOO" and is the winner.

A rule book explains scoring, penalties and other rules. It also tells in which order operations are executed.

Order from: Cuisenaire Company of America, Inc., 12 Church St., New Rochelle, NY 10805. Grade level: 4—high school. Cost: $4.95 plus 5 percent for shipping and handling.

# The Metric Mystique
by Odvard Egil Dyrli

"Metric is coming!" The intent of this message, currently being sounded throughout the land, is clear: "Look out! *You* had better be ready!" The image being projected is that of the impending arrival of the Grim Reaper.

The long-overdue changeover to the far superior metric system of measurement will most assuredly be costly for our economic system, and will require reeducation of our adult population. But what is particularly disturbing is that these facts are now being used to generate the myth that introducing the metric system in our school curriculum will be pedagogically costly—calling for "special" teaching strategies and large investments in exotic materials.

The myth of a metric mystique has meant professional recognition for individuals and groups through the establishment of "metric" associations, committees, and the funding of centers for "metric curriculum" research and development. It has opened the sluice gates to a flood of commercial materials that promise magical formulas and innovative ways to bypass the teaching problems inherent in metrics instruction. But measurement is measurement is measurement. Teachers who have successfully taught the English system of measurement will find continued success in teaching the metric system—without resorting to new devices or mysterious paraphernalia. Whether we use our own arbitrary units, the standardized English system or the standardized metric system, measurement concepts and processes are the same. There is, therefore, little need to alter the teaching strategies we now use in introducing the English system as we help students make the transition to the metric system.

**The Sequence is the Same.** The general sequence of measuring experiences should remain unchanged: (1) making relative comparisons among objects; (2) making comparisons in terms of student-devised units, leading to the establishment of the need for standard measures; and finally, (3) introducing and continuing to use a standardized system.

Young children learn the fundamentals of measuring by comparing lengths of objects and volumes of liquids and expressing these relationships in terms such as "larger than" and "less than." Later, children may start using a variety of arbitrary units of their own creation—perhaps colorfully named—measuring the lengths of objects with strips of paper, measuring volume according to "mayonnaise jar" capacity. When communication becomes a problem ("7 *Charlies*" are the same as "a little over 18 *mups*" or "almost 12 *Kims*"), the need for standard units becomes apparent and the common usage system can be introduced to the children.

Children can then begin making *direct* measurements according to the standardized system by learning to read the scales of measuring instruments. The skills required for using measuring instruments—such as rulers, thermometers, graduated containers and equal-arm balances—are identical whether the system is metric or English.

Learning *indirect* measurement is the same, too. Indirect measurement uses a single measuring instrument and a mathematical operation to obtain a desired measure—such as finding square units by multiplying length and width measurements. Even *derived* measurements, using two measuring instruments plus computations (such as time-rate-distance operations) are taught in the same way whether the goal is miles per hour or kilometers per hour.

**But Metric is Easier.** The one strategy change is a most welcome one. It involves expressing a measured quantity in terms of a larger or smaller unit—the pesky bushels-to-pecks kind of computation. Since metric is a decimal system, conversion from one unit to the next higher or lower unit simply means dividing or multiplying by ten.

Once the prefix *milli-*, meaning

"one thousandth of," is learned, it can be applied to length as *millimeter,* to weight as *milligram,* or to liquid volume as *milliliter,* and the meaning is clear. The same is true for *centi-* (one hundredth of) and each of the other metric prefixes. A curriculum shift into the metric system, therefore, will eliminate many of the problem areas we now commonly encounter in teaching measurement to children.

Once we acquire some initial experience with the simplicity of metric measurement, the imagined need for "special materials" will dissipate. However, there are some practical considerations. In the first place, physical examples of the basic units for measuring length (the meter), weight (the gram) and liquid volume (the liter) should be readily available to students. There shouldn't be, however, a need to purchase classroom quantities of metric measuring supplies. Just get a sample and devise some copies. (If you wish to use the much smaller units of millimeters, milligrams and milliliters, though, you probably *will* want to purchase several appropriate measures.)

After you have secured this equipment, give the children continuing opportunities to use metric units by recording the measurement of objects both inside and outside the classroom. The units may then be introduced into measurement problems by devising special problem sheets or by rewriting activities that are presently stated in terms of the English system. A concise and simple guide sheet useful in this regard is "All You Will Need to Know About Metric," available from the Metric Information Office of the National Bureau of Standards, Washington, DC 20234.

One note of caution: Contrary to the dictates of many metric teaching materials, do *not* waste time having students convert English measures to metric and vice versa. This activity is of limited value and leads to unnecessary confusion and even boredom. Children who learn to use the metric system by direct experience have absolutely no need to jump back and forth between it and the English system for conceptual understanding. In this connection, it is wise to resist the blitz of giveaway commercial pocket reference cards and conversion tables. These materials do little more than get product names and trademarks into the classroom, and serve to perpetuate the myth that complicated relationships and obscure units are part and parcel of learning simple metric measurement.

The basic metric system is easy to learn and easy to use. The currently popular phrase "Think metric" is incomplete. *Do* metric! There is nothing mysterious about it.

Odvard Egil Dyrli is professor of education at University of Connecticut, Storrs.

## CREATIVE EQUATIONS

☆ ☆ ☆ ☆ ☆ ☆ ☆ ☆

Take a deck of 92 cards — eight each of numbers 0 through 10 and four wild cards — and what can you play with it? No fewer than 19 problem-solving and skills-reinforcement math games for the primary through junior high grades.

The CREATIVE EQUATIONS cards are simply done, with huge block numerals nearly filling the entire card surface. Each numeral is segmented into as many parts as the number it represents (so designed for playing one of the primary level games).

The games are described in an instruction booklet, and most of them are highly flexible. Many of the games require the use of several mathematical operations while others use only one at a time. One of the games, "Sum It Up," calls for the players to turn over two cards and, as quickly as possible, give the sum of the face-up cards. (The wild cards are not used in this game.) The first person with the correct answer wins the cards. The player with the most cards at the end of the game is the winner. As a variation, players can play the same game in multiplication, division or subtraction, the last of which might result in negative totals.

CREATIVE EQUATIONS can be used with close teacher supervision to teach basic skills. Or the games make a good leisure-time resource for learning centers. The cards, booklet and a supplementary instruction sheet of games come packaged in a hard plastic storage container.

Order from: Learning Success, P.O. Box 9805, San Jose, CA 95157. Grade level: Primary — junior high. Cost: $4.50. No shipping and handling charge if payment accompanies order. Add $.50 on billed orders. School purchase orders will be billed.

# 50 MATH

## THE ABA-TEN RULE
☆ ☆ ☆ ☆ ☆ ☆ ☆ ☆ ☆

This is a poor-man's calculator that operates much like a slide rule. It can be used to perform basic computations in addition (families of facts from 1 to 20), subtraction (where the minuend is less than 21), multiplication (products up to 1,000) and division (with dividends up to 1,000 and divisors of 12 or less). THE ABA-TEN RULE may also be used for measuring linear distances in English or metrics. One side is marked in inches; the other is in centimeters.

The device itself, made of a durable white plastic, appears awesome at first, with its sliding parts and many labels. But an accompanying guidebook gives step-by-step directions for each type of computation, along with sets of problems to figure out. Pages may be duplicated for classroom use.

Though the guidebook is written simply, not all kids will be able to figure out on their own how to use THE ABA-TEN RULE. Teachers should therefore familiarize themselves with it and be prepared to demonstrate its use for students.

As with most other types of calculators, THE ABA-TEN RULE supplies answers without explaining the why or how of the processes involved, and needs the support of your regular math program. It can be a valuable shortcut for those students who have a grasp of basic facts, and a motivational tool to help those students who are struggling for mastery.

THE ABA-TEN RULE is a practical device that can be used by students at their desks or in a math learning center. Or they will enjoy using the rule much as they would a game.

Order from: Beta Enterprises, 1380 Cherokee Dr., Salinas, CA 93901. Grade level: K–6. Cost: $5.00 – includes one ABA-Ten Rule and guidebook; $2.50 – additional ABA-Ten Rules. Add $.25 for postage and handling. Payment must accompany orders from individuals. School purchase orders will be billed.

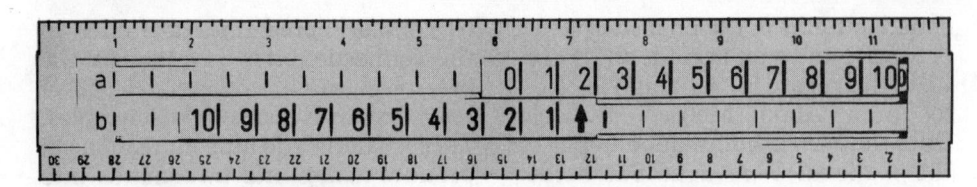

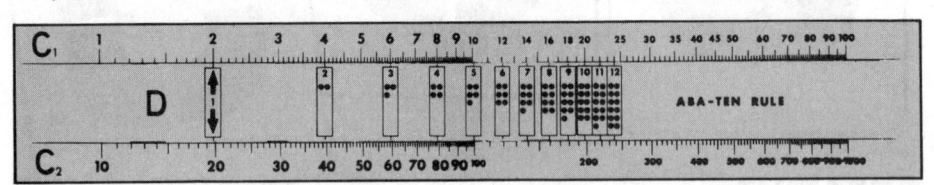

## MATH AND THE MESSAGE

What's this about?

| exponent | the | times | tells | factor |
|---|---|---|---|---|
| 8 | 27 | 4 | 3 | 11 |

| how | the | is | repeated | many |
|---|---|---|---|---|
| $4^2$ | 100 | 49 | $3 \times 3$ | 25 |

Well, it's math; that much is clear. And it's a code that's incomplete.

The numerals below each word are answers to math problems. If you match the list of problems with those answers, the words linked to the answers will come out in order.

1. $10^2 = 100$ (the)
2. $2^3 = 8$ (exponent)
3. $3 \times 3 \times 3 = 3^a$; $a = 3$ (tells)

... and so on, until the message reads: "the exponent tells how many times the factor is repeated."

The message in this case is a math-related quote. It could as easily be some other fact or even a special secret communication just between you and a student, good for a laugh or a little morale booster.

Here's the procedure:
a. Write out the message to be used. "your work is fine"
b. Count the number of words. Select and list a corresponding number of problems.

   1. $5 - 1 = 4$
   2. $5 \times 0 = 0$
   3. $5 + 1 = 6$
   4. $5 - 0 = 5$

c. Copy off the answers in order.

   4   0   6   5

d. Pair the answers with the words in your message.

| your | work | is | fine |
|---|---|---|---|
| 4 | 0 | 6 | 5 |

e. Scramble the message, maintaining the word-answer pairs. The worksheet will look like this:

| work | your | fine | is |
|---|---|---|---|
| 0 | 4 | 5 | 6 |

1. $5 - 1 =$ _____ (_____)
2. $5 \times 0 =$ _____ (_____)
3. $5 + 1 =$ _____ (_____)
4. $5 - 0 =$ _____ (_____)

Message: _____

After you try some of these with your students, don't be surprised if an epidemic of coded communications breaks out. It's bound to happen.

Idea by: Earnest Carlisle, Columbus College, Columbus, Ga.

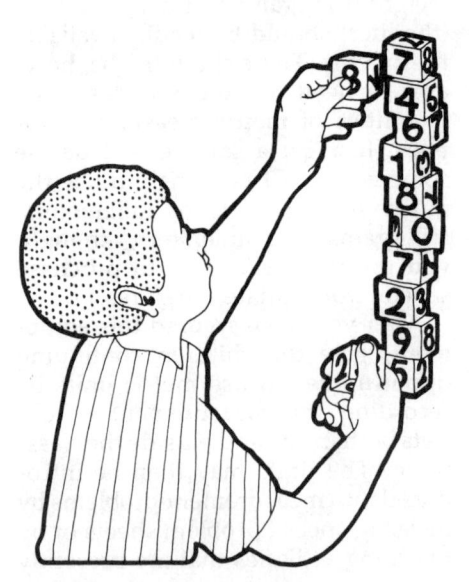

## ARITHMECUBES
☆ ☆ ☆ ☆ ☆ ☆ ☆ ☆ ☆

The box of blocks looks harmless enough—a set of 16 colored one-inch wooden cubes, with large numerals or other mathematical symbols on each. They're perfect for playing with. And perhaps that's why the many teaching-learning ways of using them make such a happy bonus.

ARITHMECUBES come with a book of directions that provides different games for ages 3 through 14. Three-year-olds can sort out the cubes and group by color, compare sizes of groups and, with a leader's help, deal with concepts of "more" and "fewer" before getting down to the symbols.

Games for older children involve all the operations plus arithmetic reasoning. Some games are designed for up to six players, but many are solitaire games, making the cubes a practical independent activity.

The first few pages of the directions booklet describe the components (pointing out the plan of the color scheme) and chart the 24 games according to difficulty. The games are also indexed by topic for most efficient use.

ARITHMECUBES are good for building towers and great long numbers such as 287,461,807,295. They're also good for learning about sets and subsets, equations, ordinal numbers and inequalities. Or you can do both.

Order from: Scott, Foresman and Co., 1900 E. Lake Ave., Glenview, IL 60025. Attn: Ordering Dept. Grade level: Preschool—junior high. Cost: $4.62. Add $.50 postage and handling on orders under $5; $.75 for orders from $5 to $10; and 8 percent of total cost on orders over $10. Payment must accompany order.

## CLIP-ON MATH CARDS

The investment in some tagboard, several spring-type clothespins and a little time can bring returns in the form of math reinforcement for your students. Cut a stack of four-and-a-half-inch squares from tagboard and mark each with a grid that divides the square into nine one-and-a-half-inch boxes.

Leave the row of boxes along the bottom of the card and the row down the right-hand side blank. The four boxes remaining in the upper-left-hand corner are for numerals. The numerals you mark in — one to a square — will depend upon the combinations the students need to practice. These combinations may be added both horizontally and vertically. The blank boxes at the right and at the bottom are the answer boxes.

The clothespins provide the answers part of the device. Each clothespin gets marked with an answer. The same answer is to be marked on both the front and back of the pin, so that it can be used either side up. (It's wise to prepare a healthy supply of answer pins with plenty of duplicates among them so that finding the needed answer doesn't become a problem.)

Each clip-on card is made self-checking by putting the answers on the back, in positions that are just at the tips of the four clothespins. A word about putting these answer-key answers on correctly the first time: with the card grid side up, clip the appropriate clothespins onto the answer boxes; then turn the card over and copy answers at the end of each pin.

This device, although developed for addition facts, could be adapted to other processes and other areas such as: (1) comparing sizes of two numbers, (2) finding a common denominator for pairs of fractions, (3) comparing vowel sounds in pairs of words — the same or different.

Just be sure the answers you'll need aren't bigger than a clothespin.

Idea by: Sister Marie Therese Kaufman, Saint Michael School, Sigel, Ill.

# CREATIVITY

## Evaluating and Using Creativity-Development Materials

by Joseph S. Renzulli and
Carolyn M. Callahan

That magic word, creativity, is tossed around so freely that one cannot help being suspicious of some claims made by publishers of curricular materials. But there is enough research on the process of creativity to allow the definition of some basic principles or criteria by which so-called creativity-training materials can be evaluated. The three principles discussed here are based on experiences and insights the authors gained from several years of developing and field testing creativity-training activities. Our concern is not with the evaluation of such creative products as poems, stories or works of art, but with materials dealing with thought processes—materials designed for the opening of options and, beyond this, encouraging and even compelling the child to go further than quick associations and common responses. Teachers should examine materials that have the words "creative" and "creativity" in the title in order to determine the goals of such

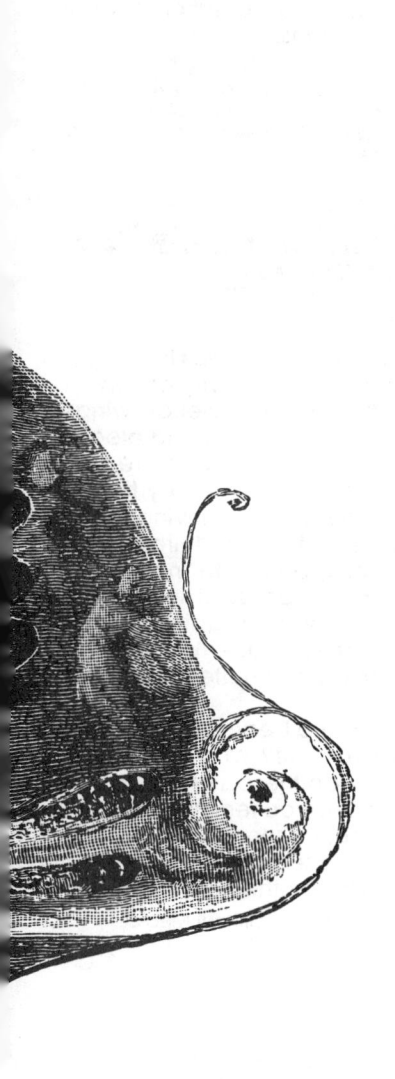

# CREATIVITY

materials and what they can expect the materials to accomplish.

▸ *Fluency.* It is obvious that the more ideas a person generates, the more likely he or she is to come up with something new and unusual. A classroom example: when a group of students was presented with the hypothetical problem of thinking up a name for a new breakfast cereal made from dandelions, most of them called the product "Dandy Flakes." Since creative ideas are, by definition, unusual or infrequent solutions to problems, and since "Dandy Flakes" was the response of more than 90 percent of the students, it was judged to be a relatively common response. The teacher then asked the students to think of five more possible names for the new breakfast cereal. Thus spurred, the students went on to develop a wide range of new possibilities, including manufacturing the cereal in the shape of lions or lions' heads and then calling it "Dandy Lions."

This example helps to illustrate the fluency principle. Unless the material encourages students to develop not a single idea but many, and unless we reward them for the sheer quantity of ideas, they may never get beyond the ordinary and the obvious. Quantity is obviously not an ultimate objective, and it is no substitute for quality; but it does increase the chance for creative thinking and moves us into the creative process. An important consideration, therefore, in evaluating creativity-training materials is to determine whether they generate a large number of ideas.

▸ *Open-Endedness.* Open-endedness is closely related to fluency. Simply stated, it means that creativity-training exercises should not have predetermined answers. A good deal of the "education game" that is played between teachers and students is based on the mental process of convergence. Teachers usually raise problems that have one predetermined solution and students are rewarded for the speed and accuracy with which they converge upon the answer. Such exercises provide students with only limited opportunities to let their minds range far and wide.

Open-ended materials can help students develop self-evaluation skills. When an answer is either right or wrong, the final source of judgment always resides with an external authority—usually the teacher or a textbook. With the threat of evaluation and the fear of being wrong hanging over their heads, it is little wonder that students are reluctant to take risks, to express thoughts divergent from the ordinary. Material with open-ended activities, on the other hand, provides students with a psychologically safe atmosphere in which to express themselves. When there are no cut-and-dried answers to problems, and when students are encouraged to generate multiple solutions, most children will review their alternative responses and select on their own the one they like best. This is not to say that the teacher and other students should not have opinions about a youngster's work. But the important thing is that the student himself pass judgment on his own work and that his opinion be regarded as valid because it is based on his own standards and criteria for self-satisfaction. We can help youngsters become more creative thinkers by giving them opportunities to practice on materials that allow for many acceptable responses and then bring their own judgmental processes to bear on their responses.

In evaluating creativity-training materials, teachers should always raise the question, "Do these exercises require a predetermined answer in order to be judged correct?" If the answer is yes, then the materials fail to meet the criterion of open-endedness.

▸ *Environmental Relevancy.* Students engaged in creativity training should not be penalized for lack of knowledge about a particular topic; the activities should allow the learner to draw upon his own background and experiences. For example, if we asked youngsters to engage in "thing listing" by listing everything they might find in a kitchen, they would not have to search through reference books in order to make several responses. Because this is an open-ended exercise based on experiences relatively common to all youngsters, it also helps to adjust for differences in background and ability level. Youngsters from affluent homes might list luxury items such as garbage disposals or microwave ovens, but students from so-called disadvantaged homes will be able to respond with their own unique selections. And while less able students are likely to focus on concrete items, brighter students may include intangibles on their lists—pleasant aromas and the warm atmosphere they associate with a kitchen.

The role of environmental relevancy in evaluation is quite clear. Unless creativity-training materials are relevant to a student's present background and immediate environment, the exercises are likely to become traditional search-for-information experiences. The major purpose of developing creativity skills can easily be lost if the student is asked to slow down divergent thinking processes in order to search out factual information.

### Sources of Creativity-Training Materials

A wide range of creativity-training materials has developed in recent years. Those interested in examining them can obtain information by writing to the ERIC Clearinghouse on the Handicapped and Gifted Children, Council for Exceptional Children, 1920 Association Drive, Reston, VA 22091. An especially valuable resource article that describes over a hundred available methods, resources and programs can be found in *The Journal of Creative Behavior* (vol. 5, no. 2, 1971, pp. 127–139). The article was written by Donald J. Treffinger and John C. Gowan and is entitled "An Updated Representative List of Methods and Educational Programs for Stimulating Creativity."

Joseph S. Renzulli and Carolyn M. Callahan are co-authors of MARK THREE — NEW DIRECTIONS IN CREATIVITY (Harper & Row).

## DEVELOPING CREATIVITY IN CHILDREN
☆ ☆ ☆ ☆ ☆ ☆ ☆

Imagination, divergent thinking and openness to inner feelings—these are some characteristics related to creativity. How can you encourage these qualities in students? And how can this creativity be expressed in positive ways?

DEVELOPING CREATIVITY IN CHILDREN, an idea book for teachers of junior high and intermediate grades, offers some concrete ways to promote creative thinking and creative expression. Activities are grouped into classifications of art, writing, dramatics and scientific thinking— more than 60 ideas in all.

The book suggests opening the way to creativity with sensory awareness experiences. Several activities for stretching the senses are described.

Throughout, diversity of ideas is the hallmark. Sometimes an idea will be a single activity, project or game. Sometimes an idea is followed up by several variations or by examples of students' responses. The ideas call for imaginative solutions to problems, unusual ways of looking at familiar experiences and everyday things, savoring words, and extending the boundaries of time and space.

The book provides a wealth of material that in the format of a teacher resource can be used in a variety of ways. Appropriate for a wide range of ages and levels of sophistication, ideas may be selected, sequenced, extended, modified and adapted to serve (the specific needs of) your class— providing an outlet for your own creativity.

The book is softcover, 8-1/2-by-11 inches in size and has 100 pages. A few carefully placed illustrations amplify the text. The table of contents lists each idea separately by name and number for easy reference.

With this kind of resource, you won't find yourself "running dry," and as your students express themselves, you'll grow in appreciation of what creativity means.

Order from: D. O. K. Publishers, 71 Radcliffe Rd., Buffalo, NY 14214. Grade level: Teachers of intermediate–junior high. Cost: $4.95. Payment must accompany orders under $5.

## LISTENING, LOOKING AND FEELING
☆ ☆ ☆ ☆ ☆ ☆ ☆

This series of four filmstrips is designed to stimulate the creativity of very young children. Its pastel drawings are simple in line, clear and pleasing. A variety of art techniques are used, all of which can be tried by the children. The accompanying records or cassettes, with their delicate music and appropriate "natural sounds," could be used separately as background for reading of original stories or poems which the filmstrip might stimulate the children to write.

Each filmstrip begins with questions: What do you see? What do you hear? How do these sights and sounds make you feel? The teacher using the series should emphasize these questions to help children consciously use their own senses.

Order from: BFA Educational Media, P.O. Box 1795, 2211 Michigan Ave., Santa Monica, CA 90406. Grade level: K – 3. Cost: $52, records; $60, cassettes.

## CREATIVE EXPRESSION
☆ ☆ ☆ ☆ ☆ ☆ ☆

The following materials—two books and a set of duplicating masters— offer practical activities for developing creative thought in students from preschool through junior high. In each of them, the process of creative thinking—stretching imaginations, making unlikely connections, conjuring up images and elaborating on them—rather than right or wrong answers, is emphasized.

**Becoming Somebody** is a teacher and parent resource book of activities for preschool and early primary aged kids.

The 68-page book by Dr. Charles Shaefer gives more than 50 activities (many with spin-offs) for stimulating creative thought and expression in young children. For example, the "Imagine Why" activity reverses the typical role of child and parent or teacher and has the adult ask such questions as: "Why is the sky blue?" "Why does the sun stay up in the

# CREATIVITY

sky?" "Why do we have thunder and lightning?" Shaefer believes that "questions such as these encourage your child to be a bold guesser in his effort to intuitively understand truths beyond his comprehension."

BECOMING SOMEBODY has sections called "Viewing the World With Wonder and Open Eyes," "Natural Artistic Talent," "Dramatic Play and Storytelling," "Poetic Expression" and "Thinking, Imagining and Problem-Solving." Because the activities are for the very young, most of the required responses can be expressed orally or through drawings.

While the activities can be used with large groups of children, they can be most effective when used with individual kids or small groups.

Order from: D. O. K. Publishers, 71 Radcliffe Rd., Buffalo, NY 14214. Grade level: Teachers of preschool—1. Cost: $3.95. Payment must accompany orders under $5.

**Put your Mother on the Ceiling: Children's Imagination Games** is a paperback book of 30 "games" that are unique in their approach to expanding the imaginations of all elementary aged kids. Written by Richard de Mille, the games take the form of guided trips into the world of fantasy.

Each game is composed of a script that is read by a teacher or parent. The script is worded so that it takes the participants gradually from the world of reality into one of fantasy. An excerpt from one script reads like this:

> "This game is called 'Captive.'
> "Let us imagine that we have a canary in a cage/Turn him green/Turn him blue/Have him jumping around inside the cage/Have him wishing he could fly outside/Have him open the door of the cage and fly out/Have him fly around the room/Have him be glad to be outside/Have him fly back into the cage/Have him shut the door. . . .
> "Now you be inside the cage instead of the canary/Jump around inside the cage/Try to get out of the cage/Bend the bars of the cage and jump out."

Though de Mille gives guidelines for using the games, there are no hard-and-fast rules. If a teacher finds, for instance, that one of the students is having a hard time shaking an image, she must use her own ingenuity to help him do it. De Mille gives examples of how this might be done, but of course each situation will be unique.

The games have one-word titles—"Animals," "Home," "School," "Helping," "Hungry," "Mirror," "Ouch!"—that usually suggest that fantasy to be played out. Teachers will probably choose to change some of the situations in the few games that project certain cultural or sex biases. The games progress in difficulty (of imagining), so it is recommended that participants begin at the beginning of the book and work sequentially through it.

The games are not for everyday use but serve as creativity exercises in preparation for other experiences. They can be especially useful with kids who have a hard time moving from the concrete to the abstract.

Order from: Educational Paperback Sales, The Viking Press, 625 Madison Ave., New York, NY 10022. Grade level: Teachers of primary—junior high. Cost: $2.95 (list); $2.21 (school price). Add $.75 for postage and handling. Payment must accompany order.

**New Directions in Creativity** is a set of three books of duplicating masters with creative activities in language arts. The activities are designed to help intermediate level kids express themselves in new ways through writing and symbol-making.

The books are designated as Mark 1, Mark 2 and Mark 3, and each contains two distinct sets of 24 exercises, or 48 per book.

Many of the activities are refreshingly original: for example, think up "alternate uses" for such things as old automobile tires, old newspapers, last year's calendar and expended ballpoint pens. A few of the activities, however, that call for creative expression are unfortunately old hat. "Making words with prefixes and suffixes" is standard fare in most classrooms.

Material for the teacher includes extensive "lesson guides," presenting teaching suggestions for each activity, stated objectives for each lesson and, in many cases, follow-up activities. Various ways of using the activities in the classroom are also described. Each ditto provides essential directions for the student. The first lesson in each pair of similar lessons always has the more detailed directions, setting the stage for both activities.

The books are not closely graded, but the publishers suggest using Mark 1 for grades 4 or 5, Mark 2 for grades 5 or 6, Mark 3 for grades 6 or 7. Students need not be familiar with Mark 1 or 2 in order to use Mark 3.

The activities can be used over an entire year for regular class work, supplementary or spare-time work.

Most of the activities can be used in learning centers where kids work at their own pace individually or in groups.

Each book provides ditto masters listing all activities. These lists can serve as individual check sheets for students to keep a record of the activities they've undertaken.

Order from: Harper and Row, Publishers, Keystone Industrial Park, Scranton, PA 18512. Grade level: 4—8. Cost: $13.98 per book.

# SOCIAL STUDIES

## SOCIAL STUDIES

# SHOP TALK

While studying different occupations, a group of students discovered a means of adding a bit of life to the classroom. Parents and relatives were invited to come in and speak about their jobs. Besides learning some practical information, the kids whose parents or relatives came to speak developed a real sense of pride in a school program that was basically theirs.

The basic plan was to send home a letter inviting parents to speak to the class. It mentioned some of the things that might be included in the talk: the preparation necessary for the kind of occupation, the type of personality best fitted to the job, and the type of activities in a typical workday. A tear-off sheet was included for responses.

After each talk was completed, a thank-you committee wrote notes to the parents involved.

Idea by: Bonnie Seitz,
Brown Deer Middle School, Brown Deer, Wis.

# SUGGESTIONS FOR A MORE CREATIVE TYPE OF TEACHING. SUBJECT: AMERICAN HISTORY

☆ ☆ ☆ ☆ ☆ ☆ ☆ ☆

This inexpensive little pamphlet is 12 pages of eminently useful ideas. It offers more than 500 American history activities. Each is described in a brief paragraph, and though none of them go into any great depth, many of the activities represent fine starting points for further probing.

Though the pamphlet brainstorms ideas for the teaching of American history, many can easily be adapted to other areas of social studies. Try these: "Present an historic skit full of errors. See if students can spot errors. Then present skit with errors corrected." "Stimulate students to search old magazines and newspapers to learn to what extent styles repeat in cycles." "Assign questions like, 'Who else could have filled X's boots?' (X can be any historical figure.) Students to defend their nominations against class criticism."

This pamphlet is the product of a creative teaching workshop held at the University of Buffalo in 1957. It has aged very well.

Order from: The Creative Education Foundation, State University College at Buffalo, 1300 Elmwood Ave., Buffalo, NY 14222. Grade level: Teachers of all grades. Cost: $.50 plus $.25 postage and handling.

# THE NEEDS OF MAN

☆ ☆ ☆ ☆ ☆ ☆ ☆ ☆

Take ten activities, add ten of humankind's physical and societal needs, mix, and you can come up with a hundred combinations for social studies projects. Taking the form of a project wheel, THE NEEDS OF MAN does just that.

The wheel itself is a cardboard circle marked into ten sectors, with the needs — food, shelter, creative arts, social institutions, transportation, clothing, natural resources, communication, interdependence, and production of goods and services — printed one to a sector. The circle is attached to a larger square on which are directions for activities — for instance, "Devise an invention man could use if he found himself without . . ." or "Plan a bulletin board to show how man requires . . ." By turning the wheel, students coordinate a need with an activity. The resulting projects are general enough to be useful in studying nearly any society in any country at any point in time.

The wheel is ideal as a project starter for independent learners in the upper elementary grades or as a resource for activities that teachers may adapt to the intermediate level. To carry out the activities, students must either have some preliminary understanding of man's needs or be prepared to do some research.

Order from: Zen-Da Productions, P.O. Box 3927, Hayward, CA 94540. Grade level: Intermediate. Cost: $1.35. Payment must accompany order.

# WEST OF CINDY BAKER ZOO

Drill at its best can be dull and at its worst can be damaging. But it's also a fact of life. Adding a personal touch may at least minimize some of the more deadly effects.

One aspect of map study that may require drill is relative location in terms of directions — Omaha is west of Council Bluffs; Boston is north of New York. But before you make out the umpteenth ditto sheet featuring the United States or your own area, consider a different sort of map. To help your students improve their abilities to use the cardinal directions, try a locale that your class can be a little closer to and a little less serious about.

Ricky Brock, your class clown, may enjoy discovering that a place called Brockville County is loaded with landmarks named after his friends — Conti Airport, Thompson Zoo, and just east of Kanner Hospital on Ronald Road, there's Gillis High School.

Try making up a map of your county, naming a river, tunnel, dam, lake, school or other item for each child. Since it is a fictional map, you can be careful in the location of landmarks so that there is no confusion about direction — Karen Village is due north of Sue City.

A worksheet accompanies the map with statements like these:
▶ Morgan Bridge is _____ of Leesville.
▶ To get from Jordan Junction to Dayton Memorial School you go _____.

The students themselves might want to contribute the map items to which their names will be attached. (The Hon. William E. Cranston Highway does have a nice ring, doesn't it, Bill?) Even older students may enjoy this approach and improve their direction skills without suffering drill doldrums.

Idea by: Gail Brown,
Milton Elementary School, Eastsound, Wash.

# 58 SOCIAL STUDIES

# A Guide to Consumer Education Materials

Resources recommended by consumer education experts contacted by LEARNING:

**Early Childhood Consumer Education; Elementary Level Consumer Education; Secondary Level Consumer Education.** Each book ($3.00 prepaid) contains about a dozen case studies of projects around the country. Highly interdisciplinary. From the Consumer Education Materials Project of the Education Division of the Consumer's Union, Orangeburg, NY 10962. (Write to Charlotte Baecher at the same address for a free examination copy of "Teaching Tools For Consumer Reports," a monthly guide of detailed suggestions on how to use CONSUMER REPORTS.)

**Let the Buyer Beware** series. Set of six color filmstrips for intermediate through junior high level ($54 with cassettes; $53.50 with records). From Eye Gate, 146-01 Archer Ave., Jamaica, NY 11435. (Individual filmstrips, $6.50; write Eye Gate for titles.)

**Consumerism Unit.** Filmstrips, games, etc., from SCHOLASTIC DIMENSION program, for grades 4–6. From Scholastic Book Services, 904 Sylvan Ave., Englewood Cliffs, NJ 07632.

**Deciding; Analyzing Advertising; Wise and Responsible Consumership.** Set of three color films (13 to 14 minutes each) for primary through junior high level ($195 per film; write for rental information). From Centron Educational Films, 1621 West Ninth St., Lawrence, KS 66044. (Write Centron for information on many consumer education filmstrips.)

**Buy and Buy.** 15-minute color film for intermediate level examines difficulties involved in making a purchasing decision ($180, purchase). From National Instructional Television, Box A, Bloomington, IN 47401.

**Learning About Consumer Education Series.** Four-filmstrip set for primary and elementary level ($65 with records or cassettes). From Doubleday Multimedia, Box C-19518, 1371 Reynolds Ave., Irvine, CA 92713.

**The Image Makers: Advertising in a Consumer Society.** 30 booklets, teacher's guide, color poster, filmstrip ($39.95 with record or cassette). From Xerox Education Center, 1250 Fairwood Ave., Columbus, OH 43216.
Also see **Economics for Primaries** and **Typical Gyps and Frauds**, both described elsewhere in this chapter.

## SOCIAL STUDIES 5

### THE MANY AMERICAN FILM SERIES

☆ ☆ ☆ ☆ ☆ ☆ ☆ ☆ ☆

The Learning Corporation of America offers a remarkably vivid and interesting series of six color films for grades two through seven about American children of different ethnic backgrounds. Each film shows in children's terms the conflicts faced by minority groups in American society. The films do not teach directly, but show life-styles and values through simple stories. A charming and interesting feature of all the films is the insertion of the child's "other" language — whether it be Chinese, Apache or Ghetto English.

GERONIMO JONES, artistically the most outstanding film in the series, was made at the Papago Indian reservation in Arizona; all the characters in the story are people who live on the reservation. The grandfather in the story, for instance, is a grandson of the great Apache chief Geronimo. The scenery and the faces of the people are exquisitely filmed.

The 21-minute story deals with an Indian boy caught between two worlds — the past as represented by his love of his grandfather, and the future as represented by his admiration of a young cousin who is working at a local scientific observatory. The grandfather gives the boy a sacred Apache medallion, which he is persuaded by a greedy white "trader" at a local store to exchange for a secondhand television set "as a present for his grandfather." The moment of truth comes when the boy and the old man are watching a program together on the newly acquired television in which white soldiers defeat Indians in battle, and the announcer proclaims that "the land is now going to be safe for the white settlers." The old man's despair causes the boy to regret deeply what he has done.

The film is marvelous for provoking discussion on the emotional conflicts of the modern Indian in our society. It is also a moving little work of art.

Order from: Learning Corporation of America, 1350 Ave. of the Americas, New York, NY 10019. Grade level: 2 – 7. Cost: $20, rental; $270, purchase.

Very briefly, the other films in the series are:

FELIPA – NORTH OF THE BORDER. A young Chicano teaches her uncle English so that he can get a driver's license and a better job. The film deals with the frustrations caused by not understanding English.

Cost: (17-min./color) $20, rental; $240, purchase.

MIGUEL – UP FROM PUERTO RICO. A Puerto Rican boy in crowded New York City uses his ingenuity to secure a fish for his father's birthday. Warm family feeling and some advantages of belonging to two cultures are shown. This is an outstanding "urban" film, understood and appreciated by city children.

Cost: (15-min./color) $15, rental; $225, purchase.

TODD – GROWING UP IN APPALACHIA. A short film which deals with the problem of poverty in Appalachia. Much respect for the dignity and courage of the characters is maintained.

Cost: (12-min./color) $15, rental; $215, purchase.

WILLIAM – FROM GEORGIA TO HARLEM. A black child from Georgia adjusts to life in a city ghetto. He meets the challenge of being "the new kid" and earns the respect of the city boys.

Cost: (17-min./color) $20, rental; $235, purchase.

SIU MEI WONG – WHO SHALL I BE? This is the tale of a Chinese girl in Los Angeles who longs to be a ballerina. The film raises the question of whether it's possible to be bicultural.

Cost: (17-min./color) $20, rental; $240, purchase.

### THE STAR-SPANGLED BANNER
**Illustrated by Peter Spier**

Children who aren't sure what the word "ramparts" means when they sing the national anthem will find out all about it in this book by Spier. It's a good antidote to mindless parroting of the 1814 lyrics.

DOUBLEDAY, $5.95 (list), $4.46 (school price). Ages 4 – 8. See page 151 for ordering information.

## JACKDAWS

☆ ☆ ☆ ☆ ☆ ☆ ☆ ☆

Realia make effective tools for teaching social studies. The problem, though, is getting hold of enough of the stuff to relate to a single topic.

JACKDAWS are reproductions of primary sources: documents, newspaper clippings, photographs, signs, maps and sundry other items related to a topic or a period of history. The packets are full of fascinating old materials that are not only useful as part of a study but are fun to examine by themselves.

JACKDAWS packets are available in categories such as American, world and English history; revolt and revolution; conflict; economics; geography and social issues. A sampling of titles includes "The United Nations," "The Depression," "The American Revolution" and "National Parks of the United States."

We looked at about ten different JACKDAWS. A typical collection, "National Parks of the United States," included the following materials: a Yellowstone National Park flyer from the season of 1885, a 19th-century railroad promotional booklet, a hand written Act of Congress setting aside the Hot Springs in Arkansas as a national park, and a current list of National Park Service recreation symbols.

Unfortunately, some of the documents bear no dates. This presents a problem in some cases, especially when the topic spans a wide time period. On the other hand, this could lead students into some creative research of their own. Moreover, because JACKDAWS are random collections, some users will want documents included that have been left out.

Teachers who decide to purchase any of the collections might wish to first write for a complete list of titles to see which will be most useful to them.

Order from: Jackdaws, Grossman Publishers, 625 Madison Ave., New York, NY 10022. Grade level: 6 – high school. Cost: $4.95 (list), $3.71 (school price). Add $.50 per package postage and handling.

## ISHI, LAST OF HIS TRIBE
**by Theodora Kroeber**

A true and haunting story of Ishi, often called "the last wild Indian," written by the woman whose husband befriended him when he first encountered white civilization in 1911. Originally published in 1961, this biography of a man whose ancestors had lived in Northern California for thousands of years should hold readers spellbound.

BANTAM, $.95, paperback. Ages 10 – 14. See page 151 for ordering information.

## YOUR CITY HAS BEEN KIDNAPPED

☆ ☆ ☆ ☆ ☆ ☆ ☆ ☆

Zephyros is an educational cooperative of teachers, toy-makers, parents and students demonstrating that "plain folks" can develop their own materials. YOUR CITY HAS BEEN KIDNAPPED, by W. Ron Jones, is one of their most popular ventures. An oversize publication, YOUR CITY originated as a series of wall placards proposing ways for children and adults to investigate their urban environment. The product can be used as a textbook, as a source book for teachers and kids, or as a game book for a rainy day. One activity:

"Where Is There Humor In Your City? Try collecting graffiti, advertisements, political promises, theater marquees, that illustrate various forms of humor."

Zephyros also offers a one-year membership in its educational exchange for ten dollars. Members are entitled to two boxes filled with learning materials created or scrounged by other members of the exchange.

A cautionary note: YOUR CITY HAS BEEN KIDNAPPED deals, in part, with grafitti containing some profanity.

Order from: Zephyros, 1201 Stanyan St., San Francisco, CA 94117. Grade level: Intermediate – high school. Cost: $1.50, includes postage and handling. Payment must accompany order.

## FABULOUS FREEBEE
## NATIONAL GALLERY OF ART SLIDE SHOWS

In teaching history, how many times have you found yourself wishing for pictorial examples to illustrate a point? If American history is the topic, access to a gold mine of such resources is available in the form of color-slide lecture sets. Teachers anywhere may borrow them free from the National Gallery of Art in Washington, D.C.

Among the topics are "American Textiles" and "Early American Crafts." One presentation of special interest is "18th- and 19th-Century Toys," which furnishes pictures of handcrafted toys: dolls, hobby horses, puppets, etc.

The Gallery lists approximately 40 different sets of about 50 slides, each with accompanying written lecture notes. In some instances, a recording of the notes is also provided. For many elementary students, the lectures may prove too sophisticated, but junior high audiences with advance preparation should have no trouble understanding the notes. The slides alone are appropriate for children in the intermediate grades.

Instead of selecting from the few titles listed here, write to the Gallery and request their "Extension Service Catalog," which lists all the slide shows and a number of free loan films as well. In lining up presentations, the Gallery requires teachers to give several alternative showing dates to allow for heavy demand.

Order from: The Extension Service, National Gallery of Art, Washington, DC 20565 Grade level: Intermediate – high school. User pays return postage and postal insurance.

## SOCIAL STUDIES

## EXPRESSION: BLACK AMERICANS

☆ ☆ ☆ ☆ ☆ ☆ ☆ ☆ ☆

How many Americans, black or white, are aware that in the year 1500 the ancient African city of Timbuktu was home for a thriving university and that books were the city's largest selling product? In fact, how many people know very much at all about the cultural heritage of black Americans? This 230-page paperback, written for junior high students by Margaret Cottom-Winslow, Agnes McCarthy and A. Okion Ojigbo, takes a cultural approach to black history.

The first of three major sections, "A Rich Heritage," relates the history of some of the old African societies and makes it clear that many of their traditions have been handed down to modern times despite the effects of slavery. "Breaking Away" covers several hundred years of cultural history, from the forced exodus from Africa through the long years of American black slavery to the present. Along the way, this section tells of the individuals who emerged as leaders of various causes and describes ways in which blacks sought relief from slavery through word (oral folklore) and action (politics). The final section, "The Arts," discusses a number of great black American artists. Included are names such as Duke Ellington, Leontyne Price, Lorraine Hansberry, Charles Gordone, Jr., and many more.

Each section of the book ends with two pages of "What Do You Know?" and "How Do You Feel?" questions asking readers both to sum up the factual information they have read and to express themselves through language and pictures. There is also an annotated bibliography describing related readings at the end of each major section.

EXPRESSION: BLACK AMERICANS is not meant to be a principal text but supplements the classroom social studies library. Its abundant illustrations serve the text well.

Order from: Harcourt Brace Jovanovich, 757 Third Ave., New York, NY 10017. Grade level: Junior High. Cost: $2.40 plus $.10 postage and handling. Payment must accompany order.

## ALONG THE NIGER RIVER: An African Way of Life

**Text and photographs by Aylette Jeness**

Jeness has brought back from her three-year stay in Nigeria a warm and natural photo-documentary of life in the market town of Yelwa, where nearly a dozen tribes, each distinctive in appearance, culture and commerce, meet to exchange goods. The reader will regret the end of this expedition to a place where the traditional (the nose rings worn by the farming Kamberi) coexists with the modern (nylon fishnets and geared bicycles).

CROWELL, $8.95 (list), $6.44 (school price). Ages 10 and up. See page 151 for ordering information.

## YELLOW PAGES OF LEARNING RESOURCES

☆ ☆ ☆ ☆ ☆ ☆ ☆ ☆ ☆

From greenhouses to junkyards, from taxicab drivers to orchestra members, YELLOW PAGES OF LEARNING RESOURCES will give you a different slant on your city, however large or small. The 94-page directory, which looks enough like the real yellow pages to fool you, is packed with practical suggestions on how to begin tapping the rich but often-overlooked learning resources of a community.

Inspired no doubt by the school-without-walls concept, the alphabetical directory (Accountant to Zoo) can help teachers extend the learning environment into the real world.

Order from: The MIT Press, 28 Carleton St., Cambridge, MA 02142. Grade level: 4 – high school. Cost: $1.95, paperback. Payment must accompany order.

# Curriculums for One World

by Patricia A. Snyder

There is a new and exciting movement making its way through the curriculum of every grade level—from kindergarten to high school. The primary objective of this movement is to develop an understanding and appreciation of the various cultures that coexist in our highly interdependent world. New texts have been written for all levels reflecting this interest, and a wide variety of curriculum materials is becoming available.

But there is a thorny problem in teaching about other cultures, a problem which has confounded anthropologists for years: Should a teacher pass on to her students judgments as to whether one culture or aspects of a culture are better than others? If she should, what are valid criteria for making such judgments? Let's take a look, in naturalistic terms, at various strategies used by teachers.

1. *The Way of the Puppy Dog*. The puppy-dog approach is simply to study the "facts" about each culture without passing judgment. Just as the puppy dog bounces out indiscriminately to greet each stranger, the neutralist teacher greets each new culture with egalitarian regard. The major advantage of this "to-each-his-own" stance is that it lessens the possibility that students will leap to unfounded judgments and thus sow the seeds for early development of prejudices. But at the same time, it makes it awkward, if not impossible, to deal with some very real cultural phenomena—headhunting, cannibalism, genocide and slavery, for example.

2. *The Way of the Crow*. The crow approach, a very popular one, demands that those aspects of other cultures which appear to us as "exotic" or "quaint" be selected as representative. Just as the crow is attracted to showy, bright objects, the *Corvus brachyrhynchos* teacher casts about the world's cultures seeking the unusual. To be sure, this can create an atmosphere of fun and excitement but it can also contribute to the creation of stereotypes, as it ignores both the subtle differences and the common denominators of humanity.

3. *The Way of the Collie*. The collie approach requires an interest in exploring other cultures, but with the predetermined conclusion that "there's no place like home." As the collie roams to investigate neighboring properties but is never fully content until it returns home, so the ethnocentric teacher directs the study of other cultures in such a way that her students will conclude that the best of all possible worlds is here, in the United States. There is something very secure and patriotic in this determinism, but students may well be left in ignorance of the brilliances of other cultures.

4. *The Way of the Bee*. Those who embrace the bee approach honor the notion that hard work is good, hard work results in production, and the true worth of a culture is reflected by its GNP. Just as the bee regards honey production as its highest calling, the work-oriented teacher regards production in general as man's end-all and be-all. This is a more scientific version of ethnocentrism, since the United States still ranks at the top. It very accurately represents the national planning objectives of many nations, but its adequacy can be easily questioned by any student bright-eyed enough to explore the cultural magnificence of those ancient and contemporary societies that by GNP standards were or are midgets.

5. *The Way of the Ant*. The ant approach views the good life in a synergistic light, a merging of the selfish and the unselfish. The superior cultures are those in which the individual can satisfy his own needs and at the same time be seen as contributing to a group. Just as the ant considers its own fulfillment as synonymous with the survival of its hillmates, the synergistically oriented teacher considers it possible for man to reach his highest fulfillment only when individual and group needs are harmonious. A teacher may find this a more humanistic basis for judging other cultures, but it can be a fuzzy yardstick to employ and poses the risk of creating images of happy, innocent natives playing with coconuts on white sandy beaches.

Which of these five strategies best fosters the understanding of other cultures? Convincing arguments can be made for any one or any combination of them. In her own wisdom, Mother Nature achieves a balance by nurturing the puppy as well as the crow, the collie, the bee and the ant.

Most teachers, however, are personally inclined toward one or two of the five approaches to viewing other cultures. For example, someone doing a unit on Asia might use as a point of major teaching emphasis the famous Filipino bamboo dance. This is clearly the way of the crow and can be highly commended for acquainting students with an exciting facet of life in a little-known culture. But how narrow, and how much better it would be to offer more: neutralistic facts (a land of more than 7,000 islands, a population of some 40 million people speaking more than 50 dialects); common comparisons to the United States (they don't have as many automobiles as we do but their traffic jams are just as bad); technological progress (small industry, electricity spreading into the rural areas); and synergistic evaluation (close-knit extended families who help each other a great deal). This example is highly simplistic, but it does illustrate the necessity for teachers to expand their own knowledge of other cultures in order to provide a balanced perspective for students. This can be pursued through one or more of a variety of channels:

▶ *Travel*—Vacation trips, study tours arranged by universities and teacher-exchange programs are excellent ways to gain firsthand knowledge of other people and to collect materials for use in the classroom.

▶ *University or home study*—Many campuses offer courses in comparative and international education, educational anthropology and a wide range of other instruction about Latin America, Africa, Asia and Europe.

▶ *Books, periodicals, newspapers, films, international organizations, art collections, music, food*—Anything that offers a new dimension to the culture being studied should be sought out and examined for classroom relevance.

▶ *People*—Perhaps the deepest understanding of other cultures comes from close association with people. Friends, friends of friends, friends and relatives of students, and community or university exchange programs should be explored as resources for people who could visit with the children and share their experiences.

Going beyond the expansion of personal knowledge, there is the area of curriculum-materials selection. Teachers should carefully select materials that represent those perspectives not already represented in the classroom. In the Philippine study, for example, the teacher may be using a core text that is rich with detail and basic facts about the islands but lacks all aspects of cross-cultural analysis. This should be her starting point for a supplementary-materials search.

Teachers, then, *can* design and carry out "One World" curriculums by emulating the various ways of the puppy dog, the crow, the collie, the bee and the ant. This requires a commitment to personal growth in the knowledge of other cultures and the courage to select some resources which might not agree with one's own point of view.

A lot of time and effort, you say? Yes, but the need for intercultural understanding and the devastating effects of provincialism can hardly be overemphasized.

Patricia A. Snyder is associate professor of education, University of Connecticut, Storrs.

## JOHN MUIR: FATHER OF OUR NATIONAL PARKS

☆ ☆ ☆ ☆ ☆ ☆ ☆ ☆ ☆

John Muir was one of those rare individuals willing to dedicate his life to a cause. His determination to help save America's natural environment established him as one of our first and perhaps best-known conservationists. Using voice-over narration and dialogue, this 15-minute color film depicts much of Muir's life and captures a feeling for the man and the forces that drove him.

Growing up in the mid-1800s on a farm where life was rugged and highly disciplined, Muir learned early to love nature. He wanted to study nature after finishing college, but economic circumstances brought him to the city, where he was temporarily blinded in an industrial accident. During his recuperation, he decided to return to his first love.

With his sight restored, Muir went out into the wilderness—only to see it being despoiled unchecked by the lumbering industry. Muir then made another difficult decision—to give up the study of nature for the fight to preserve it.

Muir was, of course, subjected to savage criticism, but he never swerved from his work. In these days of political and environmental pollution, when ideals have been compromised or abandoned and the environment is deteriorating, John Muir stands a veritable Gibraltar of integrity.

An accompanying teacher's guide gives additional background information about Muir, a summary of the film, a suggested bibliography and a few uninspired follow-up activities.

Order from: Walt Disney Educational Media Co., 500 S. Buena Vista St., Burbank, CA 91521. Grade level: 4–12. Cost: $15, rental; $210, license agreement.

## NEIGHBORHOOD NEWS

Your neighborhood—its people, its streets and its homes—is chock-full of resources to learn from and about. The exploration for one group of kids consisted of 20- to 30-minute neighborhood walks each school day for three or four weeks. Each walk was preceded with a discussion and preparation of a plan of action. Plans for a day included such activities as finding and/or investigating stores, street signs, living things, means of transportation, community helpers, houses and house numbers, colorful things, clean or dirty things, and whatever else the class's collective intelligence could define.

During each of the walks, students carried notebooks, pencils and cameras. Follow-up discussions about feelings and discoveries were tape-recorded and written up for a daily class newspaper, "The Neighborhood News." Also published in the newspaper were drawings, stories and poems related to the walks.

Everything discovered on the walks was also inscribed on a class-made map. Houses, fire hydrants, stores, telephone poles— all were drawn in on a daily basis.

Idea by: Sharon Silberman, PS 335, Brooklyn, N.Y.

## SOCIAL STUDIES

## RECYCLING STAMPS

If you can bring yourself these days to look at stamps and the prices they carry without growing bitter, you're ready for some interesting experiences with your class. And if you happen to have a stamp collector in the building—or have been known to do that kind of thing yourself—you're on your way.

For this project you'll need a variety of stamps. If you can borrow a stamp dictionary from a friendly philatelist, you can include foreign stamps, perhaps the leftovers from collectors' packets. If you can't get a stamp dictionary, better stick to commemoratives.

Clip each stamp to a three-by-five card as the focus for a research activity. Study guides might include the questions shown above. Or:
1. In what area or field was this person known?
2. Where was this person born? When?
3. What are some of the important things this person did?
... or whatever suits the content of the stamp.

Reports are written on separate paper so the cards may be reused. Reports, with stamps attached, can be used in a display. The stamps and reports generally stimulate enough interest to spark discussion and further research by others or the class as a whole.

With postage at a premium, it's a citizen's duty to get extra mileage out of those stamps.

Idea by: Alice Mangham, Boynton, Benton Harbor, Mich.

## THE PEOPLE'S BANK

Since their money isn't insured by the federal government, depositors have to have deep faith in the Jaguar Bank. They should: The bank is run by and for the sixth grade students of Johnston Elementary School. Officers, cashiers, tellers and bookkeepers—all are students in the school.

In setting up the bank, the initial step is to send letters home requesting permission for a child to participate. If it is given, the student is allowed to open a checking account. Before actually writing any checks, exercises in filling out deposit slips, writing checks, applying for loans, bookkeeping and budget preparation are given to acquaint the students with banking procedures.

To open an account a pupil must pay a 25-cent service charge. This entitles him to a special checkbook, an identification card and an account number. These items are made on the school mimeograph machine and stamped or signed by the principal.

Checks are honored anytime during the school day at several places: the school office to pay for tickets to various school activities and to pay for other items; the classroom to pay for subscriptions to school magazines, books, newspapers and other school materials and supplies; the school cafeteria to pay for lunches by the day or by the week; and the school library to pay for fines or lost books. After school, several local business establishments—a drug store, a variety store and a drive-in grocery store—participate in the project.

Idea by: Morris Foster, Johnston Elementary School, Abilene, Tex.

---

## A Guide to Games

Social studies related games recommended by game and simulation experts contacted by LEARNING:

**Starpower.** A simulation game for 18 to 35 players in which students build a society and discover the uses of power. From: Simile II, 218 Twelfth St., P.O. Box 910, Del Mar, CA 92014. Grade Level: 5–12. Cost: complete kit: $25 plus $.50 postage and handling; do-it-yourself instructions: $3 plus $.35 postage and handling. Payment must accompany orders by individuals. School purchase orders will be billed.

**Baldicer.** A simulation game for 12 to 30 players that teaches about the problem of feeding the world's population. From: John Knox Press, 341 Ponce de Leon Ave., N.E., Atlanta, GA 30308. Grade level: 5–12. Cost: $25.

**System 1.** A general learning game for 2 to 6 players for all content areas that stresses classification skills. From: ISI, 2147 University Ave., St. Paul, MN 55114. Grade level: Preschool–high school. Cost: $12.95 plus $2.50 for postage and handling.

**Ghetto.** A simulation game for 7 to 10 participants that helps children experience life in a ghetto. From: Educational Publishing Division, The Bobbs-Merrill Co., 4300 W. 62nd St., Indianapolis, IN 46268. Grade level: 5–high school. Cost: $28, school price. Add 5 percent on billed orders.

**Culture Contact.** A simulation for 15 to 30 players that teaches about the cultural differences between industrial and nonindustrial societies. From: Games Central, 55 Wheeler St., Cambridge, MA 02138. Grade level: 6–high school. Cost: $35 plus $1.50 postage and handling. School purchase orders will be billed.

**Market.** A simulation for 10 to 35 players about everyday buying and selling of food. From: Benefic Press, 10300 W. Roosevelt Rd., Westchester, IL 60153. Grade level: 5–9. Cost: $54 plus $3.78 postage and handling.

## SOCIAL STUDIES 65

## MAPLE-SUGAR FARMER

☆ ☆ ☆ ☆ ☆ ☆ ☆ ☆

Maple-sugar farmer Sherman Graff is one of a small minority of Americans who can still boast responsibility for the total production of a material good. Not only does he tap the sap from trees and boil it down into syrup, then sugar, he even whittles the wooden tapping spiles. From start to finish, he is in charge of the entire process that is captured in this 29-minute color film.

The movie follows the lone septuagenarian Illinois maple-sugar farmer through the production of syrup and sugar, revealing his processing methods as well as much about the man himself. Narrated by Graff, the movie paints a charming, sincere picture of a particular way of life where man and nature harmoniously coexist. "Man has no say-so about the production," explains Graff. "Nature and traits of the maple tree and the weather—that rules your whole harvest. You tap, you put it out there and you do everything right, but nature takes over there." Though occasional bits of information are lost by ears not tuned to the Midwestern accent, the loss detracts little from the film's total impact.

Kids viewing this film will not only get to know Graff as an individual but will gain an understanding of what it means to be a perfectionist. The maple-sugar farmer, a craftsman in his own right, knows each stage of the process and carefully inspects his work before moving on to the next step.

Social studies classes will find this film useful in studying occupations or geographical regions. In science, the film shows how one substance (sap) can be transformed into several others (syrup and sugar). And as a lesson in values, Graff's solid ideas and feelings about nature and work make for interesting discussion.

Order from: ACI Media, Inc., 35 West 45th St., New York, NY 10036. Grade level: 4–12. Cost: $370, purchase. Contact ACI for names of film libraries near you which rent this film.

## GOOD CENTS: EVERY KID'S GUIDE TO MAKING MONEY

**by Members of the Amazing Life Games Company (and friends). Illustrated by Martha Hairston and James Robertson**

Just the thing for kids who want to have fun and make money at the same time. This book covers four kinds of money-makers: weekenders, any timers, special timers and summer timers, all of which real kids (their photos are in the book to prove it) have found rewarding. MAKING MONEY is filled with surprises and has been put together and illustrated with great elan. A fitting salute to Ben Franklin's advice: "Mind your business."

HOUGHTON, $7.95, $3.95 paperback. Ages 8–12. See page 151 for ordering information.

## 66 SOCIAL STUDIES

## ENRICHED SOCIAL STUDIES TEACHING THROUGH THE USE OF GAMES AND ACTIVITIES

☆ ☆ ☆ ☆ ☆ ☆ ☆ ☆ ☆

Social studies is one of those subject areas that is frequently taught exclusively through texts. For those looking for a way to go beyond the text, this booklet offers nothing but practical activities that can be used in nearly any social studies topic of study.

Games, puzzle quizzes, writing projects and physical activities comprise the four basic types of activities (60 in all). While a few will be exhausted after a single playing, many of them will become staples for use throughout the year.

The activities are primarily for review and reinforcement rather than as a means of helping kids uncover new material. They will also be just plain fun for those social studies "buffs" who like to play around with their knowledge of the topic being studied. Directed primarily at students in the intermediate and junior high grades, the activities often require recall of specific facts.

Though the book leans heavily toward the traditional question-and-answer type games, it is still a useful addition to the social studies library of activity books.

Order from: Fearon Publishers, 6 Davis Dr., Belmont, CA 94002. Grade level: Teachers of grades 5-8. Cost: $2.50 plus $.50 postage and handling. Payment must accompany order.

## THE UPSTAIRS ROOM
**by Johanna Reiss**

This 1973 Newbery Medal Honor Book is an autobiographical account of Johanna Reiss's years as a Jewish child hiding from the Germans in World War II Holland. A gentle, very human story of the relationship between Johanna, her older sister and the family who were their benefactors, this book may very well become as popular with children as THE DIARY OF ANNE FRANK.

BANTAM, $1.25, paperback. Ages 10-14. See page 151 for ordering information.

## TYPICAL GYPS AND FRAUDS

☆ ☆ ☆ ☆ ☆ ☆ ☆ ☆ ☆

Few consumers go through life without being "taken" in one way or another. The costs, of course, vary. Some people lose only pennies or pride; others a good deal more. This set of two color filmstrips may not prevent such events but will increase general awareness about where the potential for gyps or frauds exists.

The stories in both filmstrips, which are accompanied by either records or cassettes, require the viewer to become involved in the decision-making process. Presented with a problem, the characters in the filmstrips discuss the alternatives but don't resolve the situation. In one situation, a group of high school students wants to fix up a room in order to have a dance but learns that the necessary repairs will require the services of a handyman. Uncertain of how to approach the problem, the students seek out a handyman and get his estimate for the job. Even to the unsophisticated observer, the would-be contractor's judgment seems shaky. The students then must decide between using his inexpensive services or those of a more reputable, and higher-priced, person whose work they are familiar with. The viewer is left with an open-ended situation in which he is asked to decide: "Which contractor would you vote for?"

Each filmstrip employs real characters and reasonably authentic dialogue. All the stories, two in Part 1 and three in Part 2, are short and interesting enough to involve junior high viewers and mature fifth and sixth graders.

A supplementary teaching guide suggests inquiry and discussion questions and activities that effectively take students beyond the filmstrips. There's also a separate sheet with additional discussion questions and exercises keyed to the filmstrip stories.

Order from: Changing Times Education Service, 1729 H St., N.W., Washington, DC 20006. Grade level: Junior high. Cost: $47.50, records or cassettes.

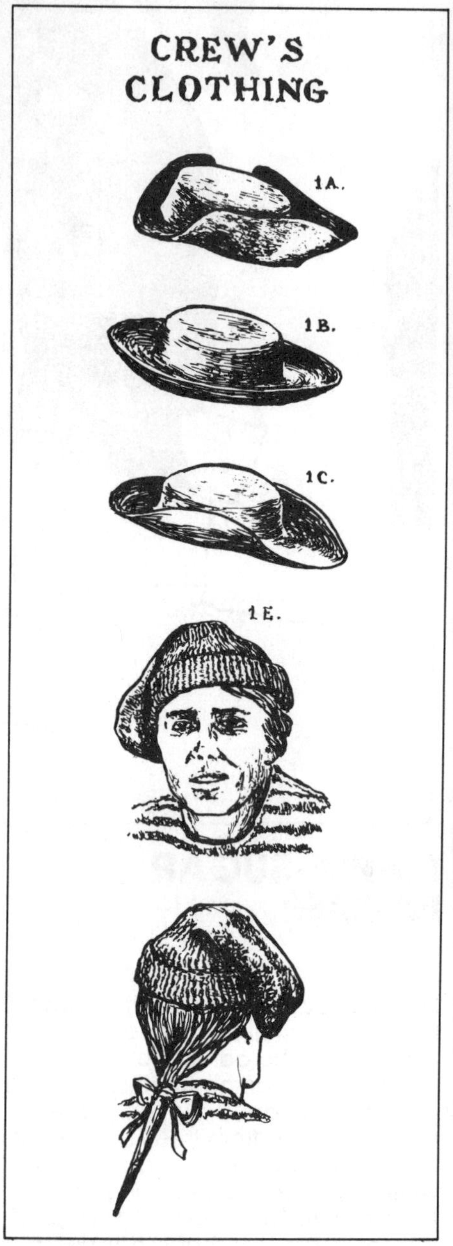

## PICTURE BOOK OF THE REVOLUTION'S PRIVATEERS
**by C. Keith Wilbur**

A gem of a resource book, this hand-lettered volume tells the true story of the American Revolution's private navy. A plethora of illustrations about victuals, weapons and navigation provide an exciting course in the seafaring of old — a time when piracy was patriotic.

STACKPOLE, $5.95. Ages 10 and up. See page 151 for ordering information.

# SOCIAL STUDIES 67

## ASSEMBLY LINE SIMULATION

If your class is studying the Industrial Revolution, the following activity may help show how the assembly line changed both the production process and the products.

Arrange most of the class in two semicircular rows with the same number in each, say, 12 and 12. These rows will be assembly lines A and B. Each student will assume the role of a worker with a specialized task.

The product is an automobile. Before class, plan an automobile consisting of 12 parts. Draw the car on the board. Each of the 12 parts will be a job for one of your assembly-line workers. For example, the outline or silhouette of the body is skill number one; the front fender, skill number two; a window, skill three. Parts should be labeled with corresponding numbers.

Assembly lines A and B will be assigned identical tasks. The first worker in each line gets 25 sheets of paper. This worker draws the outline of the car on each sheet and passes it to worker two, who draws in a fender. The papers progress down both lines and the cars grow. Each part is to be drawn identically each time — same size, same shape, no spontaneous creativity allowed.

The students not in the assembly lines are craftsmen who build cars from scratch. They begin their work as the assembly lines get started.

When the assembly lines have completed their quotas, collect their cars and the custom-built models. Discuss how and why the products are different. Have workers in both production methods discuss their feelings about their jobs. Discuss also any problems that arose — pileups, uneven distribution of work — and possible solutions.

Idea by: S. B. Hirni, former teacher at North Kansas City High School.

## FOLK PUPPET PLAYS FOR THE SOCIAL STUDIES

☆ ☆ ☆ ☆ ☆ ☆ ☆ ☆

The joys of puppet making and the benefits of puppet use are well known to teachers. Margaret Weeks Adair and Elizabeth Patapoff — with backgrounds in education, puppetry, drama and television — provide a book that helps puppet users "go from there."

The book presents 16 puppet plays based on folk tales and legends from around the world. But beyond the dialogue and stage directions (complete and detailed), there are helpful sections about dramatization techniques and practices that you can apply to other story adaptations.

The plays themselves are drawn from many different countries and traditions, including some old favorite characters, such as Paul Bunyan. Care is taken to preserve the distinctive character of the tales, with suggestions for costuming, the use of colloquial language, and the inclusion of music and special properties. Each play is followed by specific production notes. Study notes encourage discussion and suggest activities dealing with the countries and cultures represented.

The language and vocabulary used in the dialogue have more in common with literature than with basal readers, and the use of a narrator may be indicated with some classes. Junior high students may enjoy preparing and producing the plays for presentation to younger children.

A hardcover book, 8-1/2-by-11 inches in size and 120 pages long, FOLK PUPPET PLAYS FOR THE SOCIAL STUDIES is a combination of arts in a social studies setting. It should be a practical and appealing aid for those who want to make dramatization an integral part of their program.

Order from: The John Day Co., Dept. SS, 666 Fifth Ave., New York, NY 10019. Grade level: Teachers of grades 4 — 8. Cost: $9.95 (list); $7.17 (school price). Payment must accompany order.

## SIMULATION/ GAMING/NEWS

☆ ☆ ☆ ☆ ☆ ☆ ☆ ☆

In recent years, more and more games have been developed for the elementary grades. SIMULATION/GAMING/ NEWS (S/G/N) is a first-rate source for finding out about many of them.

S/G/N, which appears six times a year, can become a vital resource for anyone concerned with the use of games in the classroom. The newspaper not only discusses and reviews specific games but also suggests ways for integrating game playing into content areas of the curriculum.

S/G/N's concern is with the practical as well as the theoretical, and its inclusion of materials and feedback from classroom teachers as well as university professors makes this smorgasbord of information valuable to teachers just beginning to explore gaming as well as to those already involved in designing games.

Order from: S/G/N, Box 3039, University Station, Moscow, ID 83843. Grade level: Teachers of all grades. Cost: $6 per year; $13 for three years.

# 68 SOCIAL STUDIES

### WRAPPED FOR ETERNITY: The Story of the Egyptian Mummy
**by Mildred Mastin Pace**
**Line drawings by Tom Huffman**

Pace took two years to research this fascinating book, which could very well turn its readers into aspiring archaeologists. Who can resist mummy unwrappings, solid gold coffins, tales of ancient kings and queens, hidden tombs, grave robbers and, of course, King Tut? A simply superb book, well-designed, well-illustrated and well-written.

McGRAW-HILL, $6.95. Ages 10 and up. See page 151 for ordering information.

## ECONOMICS FOR PRIMARIES

☆ ☆ ☆ ☆ ☆ ☆ ☆ ☆

It's not clear how anyone understands economics, so there's no surprise in the fact that it's a difficult topic to adapt to the elementary grades. But the problem has been tackled successfully in this discovery-oriented series of filmstrips from Q-ED Productions. By dealing with some key economic concepts in real-life situations, the authors have created materials which can be easily understood even by kindergartners.

In unrelated stories, each of the four filmstrips approaches a different aspect of economics: wants and consumerism ("The Toy Store"), production ("The Doghouse"), division of labor ("The Breakfast"), and choices and opportunities ("The Garden"). In "The Breakfast," for instance, two sisters with different household responsibilities begin arguing about the messiness of the lunches one of them prepares for school each day. The disagreement leads to a decision that the chores will no longer be split; instead, each girl will make her own lunch and bed. Their mother takes it a step further by suggesting that every household task be done individually — no one helping anyone else.

The results are predictable, but they aren't handled in a routine fashion. At breakfast, too many hands reach into drawers and cupboards at the same time, pots and pans are too scarce to go around, the kitchen falls into general disarray, and finally, the girls end up late for school.

Throughout, discussion revolves around how awful it is for everyone to be doing the same thing at the same time. But, as in all the filmstrips, "The Breakfast" refuses to make any judgments about how things should be done. It presents a problem with a number of alternative solutions and ends with the problem still unresolved. Teachers and students must take over from there. And to help them, there is an excellent accompanying teacher's manual which contains, for each filmstrip, far-reaching questions and projects for follow-up, explanations of the economic principles involved, transcriptions of the tapes, and summaries of the stories. A poster describing the development of a loaf of bread from the farm to the consumer is also included.

The filmstrips are colorful and the stories are tight, flowing smoothly from frame to frame with no abrupt or confusing changes in situation.

Advertised for primaries, the filmstrips need not be limited to kindergarten through third grade. The stories are mature enough to involve and interest, without insulting, upper elementary kids. Language arts teachers will also find these filmstrips useful as starters for discussion and writing about values.

Order from: Q-ED Productions, P.O. Box 1608, Burbank, CA 91507. Grade level: K — 5. Cost: Four color filmstrips with records, $76; with cassettes, $84.

## SOCIAL STUDIES

## FIVE CHILDREN AND FIVE FAMILIES

☆ ☆ ☆ ☆ ☆ ☆ ☆ ☆ ☆

There aren't many teaching aids that actually accomplish with children all they are touted to do, but these two complementary sound filmstrip kits do just that. FIVE CHILDREN introduces basic concepts that range from those related to geography to self-awareness and cultural identity. A charming series, it shows events in the lives of five American children, ages four through seven, who represent very different life-styles and cultural backgrounds. The photography by photojournalist Ken Heyman is excellent, and the background music (on cassettes or records) is appropriate to each given location.

The accompanying teacher's guide includes words of songs that many children will enjoy making part of their repertoires. It also suggests related arts-and-crafts activities and follow-up book and record lists. A full-color poster is included in the kit.

FIVE FAMILIES provides lessons about the family as a social unit, as well as dealing with the concepts emphasized in FIVE CHILDREN. The authors of the program point out that children, even those in large cities, often live in isolation from people with life-styles different from their own. These delightful filmstrips provide an expedition into the homes of a wide variety of cultural backgrounds. Both the constants and the differences in the family situations intrigue young children.

Again, the photography is superb, the scenery and people sensitively captured on film. Poverty, where it exists, is not minimized, but in all cases the creative aspects of that family's life are emphasized. The excellent teacher's guide includes activities involving dramatic play, language development, music, dance and games, as well as a bibliography and record list.

The two series are captivating, imaginative and sensitively put together.

Order from: Scholastic Book Services, 904 Sylvan Ave., Englewood Cliffs, NJ 07632. Grade level: Preschool—3. Cost: $69.50 per set. Add 6 percent for postage and handling on billed orders.

## THE GOOD OLD DAYS?

How can a class of fifth grade TV addicts understand a pioneer school day? By reliving it.

Armed with research into pioneer education, family life, customs and recreation, students can prepare to establish the classroom atmosphere of those early schools. The strict and structured curriculum of the Latin grammar school and the warm, practical arts of the dame-school return—just for a day.

Appropriately costumed, the students enter the world of earlier times. No electric lights—only the dim glow of candles. No running water—unless some sturdy lad takes an oaken bucket down to the nearest stream (the water fountain down the hall). No heat—the long skirts and heavy shirts have more than fashion to recommend them.

After the initial shock of a familiar environment transformed, the boys and girls go to their places—at opposite ends of the room—to begin the day's lessons. The boys are instructed in ciphering, Latin, reading and writing. The girls are taught the finer points of domestic arts and allowed to read from the Scriptures. Students are reminded about the consequences of unseemly behavior. Smiling or talking out of turn might be punishable by a good switching. Conversing with someone of the opposite sex is frowned upon and could result in a dunking.

Surviving the strain of "roughing it" into the afternoon, students can be treated to entertainment— bobbing for apples, cutting out a jack-o'-lantern, square dancing and telling tall tales.

When students discuss their feelings and ideas about their "ordeal," expect reactions such as "Thank goodness that's over!" "I'm sure glad I didn't live back then." Most will express appreciation for modern conveniences.

A better understanding of people who live under conditions different from one's own, and a respect for our pioneer heritage, can grow from such an experience with the "good old days."

Idea by: Ralph Covington, Jr., Concord, N.C.

## THE HOW AND WHY OF DJI

By the time students reach the upper elementary level, most of them feel comfortable with such nightly news terminology as "informed sources on Capitol Hill," "semifinal match" and "measurable precipitation." But along with weather watching, politics and sports, students are confronted with the "Dow-Jones industrials."

For some youngsters, Dow-Jones may be as familiar as a member of the family. But for the others, unraveling the mysteries of the DJI may represent an out-of-the-ordinary social studies activity.

The project begins with library research to find out which stocks comprise the Dow-Jones industrials. Further investigation into the background of the Dow will reveal additions and deletions of stocks in order to maintain a roster representative of the American economy.

Each student may then be given one of the 30 industrials to study further. Letters can be composed requesting each company's latest annual report. Though students will find most reports full of formidable figures, other features of the brochures may prove more interesting; photos, graphs, cover designs, general format and even the use of recycled paper may tell something about the company. The reports can help students become a little better acquainted with "their" companies and can provide data to share with the rest of the class.

Students may contribute the covers and selected photos from their reports to create a cooperative montage display—a bird's-eye DJI.

THE WALL STREET JOURNAL and business sections of other major newspapers can be other resources for these studies. Students will find charts of market activity and articles dealing with their or similar companies.

The world of the DJI is a not-so-remote factor in the lives of your students—students who brush their teeth, take photos, talk on the phone, eat cereal and use electricity.

Idea by: Joan Mary Macey, Binghamton, N.Y.

## MOVING PEOPLE AND THINGS

☆ ☆ ☆ ☆ ☆ ☆ ☆

Jeeps and motor homes, little red wagons and shopping carts, biplanes and moon rockets, submarines and hydrofoils are but a handful of the vehicles used to move people and goods.

These conveyances and many others are examined in four separate filmstrips—"Cars and Trucks," "Things That Fly," "Things That Float" and "Other Vehicles," all comprising this series about transportation.

The filmstrips present information in a straightforward way about different vehicles and their roles in our lives.

A short teacher's guide comes with the set. It suggests skills to be developed and gives rudimentary follow-up ideas for each filmstrip.

Order from: Learning Tree Filmstrips, 934 Pearl St., Boulder, CO 80302.
Grade level: 4—6. Cost: $48, four-filmstrip set and teacher's guide.

## WANT A JOB?

"The job market is saturated." "Unemployment is high." "Welfare rolls are up." We say and hear these things so often, yet are young children ever encouraged to explore the significance of these statements? Here is a way to do just that.

Establish a list of approximately 20 jobs on an employment board in your class. A sample list would include "board eraser," "messenger," "shades," "maintenance," "baskets," "windows," "audio-visuals," "first substitute" (to substitute for absentees), etc. To begin the project assign everyone to a job on a completely arbitrary basis. Then, after one month, you are ready to shift into phase two.

Obtain a job application form from any large company in the area and make ditto copies for each member of your class. If this is not practical, it is easy enough to construct your own forms. Be sure to include items such as "previous experience" and "reason for applying for position." Now distribute the forms and have each child interested in a position make a formal application.

At the conclusion of the application period read aloud all applications, excluding the students' names. A class vote should decide on the best applicant for each position for that month.

Reading aloud four or five applications for the same job may not provide enough information for the class to make a wise decision. In this case the applications should be returned with the request that they be resubmitted with the addition of two letters of reference (from classmates, teachers, parents, anyone). Once again, the information should be read aloud and a final vote taken.

Once the job positions are filled, don't stop there. In math class, compute the unemployment rate and graph employment by monthly totals and by the number of applications for each position. For further curriculum integration relate current events through news articles dealing with employment.

The possibilities are many. And, as a teacher, you'll learn a wealth of worthwhile information about your kids.

Idea by: Thomas Finn,
Rice Elementary School, Pittsfield, Mass.

## THE CAREER TREE

The world of work is richly diverse, and career kits can help broaden your class's awareness of it.

Creation of the career kits works best as a cooperative, continuing project. Involvement of other classes will yield a greater variety of materials, and continuous updating will sustain student interest.

Clip informational items and collect pictures from magazines, newspapers and pamphlets showing people in various kinds of work. To complement and extend these materials, add cassette tapes of interviews with people at work. Tapes can also provide factual information about different kinds of

# SOCIAL STUDIES

work. Some parents may be willing to participate through a questionnaire which you and your class could draw up. Sample questions: Where do you work? What kinds of things do you do? What do you like best about what you do?

This information collection can then be categorized — sports, forestry, health care, education, transportation, communication, store work, social work, repair work. When the categories are sorted out, prepare a paper grocery bag to hold each classification. Make handles at the top of the bag by cutting out slots and reinforcing them with tape. Each bag is then labeled with its appropriate category and further identified with a picture.

If you can commandeer a hall coat tree, you'll have a fine display device. You may have to add a few hooks to accommodate all your kits. (An alternate display: a pegboard with hooks.)

The kits can serve as resource information for study units, panel discussions, story writing and displays of career opportunities. But mostly the career tree is for independent student browsing.

You don't often find jobs on trees, but a career tree might provide the first steps toward greater job awareness for some of your students.

Idea by: Florence Rives, Selma, Ala.

---

## FABULOUS FREEBEE
### RAILROAD PICTURES AND MAP

Whether trains and transportation comprise a unit of study for your entire class or interest just one youngster, this set of eight prints from Union Pacific Railroad is worth the effort required to obtain them.

Each of these full-color pictures shows a train in one of a variety of settings — beside a river, on a bridge, crossing the mountains.

Also offered is the "Union Pacific Map of the United States" showing the railroad's different routes.

Requests should be made by teachers only.

Order from: Union Pacific Railroad, Dept. of Public Relations, 1416 Dodge St., Omaha, NE 68179
Grade level: K – 8

---

## LIFE IN RURAL AMERICA

☆ ☆ ☆ ☆ ☆ ☆ ☆

The National Geographic Society has taken several feature articles from issues of its NATIONAL GEOGRAPHIC magazine, added a few topics and successfully turned them into a series of five color filmstrips.

By focusing on real people — family farmers, harvesters, cowboys, coal miners and Alaskan pioneers — each filmstrip describes one type of rural occupation as it is performed today, and to some degree, as it was performed in the past. Though the filmstrips tend to romanticize some of the hardships of rural life, the viewer becomes keenly aware of the potential difficulties and dangers of extreme rural living. The Alaskan pioneers not only build their own log cabins but travel three hours each way to stock them. The coal miner falls victim to the occupational hazard — black lung disease. Shortness of breath renders him disabled

Typical of National Geographic Society productions, the photography is superb, the narration always interesting and absorbing. A teacher's guide for each filmstrip includes a summary, key points, objectives and a text of the filmstrip as well as questions for discussion and follow-up activities. The series provides an excellent resource for intermediate and above social studies groups.

Order from: National Geographic Society, Washington, DC 20036. Grade level: 5 – 12. Cost: $67.50 with cassettes or records.

---

## PEOPLE WHO ORGANIZE FACTS

☆ ☆ ☆ ☆ ☆ ☆ ☆

What do an automotive researcher, a TV sports editor and a bakery forewoman have in common? All must gather, sort and organize facts to do their jobs. These three occupations, plus an overview of several other careers which involve fact-organizing skills, are the focus of this set of four color filmstrips from Guidance Associates. The set, which comes with a discussion guide, is part of a larger "Careers Discovery" series designed for teaching career awareness.

The filmstrips give a good feeling for what is involved in organizing facts and how certain careers demand fact-organizing skills. The automotive researcher, for instance, describes how an old auto in poor condition is restored to look and run precisely as it did when it was new. The job requires plenty of data gathering and organizing — digging into old manuals, sales brochures, picture files and advertisements — to come up with exact details for a perfect restoration.

In addition to their value in career education, the filmstrips can be used just as effectively for teaching research skills. Three of the filmstrips present problems which require some form of research and then follow them through to their solutions. From this, kids develop a sense of how to tackle research problems of their own.

Order from: Guidance Associates, Customer Service, 757 Third Ave., New York, NY 10017. Grade level: 5 – 9. Cost: $59.50, records or cassettes.

# SOCIAL STUDIES

## TURNING ON TO THE WORLD

"Bringing the world into the classroom" sounds like an impossible task. But with a shortwave radio, it's as simple as turning a dial. International broadcasts carry a wealth of current and relevant information about other countries. In a sixth grade social studies class, this was found to be a useful supplement to a study of different cultures.

To use the broadcasts in the classroom, segments are taped from English-language broadcasts from around the world. The tapes are edited to 15 or 20 minutes in length, and only material relevant to the study of a particular country is included in the final tape. The cassettes are either played for the entire class or they are used at listening centers by individuals or small groups with headphones.

After the listening sessions, class discussion is conducted or written exercises are used to check the students' comprehension. Students are then encouraged to use other resources for additional research about the country. The results take the form of oral or written reports or notebooks.

Among the broadcasts used are "Call of the Andes" from radio station HCJB in Quito, Ecuador, and "North American Mailbag" and "Club Forum" from Radio Australia. These programs emphasize local traditions and customs.

In addition to listening to the broadcasts, the class has corresponded with several international radio stations. A special highlight was the correspondence with a broadcaster from Radio Australia. After sending him letters, he beamed a special message to the class on "North American Mailbag."

Idea by: John Glenwright, Oakland School, Bloomington, Ill.

## SPORT GEOGRAPHY

With the correct guidance, an interest in sports, professional and college, national and international, can be used to generate a wide range of curriculum-related activities.

Here are a few classroom ideas that can be adapted to the various seasons of the year — athletic seasons, that is.

▶ Using wall maps, atlases, textbooks and homemade maps, have the class members trace the travel routes of their favorite teams. Discuss the cities, states and parts of the country in which the teams are situated.

▶ Plot and compute distances. What are the greatest and shortest distances your favorite team must travel away from home in order to play a game? How far must the Mets go to play the Giants? Who must travel the greatest distance to play the Reds, the Braves or the Phillies? By how many miles?

▶ Write to a favorite player on a team in a distant city (best not to have too many kids write to the same one) and ask the player to describe the city where his team plays. He might be asked to include the city's climate, terrain and relationship to other cities, among other things. The player could also compare his hometown to the one in which his team plays.

▶ Have a committee record — on maps — the cities and states from which players respond.

▶ Compare the climates where different teams play. Will performance be affected when a team plays on foreign turf? Does it ever snow on the Miami Dolphins when they play home games?

With a little imagination, mathematics can also be reached through an interest in sports. League standings, player records and stadium dimensions all lend themselves to skill practice and problem-solving techniques.

Idea by: Lou Foleno, Mercer County Community College, Trenton, N.J.

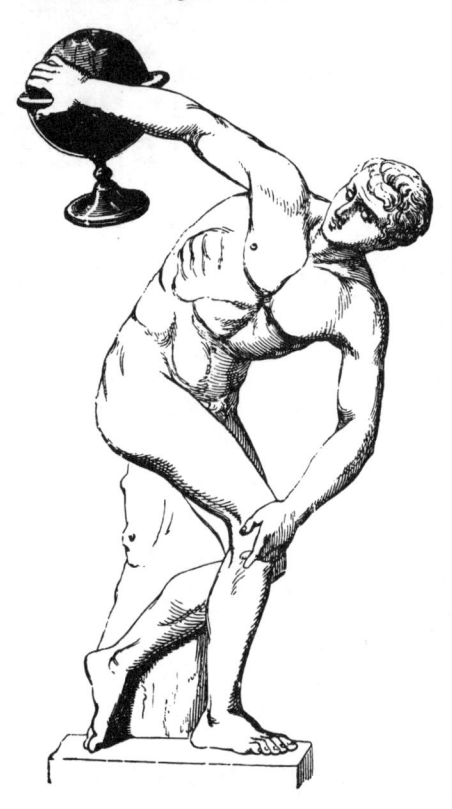

## SOCIAL STUDIES

### FABULOUS FREEBEE

#### TRUCKS AND THINGS YOU'LL WANT TO KNOW ABOUT THEM

This colorful 13-page booklet transports kids through the role of trucking in the United States. They find out how trucking began, what kinds of things trucks carry, and how to identify different kinds of trucks. Of special interest is a dictionary of trucking terms. In it you'll find that a "bareback" is a tractor without a trailer, and that a "milk run" is an easy trip. The covers of the booklet serve as a quiz about the kinds of trucks described inside.

Written and illustrated for kids, the booklet (available in classroom quantities) opens the way to a careful inspection of the kinds of trucks that are likely to affect the daily lives of all of us.

Order from: Educational Services, Public Relations Department, American Trucking Associations, 1616 P St., N.W., Washington, DC 20036
Grade level: 3–6

## PRESENT-PAST

To most people, "building a society" sounds like a lofty political slogan. Not so with at least one sixth grade class. To them it means designing and constructing an imaginary society out of assorted materials.

This project is undertaken after the class has studied an ancient civilization such as the Aztecs, Incas, African tribes or American Indians. Several specific concepts that will be applied later when the kids begin to design their own societies are emphasized during the study. For instance, when they're studying Eskimos, it's apparent that the Eskimos' diet consists largely of food from the sea, because they can't farm in such a cold climate. Similarly, igloos are made of ice and snow because they are the most abundant building materials available. This leads to an understanding of an important concept: that pretechnological societies are greatly shaped by the geography, climate and natural resources of the area in which they exist. Additional probing and comparison highlights a second important concept: that certain factors found in Eskimo society (food, clothing, shelter, tools, weapons, communication, religion, education, government, law, art, transportation) are universal to every society, though naturally they differ in applied detail.

Armed with this knowledge, the class then breaks into groups of three to five students. The job of each group is to create a society that has just developed the wheel. Each group then draws from a hat a location in which their civilization must survive. Such locations might include the Amazon Jungle, the Mojave Desert, the Rocky Mountains, the tundra, the Nile River Valley or a tropical island.

Each group then does research (using encyclopedias, almanacs, flora and fauna maps, atlases and anything else they can get their hands on) to find out as much as they can about the geography, climate, plants, animals and mineral resources of their region.

Each group is then ready to plan a civilization that can exist in its location, using the resources and conditions they found in their research. Through group planning (with a chairman and recorder) each committee decides how to make its civilization consistent with the concepts developed in earlier study.

It should be noted that food, clothing and shelter are easier concepts for the students to handle than government, religion and education. Younger or less sophisticated groups will probably have greater success dealing with the more concrete variables. Older groups will have their fun creating languages, transportation systems and religions.

Once the research and planning are finished, civilizations begin to spring up all over the classroom. They usually exist on large (approximately 2-1/2-by-4 foot) pieces of cardboard or plywood. Houses and huts are erected from tongue depressors, covered milk cartons, small boxes and cardboard sheets. Mountains arise out of painted cardboard cones, papier-mache, and paper-towel rolls covered with gauze. Roofs are covered with grass or mud. Temples are built from small blocks, large boxes and sugar-cube pyramids. Tools are made from toothpicks, cardboard cutouts and twigs. Plants made of small twigs grounded in clay and paper or cardboard cutouts grow everywhere. The ground is covered with paint, dried grass, dirt, rocks or dried coffee grounds, which are all glued into place. Sometimes people made of aluminum foil and covered with plaster of paris, gauze or hand-sewn clothing roam the streets. Cardboard people are found in other models.

The ideas and possibilities for constructions are endless. There have even been simulations of sacred ritual areas, suspension bridges (tongue depressors and yarn) and underground storage areas.

If model building is not convenient, murals are also an excellent way of depicting a civilization.

Idea by: Jan Shapiro,
Lakeview Elementary School,
Oakland, Calif.

BACK VIEW OF PHONOGRAPH WHEN OPEN.

# DO-IT-YOURSELF GAMES & MEDIA

## "U" FILM FILMSTRIP KIT AND SLIDE KIT

☆ ☆ ☆ ☆ ☆ ☆ ☆ ☆ ☆ ☆

"U" FILM is one of those simple but profound inventions—like the safety pin or adhesive tape—that can be used in seemingly endless new ways.

The stuff itself is blank 35-mm film chemically treated so that it can be typed on, or written and drawn on with ordinary pencils, felt-tip markers, wax crayons or water colors. The material is also erasable.

While "U" FILM has many obvious instructional possibilities, the real fun begins when youngsters get to use it themselves. They must draw compactly to fit their images into the 35-mm format, but the results will be enormous since "U" FILM can be projected by any standard filmstrip or slide projector.

Youngsters can create all-picture stories, or illustrations for written stories or book reports, visuals for science reports, pure artistic statements or multimedia extravaganzas. All this for about two cents a picture.

The filmstrip "U" FILM kit contains, among other things, a 25-foot roll of film, 10 plastic filmstrip cans, a how-to-do-it manual, a splicer, splicing tapes and colored pencils. The slide-making kit includes: a large roll of "U" FILM, slip-in slide mounts, colored pencils and an instructional manual.

Order from: Prima Education Products, 2 South Buckhout St., Irvington-on-Hudson, NY 10533. Grade level: Primary—high school. Cost: $15, filmstrip kit; $12, slide kit. Payment must accompany order.

## RECYCLING FILMSTRIPS

Are there any antiquated or damaged filmstrips sitting idly around your school? If so, there is a way to process them so that the film can be reused to create a new and useful filmstrip.

Soak the filmstrip in household bleach until all the pictures and print are removed. Allow it to dry. Using another filmstrip as a guide, mark off the proper size of filmstrip frames. Use a permanent fine-point felt-tip marker for writing or drawing on the filmstrip.

Rather than print detailed explanations on the filmstrip, you may want to have your students tape-record a narrative and play it along with the filmstrip.

Idea by: Kay Olson, Lenox Elementary School, St. Louis Park, Minn.

# LEARN-ALOT-ALOPOLY

All too often students are forced into hours of monotonous drill with justification that there is a need to practice newly learned skills and review new content. One solution to that problem is Learn-Alot-Alopoly. It is a homemade game that provides practice with the added ingredients of fun, involvement and playful competition.

Alopoly is played like most commercial board games—Monopoly, for example. Students move their game piece along a determined route by answering questions and rolling a die. The game is appropriate for any subject area and any grade level.

PLAYERS: Three or more.

EQUIPMENT: Game board, one die, markers (such as ten-cent animals from the dime store), question cards, chance cards and an answer sheet.

QUESTION CARDS: Thirty or more numbered questions printed on oak tag cut to the size of a playing deck of cards.

CHANCE CARDS: Same size and number as above. They are drawn when a player lands on "chance" on the game board. Examples: " 'A' on spelling test—go ahead two spaces." "Not feeling well—go back one space." "Helped the new student—take another turn."

GAME BOARD: It can be of any size and shape with at least 24 spaces—one labeled "start," another "finish," and approximately four labeled "chance." Other spaces should be labeled with things that are relevant to the kids. Example: "Mr. _____ [the principal's name] tells you you're doing well in school—go ahead one space."

ANSWER SHEET: Held by a neutral player, who tells whether answers are right or wrong. The numbers on the answer sheet correspond to those on the question cards.

RULES: (1) First player takes the top card and tries to answer the question. If the answer is correct, he rolls the die and moves his piece the indicated number of places. (2) The player whose turn is next can challenge any answer. If it is a correct challenge and he can supply the proper answer, he has an extra turn. If it is an incorrect challenge or he too gives a wrong answer, he misses his turn. (3) Play moves clockwise and the first player to reach "finish" is the winner.

Idea by: Barbara Welty, Washington Elementary School, Oakland, Calif.

# QUICK SLIDE

☆ ☆ ☆ ☆ ☆ ☆ ☆ ☆ ☆

Ever have to pass up clipping a magazine picture because it was too small to share with a large group? Here is a process for rescuing those gems in the future and for turning them into permanent two-by-two-inch slides.

By this method any picture printed on a slick magazine paper can be "lifted" from the paper and transferred to the plastic slide. The transfer takes only a matter of minutes, and the easy-to-follow directions, the materials in the kit and a bowl of tap water are the only equipment needed. The resulting slides are an ideal size for use in most projectors.

Another advantage is that even young children can make good-quality slides. Older kids can make and use the slides in class presentations and slide shows.

Order from: Quick Slide, P.O. Box 517, Englishtown, NJ 07726. Grade level: 3–12. Cost: $5.75. Postage and handling free when payment accompanies order; otherwise add $1.

# FABULOUS FREEBEE

## PHOTOGRAPHY— HOW IT WORKS BOOKLET

Whether they cost 50 cents or thousands of dollars, all cameras have four basic needs—film, light, a lens opening and a shutter.

This and other illuminating information which helps to demystify the process of photography can be found in PHOTOGRAPHY—HOW IT WORKS, a 19-page booklet based on a film of the same title. The components and operations of a camera are explained through small, colorful illustrations with descriptive captions. Kids first getting involved in photography will find the booklet an excellent resource for answers to questions that traditionally plague the more curious set.

Available free in single copies or in quantity for 10 cents per copy, prepaid. Include a legal-sized, self-addressed, stamped envelope.

Order from: Eastman Kodak Co., Dept. 841, 343 State St., Rochester, NY 14650
Grade Level: 4–12.

# THE CAMERA COOKBOOK

☆ ☆ ☆ ☆ ☆ ☆ ☆ ☆ ☆

If you have some camera buffs in your class, or perhaps have been thinking about doing some camera work "one of these days," THE CAMERA COOKBOOK has some valuable suggestions for you. Beginning with a few hints about shutter openings and speeds, the book concerns itself primarily with what happens after you get to the end of the film.

The mysterious processes by which films become photos are taken up step by step. Recipes for developer solutions and fixer solutions are given on colored pages easily located in the center of the book. Explanations cover getting the film into the developing tank, the five steps in the developing of negatives, and several methods of making prints.

After providing the principles of the developing process, the book tells how to set up for film processing in the classroom, working with eight to ten students at a time. And in case you have qualms about five pails of water and chemical "stuff" and a group of active students, the book assures you that all procedures have been tried in classrooms and workshops.

THE CAMERA COOKBOOK is 8-1/2-by-11 inches in size, soft-cover, and spiral-bound to lie flat while in use. Instructions are clear and in a simple, uncluttered format. Notes anticipate possible problem areas and offer hints for best results. With this handbook your camera kooks can become camera cooks, turning out nicely done batches of photographic creations.

Order from: Workshop for Learning Things, Inc., 5 Bridge St., Watertown, MA 02172.
Grade level: Teachers of all grades.
Cost: $4. Payment must accompany orders under $20.

# LIGHT WRITING
### by Donald Roman

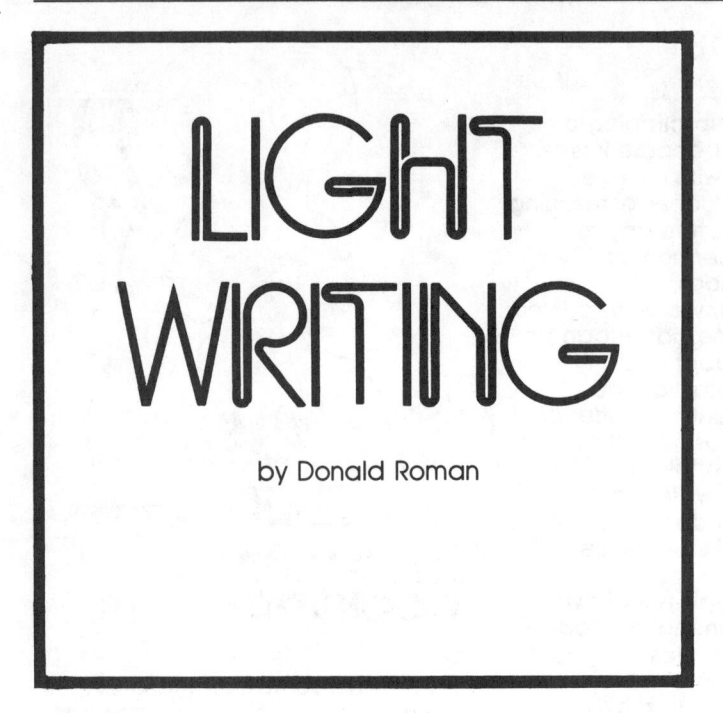

Almost everyone who has held a camera knows that when light strikes photographic film, an image is formed. Controlling this image is the name of the game in photography. Professional photographers invest heavily in lenses, lights and other exotic equipment to insure that they can control the images they create. But you don't need all that to produce brilliant images on slide film. Here's a technique that is so easy, it's almost too good to be true.

The process may, in fact, be one you are already familiar with. If you have ever seen a time-exposure picture of a city-street scene taken at night, you may have noticed that the streets were filled with long streaks of white and red light. The picture was made by opening the shutter on the camera for an extended period of time. The glowing lines of red and white were made by the moving taillights and headlights of cars traveling on the street. This same effect is produced when a time exposure of the night sky is made. The rotation of the earth causes the stars to produce curved lines of light on the film.

"Light-writing" makes use of a similar process. The main difference is that a flashlight is used as a light source rather than stars or headlights.

The equipment needed is probably available to most classroom teachers. The key item is an adjustable camera that has a shutter that can be locked open with a cable release. On adjustable cameras, this is usually indicated by the letter "B" on the shutter-speed dial. Next, a tripod or other device is needed to hold the camera steady during the exposure. Finally, you will need a small flashlight. The type that operates on one battery works quite well. Anything larger than this will produce streaks of light that are too wide.

This is roughly comparable to choosing either a wide or narrow brush when painting a picture. In this case, the small light produces a sharper, clearer line.

To begin your light-writing, load your camera with slide film. (When using Kodachrome II daylight film, set the aperture at F 4.) Set up your equipment in a room that can be darkened completely. (You can also

## NEW IDEAS FOR USING OLD FILMS

What teacher hasn't had the unhappy experience of obtaining a film from the A-V library only to have it be so outdated that it turns the students off? If you were burned badly enough, you may even have resolved never to show such films again. But a more positive remedy for old flicks is within reach.

1. LIVEN UP OLD BLACK-AND-WHITE FILMS. Buy a selection of small pieces of cellophane in different colors. As the old movie flashes on the

## DO-IT-YOURSELF GAMES & MEDIA 77

work at night, but if you plan to have your students take part, this might not be practical.) You can get striking images by using such simple objects as bottles and candleholders. People also make excellent subjects. Pose your subject and compose the picture in the viewfinder. Turn off the room lights and open the camera shutter. With the flashlight turned on and aimed at the camera, move it slowly around the profile of your subject. When you finish, turn off the flashlight and close the shutter.

Making an exposure by tracing around an object or person is so easy that even elementary students can do it with little trouble. The butterfly above was first drawn on a window with a grease pencil. The exposure was made while a flashlight moved along the outline of the figure. A more difficult approach, which yields somewhat unpredictable results, is simply to draw freehand in the air with the flashlight. Since you are working in a pitch-black room, there is a danger of going over the same area with the flashlight more than once, but even then, the results can be very effective.

When your processed slides are returned, you will be in for a mild surprise. Even though you began with color slide film, your finished slides will be black and white. The explanation is quite simple. The film responded only to the white light from the flashlight and the blackness in the room. To add color, take some transparency markers and draw in the colors you want. Use transparency markers for adding color rather than ordinary felt-tip pens, because the latter do not adhere well to the surface of the acetate film.

You may have to experiment a bit with exposures because each flashlight is somewhat different. If your images are too faint, widen the aperture to the next larger opening. If your images are too bright, bring the aperture down to a smaller opening.

No doubt your best effects will be the results of your own experiments. Let your students loose with flashlights and see what they can create.

Donald Roman is assistant principal,
Broadmeadow-Harris Schools,
Needham, Mass.

---

screen, brighten it up by holding the colored transparent material in front of the lens. To free yourself for teaching the film, invite some of the students to manage the color effects. (For a quality "performance," ask the students to preview the film and practice selecting appropriate colors for various parts of the movie.)

2. START WITH HALF A MOVIE. To convert almost any old film into a fine stimulus for imagination, first run it so only the sound track is heard.

Let the students listen to the narration and the music and imagine what the visuals would be like. Then have the students discuss (and/or draw) the visual scenes they created in their own minds.

By this time, most of the students will be eager to see what the film really looks like. Play it again, this time with both picture and sound. Your follow-up discussion can touch on many points: Were the visuals on the screen what the children had seen in their minds? Which visuals do they prefer— the film makers' or their own? Why?

3. MAKE NEW SOUND TRACKS. Often the weakest part of old (and even new) educational films is the sound track. It can be boring to listen to the narrator tell exactly what's going on in the visuals. Your students can probably construct a much more exciting set of sounds.

For instance, let them bring in their favorite records — pop, jazz, western, folk or classical. After watching a few minutes of film with the original track, the students can experiment by providing their own musical scores. Through careful planning, students can construct an entire sound track that is fast and loud when the visuals call for it, calm when the pictures are calm. Student-made sound tracks, of course, can include homemade sound effects, narration and — often very effective — moments of silence.

Idea by: David Doty,
Brightwood School,
Monterey Park, Calif.

# 78 DO-IT-YOURSELF GAMES & MEDIA

## KIDS AND FILMS
☆ ☆ ☆ ☆ ☆ ☆ ☆ ☆

Whether you believe in studying film for film's sake or are simply convinced that film study and production can be an effective means for developing basic skills, the following books should be of interest. One book is a descriptive guide to films kids have consistently enjoyed and the other shows how to set up for film production in school.

**Films Kids Like.** THE RED BALLOON, BRAKE FREE, TADPOLE TALE and most of the 217 other films described in this book are proven winners with children. That's what Susan Rice, the editor of FILMS KIDS LIKE, found when showing the films to groups of children aged 3 to 12 in the Children's Film Theatre in New York.

A 150-page softcover book, Rice's work provides brief descriptions of the films and the children's reactions to many of them. The films themselves are mostly of the language arts variety. They can be used for straight film study or as a supplement to the content areas.

In addition, the book gives names of distributors, an explanation of the conditions under which the films were viewed and some of the follow-up activities used with children after showings. Stills from many of the films are reproduced in black and white throughout the book.

Teachers who are interested in renting good films for their classes or want to influence school district film-purchase decisions will find a wealth of fine material here.

Order from: Order Dept., The American Library Association, 50 E. Huron St., Chicago, IL 60611. Grade level: Teachers of grades K–6. Cost: $5.50. Add $.75 for postage and handling if order is not prepaid.

**Children as Film Makers.** Much of learning involves converting some form of input into a related form of output — listening becomes speaking, reading becomes writing. For some reason, the analogy usually breaks down where certain visual experiences are concerned. Kids spend hours watching television and movies but little or no time producing film. That's largely a question of opportunity, say authors John Lidstone and Don McIntosh. Give kids a real chance, and they'll prove themselves quite capable of making intelligent and worthwhile films. They explain the rudiments of filmmaking in this 111-page hardcover book and tell how to set up a film program.

The book contains sections on "The Camera and How to Use It," "Projectors," "Organization and Supervision," "Editing," "Sound," "Animation and Titling" and "Creative Film Presentation," as well as several descriptions of films made by elementary level children. A final bibliography lists other sources of information about films and filmmaking.

The authors explain the technical procedures of filmmaking in simple terms, using plenty of diagrams and photographs. Grasping the basics should be no problem, even for those inexperienced in photography.

Order from: Van Nostrand Reinhold, Dept. RB, 450 W. 33rd St., New York, NY 10001. Grade level: Teachers of grades 3–12. Cost: $8.06. Payment must accompany order.

### FABULOUS FREEBEE

## MOVIES WITH A PURPOSE AND SLIDES WITH A PURPOSE

MOVIES WITH A PURPOSE is a booklet that deals primarily with the planning and producing of Super 8mm single-concept films. The topics covered give the amateur filmmaker the basic technical information needed in order to move from simple to more sophisticated film endeavors.

SLIDES WITH A PURPOSE presents topics unique to slide presentations. Included in this booklet are plans for building a low-cost copystand and a selection of projectors and accessories.

Order from: Eastman Kodak Co., 343 State St., Rochester, NY 14650 Grade level: Teachers of all grades.

of picture lifting. Mel Fuller, assistant professor of education at Southern Methodist University, has a number of suggestions:
1. Overhead transparencies.
2. Collages of pictures to be used as window murals.
3. Book and notebook covers—colorful and original as well as durable.
4. Mobiles and other decorations with a stained-glass effect.

The process for these picture-lift projects is essentially the same as for slide making. For collages, arrange pieces as you want them on a counter or desk, face up. Cover with Con-Tact and rub carefully over all areas to be lifted. (Enlisting the efforts of a group will cut down on picture-lift fatigue.) Soak Con-Tact to remove paper, as with slides. The colorless areas between pictures will still be sticky. This means you can stick the collage onto a window as is.

For overhead transparencies, apply an acetate backing sheet or another sheet of Con-Tact. For book covers you'll also need a second sheet of Con-Tact for backing.

The raw material for picture lifting is almost limitless. Both color and black-and-white pictures may be used. And though simple composition and strong contrast will produce the sharpest transfers, you may get interesting results by experimenting with softer tones. And don't overlook the printed word. Advertising is full of bold lettering just begging to be lifted. Students may enjoy the creative writing involved in assembling out-of-context words and phrases.

With this medium in mind, your students may be motivated to start their own collection of picture-lifting possibilities. You knew you were saving those old magazines for something special!

Carolyn Paine is a staff writer of LEARNING.

## FILMSTRIP REPAIR KIT

☆ ☆ ☆ ☆ ☆ ☆ ☆ ☆

Even when teachers run them, the best filmstrip projectors and viewers chew up their quota of sacrificial filmstrips each year. And now that more schools are purchasing their own filmstrips and kids are using them independently, the toll of damaged filmstrips is inevitably rising.

In the future, instead of waiting for injured filmstrips to be mended at the district office, why not repair the casualties right in your classroom? An inexpensive repair kit, available from Prima Education Products, makes the process of patching tears and torn sprocket holes, splicing filmstrips together or adding an extra leader so easy that even first attempts are successful. The kit is also handy for classes making their own 35-mm filmstrips.

Comprising the kit are a few simple items: a roll of 100 transparent repair tapes guaranteed not to "shrink, dry out or become brittle with age"; a plastic film holder with sprocket guides for placing the tape on evenly; a guarded razor blade for evening filmstrip edges; and a set of uncomplicated instructions. Everything is included in a convenient storage case. Additional repair tapes can be purchased separately as needed.

As a test, we rehabilitated a thoroughly battered five-year-old filmstrip with this kit. It has held up perfectly over several months through numerous showings using different types of projectors.

Order from: Prima Education Products, 2 South Buckhout St., Irvington-on-Hudson, NY 10533. Grade level: Teachers of all grades. Cost: $7 plus $.50 shipping and handling. Payment must accompany order.

## THE SNAPSHOOTER

☆ ☆ ☆ ☆ ☆ ☆ ☆ ☆

You say what this country needs is a good three-dollar camera? Then be advised it has one, and it comes with a roll of film. The camera is the SNAPSHOOTER. It's a small, American-made plastic box with one side open. Any Instamatic-type 126 cartridge snaps on the back to create a camera that takes both black-and-white and color pictures.

Despite the fact the camera is cheaper than most, you can do things with it you couldn't—or wouldn't—do with equipment costing hundreds of dollars. One reason is that the camera is snapped together rather than glued. Thus, when accidentally dropped it is more likely simply to pop apart than shatter.

You can be daring with the camera just because it is so inexpensive. One teacher wrapped the camera in a plastic bag, fastened it with a rubber band and took some underwater shots one bright summer afternoon. The pictures came out fine.

So if you're looking for a basic photo tool, try the camera nicknamed "The Nickle Nikon"—the SNAPSHOOTER.

Order from: Visual Motivations Co., Regal Rd., King of Prussia, PA 19406. Grade level: Primary—high school. Cost: $3 plus $.50 postage and handling. Payment must accompany orders from individuals. School purchase orders will be billed.

## FILMSTRIPS IN THE MAKING

Your own custom-made filmstrips can be especially useful in your teaching. The standard 35 mm camera produces pictures too large for most filmstrip projectors. But try using a half-frame camera (the Olympus—Pen F) held as shown in the illustration below.

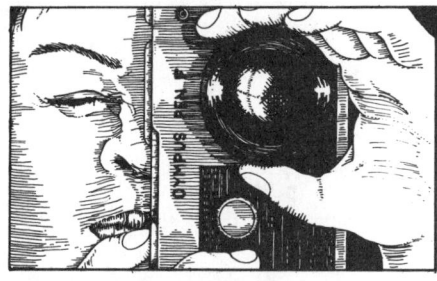

When you have the film processed, ask that it be developed only, not cut or mounted.

On half-frame cameras, a 20-exposure film gives 40 exposures. With five frames each for leader and trailer, you'll have 30 frames for your story. Plan each frame carefully before you start shooting.

Custom filmstrips can focus on many topics—preparation and follow-up of a field trip, step-by-step construction projects, how to use equipment. They can also be used to record special activities—plays, puppet shows, open house presentations. They make fine review and reinforcement aids, and may serve equally well with future classes.

As your students help make filmstrips, they see themselves as teachers and take special pride and care in their work. Film makers, get snapping.

Idea by: Roberta Naus,
Cathedral Oaks School, Santa Barbara, Calif.

# LANGUAGE ARTS

# LANGUAGE ARTS

## TEACHING WITH THE TOP TEN

> The TV's been broken since
>   Tuesday;
> We're out of bologna and bread.
> There's nothing to do,
> So I think of you—
>
>                 Winifred

Students will listen to lyrics like that (well not like that, exactly) a lot more attentively than they will to the things you or I might say. While they're at it, here are some suggestions of things they might listen for:

### The Language of Lyrics

Popular music can be a unique addition to your language arts program. Interest is inherent. And the lyrics can serve as a form of literature as well as a stimulus for creative-writing projects.

Have students bring in favorite 45s, LPs and cassettes. Ask them to listen to the lyrics for content and style, as they would a story or a poem. A few questions may help to guide students in their listening. Does the song tell a story or outline a series of events? Are the lyrics describing a feeling or mood rather than telling a story? Is there a "message" in the song—is it meant to make you think about something? Students may be interested in hearing "message" songs from times past.

Popular music can be used as a starting place for numerous writing projects, such as: (1) translating the events of a narrative-type song into a prose story; (2) writing a letter (serious or otherwise) to the main character or the "I" of the song, offering advice or just an opinion; (3) creating additional verses for the song; (4) writing parodies.

Song preferences likely will differ from student to student. Have each student select a favorite and decide what sort of language-related extension to undertake, and popular music becomes an instant individualizer.

Idea by: Joanna Spampanato,
Most Precious Blood School,
Long Island City, N.Y.

### Painless Parsing

If learning parts of speech is going to remain unavoidable, then using popular music may make the chore a little less like work.

Ask each student to divide a paper into columns labeled "noun," "verb," "adjective," etc. Select a song from those your students have been invited to bring in from home and share with the class, and ask students to listen for a word you've chosen. When they hear the word, they're to write it in the appropriate column.

Vary this by having students make up their own lists of words from the songs and put them in the proper classifications. One song will be good for quite a few rounds.

And since popular music isn't confined to the classroom, some of the parts-of-speech associations may carry over into the after-school hours. Rock might just become the fourth R.

Idea by: Mrs. Nakaoka,
Newton Junior High School,
Hacienda Heights, Calif.

## MYSTERY WRITING

Secret messages and invisible writing always seem to appeal to young children. This interest factor can be put to work in almost any beginning reading program.

To produce your invisible writing, print a letter or word with white crayon on white paper. To make the word visible the child must paint the paper with a tempera wash. The wash can be made by adding water to any color of tempera paint. The wax of the crayon resists the paint and allows the word to show through.

The technique works very well in a learning station or activity center. The station could be set up using a game approach with two children working together—one making up a mystery word for the other.

Idea by: Nancy Hamilton,
Joppatowne Elementary School,
Joppatowne, Md.

## A KITE STORY

☆ ☆ ☆ ☆ ☆ ☆ ☆ ☆

There are two sure-fire subjects for an effective children's film: balloons and kites. THE RED BALLOON was one of the first and most successful films of this genre. Now Churchill Films gives us a 25-minute color film, A KITE STORY, which is almost certain to become another classroom classic.

The viewer follows a young boy as he meets a mysterious kite maker and is given a plain white kite, which he promptly decorates with a smiling face. However, the boy's attention soon turns to a flashy rocket kite and the plain kite is discarded. It is at this point that the white kite takes on personification and follows the boy home at night. (Young children prove to be particularly sympathetic towards the white kite, perhaps knowing what it feels like to be ignored.)

The next day the boy goes to the kite maker, while the white kite follows behind, forgotten, finally becoming caught in a tree. While flying high, the beautiful rocket kite gets caught in a turbulent wind and crashes. Now both kites are gone. The boy runs quickly to the encampment of the kite maker, only to find him gone. End of movie.

Cinematically, the film is superb. The muted tones in the outdoor scenes and the bright paints of the kite maker combine in a sumptuous feast of color.

Symbolism is present, yet all age groups can understand the message. An audience of younger children easily understood that the boy "had nothing because he didn't take care of anything." An older audience felt that the film "was trying to say that we must value our possessions and love those we have."

Because of its universal theme, the movie seems an ideal purchase for school or library, and is certainly worth the low rental fee.

Order from: Churchill Films, 662 N. Robertson Blvd., Los Angeles, CA 90069. Grade level: K–8. Cost: $25, rental; $310, purchase.

## 84 LANGUAGE ARTS

## BOOKS TO FILMSTRIPS

☆ ☆ ☆ ☆ ☆ ☆ ☆ ☆

The Great Debate about converting books into sound filmstrips continues. Some believe that such strips discourage kids from reading the books on their own because the passive experience of viewing is easier than reading. Others feel that the filmstrips encourage and motivate slow readers to tackle stories and books they would otherwise ignore.

Controversy or not, a variety of book-based filmstrips continues to be released. The following selections represent three fine adaptations:

**Charlotte's Web** may be the most adventurous adaptation yet of book to filmstrip. Stephen Bosustow Productions has accomplished the herculean task in a set of 18 filmstrips, with over 1,000 original illustrations and a narration by author E.B. White himself. The result has the potential of becoming as much of a classic as the book itself. White's simple, low-key reading of every word in the book works magnificently, despite the lack of musical embellishment or sound effects.

A carefully planned teacher's guide deals with CHARLOTTE'S WEB chapter by chapter, giving brief synopses and plenty of useful cross-disciplinary follow-up activities. Three copies of the guide come with the set.

Order from: Stephen Bosustow Productions, 1649 Eleventh St., Santa Monica, CA 90404. Grade level: Intermediate. Cost: $225, with cassettes or records.

**Threshold Filmstrips** is a collection of 13 primary stories. The illustrations in the strips come directly from the original books and involve a range of artistic styles. In general, adaptations have been executed nicely, though a few strips have minor technical problems. In "The Toolbox and Machines," a single strip with two stories, for instance, the child narrator's voice is occasionally difficult to understand. The 11 other titles in the set are "The Little Brute Family," "City in the Summer," "The Box With Red Wheels," "Three by Three," "Hi, Cat!" "The Green Grass Grows All Around," "City in the Winter," "The Turnip," "Will I Have a Friend?" "The Little Wooden Farmer" and "Ask Mr. Bear."

Order from: Macmillan Library Services, 866 Third Ave., New York, NY 10022. Grade level: Primary. Cost: $129.95, set of 12 filmstrips with records; $153.95, set of 12 filmstrips with cassettes; $12.95, individual filmstrip with record; $14.95, individual filmstrip with cassette.

**Sound Filmstrip Sets 37 and 38** include eight adaptations, four per set, of outstandingly illustrated children's books. SET 37 includes "Goggles!" "Harold's Fairy Tale," "The Little Red Hen" and "Bill's Balloon Ride." Comprising SET 38: "The Beast of Monsieur Racine," "The Sultan's Bath," "Anansi the Spider" and "Through the Window."

As usual, Weston Woods has created flawless filmstrips. In addition to the extraordinary visuals, the narrations make for exciting listening, with original musical compositions complementing the readers.

Order from: Weston Woods, Weston, CT 06880. Grade level: Primary. Cost: $32.50 per set with record or cassette; $9.20, individual title with record; $12.75, individual title with cassette.

## WRITER'S FILE BOX

Despite their widely varied experiences both in and out of the classroom, students often announce that they have nothing to write about when it's time for a free writing assignment. To help them overcome this "writer's block," borrow a technique from professional writers.

Every student maintains an idea file box at his desk. The box is stocked with three-by-five-inch cards. Whenever the student is struck by an interesting thought, he or she makes a brief note of it, dates it and drops it into the file box.

Later, when it's time for writing, the student can flip through the cards. Very often the student will find some idea there that will spark a story, a poem or a nonfiction research piece.

The approach not only helps break writer's block, it also teaches students a work habit which will be useful in future years.

Idea by: Frank Lyman, coordinator, Southern Teacher Education Center, University of Maryland.

---

MODERN POETRY, TEACHER STYLE

A harsh, jagged streak of lightning
Stark against the black
Then quiet
And a heavy snowfall.
(Translation: Find Mr. Miller
to fix the TV set.)

A figure stands against the sky
A roar
Wells up from
The dark reaches of below
Turbulence
The storm clouds gather
And the heavens shake.
(Leroy, no one has your pencil.
It's in your book.)

Anne H. Friend,
Teacher, Henrico County, Va.

# LANGUAGE ARTS 85

# Joking Around

by Louis Phillips

Here are some ways to put jokes to practical use in the classroom:

▸ In the lower grades, create a class scrapbook of cartoons and jokes submitted by the students. Encourage the kids to read joke books and copy out the jokes they like (it's fine extra practice in reading and writing skills).

▸ Set aside time for each willing student to tell a joke, either from the class scrapbook or one of his own choice. Use the response to the joke as a springboard for discussion. Why did those who laughed at a joke do so? Why did those who didn't laugh react that way?

▸ In the upper grades, bring in from the school library or other source a collection of joke books from the past. What does early American humor tell us about our national character? about our values? about our attitudes toward ethnic and minority groups? Do modern jokes indicate any changes in those attitudes?

▸ Select a television show—or let the students pick their own—and have the students write down and bring to class those jokes or comedy situations they most enjoyed. What does such humor tell us about the world today?

▸ As a creative-writing exercise, have your students rewrite a joke as a short story or poem.

▸ In a film-making class, compile a visual anthology of jokes. Can the kids tell their jokes in such a way that they can be filmed? What is each joke teller's response to seeing himself being funny on film? (Films of Chaplin, Keaton, Langdon, Sennett, et al., not only help identify what makes a joke funny but can serve as starting points for wide-ranging discussions.)

▸ Invite a professional comedian, gag writer or cartoonist to visit the class, not simply to entertain but to discuss what humor is—and isn't.

▸ Assemble an assortment of cartoons without captions and written jokes with punch lines missing and have students compose their own. A variation: scramble the captions and punch lines and let the kids sort them out.

▸ In foreign language and social studies classes, jokes or cartoons in French, Spanish or other foreign languages make good translation exercises and provide insight into the national character of foreign lands.

Louis Phillips teaches in the Film Studies Program, Brooklyn College, New York.

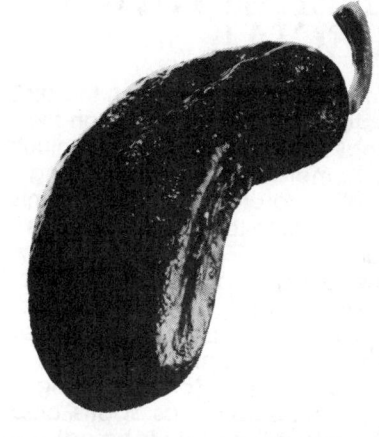

## MAKING IT STRANGE

☆ ☆ ☆ ☆ ☆ ☆ ☆ ☆

"Which takes up more space—a pickle or a pain?

Which is angrier—the kitchen or the living room?

What fruit is like yourself? And why?"

Welcome to the world of MAKING IT STRANGE.

MAKING IT STRANGE is a series of four workbooks appropriate for use in grades two through five. The booklets contain questions, exercises and activities designed to help youngsters see, think, say and write with the kind of creativity that powers productive writers, scientists, inventors and artists.

Each 80-page volume is packed with activities that invite the student to look at the world in a new way and with a new kind of awareness and intensity.

Assignments build through a series of ever-more complex lessons. The startling—and often humorous—drawings and photographs provide excellent visual support.

Order from: Synectics Education Systems, Order Dept., 121 Brattle St., Cambridge, MA 02138. Grade level: 2–5. Cost: $6 per workbook for 1–4 copies; $3.50 per copy for 5 or more copies. Add $.75 for postage and handling for one workbook; $.10 for each additional.

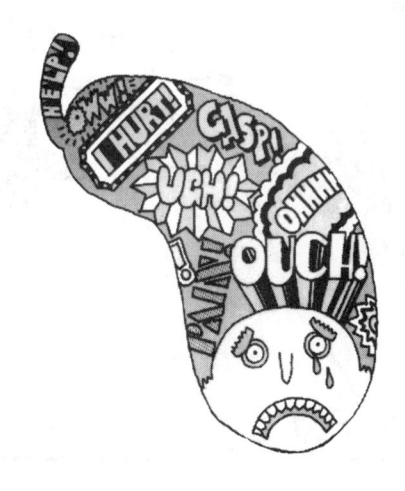

# 86 LANGUAGE ARTS

## WEEKLY NEWS SPECIAL

"Station WOWW news is on the air."

Actually, WOWW news is on the school's intercom, the last 15 minutes of a homeroom period. It's giving seventh and eighth grade students a try at a little journalism and lots of fun.

The format of a student-produced weekly show might run as follows:

1. World news briefs (two or three simply written summaries).
2. School news (cheerleading tryouts, class field trips, sports, clubs).
3. Editorial (clearly labeled).
4. Student opinions (collected and compiled comments from various individuals on a particular topic).
5. Commercial (clearly labeled).
6. On-the-spot report (faked interview just for laughs).
7. Birthday roundup (listing of students and teachers whose birthdays fall within the coming week).
8. Sign-off.

The news staff includes an anchor person who introduces the show, brings in the reporters and their stories and signs off; a student program director who schedules the order of the stories; and a cast of reporters and writers. (Role assignments change from week to week.)

Students learn that even a short news program requires a great deal of planning and decision making. What items will be of most interest at air time? What proportions of time should be devoted to world or national news, to local events, to special features or humor? How much time does it take a reporter to read a story that is two handwritten pages long?

Mechanics are important. Materials to be broadcast are written (no ad-libbing), timed to the second, edited and copied over—double-spaced for easy reading. Legibility is critical if a writer prefers to have someone else do the reporting.

Be prepared for some editorial and technical difficulties. The accuracy of a story may have to be rechecked. Gossip or items of questionable taste may creep in and need to be discussed. And a fickle intercom may reduce your news special to a series of shrill whistles and explosive pops.

These minor mishaps shouldn't discourage your news hounds. They might like to know that the WOWW news crew at Constitution Hall Junior High got a bid from a local station to televise a show. Are you ready for the big time?

Idea by: Dorothy Stout Janz, Constitution Hall Junior High School, Johnson City, Tenn.

## PUPPET MAKING

☆ ☆ ☆ ☆ ☆ ☆ ☆ ☆

Puppets go where humankind fears to tread and can speak up bravely when shy voices falter. Beloved bits of fabric and paper can become alter egos for their handlers. And

# LANGUAGE ARTS 87

how much greater the feeling of identification when the puppet is one a child has made himself.

Almost everyone is familiar with button-eyed sock puppets and brightly crayoned paper-bag puppets. But here are two books that offer dozens more forms and styles for the creative puppet maker:

**Aha! I'm a Puppet** by Avis Reid is a collection of more than 50 ideas for puppet making. The book represents ideas from in-service workshops conducted by the author and was developed at the request of workshop participants.

Without fuss, in an uncomplicated style, the book features a puppet a page with large, bold diagrams and simple directions. Suggestions for the use of particular kinds of puppets in the classroom are often given.

Puppet-making materials include cereal boxes, paper plates, plastic bags, spools and other such "found" supplies. Even the child's own hands and fingers can be transformed into puppets by following directions.

The book is of an 8-1/2-by-11-inch size, soft-covered and spiral-bound to lie flat while in use.

As the foreword suggests, this book would be valuable for hobby and recreation programs, Scouts and other groups, as well as the classroom. The easy directions and almost self-explanatory diagrams make the book useful to children with a minimum of guidance from group leaders.

Order from: The Open Door, 205 W. 16th St., Glencoe, MN 55336. Grade level: Teachers of all grades. Cost: $5 plus $.50 postage and handling.

**Puppet Making Through the Grades** by Grizella H. Hopper is a hardcover, 64-page book that gives directions for making puppets, suggestions for dressing them, and concludes with ideas for creative dramatics and the staging of puppet plays in the classroom.

A wide variety of puppets are described, from simple paper-bag ones to handsomely attired Styrofoam and sock puppets, and even the more sophisticated papier mache-over-clay models. Complete and detailed directions are supported with clear illustrations of basic steps. More than 100 photographs show actual results — unique, creative and charming — of each puppet-making technique. You've never seen such a show of curly eyelashes, buck teeth, furry heads and expressions of evil glee!

The book has new ideas for old hands at puppet making as well as solid help for the newcomer to puppetry.

Order from: Davis Publications, Inc., 50 Portland St., Worcester, MA 01608. Grade level: Teachers of all grades. Cost: $5.75. Add $.50 on billed orders. Payment must accompany orders from individuals.

## STORY STARTERS
☆ ☆ ☆ ☆ ☆ ☆ ☆ ☆

For the student who "never has anything to write about," here are 50 places to begin. Each set (one for the primary level and one for the intermediate level) of activity cards from Creative Teaching Press offers students many original writing topics.

Among those in the primary set are "Animal Crackers" ("You open the lid and the animals come alive. Tell what happened"), "The Magic Car" ("It will take you anywhere. Where will you go? What will you do?") and "Raindrop" ("You are a drop of rain. Tell where you go. What does it feel like to fall?"). Though the vocabulary is geared toward the primary student, some kids may still have trouble reading the cards. In that case, the topics can just as easily be assigned by the teacher.

Some of the STORY STARTERS in the intermediate set ask the student to tell about an adventure in the desert while riding a new "Trail Bike," to describe what is found on a beach after following the "Footprints in the Sand" and to tell what would be seen on "The Other Side of the Moon."

With each story starter, there is a brief description of the topic, some optional vocabulary for use in the story and an interesting sketch, all designed to motivate kids to write. For the teacher there are suggestions on how to use the cards and how to administer an independent creative-writing program.

Each of the five-by-seven cards is designed to be handled and read independently by the students. The cards as manufactured should last through more than one school year, and if time is taken to mount them, they'll last indefinitely.

Order from: Creative Teaching Press, 1900 Tyler #22, South El Monte, CA 91733. Grade level: 1–3 (Primary Set) and 4–6 (Intermediate Set). Cost: $4.95 per set plus $1 postage and handling. Specify which set when placing order. Payment must accompany order.

## JUST SO STORIES
☆ ☆ ☆ ☆ ☆ ☆ ☆ ☆

These familiar stories are charmingly illustrated with bright colors and bold and amusing pictures in this set of four filmstrips. The artist's fine sense of design and drama are evident in the way animals and foliage complement and interweave with each other. The backgrounds are well researched with accurate representation of the flora and fauna. Judicious and sensitive cutting of Rudyard Kipling's "How the Leopard Got His Spots" eliminates the racially offensive overtones of the original text and makes it a story not only acceptable but delightful to all primary grade children.

The titles of the filmstrips are "How the Elephant Got His Trunk," "How the Camel Got His Hump," "How the Animals Came to Live With Man" and "How the Leopard Got His Spots."

Order from: Coronet Instructional Media, 65 E. South Water St., Chicago, IL 60601. Grade level: K–2. Cost: $48, records; $53, cassettes.

# Comics FOR FUN AND PROFIT

by Carolyn Paine

While you're getting a few extra minutes of Sunday shut-eye, a marvelous teaching aid may be arriving on your doorstep (or possibly under your hedge). The big, colorful comics section of Sunday's paper deserves a second look in the cold light of a Monday morning. These comics can be a tool for teaching logic, sequencing, creative writing, reading skills, punctuation and other assorted esoteric etceteras.

Collect the comics over several weeks' time. Have the class help in this to assure a wide selection of strips. You'll also need duplicates, allowing the use of both the front and back of each page. (For younger children, also collect daily papers with the shorter three- or four-frame stories.) You may want to sort strips by title, length or type, e.g., continuous story versus complete-in-this-issue. Children can help in cutting up the papers and sorting out the strips, thus getting some extra classification practice.

You can use a comic strip as is for a number of language activities. For beginning readers, a comic strip can be a step-by-step guide for story telling. Children can tell about the action in each panel of a comic strip in the same way they "read" books by using picture clues to recall the story. Obviously, in selecting a comic strip for this kind of picture reading, you'll want to look for those in which the weight of the story is carried in the pictures, not in the dialogue.

Mary Ellen Erdo, who teaches sixth grade at Central Elementary School in Allentown, Pennsylvania, finds that in working with her slower readers, comics are a "sneaky" and quite acceptable substitute for books. In addition to being colorful, current and completely unrelated to past reading failures, comics have other attributes that make them ideal for older students with reading problems: The stories are short and have a definite point,

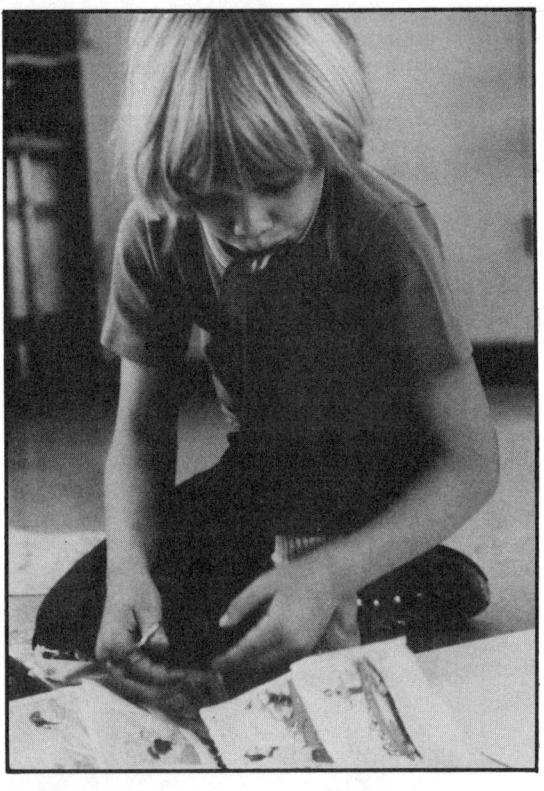

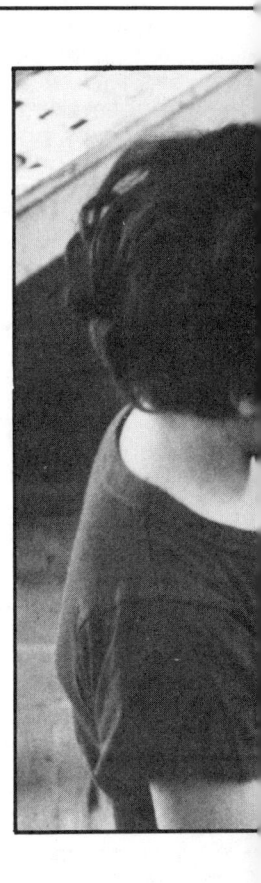

SHAZAM! Logic, sequencing, creative writing . . .

feature familiar characters with amusingly predictable personality traits, and highlight humor. Moreover, the serial-type strips feature mystery and adventure.

Some students may enjoy analyzing the elements of humor in comic strips. What brings the laughs and why? Can you find examples of play-on-words humor? Unexpected or inappropriate responses? What strips would be funny even to someone who didn't understand English? (Test this by masking the speech balloons.)

**Giving Dialogue a Lift**
Speech balloons carry almost all the reading in comic strips—except for the occasional "Early next morning..." or "ZAP!" The speech balloon is the cartoonist's equivalent of quotation marks, and it could be the answer to some of the quotation mark difficulties that students encounter when they try to capture dialogue in writing.

Camille Blachowicz finds that her students at Queen of All Saints School in Chicago have problems with quotations in several areas: (1) forgetting the quotation marks altogether, (2) including extraneous material inside quotes, (3) puzzling over periods and commas, (4) forgetting to start a new paragraph for each speaker. She suggests using cartoons as aids in teaching about quotations.

Focusing on a single comic-strip panel, students can easily observe the function of the speech balloon. They will note that the balloons carry spoken words only. Scene-setting words, sounds and "she said quickly" are not found inside the balloons unless someone is actually saying them. Familiar marks of punctuation may appear inside the balloons—with the fairly general exception of final periods, which are usually missing. Each speaker gets a separate balloon. The parallels between the function of the speech balloon and role of quotation marks are easily drawn.

To put these parallels into practice, students can copy conversations from a single comic-strip panel, enclosing the words of each speaker inside a set of quotation marks. What is inside the speech balloon goes inside the quotation marks, punctuation and all. (Students should add periods where needed.) Since each speaker uses a different balloon, there's a visual reminder for beginning a new paragraph for each.

Students may be anxious to add some "said So-and-So"s to identify the characters. Comics can help here, too. Traditionally there's a problem with "said"s when the quoted material ends with a period. But since that final period is often missing in speech balloons anyway, students who are translating comic-strip speeches into prose are reminded that they have a choice to make: If the "said" precedes the quote, they'll need to add a period at the end of the quote; if the "said" follows the quote, they'll need to insert a comma instead. All other speech balloon punctuation stays the same. No problem.

Mary Ellen Erdo's sixth graders also learn about quotes from comics. She suggests that students create conversations for cartoons. A collection of cartoons with masked speech balloons can be posted around the room. Each student chooses an intriguing situation, draws large speech balloons on separate paper, and makes up dialogue to fit the action pictured. (Numbering the cartoons helps in the matching-up process—or some students may want to sketch the cartoon for a completed look.) Then comes the moment for "breaking the balloons." Each student erases the balloon he had drawn and adds quotation marks to the

Good Grief! Reading skills, punctuation too...

speech that remains.

Students who've already worked with single panels may try three- or four-panel strips. Camille Blachowicz has each student bring in a favorite strip, paste it on newsprint and copy the conversations, with appropriate punctuation, beneath each panel. Later, speeches may be incorporated into story form on separate paper. Students will appreciate the fact that conversation outside the context of its picture loses some of its clarity and emphasis and will need to be augmented with "connective tissue." ("Have one" will have more meaning when accompanied by "said Linus, offering Snoopy a peanut butter sandwich.")

The process of reverse translation — making a cartoon out of written dialogue — may help students having trouble knowing what to put inside the quotes. The speech balloon quite effectively isolates the spoken words.

**Comic Cut-ups**
Drenda Underwood, who teaches at Washington Elementary in St. Louis, recommends cutting comic-strip panels apart for students to reassemble in their original order. To do this, students need to study a set of individual panels for clues to chronology, logical sequence or natural groupings—such as a question and its answer, a fall and a landing, movement from some place to some place, a telephoning segment, or panels showing the same setting.

To help your students with the reassembling of panels, examine the comic strips carefully, selecting those that can go together in only one order. (Sometimes the addition of critical punctuation can make a borderline strip into a usable one.)

Cut apart the panels of a selected strip and glue them onto construction paper. Caution: Don't glue the whole strip on paper and then cut the panels apart; the kids will match the cut edges to reassemble the strip.

Label each panel in the strip with an identifying letter and copy off the correct order for an answer key. Each cut-up strip can then be placed in a separate envelope and stored in a shoe box. The answer key for the whole collection can be put in a separate envelope and stored with the rest. Then the kids can help themselves to the puzzles.

Lucila Dypinagco, teaching at Edison Junior High School in Los Angeles, encourages her students to make their own comic cut-ups to exchange with their friends for solving. Students mount separate panels on index cards. The cards are then arranged in order, turned over and marked with a code. Devising the code can become an interesting challenge in itself, particularly if the code is to be self-correcting. Possibilities for a self-correcting code might be: sequential patterns using numerals or letters, a symbol graduated in size, letters that spell a word when copied off in the correct order. Each puzzle maker should test out the code for bugs—as well as checking the order of the panels—before springing the puzzle on a friend. An answer key may be deemed necessary in some cases.

Solving puzzles of the complexity that junior high students devise will definitely involve reading-comprehension skills. In most cases the correct order of the panels can be achieved only by reading and interpreting what the characters are saying. But the challenge and fun of puzzle solving and the humor of the content make comic cut-ups an appealing and absorbing activity even for so-called reluctant readers.

The cut-up comics can serve other uses: (1) Students may want to try some "creative sequencing," changing the order of panels

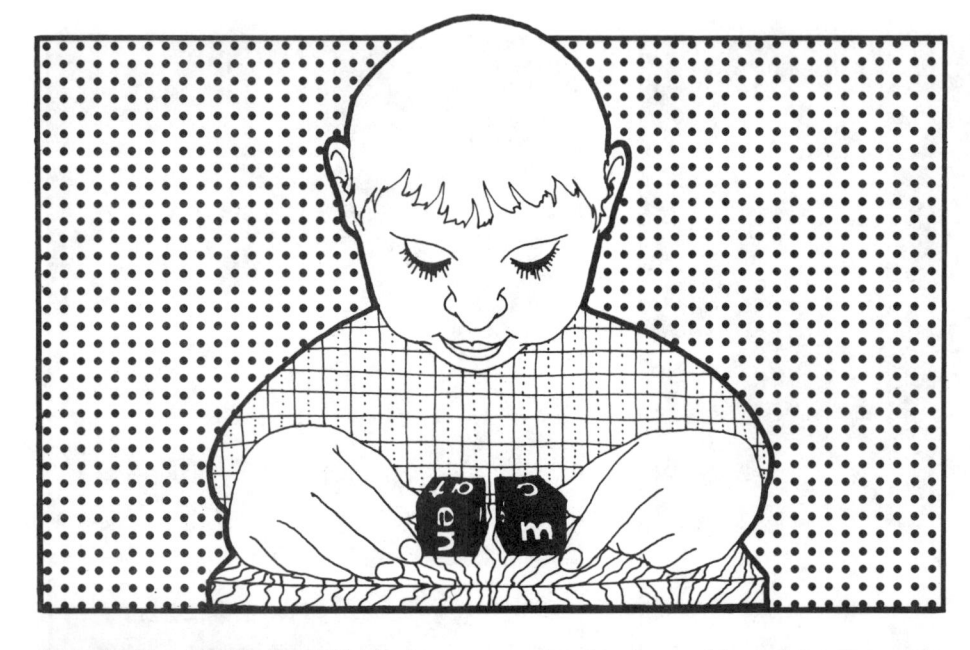

## BLEND AND BUILD 1

★ ★ ★ ★ ★ ★ ★ ★ ★ ★

Seeing it, saying it (blending it) and spelling it. These are not only good ways of learning a word, they're also the rules of BLEND AND BUILD 1.

The basic equipment for BLEND AND BUILD 1 is a set of 29 word-building cubes. The ten green cubes show initial consonants: five cubes show single consonants; five show blends. The 19 red cubes show short vowel phonograms (AN or UT, for example). A plastic shaker, score sheets and a storage box with a "place for everything" round out the components.

Play follows this basic form: A number of cubes are shaken out and separated into two columns by color. Player one selects a consonant cube and blends it with each vowel phonogram. If the combination makes a word, the player not only pronounces it, he also spells it for the next player to record. Points are given for correctly identified—pronounced and spelled—words. Challenges are invited. Proofs are through use in a sentence or definition.

To help referee rounds of sense-nonsense controversy, the teacher's guide provides lists of acceptable words. (You'll note that alternative pronunciations for some phonograms pop up—like RAN and SWAN, BUT and PUT—so there'll probably have to be discussion of them.)

Beyond the basic game and its instructive fun, there are suggestions for use of the cubes for diagnostic work, with special education, regular classroom, or home tutoring applications. The cubes can be a motivating factor over pencil-and-paper approaches. Areas of deliberately to make a different ending or introduce a new twist. (2) Arrange all but the last panel of a strip in a pocket chart and have children discuss possible endings. Or put the "hole" in the middle of the sequence; children can then study the panels that precede and those that follow for clues in determining what might logically fit in the opening. (3) Separately mounted panels of a strip might be stacked and stapled together to produce a one-story book. A collection of such books might be a welcome little library for children who are having difficulty in finding materials they can read and enjoy. (4) Mount and mix up separate panels from a particular strip over a month of Sundays. Students can try creating short four-panel stories, drawing separate out-of-sequence frames from a stockpile of 24 or so scenes.

The Sunday comics may give you the Monday "morning-after" lift you need. Let Charles Schultz and others take over, providing sequencing exercises, punctuation practice and creative-writing opportunities, not to mention laughs. And you'll probably think of lots more things to do once you get started with this funny business.

Carolyn Paine is a staff writer of LEARNING.

concentration include visual matching, visual-auditory integration checks, and the use of words produced in story telling. The guide describes several variations of the game, too, involving different numbers of players and varying complexity.

Though not mentioned among the game variations, a version recognizing blending of nonsense syllables might be worth trying with older children. A round of accepting only nonsense syllables and later making up sentences using them could be a different and creative activity. (Of course, this would mean deciding whether "grat" is something you do on Wednesdays, something you eat with mustard, or a small kind of pet.)

BLEND AND BUILD 1 has the virtue of being a teaching tool as well as a game. The elements have within them the possibilities for many different kinds of group and individual activities, all involving the way words are made.

Order from: Robert Rosche, Inc., 711 Apple Tree Lane, Glencoe, IL 60022. Grade level: K–4. Cost: $12.95 plus 10 percent postage and handling. Payment must accompany order.

## CREATIVE-WRITING IDEA FILE

"Starters," "Stimulators" and "Prescriptions" for creative tasks come in color-coded packets, pouches and boxes. And they're good. But you might be surprised at the idea file you're able to create yourself, given a little time.

The element of time is important — and perhaps there will be a chance of getting some of it next vacation. Start clipping magazine and newspaper pictures, headlines, cartoons, advertising captions — anything that is visually appealing or thought-provoking. To be useful as creative-writing stimulators, the items must have an open-ended feeling in themselves, or must be augmented with questions and suggestions that give the students reasons to react and respond.

File folders become activity cards for your creative-writing project. On the outside of each folder goes a number — just for organizational purposes. (Are all the folders back in the box?) Inside, on the left-hand side, goes a "stimulator," one of the clippings that you've collected. On the right goes a ditto sheet, a form that you'll fill in for each stimulator.

Sections on the form might include: (1) possible titles, (2) words you may want, (3) questions to think about, (4) reminders (on mechanical matters, like proofreading). The sections you use, and what you write for each one, will depend upon the ability level of your class and on the stimulator itself.

Give yourself time to assess the possibilities of each stimulator before completing the forms. Here's where you'll need to exercise your own creative thinking. Open up the picture situation or the headline context to a number of different angles. But be careful not to overhelp, or you'll get homogenized results.

With the help of some rainy vacation days or other such crises of forced at-homeness, you'll have a good start on a creative-writing idea file. Then your students can browse among the folders for ideas and guidelines meant to help them get ready to write.

Idea by: Mary Jo O'Hanlon, Santa Cruz, Calif.

## THE SELFISH GIANT

☆☆☆☆☆☆☆

Here is a welcome film version of the classic story by Oscar Wilde. Animated in rich color, this 26-minute film does ample justice to the original fairy tale.

For those who are unfamiliar with it, the story tells of a selfish giant who, after seven years' absence, returns to his home and finds children playing in his beautiful garden. Because he is too selfish to share, he builds a high stone wall to keep them out. But without the warmth of the children, the garden remains in a perpetual state of winter.

Much later, when a bird alights on the giant's window sill and begins to sing, he recognizes its beauty and realizes how foolish he has been. Whereupon he tears down the garden wall and welcomes the children to play within. He immediately befriends a very weak and tiny child who later disappears. Though the giant constantly asks for him, the child does not return.

Years slide by and the giant grows old and feeble. But he continues to be generous with his garden and his love. For this he is repaid with the love of the children and townfolk.

At the end of the story, the weak child (a Christ-like figure with nail scars on his hands and feet) returns and leads the giant to paradise.

Startling animation is the film's highlight. A great deal of attention is paid to color and detail. The characters acquire personalities through words, actions and unique appearances.

There is something of value in this story for all ages. Younger children will view it as a fine fairy tale, older kids will understand much of its symbolism, and everyone will be touched by its sensitivity.

Order from: Pyramid Films, P.O. Box 1048, Santa Monica, CA 90406. Grade level: Primary–high school. Cost: $25, rental; $350, purchase. Add $2 for postage.

## IMPROVISATION FOR THE THEATER

☆☆☆☆☆☆☆

Many teachers would like to introduce creative dramatics to their students but just don't know how to get started. Others are well into dramatics and improvisation and are looking for ways to enrich their program. For either of these groups, here is a book, written by Viola Spolin, which has long been used by a small but enthusiastic group of elementary, junior and senior high school teachers. It is the reference most often recommended by experts in the field.

Though the book deals with most aspects of theater — directing, acting, producing — its highlight is a large section with suggestions for over 200 informal creative dramatics activities. These activities help develop skills in acting and self-expression as well as provide techniques for making traditional subject areas take on new life. The "What Do I Do for a Living?" exercise, for example, could readily be used as a social studies lesson in which students simulate a job-hunting experience in whatever period of history they are studying.

Order from: Northwestern University Press, 1735 Benson Ave., Evanston, IL 60201. Grade level: Teachers of all grades. Cost: $7.50 (list); $6.75 (school price). Add $.31 per book for postage and handling. Payment must accompany order.

## WRITING FOR THE FUN OF IT: An Experience-Based Approach to Composition
**by Robert C. Hawley and Isabel L. Hawley**

More than 60 catalytic activities (writing name poems, brainstorming, writing about utopias) are neatly wrapped up in this little book. The authors, who between them have taught English composition for 26 years, also provide model forms for both student and teacher self-evaluation and student feedback.

Order from: ERA Press, Box 767, Amherst, MA 01002. Grade level: Teachers of intermediate–high school. Cost: $3.95. Payment must accompany orders from individuals.

## OH SAY WHAT YOU SEE

House. Tree. Child. These words name things, but they don't tell what kind. It's quite unlikely, for example, that you'll see exactly what I see when I say "house." And thereby hangs a communications problem.

You can help your class appreciate the problems of strictly verbal communication through a draw-what-I'm-drawing experiment. Equip each individual with drawing paper and crayons. Pair the children and have the partners sit back-to-back.

Child 1 of each pair begins to draw a picture (or design). As each item is added to the picture, child 1 describes it to child 2, who tries to duplicate it exactly. The partner may ask about size, shape, color, etc., but only with questions that can be answered yes or no. (You may wish to disregard this rule with your group.)

When they've finished their pictures, the partners compare the original with the interpretation. Have children look for features that seem to have been communicated and those over which there was some misunderstanding. (Children may discover that "little" was not really specific enough.) Discuss ways of describing features more precisely.

You may wish to use this activity to stimulate deeper discussion of problems in communication. Tell about times when you misunderstood what somebody meant or when someone didn't understand you. What was the cause of the problem? What did you do? In what ways can we work for better communication in the classroom? Outside? What are forms of communication that don't rely completely on words? What factors help you decide what form of communication to use in various situations? Think of instances when you felt someone deliberately communicated poorly. What made you think so?

As the school year progresses, this drawing activity might be a reference point for both you and your students when a misunderstanding occurs. It's not always easy to say just what you mean.

Idea by: Linda Sylva, Ridgecrest Elementary School, Houston, Tex.

## DAFFODILS
☆ ☆ ☆ ☆ ☆ ☆ ☆ ☆ ☆

Using William Wordsworth's poem DAFFODILS, this 11-minute color film explores the arrival of spring in the city. No flowers bloom in the asphalt playground surrounding the city school. Indeed, the only signs of spring are the paper cutouts on the windows and a plastic daffodil the teacher has invited her students to focus on as she reads the Wordsworth poem. One black student, remaining under the spell of the poem even after the recess bell rings, suddenly finds himself in a field of daffodils. But the second ringing of the bell breaks his fantasy, and he finds himself again in a world without greenery.

Both inner-city and suburban children respond positively to this exquisite film. The color is lovely, and the motion graceful. The sound track, with its muted, subtle sounds of water, wind and living creatures, appeals to the children, as does the electronic music in the urban sequences.

Order from: ACI Media, Inc., 35 W. 45th St., New York, NY 10036. Grade level: Primary–high school. Cost: $130, purchase; inquire about rental prices.

## LANGUAGE BLANKETS

Colorful crazy quilts from Grandma's day could have been the inspiration for this teaching aid. A patchwork chart made of fabric squares is an interesting alternative to the standard tagboard and just as useful.

This idea was used in one classroom to reinforce parts of speech, but it could have been used with "ch" words, "short a" words, rhyming words or any of a zillion other classifications.

An old sheet cut into ten-inch squares was the raw material. Each child received a number of squares on which he illustrated a noun or verb. The illustration was then colored in. (Try fabric scraps, trims, sequins, etc.) Each illustration was labeled with the word pictured. Then the children sewed the squares together to form a noun blanket and a verb blanket.

Blanket lists can serve as attractive reminders of vocabulary, facts or ideas, and might even inspire the creative energies of the needlework enthusiasts among your teaching colleagues.

Idea by: Sally Gordon, Irving, Tex.

# Science Fiction: Curriculum for the Future

by Barbara Gay Ford
and Ronald D. Ford

1984 is less than a decade away. Life then may or may not reflect Orwell's prophecies, but there's no doubt it will be different from what it is now.

Present-day prophets proclaim that change is the only predictable element of the future. It seems wise, then, to prepare for a variety of alternate futures. And one of our most important goals in education should be preparation of students for the unexpected—indicating a need for increased emphasis on creative problem-solving and divergent thought.

Such processes can be encouraged through the study of imaginative literature, particularly science fiction. Writers of science fiction deal with supposition and prediction, evoking a sense of probing curiosity and wonder as they travel into the world of "if." This emphasis on speculation is the quality that makes sf most valuable for today's classroom.

**Kaleidoscope of Themes.** Science-fiction literature deals in both classic themes of human conflict and unique situations, and presents students with surprising, exciting and imaginative views of the universe. Recurring themes involve problems of communication, socialization and relationships with nature, the advent and use of new technologies, the "inner space" of the mind, and scientific triumph over death. Many stories suggest that no problem is too complex to solve if possible solutions are approached with an open and creative mind.

Some stories are instruments of social criticism, exposing weaknesses in various social systems by use of frontal attacks or biting sarcasm. Many teachers have used works such as *1984*, *Brave New World* or *Fahrenheit 451* to show the pitfalls in some kinds of political organization. Myriad other stories relate to the same idea.

The role of prophecy in sf is both large and diverse and usually offers so many alternatives that students are not bound by any one view. Science fiction has continued to explore the possibilities of alien life, the implications of space travel, and questions regarding time travel and the fourth dimension.

**An SF Curriculum Gap.** Science fiction and fantasy have been included in the curriculums of numerous American colleges and universities in the last several years. A growing number of high schools also offer sf courses. More recently, instructional catalogs have begun to show a few sf materials for the elementary student.

Unfortunately, the "imagination gap" between the fairy tales of the early grades and the social satire of college-level sf is still vast and deadening. By the time children enter the fourth grade, the focus of their studies has switched from storytelling, fantasy and creative thought to facts, figures and ideas—all with predictable obsolescence. If students were consistently encouraged to read and study quality sf, perhaps their imaginative powers and creative abilities would be as strong in adulthood as they are in early childhood.

**Filling the Void.** How does one find good sf for classroom use? Some novels are inappropriate for younger readers, but a vast amount of sf literature is well suited for use as an educational resource in elementary and junior high schools. We recommend short stories, because they develop their themes with a minimum of complications and often have unexpected endings. When considering a story for your class:

▶ Make sure it quickly projects a mood that will catch the interest of young readers. The tone may be that of adventure, suspense, melancholy or humor, but it must hook the child early in the reading experience.

▶ Check the publishing date and the language; if certain scientific references are obviously dated, or if the writer is condescending in his attitude toward children, your students will probably be bored very quickly. They see sf cartoon series on Saturday mornings that are more sophisticated than many of the stories written for youngsters in the 1950s.

▶ Look for the introduction of unusual characters with special skills or qualities; an unpredictable and alien environment; fantastic machines or inventions; strange, unexplained phenomena; or weird unearthly creatures. And the sooner they appear in the tale, the better.

▶ Check to see if the theme is well developed and the ending is satisfying. If the tension of the story is not resolved, or the conclusion is too obvious, your readers will feel frustrated or let down. (See *Zoo 2000* by Jane Yolen [Seabury Press, 1973] and *The Calibrated Alligator* by Robert Silverberg [Holt, 1969] for younger readers. More advanced readers would enjoy the *Science Fiction Hall of Fame*, vol. 1, edited by Robert Silverberg [Doubleday, 1970].)

Anthologies of short stories are numerous and easy to come by at libraries or bookstores. The brevity of the stories makes them practical for the younger student.

[*Editor's note:* An excellent set of eight science fiction anthologies, *The Lerner Science Fiction Library*, is available from Lerner Publications Company, 241 First Ave. North, Minneapolis, MN 55401. The books are written on a fifth grade reading level for intermediate and junior high students.]

Inexpensive sf magazines and "fanzines" (magazines written by and for science-fiction fans) are available on the newsstand or by mail. These are sources of good short stories and short novels, sf criticism, and news about the field. Among the best on the newsstand are *The Magazine of Fantasy and Science Fiction*, *Analog: Science Fiction–Science Fact* and *Vertex*. By mail, try *Locus*, Box 3938, San Francisco, CA 94119. If you wish to read views on major novels or films, try *SF: The Other Side of Realism* by Thomas Clareson (Bowling Green University [Popular Press], 1971), and *Science Fiction in the Cinema* by John Baxter (Warner Paperback Library, 1970).

Older students can find critics who express opinions about the ideas of certain writers or stories, and may enjoy reading the analyses of certain films like *2001: A Space Odyssey* and *Planet of the Apes*.

**SF Can Be Integrated.** The ideas, problem-solving approaches and predisposition to speculation in sf have applications in many curriculum areas. Besides creating their own sf stories, students may enjoy rewriting endings of familiar stories in sf style—"saving the day" for the characters through futuristic devices or the harnessing of unearthly forces. Or consider the adventures of a robot as the basis for creative writing: what does it look like, what does it do, and how does it affect the lives of people? Students might try developing an ideal language for the future, avoiding the problems and inconsistencies encountered in our present language and, of course, including words to name and describe objects and events as yet unknown.

Social studies units might be expanded to include a future dimension. TV news progams could be created in which correspondents report on local conditions and world events in some future time. Sf stories of new societies—both those reflecting utopian views and those of a more pessimistic persuasion—may motivate students to try planning their own versions of a future society or future city. Planners of new societies may take into account the benefits (and problems) of an altered technology. And, unless it's a robot society, meeting human needs must be a consideration. Ecology principles as well as social studies concepts will likely influence the designing of these new societies.

Science-fiction stories may interest the class in both practical and theoretical aspects of science. Astronomy may suddenly become very relevant. Students may draw on science facts and findings to bring authenticity to the sf stories they write and to other sf-related creative projects as well.

Allied with reading and creative writing efforts, drama is a natural outcome of sf studies. Staging scenes and playing characters from sf can be more exciting than drama drawn from other kinds of literature because of the freedom fantasy affords. And in a similar vein, since unreality gives all kinds of comfortable license to artists, sf may stimulate illustrations, constructions and other art forms of striking originality.

The special relevancy and appeal of sf lies in its ability to stimulate thought and open the mind to imagination and speculation. Through it, students can experience other worlds, focus imaginative skills on the conflicts presented, and probe the place of humankind in the universe of 1984 and beyond. They might even conjure up some innovative approaches to the problems of today.

Barbara Gay Ford is assistant professor, Northern Illinois University, Dekalb.
Ronald Ford is a free-lance writer.

## TURN NOT PALE, BELOVED SNAIL: A Book About Writing Among Other Things

**by Jacqueline Jackson**

Here's an author (of children's books) who doesn't think much of the way teachers teach writing (they mark things up with red pencils and spoil the fun and fantasy). This book is intended for young writers of poetry and prose (aged 10–15), but teachers can use and adapt the suggestions. Just forget that red pencil for a while. (The title is from "The Lobster-Quadrille" in Lewis Carroll's ALICE IN WONDERLAND: "Then turn not pale, beloved snail, but come and join the dance.")

Order from: Little, Brown and Co., 34 Beacon St., Boston, MA 02106. Grade level: Intermediate–junior high. Cost: $7.50.

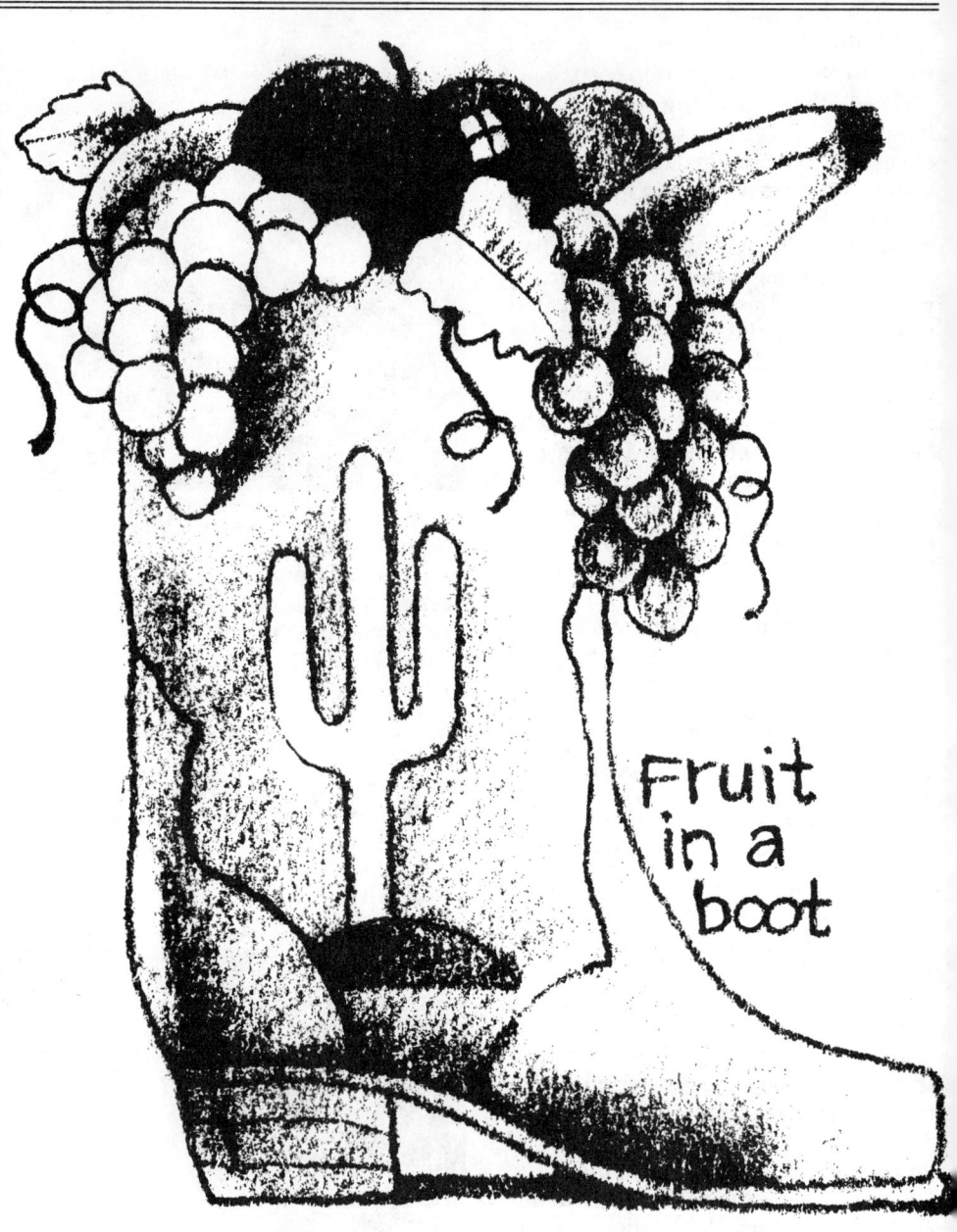

## DRAW A RHYME

Silliness seems epidemic among students at certain times of the year. You might consider channeling some of it into nonsense rhymes. No epic OWL AND THE PUSSYCAT verses, no special rules, just connecting two rhyming words in a phrase that projects an image: "a wagon for a dragon", "knight with a kite", "a muff made of fluff", the gizzard of a wizard." Students may even find themselves consulting those dusty dictionaries in order to lengthen their lists.

There's method in this madness beyond therapeutic considerations. Some of these rhyming pairs can be turned into reading aids for lower grades. Teachers of beginning readers may be able to use the rhymes for extending reading vocabularies, in auditory training exercises and in introducing variant spellings.

Of course, the lists will be needing some weeding. Some of the rhymes that beguile the sophisticates in grade five may not be much help to the novice reader. Have students decide which rhymes (1) might be enjoyable for younger children, (2) can be effectively illustrated, (3) use familiar phonograms and simple spellings for the most part.

Once a working list of rhymes for this project has been compiled (and the others reserved for class use), you're ready to begin illustrating. For this you may want to enlist the services of your art teacher—who might welcome a less complicated project for a change. The art teacher may help students find ways of illustrating their rhymes, either in a compact format for ditto sheets, or in a larger-sized poster layout. In both cases, plan space for writing in the rhymes. The art teacher may also see the need for conducting a short refresher course in manuscript lettering before the students start captioning their work.

If the finished rhyme pictures go on dittos, they can be duplicated and stapled into booklets. Copies can then go to primary classrooms and also to the rhyme originators.

There is much rhyme, considerable reason and more than a few giggles in this project.

Idea by: Martha Snyder and Margaret Clayton, Reynoldsburg, Ohio.

# FIVE LINERS

When providing outlets for creative expression becomes a problem of time, try out "five-line themes" — a fairly simple way to help students exercise creative thinking.

Supply the class with a one-word title: patience, hollow, bananas. Students try to write five lines — no more, no less — on the subject.

Some students, who seem to draw a blank on any writing topic, must really dig for the five lines. Many students need practice in the creative thought processes of stretching the imagination, reaching for associations. At first you may want to offer some thought-starters: What impressions, pictures, experiences, feelings does the word bring to mind? Are times, places, people involved?

At the other extreme, students who tend to write on and on may feel cramped by the five-line ration. But being able to confine expression within limits and still have a satisfying experience is part of creativity, too.

Have the class try a new title each day for several days, and see if the five-liners begin to come more easily for most of your students.

You (and they) may be surprised by the creative thinking and writing that can come through in just five lines.

Idea by: Jule E. Marine, Jr., Jordan Junior High School, Salt Lake City, Utah.

# FOG

☆ ☆ ☆ ☆ ☆ ☆ ☆ ☆ ☆

Using the Carl Sandburg poem "Fog" as a point of departure, this 9-minute film focuses on the mood, forms, textures and motions of fog. The photography is outstanding, and the background noises and music serve to intensify its emotional impact. The purpose of the film is to inspire a variety of creative activities (poetry, music, art) in the classroom.

After students in a kindergarten class had studied Sandburg's poem, they used the film as a guide for dramatizing the movement of cats and wrote group stories and poems about them. Finally, they did improvisations of wind, fog and other subjects of the film. It proved useful in increasing the children's scientific knowledge and added many new words to their speaking vocabulary.

Order from: Encyclopaedia Britannica Educational Corp., 425 N. Michigan Ave., Chicago, IL 60611. Grade level: Primary–high school. Cost: $7.50, rental; $115, purchase. School purchase orders will be billed.

# AARON ZWIEBACK AND HIS WORLD OF WORDS

☆ ☆ ☆ ☆ ☆ ☆ ☆ ☆ ☆

Although words hold a fascination for beginning readers, they often lose their luster when assembled, alphabetized and packaged in a dictionary. Ask any fourth grader. But AARON ZWIEBACK (the first of the a's and the last of the z's, get it?) shows how to make dictionary work most unworklike.

Within this 80-page workbook, students do deal with alphabetical order, pronunciation keys and phonetics, definitions, idioms and guide words. But they'll also be using a glossary to translate nonsense sentences such as "Each robelf was zeeing with a dotion flouse," turning dictionary entries into cinquain and drawing pictures of happiness.

Heavily illustrated with cartoon drawings, the book has an appealing look. The style is light and humorous, and the dictionary skills are solid and well developed.

AARON ZWIEBACK was designed for use with editions of WEBSTER'S NEW WORLD DICTIONARY. You should be aware of this, although in most cases where reference is made to specific pages, you can adapt the material with no difficulty.

A 48-page teacher's manual is also available. It provides interesting background information, teaching suggestions and many additional activities. Its bibliography supplies enrichment sources, and a chart relates each lesson to dictionary and language arts objectives.

The philosophy of AARON ZWIEBACK is that a dictionary should be a "source of interesting and important data" and a "starter for creative activities." That attitude could catch on, so don't be surprised if you discover a child curled up reading a dictionary.

Order from: Prentice-Hall, Inc., Educational Book Division, Dept. KH-112, Englewood Cliffs, NJ 07632. Grade level: 4–6. Cost: $1.62, student workbook; $1.41, teacher's manual. Add 3 percent for postage and handling.

## LANGUAGE ARTS

# PRACTICE PATTERNS

Introduce them on Monday, check them on Wednesday, test them on Friday. And on Tuesday and Thursday? Practice! The time-honored spelling words cycle. Maybe your class undergoes a somewhat modified routine, but practice is bound to be in there somewhere.

Spelling practice sometimes gets combined with "creative writing" (one sentence per word) activities and with handwriting. How about combining spelling practice with pictures and patterns?

Using the eraser ends of their pencils, students outline designs or pictures on practice paper. Then, armed with their spelling lists, students pencil in the perimeter of the pattern with spelling words. Using each word at least three or four times will assure a satisfactory session as regards spelling practice.

And for the truly committed, there's the practice picture of the fill-in-border-to-border variety. After completing the outlines of the pictures, students can fill in all the empty spaces with more spelling words. Color? Why not? Inventiveness will be rewarded by the creation of graphics masterpieces and maybe a few more 100s for the old spelling graphs.

Idea by: Carol Cushner, Upham School, Wellesley Hills, Mass.

## JOSHUA IN A BOX

☆ ☆ ☆ ☆ ☆ ☆ ☆ ☆ ☆ ☆

Joshua is a strange little creature who spends most of this five-minute, animated color film trying to escape from inside a box. During his many efforts to get out, he expresses a variety of human emotions.

The film begins with Joshua's puzzled explorations of the box. Then he realizes he is trapped, and smashing and kicking, he tries in vain to break out. Finally Joshua discovers a crack in one of the sides, and after one futile attempt, he manages to slip out through the tiny opening.

Elated, Joshua sticks out his tongue at the box. But his emotions quickly change, and he sheds a tear as depression sets in. His body then transforms itself into another box identical to the first with him inside once again.

During the action, the viewer not only sees but in some instances experiences Joshua's feelings of puzzlement, anger, hysteria, frustration and elation. There is no dialogue, but the many emotions are conveyed through facial expressions and a guitar accompaniment which reflects Joshua's moods and actions.

In its unique way, the film shows something about man's gut-level reactions to freedom and confinement. Younger kids understand the film in terms of their own experiences: what it has felt like to be enclosed or confined within a small space — perhaps a closet or a box. Discussion can help older viewers to understand the broader, more abstract concepts and meanings of freedom implied in the film.

Order from: Stephen Bosustow Productions, 1649 11th St., Santa Monica, CA 90404. Grade level: 3–12. Cost: Rental, $15 first day, $7.50 each additional day; purchase, $115. Postage and handling extra.

## FILL IN THE BLANKS

The <u>TREMENDOUS</u> man <u>WALKED</u> over
     adjective          verb

to the <u>SILLY</u> girl and gave her a
      adjective

<u>SOFT</u> <u>ORANGE</u> <u>AIRPLANE</u>. The
adjective  adjective   noun

<u>ELDERLY</u> man <u>SWAM</u> over to
adjective       verb

the shy girl and gave her a <u>CONCEALED</u>
                                adjective

<u>TIMID</u> <u>GIRAFFE</u>.
adjective  noun

Have you seen books or card games at novelty stores that leave out words in strategic places? Someone first asks volunteers to provide a list of nouns, verbs or adjectives — whatever the story has missing. The blanks are then filled with the supplied words. Of course, since the volunteers must respond without knowing the nature of the story, the completed story can be laughable when read back.

You or your students can make up stories which can be read in small groups or with the entire class.

This is an involving way to teach parts of speech. The activity will also help students to better understand how important context clues are in reading. And _____
                              adjective

of all, it's a lot of _____.
               noun

Idea by: Irwin Hill, Hollywood, Florida.

# LANGUAGE ARTS 99

vocabulary building, making a newspaper, and an approach to essay writing that could become a helpful addition to your language arts program.

Each booklet is composed of 22 typed and duplicated pages stapled into a paper cover. Both booklets have bibliographies, and information about the services of the Home and School Institute is included.

Order from: The Home and School Institute, Trinity College, Washington, DC 20017. Grade level: Teachers of preschool—grade 3. Cost: Each booklet, $2. Orders must be prepaid. (The Home and School Institute is a nonprofit organization; to keep distribution costs low, its general ordering information suggests a $2.50 minimum order.)

## LIVING SENTENCES

"Who's a verb?"
"I am, Light."
"Light's a noun."
"It's a verb, too, like 'light a fire.'"

Students can do some real thinking when winning a game is at stake. Creating sentences can be a game in which parts of speech suddenly take on new importance.

Make a set of word cards—one word per card—that has at least nouns and verbs, and as many other parts of speech as the class can handle. Divide the class into two teams and deal the cards. Each team member now becomes a sentence component. The object of the game is to see how many sentences each team can make. Teams must decide among themselves how to use each word. Then members must arrange themselves in order with their words reading left to right—from the audience's point of view.

Depending upon the level of your class, you may need to discuss and demonstrate what is needed to make a sentence and how each part of speech functions in the sentence. With some levels you'll want to guide the sentence-making process: What parts do we need first? More advanced levels will be able to organize themselves and present sentences within a time limit.

Variations of the game might be to see which team can use all of its members in the sentences it makes, or to try to make the longest sentence with the given words. Including words that can be used in a number of ways adds to the sentence possibilities. Be prepared for much scrambling and some silly sentences.

Idea by: Kay Califf, Nauvoo-Colusa Community Unit School, Colusa, Ill.

## READING/WRITING: SUCCESS FOR CHILDREN BEGINS AT HOME

☆ ☆ ☆ ☆ ☆ ☆ ☆ ☆

Two booklets from the Home and School Institute offer teaching suggestions in the vital curriculum areas of reading and writing. The booklets are written primarily for parents who are interested in working with their children in ways that will complement the school's program.

READING: SUCCESS FOR CHILDREN BEGINS AT HOME briefly explains the controversy about early reading and stresses the importance of the child's feelings and attitude in determining approaches and activities. The activities suggested involve visual perception and discrimination, listening skills and the development of reading habits. Ways of working with teachers are suggested to parents.

WRITING: SUCCESS FOR CHILDREN BEGINS AT HOME includes activities for

## IN OTHER WORDS: An Introductory Thesaurus

☆ ☆ ☆ ☆ ☆ ☆ ☆ ☆

When is happy not happy? When it's joyful, merry, gay, jolly, cheerful, delightful, etc. That's the kind of news that should make you and your creative writers pleased and glad.

Finding another word, a more precise word, a more colorful word, for one already worn thin is a constant struggle for all writers, whatever their experience. IN OTHER WORDS helps. This word book lists 2,500 words with synonyms and antonyms for each.

The format of this thesaurus makes it easy for elementary students to use. The source words are shown at the left on a colored panel, alternative words are shown on a white center strip, and contrasting words are listed at the far right on a light-tint panel. The center strip also provides sentences using each of the source words. Words that can be used as more than one part of speech are pointed out, and alternatives are given for all usages.

The book is a Canadian publication, and thus has some entries for which there are two spellings, e.g., colour, color. Each of these words is marked with an asterisk indicating an alternative spelling in a footnote.

Taking into account the hard use given reference books, the publishers offer IN OTHER WORDS on heavy stock with a durable soft cover.

This first thesaurus should provide your young writers with a quite adequate, ample, sufficient supply of emphatic, eloquent words.

Order from: Lothrop, Lee & Shepard, 105 Madison Ave., New York, NY 10016. Grade level: 3–8. Cost: $5.81.

# 100 LANGUAGE ARTS

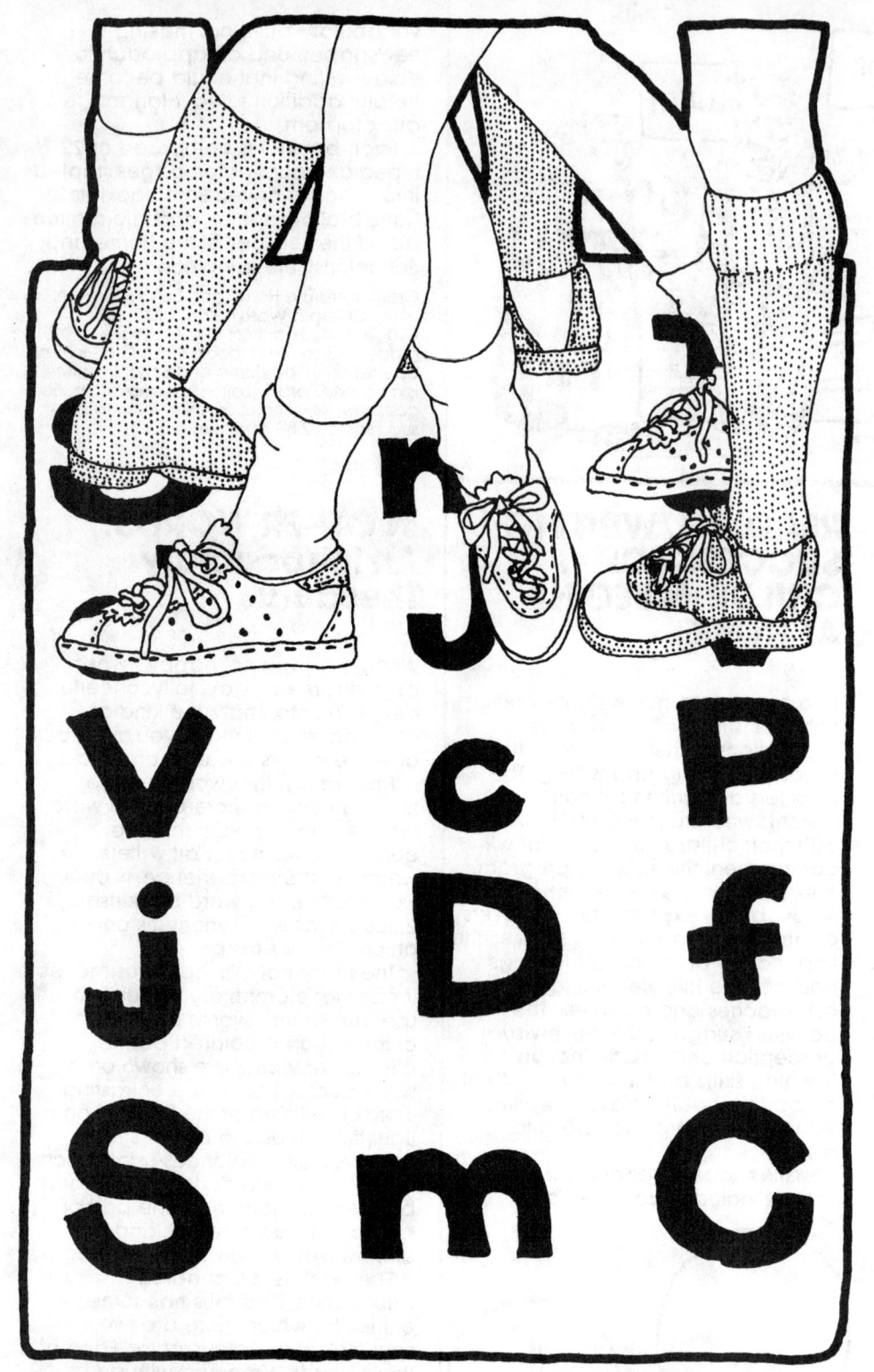

## CONSONANT JUMBLE "Magic Carpet" Floor Game

☆ ☆ ☆ ☆ ☆ ☆ ☆ ☆ ☆

"With your right foot firmly on the b, reach out with your left foot and find the B—and don't step on Kathy, and try not to fall down." Here's a way both to reinforce the capital letter and lower-case letter pairs and give those wiggly children a chance to move around. The CONSONANT JUMBLE game starts with a Mylar-coated (smooth, tough) floor mat about 3-1/2-by-6-1/2 feet in size, with large colorful consonants lined up on it. Both capital and lower-case forms of 19 out-of-order consonants can be found on the mat. A twist of the spinner tells the child which letter to look for. He must find both forms of the letter and stand with one foot on each. He continues to stand on his letters while others play and the mat fills up.

The back of the spinner serves as the rule book. It has suggestions for letter recognition and identification activities that allow children who are not quite ready for the JUMBLE game to utilize the floor mat. The card also gives suggestions for more complex versions of the game.

The mat and spinner come in a heavy plastic slip case. All items are designed for hard wear and easy cleaning.

This "magic carpet" offers a way to work with consonants that will soon have children standing on their own feet—or maybe somebody else's.

Order from: Society for Visual Education, Inc., 1345 Diversey Parkway, Chicago, IL 60614. Grade level: K–1. Cost: $14.50 plus $1 postage and handling. Payment must accompany orders from individuals.

## THE QUILTED STORY

This is a group construction. Very free, playful and unpredictable, it has in it elements of collage, mural painting and story telling. The actual "event" will have the children cooperate in building a story out of photographs, paint, crayons and found objects.

To prepare for the experience, tack a long piece of wrapping paper to the bulletin board or chalkboard as if you were setting up for a mural. Gather, or have the children collect, a large stock of pictures from magazines or from personal (but expendable) photo collections.

The photos can be spread out on tables so that all the students can become familiar with them. As an alternative, each child can choose or be given several photos to use in the activity.

Someone might start things off with a photo of a family, pasting it on the left side of the paper. "This is Sam," the student says as he or she taps a child in the photo. "And this is Sam's family at home."

A second child, inspired by the first, comes up with a photo of a school, pasting it under the first photo and saying, "This is the school Sam goes to," and then painting a path from Sam to the school.

Children take their turns as they see ways to tie in given photos to the flow of the story.

By large and small steps, the pageant develops as each child adds whatever makes sense to him or her.

In case the story moves in a direction in which there happen to be no photographs immediately available, there are several options. Students can hunt for additional photos, or they can draw in the necessary elements. In a pinch, you can have the students empty their pockets or search in their desks for some real object—a key, a piece of string, a comb—that can be fastened right onto the mural.

If the teacher records the story as it is told, the tape can later be enjoyed by visitors as well as by the children themselves. The total work, in fact, can be sent on a traveling show around the school.

Idea by: Ronald Goodman, Hinton, W.Va.

## TALES OF THE HOPI INDIANS

☆ ☆ ☆ ☆ ☆ ☆ ☆ ☆

In this age of multimedia, storytelling in its purist form is a nearly lost art. But not altogether. Using nothing but her voice, master storyteller Diane Wolkstein brings three Hopi Indian tales vividly to life in this record album written by folklorist Harold Courlander. Because all of the characterization and drama are achieved simply through the telling, the record makes for exciting and absorbing listening.

Two of the tales, "The Sun Callers" and "Coyote and the Crying Song," are short and simple enough for older primaries to understand and appreciate. The longer and more complex "Sikakokuh and the Hunting Dog" requires greater concentration and is more appropriate for intermediate and upper grades.

Each of the tales gives some meaningful insights into the Hopi way of life. As a social studies aid in looking at a particular Indian culture, or as a language arts supplement, this record can be a valuable tool.

Order from: Spoken Arts, 310 North Ave., New Rochelle, NY 10801. Grade level: 2–12. Cost: $6.98 plus $1 postage and handling. Orders for single copies must be accompanied by payment.

## ENCYCLOPEDIA TELEPHONIA

Almost every home has at least one. It's white and yellow on the inside, and it's not an egg. It's your telephone book—a reference tool of many mysteries.

The telephone book can serve as a take-home test of research skills such as: (1) knowing alphabetical order, (2) using guide words, (3) recognizing symbols, (4) using the table of contents with flexibility and resourcefulness, (5) following cross references, (6) substituting synonyms, (7) obtaining information from maps and diagrams, (8) "reading the fine print."

Each locality would require its own set of questions, but the following items may serve as examples:

WHAT DO YOU KNOW ABOUT YOUR TELEPHONE DIRECTORY?

1. What single number do you dial in case of a serious emergency? On what page did you find this information?
2. What is the phone number of the North Dartmouth State Police? On what page can you find it quickly?
3. What is the area code for Chicago? In how many places can you find this?
4. What is the zip code for Tisbury?
5. What are the guide words on page 116? Will you find Earl Phipps on that page?
6. What is the address of Manuel Souza whose phone number is 758-3803? (This was tricky. The name was common, but the exchange, 758, helped. There were only two Manuel Souzas in the town served by that exchange.)
7. If you put in a call to Oregon from Dartmouth, what difference in time should you allow for? Where did you get this information?
8. What is the symbol of the Coast Guard? What number do you call for a Search and Rescue operation?

YELLOW PAGES
1. How many places are listed where you can get a knife sharpened? (This was a "See also.")
2. How many pediatricians are listed? (Students had to translate "pediatricians" to "physicians—practice limited to children.")
3. You need to rent a pair of metal crutches and a wheelchair for an elderly relative. What company advertises that it can furnish both?

Don't be surprised if you learn something new about your telephone book in making up your test!

Idea by: Mildred Berkowitz, Dartmouth Middle School, North Dartmouth, Mass.

## CREATIVE WRITINGS REVISITED

Running dry on creative writing projects? Try recycling some of the old ones. Go back to things that the students have already done and suggest ways to give the topics a new look:

1. Write the story so that the sequence of events is reversed.
2. Add five new details.
3. Make it funny.
4. Write it as a telephone conversation.
5. Write it very formally.
6. Write it very informally.
7. Write it in as few words as you can.
8. Write it for a particular person; describe the person—age, interests, etc.
9. Write it as a poem or as the lyrics of a song.
10. Write it so that readers will be moved to some kind of action.

Idea by: Robert H. Weston, Seattle, Wash.

## The Language Arts: A Revolution

by Arthur Daigon

New revolutions are brewing in the classroom world of talking, reading, writing and listening. These revolutions may point the way for intermediate and secondary teachers interested in alternatives to language and literature instruction that until now has changed very little language or literary behavior.

Having long ago overturned the regime based on diagraming other people's sentences and correcting other people's errors, having banished the literary priesthood and the mandatory worship of Hiawatha, Miles Standish, the Ancient Mariner and company, the revolutionaries are now turning their energies to the succession of shaky interim establishments that promise solid educational reforms but deliver only token concessions.

Members of the establishment claim they *have* made substantial improvements in the conditions of teaching and learning. They have given space: large rooms, small rooms, open corridors and interest corners. They have given time: modular schedules, rotating schedules and flexible schedules. They have granted permission for large group meetings, small group meetings and individual study. They point to the new technology—the picture-sound machines—they have provided.

For the revolutionaries, these are stopgap measures. Has anything been accomplished, they ask, if the parts of speech or the definition of *alliteration* or the difference between synonym and antonym is taught in large or small rooms, during rotating modular schedules, to individual students or masses of them, by teams of teachers using an arsenal of electronic equipment? Increased efficiency in teaching the inconsequential is the only breakthrough for which the technology promoters can take credit.

"Openness" is the term most frequently seen in the manifestoes of the rebels. Their openness, however, has nothing to do with the availability or arrangement of space, but with a flexibility of mind. The language arts they want to see come to life call for three kinds of openness:

1) Openness to the ideas and subjects that may be explored in a classroom.
2) Openness to the media and materials that may be used for such exploration.
3) Openness to the kinds of responses students may use.

*Openness to ideas and subjects* is central to this view of language arts. It suggests that the language-arts classroom is the place where young people consider what they judge to be important: families, money, violence, minorities, fantasy, crime, buying and selling, heroes and villains, right and wrong—all of the puzzling, exciting and frightening subjects calling for scrutiny and understanding. Teachers do not abdicate commitments to language when they go to the social sciences for the stuff of instruction. We must *language* about something, and the interests of young people seem to provide the most promising means of generating language situations calling for reading, writing, speaking, listening, viewing and acting—the grist of the language-arts classroom.

*Openness to the media and materials used to explore subjects* separates the new language arts from the conventional "thematic" approach—the brief foray into "Courage" or "Who Am I?" through the reading of some stories, poems and biographical sketches, or the viewing of a film, all supported by the usual showing, telling and writing activities. The crusaders for a language arts that carries over into the world beyond school would insist on using all evidence that sheds light on an important or interesting subject.

Our materials then should include the handbills, posters, headlines, news stories, articles, letters to the editor; the photos, cartoons, comic strips, paintings, sculpture, graffiti; the charts, graphs, polls, questionnaires, quotations, speeches, epigrams; the forms, lists, songs, slogans—and a hundred other kinds of verbal and pictorial evidence that may be used along with more conventional materials to open minds and generate response.

And *openness to the kinds of responses* available to students ready to say or do something about a subject is the last nonnegotiable demand of the language-arts militants. Responses, or "feedback," from students tell us how our talks, short stories, films, and so on, have been received and internalized. Responses generated by interesting materials about interesting subjects should not be allowed to evaporate through overreliance on "discussion" (teacher-talk with occasional monosyllabic replies by two kids sitting in the first row), formal exercises and testing.

What is important is that students are actively synthesizing ideas and their vehicles rather than passively receiving them.

It is here that the revolutionaries confound their enemies by a brilliant piece of classroom strategy certain to win new adherents to their cause. Rigor and discipline (of all things!) are wedded to openness, as instruction is focused on ways to clarify and intensify meanings of important messages sent and important messages received. Basic skills, the conventions of various media and details of linguistic etiquette are learned as they are needed to explore and to communicate. Drills become an aid to instruction rather than its mainstay.

Among the various groups blocking significant change in language-arts instruction are two that are particularly powerful—one established and respected, the other, newly arrived and intimidating. The first is the Reading Hierarchy, whose dogmas and mysteries can be fathomed only through special kits and boxes, and who perform their reading rituals only on brightly colored, secretly sequenced cards. Their followers are unusually adept at reading these and other cards, but are woefully deficient with newspapers, magazines and books.

The second group has produced comprehensive lists of acceptable behaviors and promises to hold everyone accountable for their performance. Its own objectives call for a purge of affect/value-centered learning and a restoration of the absolutism of narrowly defined basic skills. This group is, of course, none other than the old Rote-Learning Formalists, returned with a new pitch.

When and where will the revolution be fought? In September, after teachers choose their weapons—rules, definitions and "safe" materials, or the openness that brands them converts to the cause. The first shots will be heard in thousands of classrooms—and the revolution begins again, and again, and again.

Arthur Daigon is a co-author of DIG/U.S.A. (Bantam).

## CREATIVE DRAMATICS FOR THE CLASSROOM TEACHER
**by Ruth Beall Heinig and Lyda Stillwell**

Those teachers looking for a practical guide to introducing creative dramatics in the classroom will find real help in this book. It offers close to 300 pages of suggestions for narrative pantomime, creative pantomime, dialogue scenes and story dramatizations. Extensive and well-annotated lists of stories to use for dramatizations are also included.

Order from: Prentice-Hall, Inc., Englewood Cliffs, NJ 07632. Grade level: Teachers of primary–intermediate. Cost: $8.95.

## THE WRITING CENTER KIT

☆ ☆ ☆ ☆ ☆ ☆ ☆ ☆

As the name suggests, this kit of large-sized, colorful and stimulating cards can become a center for creative-writing experiences. Each of the 56 cards presents a separate writing stimulator. Distinctive art establishes mood and setting, while the text provides story bits or thought-provoking and thought-organizing aids. The cards pose unusual situations, feature unique settings and offer a good supply of humor as well.

The kit provides stimulation for five creative-writing themes or forms: adventure, animals, fantasy, mystery and poetry. Designed for use in grades 3–8, the cards are not intended to comprise a total creative-writing program; they do, however, provide a wide variety of creative-writing possibilities that can be used by the children independently.

The price may be a problem for some, but sharing a kit among classrooms is perhaps a solution. The cards are heavy, of very durable stock, and should hold up well.

Order from: Order Dept., Winston Press, 25 Groveland Terrace, Minneapolis, MN 55403. Grade level: 3–8. Cost: $27 plus shipping and handling.

*It is the last minute of play in the game. The coach has pulled the goalkeeper, and has put another attacker on the ice. You are that extra attacker. Tell what happens.*

## THE LEGEND OF JOHN HENRY

☆ ☆ ☆ ☆ ☆ ☆ ☆ ☆ ☆

John Henry, the steel-driving, black folk hero, lives again in an 11-minute, animated color film narrated in song by Roberta Flack.

In a folk tale which epitomizes the confrontation of man and machine, John Henry displays a level of determination that can serve as a model for all children. Pitching himself against technology's steam drill – a standoff in brute strength – John Henry proves the worth of motivation and desire in reaching one's goals.

The colorful, impressionistic animation and the beautiful singing of Roberta Flack are the film's greatest strengths. Lyrically, though, the ballad narration focuses more on the story itself than on John Henry's background and character, which is so necessary to fully understanding his personality. This problem can be overcome, however, by reading or telling students a version of the story before viewing.

Order from: Stephen Bosustow Productions, 1649 Eleventh St., Santa Monica, CA 90404 or Pyramid Films, Box 1048, Santa Monica, CA 90406. Grade level: 3–12. Cost: Rental, $15 for the first day, $7.50 per day thereafter; purchase, $160. Postage and handling extra.

## VIVE LA DIFFERENCE!

In these days of unisex, there are still some corners of the curriculum where determining what's feminine and what's masculine is critical. The proper use of the LA's and LE's, the DIE's and DER's is a constant trial for the student of foreign languages.

Reason and logic – or, if you will, stereotypes – play no part in the struggle. What's feminine about ROAD or masculine about BOOK? In French, PURSE is masculine, TIE is feminine. It's easy to see why rote memory turns out to be the only way to a workable vocabulary.

If memorization has to be the route, there's no reason to condemn the gimmick that aids the process. (How many of us rely on ancient crutches and jingles to recall the spelling of the "demons"?)

Try running off lists using blue spirit master backing for masculine nouns and pink spirit master backing for feminine nouns. Like nouns are then associated with each other and with a color. (If pink and blue disturb you, select whatever color system your duplicating method can manage.) Color coding might also be used to separate two languages being studied concurrently.

Whatever your feelings about unigarb, or unijob, better not try LA CRAYON or LE PLUME. The French will get you for it.

Idea by: Thomas J. Sacco, Columbus, Ohio.

# AN IDEA BOOK FOR ACTING OUT AND WRITING LANGUAGE

☆☆☆☆☆☆☆☆☆

In addition to hundreds of topics for acting out and writing language, this book details the mechanics of the small group process in the classroom.

Teacher Gary L. Gerbrandt wrote AN IDEA BOOK "to give a new dimension to James Moffett's ideas and philosophy on the teaching of language arts." (Moffett's conviction is that kids learn language best by moving in small groups from dramatics activities to writing experiences.)

"The Small Group Process" is the Gerbrandt book's first section. It provides a rationale for the small group approach, describes nine different kinds of small groups, explains student and teacher roles in the groups, and, most important, tells how and when to implement the grouping process.

The second section, "Acting Out Language," briefly defines four kinds of dramatics activities—pantomine, guessing games, charades and small group improvisations—that develop unwritten communication skills. Suggested situations for acting out follow the development of each activity type. In some cases, situations are organized by grade level.

The final chapters, "Writing Out Language" and "Writing Down Language," call for two different kinds of writing experiences: writing out is actually creative writing; writing down develops skills in structuring and transcribing sentences.

In "Writing Out," the child thinks out and writes a story in response to a stimulus. Stimuli take the form of to-be-completed sentences ("The chipmunk had filled his cheeks with nuts after _____"), morals which may suggest fables ("If you don't know where you're going, any road will take you there"), and high-interest or suspenseful situations on which to build stories ("You are a passenger on an airplane and see a man pass a note to a stewardess").

In "Writing Down," kids straighten out scrambled sentences and take down sentences from dictation.

Besides its use as a teaching reference, AN IDEA BOOK is an excellent guide for presenting workshops in the use of small groups.

Order from: Order Dept., National Council of Teachers of English, 1111 Kenyon Rd., Urbana, IL 61801. Grade level: Teachers of grades K–8. Cost: $4.75 (add $.60 for billed orders). Use stock number 22213 when ordering. (NCTE members pay $3.95.)

# IT'S IN THE BOOK

What does the capital of Delaware have in common with the name of the first successful Mickey Mouse film? They're both found in encyclopedia "D."

A good way to provide practice in using reference books is to set up sessions for tracking down trivia. Assign each student an encyclopedia. The student is to peruse the volume for five facts and turn those facts into questions. In order to maintain the middle ground between the obvious and the obscure, guidance may be needed in selecting facts for the first go-round.

Samples of "D" questions:
1. Where are the three most important diamond fields in the world located?
2. How often does a male deer grow a new set of antlers?
3. Who was John Davenport?

Students should first list their facts along with the page where each was found. These fact lists become answer keys. Questions drawn from the facts should go on separate paper and be placed inside the appropriate volume.

Now students swap encyclopedias, take out the question sheets and start searching. Research skills—isolating key words in the questions, using alphabetical order and subheads, skimming, reading for detail and documenting answers with page numbers—get a workout.

The author of each question sheet might also be keeper of its answer key and judge of the correctness of responses. Remind your judges that variation in page documentation may be acceptable. (Here's an opportunity to reinforce the fact that there may be more than one place to find the same information. Students may discover that the capital of Delaware is on a number of maps as well as in the text.)

Questions will vary according to students' reference experience and may be channeled along specific lines if that's needed—questions based on maps and graphs only, for instance.

While retention of specific minor facts is not the goal of the activity, don't be surprised if spontaneous trivia tournaments spring up.

Idea by: Esther Truesdale, Quincy, Mass.

# AMERICAN FOLKLORE

☆☆☆☆☆☆☆☆☆

Paul Bunyan and five other American folk heroes are the subjects of this series of six filmstrips, available with accompanying records or as fully captioned silent strips. Students will meet Mike Fink, Pecos Bill, John Henry, Joe Margarac, Casey Jones and Bunyan. The sound version of these filmstrips includes excellent storytelling, sound effects and related folksongs. Children observed using the filmstrips were delighted with the music and were anxious to learn and sing the songs for themselves. The silent version makes a high-interest reading lesson, as well as being useful for social studies or work with American folklore. The drawings in the filmstrips are clear and pleasant, and the colors are superb.

The materials were particularly successful in a class of dyslexic children, who used the sound version, viewed each story a number of times, learned the songs and retold the stories in their own words. When their teacher finally presented the children with the stories in book form, they were quite excited at being able to read the fables with a minimum of difficulty.

Coronet Films also produces a related series of filmstrips: TALL TALES IN AMERICAN FOLKLORE.

Order from: Coronet Instructional Media, 65 E. South Water St., Chicago, IL 60601. Grade level: 1–6. Cost: $70, records; $78, cassettes; $47, captioned. Available also in a Spanish-English version with cassettes only, $78.

## THE WRITING BUG: A SWARM OF WRITING EXPERIENCES

☆ ☆ ☆ ☆ ☆ ☆ ☆ ☆ ☆

Multimedia kits are all too often bundles of vaguely related materials loosely strung together under the guise of relevancy. THE WRITING BUG, however, is a materials kit that demonstrates careful planning, a clear interrelationship among the components and a joy in the subject matter.

The core of the kit is a set of 63 writing activity cards with contemporary color illustrations. The cards are divided into three categories — describing, explaining, storytelling — with 21 different activities in each. The 8-1/2-by-11-inch cards are numbered and coded according to both their categories and whether they are intended for individual or group activities. (There are seven group activities in each section. Two extra copies of group activity cards are provided.)

The high-interest activity cards derive their penetrating questions and writing assignments from a picture, a prose passage or a poem. Assignments fall into several stages: "Warm-Up" questions based on the picture or reading, a "Round One" preliminary writing activity, and a lengthier "Round Two" writing assignment. The group cards include a "Round Three" writing project. Some of the cards link neatly with the four filmstrips (including a make-it-yourself strip), posters and tape cassette that come with the kit, although none are totally dependent on the other ingredients.

A comprehensive and thorough teacher's guide accompanies the program. In a useful section entitled "Working Through the Program: Classroom Management Systems," it offers alternative methods for utilizing the kit. Other practical sections introduce the program to the class, define the role of the teacher and the teacher-pupil conference in the program, provide a skills and objectives chart for each card, and give additional suggestions for using the cards.

The kit comes packaged in a notebook-like folder that unfolds three times and stands up to become a display writing center. So that students can keep records of the activities they have completed, there is a ditto master with a check list of all the cards.

Order from: Random House, Inc., 400 Hahn Rd., Westminister, MD 21157. Grade level: 4–6. Cost: $113.46, complete kit; $53.13, activity cards; $12.90, ditto master and posters; $8.58, cassette; $26.55, filmstrips 1, 2, 3; $6.30, U-Film can and template; $8.34, teacher's guide.

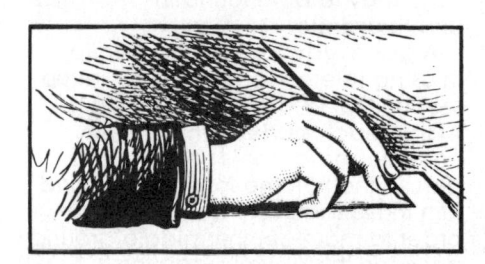

## GRUESOME GARBAGE, ALIAS DAILY NEWS

There's a way to avoid collecting, copying, collating and stapling a school newspaper and still reap the benefits of junior journalism. Just expropriate a prominently located bulletin board where your class may post its news-writing efforts. With an imposing masthead, headlines, by-lines and several regular columns, a bulletin board newspaper will draw a wide readership from the students and faculty alike.

News can be school-related — coming events, honor roll, sports scores. Items may also be picked up from local newspapers and rewritten. Some students like making up phony news items — pure fiction, but written in a believable news style. (Such items need to be posted under an appropriate label so that no one takes seriously the announcement that the entire male faculty is being auctioned off after lunch on Friday.) Another favorite is the takeoff on "Dear Abby," offering solutions to far-fetched problems.

Topics and emphases can be suggested to the class and occasional assignments made to keep things moving. Offerings are checked over for corrections and rewrites — if it's going to be "printed," it should be correct. Each day, select two or three finished items, seeing that each student has something chosen every few weeks. Rotate items daily. Give the paper a new look with some seasonal mastheads; designers get by-lines too.

The newspaper can lead to other projects: a readership poll or a schoolwide fiction contest, with winning stories running in serial form in the newspaper.

Idea by: Dorothy Stout Janz, North Junior High School, Johnson City, Tenn.

## READING REEL AND TITLE TWISTER

☆ ☆ ☆ ☆ ☆ ☆ ☆ ☆ ☆

These two language arts aids are designed to keep ideas in motion. Book report ideas? Leave them to the READING REEL. Whether the student has read a mystery, a biography or an animal story, the READING REEL offers suggestions for follow-up activities.

The READING REEL is made up of three layers of cardboard wheels that can be rotated separately. The base card arranges in a ring the names of ten literature forms that students may encounter in their recreational reading. Inside this ring, a movable wheel provides ten suggested writing assignments that extend ideas from the books. "Change the ending of the story," the wheel suggests, or "Write a personal letter to a character in the story."

The innermost wheel offers ten art or construction activities that again may be matched to the book that the child has read.

Turning the wheels and lining up the suggestions may be just enough of a novelty for the students that it puts new life into reading follow-ups.

TITLE TWISTER is an aid that may find itself happily occupied in your creative writing center, where students go individually, independently, for ideas and "starters." On the outer ring of the cardboard base there are the beginnings of 20 titles — "One Day in the Life of _____"; "Why I Can't Stand Kids, by _____." The inner wheel supplies the endings — "Super

Rooster" or, perhaps, "Uncle Grouch."

With a turn of the wheel, the TITLE TWISTER provides some impossibly silly, intriguingly obtuse and even a few fairly believable titles to start the creative kernels popping.

Of course, these are only titles, and what a child does with them will depend on the way he is able to use language and his imagination. For your "self-starters," the TITLE TWISTER will provide enough of an "angle" to stimulate a story. But for students who have difficulty putting together stories, a catchy title needs some developing. These students may benefit by a discussion of the story possibilities that the title brings to mind. A few open-ended questions about the suggested situation may help these students on their way. Your own creativity and common sense will extend the use of this aid.

In all, TITLE TWISTER offers 400 title combinations. Most students will find something in a set that size.

Order from: Teachers Exchange of San Francisco, 600 35th Ave., San Francisco, CA 94121. Grade level: 4–8. Cost: $1.25, Reading Reel; $.75, Title Twister. Add $.50 for postage and handling.

## THE MOLE FILM SERIES

☆ ☆ ☆ ☆ ☆ ☆ ☆ ☆ ☆

Zdenek Miler, the award-winning Czech animator, has done an outstanding job with this series of four films. The stories are charming, full of healthy action and excitement. The lifelike animals, particularly Mole, are beautifully characterized. Children find them a sheer delight, both visually and emotionally.

These films fit into that grab-bag category of "children's films/ language arts." Like children's books, they exist to provide pleasure. They're also excellent catalysts for the language arts activities of writing, discussion and dramatics. Each film is problem-centered. In THE MOLE AND THE GREEN STAR (8 minutes), Mole discovers a green stone that he is sure must be a star fallen from the heavens. Mole's problem: to get it back up there. THE MOLE AND THE HEDGEHOG (10 minutes) deals with an interpersonal problem with the lazy Hedgehog.

Mole finds a strange, round and shiny object in THE MOLE AND THE LOLLIPOP (9 minutes) and proceeds to take it home to investigate its properties. The last film in the series, THE MOLE AND THE UMBRELLA (9 minutes), has Mole and friends experimenting with another found object. The sense of adventure and discovery that fills the films should spill over into the classroom.

Order from: McGraw-Hill Films, 1221 Avenue of the Americas, New York, NY 10020. Grade level: K–8. Cost: Rental – $10 per film; purchase – $130, The Mole and the Green Star; $160, The Mole and the Hedgehog; $145, The Mole and the Lollipop; $145, The Mole and the Umbrella.

## THE VIEWER'S VOICE

Have you – or anyone else you know – ever written to the sponsor or producer of a television show? Of all pressure groups, one of the largest and least responsive, at least as measured by letter writing, is the TV viewing public. And it's a group in which children can have an active voice. Television is an important part of their environment, and they have a responsibility to voice their opinions about its offerings.

The beginning of a new TV season, with its rash of "premieres," seems an appropriate time to encourage viewer response. But "I like your show," or "I never watch you any more," needs the support of some specific becauses. Discuss what makes a situation comedy, or a family show, or a mystery show, enjoyable. Are the stories fresh and original, or are they predictable and repetitive? Which episodes of a program did you especially like? Which members of your family like the program? Which characters do you like best, and why do you like them? What improvements would you like to suggest? List the questions on the board for reference as students begin to write.

Before students take up the questions, they should gather some vital statistics: (1) the name of the show, (2) the station on which it is seen locally, (3) the day and time of the show. Some students may want to address letters to the stars – and conclude with a request for autographed pictures.

You might want to encourage students to respond similarly to TV "specials" or documentaries. The preparation and follow-up you arrange in connection with these shows – research, discussion – should provide background for students in writing their letters.

Student letters won't bring back "My Mother the Car," but writing letters in support or in protest can have far more far-reaching effects than you might suspect.

Idea by: Frank W. Sosnowski, Our Lady Queen of Peace School, Harper Woods, Mich.

## A STORY A STORY

☆ ☆ ☆ ☆ ☆ ☆ ☆ ☆ ☆

The "trickster" has always figured prominently in the folklore of black people – from Africa to the United States. A perpetual underdog, the trickster is a clever but physically weak character who constantly uses his brain to outwit individuals stronger than himself. This beautiful ten-minute color film, written and illustrated by Gail Haley, tells of an adventure of one of the best-known tricksters: Anansi the Spider.

Anansi (in this version not actually a spider but a weak old man with gangling, spiderlike arms and legs) wants to bring the sky god's box of stories to the people of earth so that humans will have stories, too. The sky god offers his treasure in trade for three formidable creatures: the leopard-of-the-terrible-teeth, the hornet-who-stings-like-fire and the fairy-whom-men-never-see. Anansi cleverly captures each of them, spins a web to the sky and delivers them up to the sky god. In return, Anansi receives the promised story box which he brings to earth and opens so that stories – including this one – spread to all corners of the earth.

The mood of this superb film is pure African – from the animation comprised of brilliantly colored woodcuts to the accent of the narrator and the accompanying beat and melody of African drums and kalimba.

The film is ideal for a study of Africa or as motivation for writing and discussion in language arts.

Order from: Weston Woods, Weston, CT 06880. Grade level: 2–12. Cost: $10 per day, rental; $150, purchase.

## Spelling Flunks the Test

by Masha Kabakow Rudman

*... and I called my dog Mischiff–Mischeff—Mischuf . . . ?*

Any teacher who's plowed through the pages of a spelling text knows there is absolutely no correlation between a child's performance on spelling-lesson chores and that child's real-life spelling proficiency. The child who spelled *Istanbul* perfectly on a Friday spelling test misspells it repeatedly in his social studies report. Spelling demons conquered for the weekly quiz return unvanquished when the child submits a creative-writing effort.

It's not for lack of trying that traditional spelling lessons fail to produce the intended effect. It's just that their tactics are an inappropriate means to a desired end. If a teacher wants to provide experiences with short-term memory tasks, then spelling as it is now taught is a fine idea. If a teacher wants to measure a child's facility in using some mnemonic devices, the spelling test is an adequate tool. But if the teacher is interested in helping children reach the ultimate spelling goal—the ability to reproduce words in writing with consistent accuracy—traditional spelling pedagogy is irrelevant.

In theory, spelling is the reverse side of the reading coin: reading primarily involves decoding skills, the unscrambling of symbols from print to speech, while spelling involves encoding—assigning written symbols to our language phonemes. In application, however, the simple reversal phenomenon just doesn't hold. Given the notorious inconsistencies of the English language, there is nevertheless a smaller chance for error in sounding out a word for reading purposes than there is in encoding the sounds of a word into written symbols. There are many more written symbol possibilities for a given sound than there are sound possibilities for a given symbol. There are only a few pronunciation possibilities for *rain*, but try listing the orthographic alternatives.

While reading can be accepted and taught as a skill, or a set of skills, spelling cannot be similarly classified. For the most part, people learn spellings, not how to spell.

**An Alternative to Spelling Lessons.** A curriculum shift appears to be in order. Spelling, as we know it, a separate emphasis with its own particular and peculiar pedagogy, must go. This is not to down-play the importance of spelling proficiency—a goal to be stressed for every child. Rather what is suggested is that spelling be absorbed into a larger context, within the scope of something that does require skill building, something that can be learned, and something that has relevance in the wider curriculum—namely, proofreading. Proofreading tasks will out of necessity include a great deal of spelling practice. And proofreading should be an integral part of science, social studies, mathematics—any curriculum area that requires some form of writing.

The first pair of spelling-related proofreading tasks is to recognize and then correct a misspelled word. But how do you recognize that a word has been misspelled if you're not sure how it's *supposed* to look? By being constantly suspicious and skeptical. Students must develop an appreciation for the need to question the spelling of every word they are not absolutely sure about. If this means that proofreading assignments will require a child to refer to a spelling resource for a great percent of the words in a report, so be it. Words checked often enough will eventually be learned.

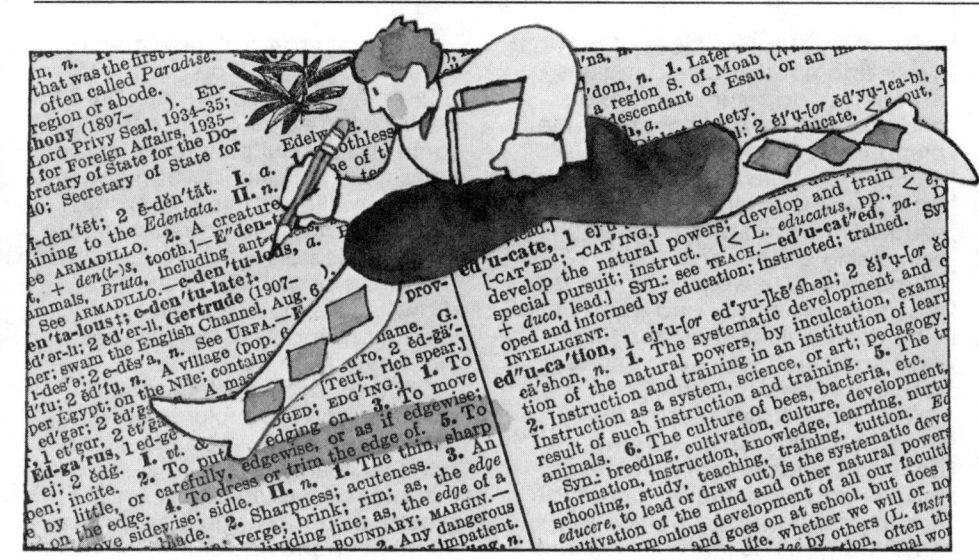

The implication here is that a good proofreading program will include enjoyable, uncumbersome exercises for effectively using the dictionary. Other sources of correct spellings can be glossaries and word lists that appear in student texts. Newspapers, magazine articles and books that the child has read are often useful places for locating correct spellings. The child or the class collectively may compile word lists as references. And don't overlook human resources. Children may locate other people whom they judge to be good spellers and ask them for correct spellings. Sometimes a child will learn to check out an answer by asking more than one person. All the better. That child is practicing some excellent research skills.

**Creative Work Need Not Be Slop Work.** The shift from spelling to proofreading should also help put one curriculum wives' tale to rest. The old argument that creative writing and correct spelling do not mix is utter nonsense. Creativity should not be used as an excuse for sloppy work, and it need not be used as such if we accept proofreading as the second step in all our daily work. Proofreading, by definition, is an after-the-fact activity, and thus in no way should it inhibit the primary writing act. In fact, a second reading can do no less than enhance the first rough draft. A classroom visit by almost any local newspaper writer or editor should assist in communicating this concept. Indeed, a classroom newspaper or magazine is an excellent vehicle for providing proofreading practice and for motivating the students to deliver accurate work.

Spelling is only the tip of the proofreading iceberg. All the language skills of punctuation, capitalization, word usage, etc., fall under this umbrella curriculum area. Proofreading, unlike some of the conventional language arts exercises and spelling lessons, is totally functional. Children became proficient for the sake of clarity, not to receive 100 percent in memory and regurgitation.

**Copy Editor's note:** An excellent quick reference source for proofreaders of all ages is *Webster's Instant Word Guide* (Merriam, 1972, $2.95), a pocket-sized book containing 35,000 words spelled and divided.

Masha Kabakow Rudman is associate professor of education at the University of Massachusetts, Amherst, and codirector of the Integrated Day Program.

# SPELLING SURVEY

Does your dictionary tend to fall open at the page for "accommodate," or "relevance," or "changeable," or maybe "desperate?" Most adults who are otherwise quite literate, capable and self-sufficient will admit that they find certain words hard to spell. And in the cause of correct spelling, numerous mnemonic devices have been conjured up. A spelling survey conducted by your class may uncover some fascinating data about the tortuous trails to spelling accuracy.

First, have students collect and analyze their own spelling errors over a period of weeks. By studying the various misspellings, students may be able to discover some patterns and also speculate on the reasons for making errors: the problems of silent letters, sound-alike letters, doubling letters and dropping letters (when to), and a host of foreign-language enrichments such as "eau."

Next, devise a survey sheet with questions such as the following: (1) What words do you find difficult to spell? (2) Why do you think these words give you trouble? (3) Do you have any tricks to help you spell words (not just the words you've mentioned)? (4) Why do you think people misspell words?

Each student is then responsible for interviewing three persons who are at least 16 years old—friends, neighbors, parents. A master list of difficult words is compiled and a frequency of response tallied for each word. Words from this list may be selected on the students' recommendation to add to their regular allotment. (Individual goals for mastering these new words may be contracted.)

A compilation of the survey's "reasons for misspellings" can be compared with the reasons the students have given. A study of the tricks people use for remembering spellings may yield some valuable devices worthy of adoption.

The spelling survey may underscore the fact that spelling is a personal thing, that people of all ages may have difficulty with spellings, and that the ways of remembering spellings are as individual as the people who rely on them.

Idea by: Lola R. Mapes,
Des Moines, Iowa.

## B.L.T. IS G.O.O.D.

Food is a favorite fantasy among children, sparked by the appetites of the growing years. To spread some of this food fascination over your phonics class activities, try making imaginary sandwiches.

Suggested materials for this project include brown wrapping paper, crayons or markers, scissors and paste. From the brown paper each child cuts two slices of bread. (More imaginative bread makers may select paper in other colors and textures. But don't overlook the blend reinforcing potential of phrases like "brown bread.")

Now for the fillings. Prepare squares of paper and mark each with a single letter or blend—whatever you're working on. All the letters go into a box and each child may draw out three or four. (More if the sandwich is to be a grinder, sub, hero, hoagie, or just BIG.)

The letters drawn dictate the sandwich filling. Thus, a H.G.W. becomes a taste treat of honey, grapes and watermelon, or maybe hominy, goulash and waffles. Anything goes as long as the items begin with the correct letters. (Food items are favored, but if somebody wants to fill a sandwich with hammocks, grommets and widgets, to each his own.)

Children now draw, color and cut out their filling items, or they may find some of the less exotic things in magazine pictures. Children then make individual sandwiches by pasting their fillings onto one of their bread slices. The letters describing the sandwich may be pasted—or copied—onto the top slice. Slices may be joined at one edge so sandwiches may be opened and "read."

A different sort of sandwich-making session could yield an activity for a learning station. Have all "bread" cut from the same color and in the same shape. Cut pictures of single items from old phonics workbooks to use as fillings. (This is to ensure that the pictures will be identifiable to most children without interpretation.) The letters prepared for the letter-draw will be those representing initial consonants of the pictures that have been cut out.

Children draw out their quotas of letters, find the pictures as before and prepare the slices. The slices can then be mixed up to be sorted out later by individuals or small groups as a matching activity. You might even provide sandwich bags for the properly paired sandwich slices.

Bon appétit!

Idea by: Linda Gutlohn,
San Francisco Unified School District,
San Francisco, Calif.

## PRINT IT!

How can your beginning writers write without putting pencil to paper? With a homemade print kit. Letter blocks and an ink pad can expand the horizons of your not-so-confident young pencil-pushers.

Making a print kit involves few

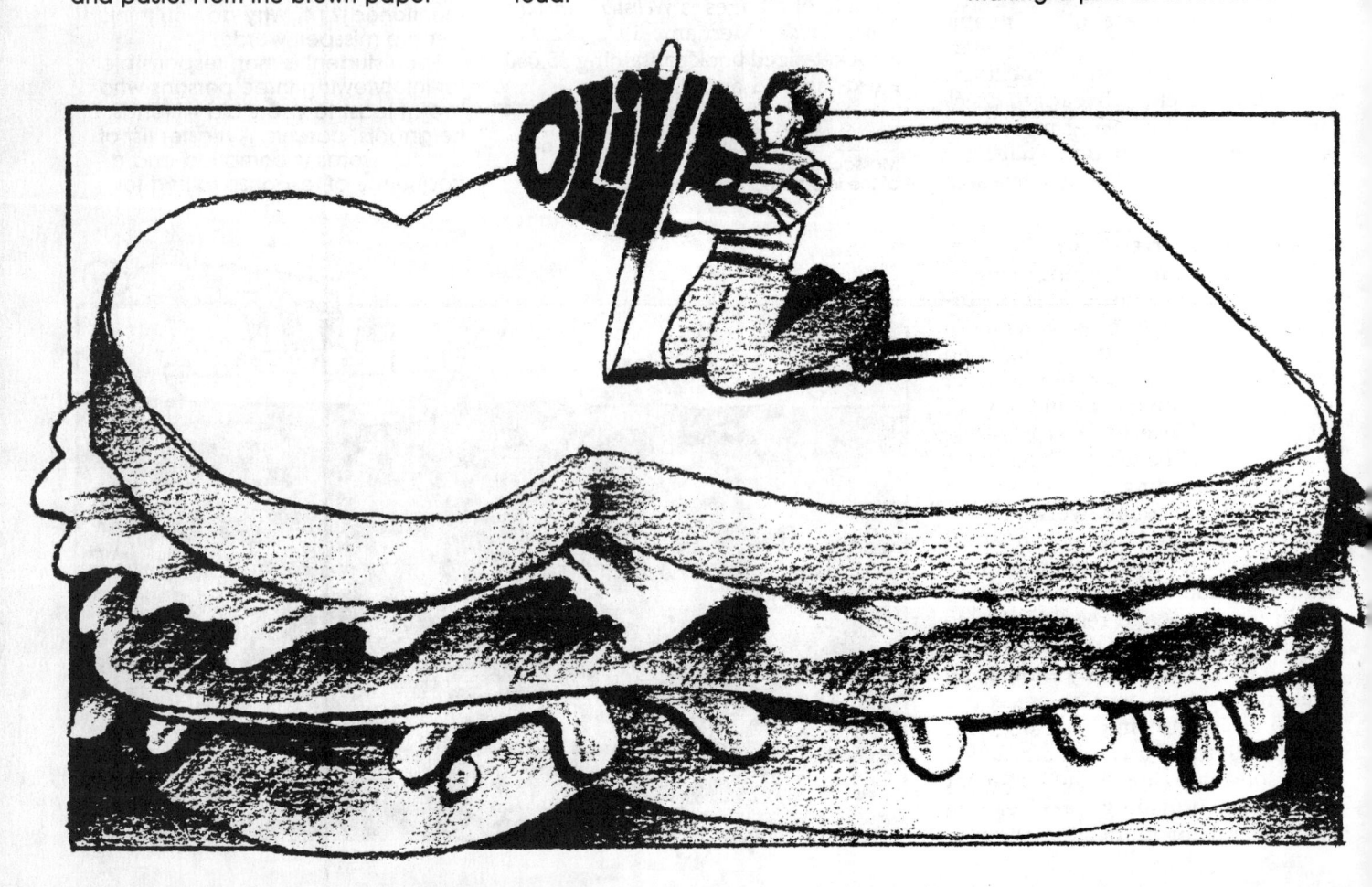

materials (and is a project that upper grade students might like to try on their own). Materials include:
- plain wooden blocks, one-cubic-inch size (these may be purchased through math materials suppliers);
- flocked Con-Tact paper (feels like velvet or felt and may be found where wallpaper is sold);
- plastic ice cube trays (to keep blocks in order);
- large shallow box to hold the ice cube trays;
- soap dish with cover;
- sponge cut to fit soap dish.

Procedure:
1. Draw or trace your letters right on the Con-Tact backing, which is marked into one-inch squares—accommodatingly enough.
2. Cut out letters. Use a razor knife for a more accurate job.
3. Peel off backing and stick each letter onto a cube. The letter should be backwards, which will make it right when printed.
4. On the opposite face of the cube copy the letter with a flow pen. In this way you can identify the blocks when the inked side is down.
5. Dampen sponge and insert it into the soap dish to make an ink pad.
6. Make "ink" of two parts poster paint and one part white glue. Apply mixture to ink pad. (You may want to experiment with ink recipes to determine what works best for you.)
7. Print it! Don't expect absolutely "clean" results. Some of the cube may show around the edges.

Depending on the ages of the printers, the printed products might be signs, labels, flash cards, spelling words or dozens of other things. You probably won't get any lengthy manuscripts, but you may acquire some very professional-looking DOOR, TABLE, or HAMSTER labels.

Idea by: Patricia Hall,
Patterson School, Fremont, Calif.

## WRITE ON!

☆ ☆ ☆ ☆ ☆ ☆ ☆ ☆ ☆

Most teachers seem to be engaged in a never-ending quest for good creative writing activities. If you're among them, WRITE ON! should help meet your need. WRITE ON! consists of two separate boxes of four-by-six-inch activity cards: one box is a teacher idea file of 70 creative-writing assignments; the other contains 50 writing activities to be used directly by students. Try the following activity from the student cards:

"The Stamp Takes A Trip
"You are a stamp living happily in the post office. One day someone buys you and puts you on an important letter.
"Write a story telling: Who bought you? Where are you going? What is inside of this very important letter?"

Teacher assignments are organized by categories: "Writer's Workshop," "Motivators," "Word Power," "Flair for Fantasy," "Holiday Happenings" and "Potpourri." The cards tell what materials, preparation and background are necessary for each writing activity. Included within the cards are instructions for setting up a classroom writing center.

The student cards are plasticized for durability, and activities are written in language upper primary students can understand on their own. Teachers may adapt the student cards for use with younger children. An introduction to the student cards supplies teachers with alternative methods for presenting the activities.

Order from: Educational Insights, Inc., 20435 S. Tillman Ave., Carson, CA 90746. Grade level: 3–6. Cost: $4.85, 70 teacher cards, #9124; $4.95, 50 student cards, #9125. Add 10 percent for postage and handling. Payment must accompany orders from individuals.

## TO THE BEST OF MY RECOLLECTION...

English period. You're using the overhead projector. Class attention is focused on the screen. Enter Mr. Smith, a fellow faculty member, to begin the enactment of a prearranged scene.

Mr. Smith tells you he needs the overhead projector this period. In fact, he signed up weeks in advance for this particular time. You say you'll be finished in a few minutes anyway. He insists he needs it now. You try reasoning with him.

His voice goes up a notch. You stand your ground. (Stifle the urge to overact, or you'll blow the whole thing.) At last he leaves—with or without the projector; you decide. End of scene.

Immediately have the students take out paper and pencils. Ask for written answers to the following:
1. Does Mr. Smith wear glasses? How was he dressed? What colors was he wearing?
2. Was Mr. Smith carrying anything?
3. What time did Mr. Smith come into the room? How long did he stay?
4. What started the argument?
5. How would you describe the actions and voices of the persons involved?
6. Give some direct quotes from the discussion.

(You can add other questions, of course.)

When the students are finished, have them read their answers aloud. The reports will probably vary widely. Individual opinions will enter into descriptions of the action. Feelings about the participants will influence what students thought they heard or saw. Have students listen for the points of difference and the areas of general agreement. Have discussion of the reasons for the differences in answers.

Have students tell how accurate they feel their own reports are. For instance, how would each person rate his answer on a scale of "absolutely sure" to "really couldn't say for certain?"

Besides waking up—and possibly shaking up—a few students, this activity serves other purposes: (1) It can help students gain experience in reporting—describing general action and important details. (2) It can help students appreciate the difficulty of recalling accurately an event they've witnessed.

Be sure to exonerate Mr. Smith, in case some of the kids forget the whole thing was a put-on.

Idea by: Ben Neideigh,
New Hampton, Iowa.

## THE MARBLE

☆ ☆ ☆ ☆ ☆ ☆ ☆ ☆ ☆

A boy's relentless pursuit of a lost marble takes the viewer on a voyage from the real into the surreal in this 10-minute color film by Jan Oonk.

After polishing a favorite marble, a boy becomes involved in a game with some friends until his marble disappears into a gutter. In vain, he attempts to find it.

While the boy is figuring out what to do next, a man in a horse-drawn carriage stops and lifts the marble from the gutter — as if it were a treasure he had been sent to find. Hopeful of retrieving the marble, the boy picks up his scooter and follows the man. The scene turns into a classic chase as the carriage and scooter pick up speed — the man constantly looking behind to see how close the boy is getting. At last the boy catches up, only to see the man hand the marble to a train conductor. Once again, the chase resumes. This time the boy's frantic pushing of the scooter, in an effort to keep up with the train, becomes so frustrating that the scooter is suddenly and inexplicably transformed into a motorcycle with the boy astride.

The last person to accept the marble is a military officer in some unnamed army. He tosses the marble into the barrel of a cannon just as it fires. The boy chases after and catches the marble only to be pursued by the entire army, guns and tanks blasting. In the end, the boy puts the marble to his eye, and through it, sees a path through the soldiers to freedom.

The unnarrated film is seen primarily from the boy's viewpoint, but on occasion it is through the distorted, imaginary eye of the marble. This latter effect combines with an eerie sound track and some events of fantasy to produce a mildly surrealistic story that will provoke discussion and writing even among primary-age kids.

Order from: Pyramid Films, Box 1048, Santa Monica, CA 90406. Grade level: K–high school. Cost: $15, rental; $150, purchase. Add $2 for postage.

---

## Simple Word Games and Books to Make

### by Celia Houghton

**Word Bingo** (for pre-readers)
If five players are involved you need five sheets of manila paper and some chips (or construction paper cut into small squares).

Rule the manila paper into nine rectangles and write one word in each space. Write the same words on each of the five sheets, but mix up the order in which they are written. Cut up one of the sheets so that you have nine separate word cards. These are for the "caller," who sits at a table facing the other four players, holding the cards.

Give a sheet of the ruled paper and some chips to each of the four players. The caller then "reads," with your help, a word off one of the cards and places the card on the table, so that the players can see it. Each covers the word on his sheet with a chip. He doesn't have to be able to read the word; he is matching it.

The caller continues to read off the words. The first child to cover a row of three words (horizontal or vertical) wins the round and becomes the caller.

After a few rounds, you'll find that the children begin to recognize the words. The important thing is to stick with the same words for far longer than seems necessary, adding a word or two but keeping the basic words constantly in practice.

**Finding Words** (for one or more children)
Use a book, chips or small objects children can count with, and a paper cup. Write a word on the cup and ask the child to place a chip in it each time he finds the word in his book. If two or more children play, give each a cup or dissimilar chips. Use only high-frequency words.

**Twins** (for two children)
Rule two sheets of manila paper into 24 rectangles; write each of the dozen words you are working with in two rectangles on one of the sheets. Leave the other sheet blank. Cut up the sheet with the words on it, then mix up the words and have the children place each word in a space on the blank sheet, face down. (You can obviously adapt this game for use with any number of words.)

When all the word cards are down, the first player turns up two. If they are "twins," he wins them. The second player then turns up two cards. If the first play did not produce "twins," the second player only turns up one card. (There must always be at least two cards face up.) The players read the words as they play, keeping any matches they turn up. When all the cards have been paired and taken, the player with the most cards wins the game and the children read their words to each other.

**Making Books**
Good heavy-duty class books can be made with construction paper pages and heavy cardboard covers, using nuts and bolts (and washers) to fasten covers and pages together.

Cut through the cardboard on dotted line and join the cut edges with one- or two-inch plastic tape, leaving a little space between the edges.

Less sturdy but just as useful books can be made with construction paper for the covers and newsprint for the pages. Fold the sheets and staple at the fold, outside to inside. Try making the cover shape fit the subject.

Celia Houghton is director of the The Teachers' Center at Greenwich, Conn.

# CREATIVE MOVEMENT & PLAY

## KING-SIZE KICKBALL

Proposed rule changes are certain to cause all kinds of debate and discussion if you're dealing with major-league baseball. But changing kickball (or baseball or softball) rules on your home playground shouldn't raise too much dust. Why not alter the rules to get more kids into the action at one time—cutting down on waiting in line and its attendant woes?

Try increasing the number of bases. The addition of two, three or even four bases can open up new defensive positions and provide opportunity for more players to be on base at once. The base path may actually extend into the regular outfield. This means more chances for defensive plays at that part of the field, so more kids can be where the action is. And imagine a grand-slam home run that brings home six or seven runs!

The change in the number of bases may increase the total distance around the circuit and back to home plate. (Distance between bases would, of course, vary according to the grade level of the players.) If this change tends to cut down too much on scoring, other rule changes may be needed. How about allowing four or five outs per inning?

Even if a kickball league—American, National or perhaps a WKL—arises, it seems likely they'd approve of changes like these. And anything that allows greater participation ought to boost morale around the kickball clubhouse.

Idea by: Earl Hoffman,
Northern Illinois University, De Kalb, Ill.

## THE LANGUAGE OF MOVEMENT

[Note: Dr. Van Slooten planned these activities around the use of hula hoops, one for each child in the group. This means you might (1) put out an APB to let other classes know you need hula hoops, (2) ask your phys. ed. people about getting hoops, (3) use large boxes open at both ends and cut down to a manageable height.] Moving along now...

Movement exploration challenges children to explore ways of moving. But children must also comprehend the language of the challenges. These spoken commands can be used to develop vocabulary of place and position — part of most kindergarten or first grade programs.

Spread out hoops (or boxes) on the gym floor and have children try some of the following:

1. Find a hoop and sit inside it.
2. Jump into the hoop. Jump out.
3. Skip around the hoop.
4. Move around inside the hoop without using your feet.
5. Pick up the hoop without using your hands. Put it on the floor.
6. Put the hoop behind you, against the back of your legs; now turn slowly around until the hoop is in front of you.
7. Choose a partner. Both sit inside one hoop. Hold a hoop above you.
8. Hold one hoop so your partner can crawl through it. Hold the other hoop so your partner can crawl under it.
9. Place your hoops on the floor. Leave just enough room to walk between them. (Some children enjoy imagining the area outside the hoop as being "in the water.")

As a culminating activity, you might consider an obstacle course using the hoops. Directions for the course would be built around the position words that have been developed. (Directions may be given one step at a time, or in several steps that must be recalled in order.) Children may wish to design obstacle courses for others to try.

Or how about a game of musical hoops? Around and around the hoops while the music plays. Then jump inside the hoop nearest you — if someone else doesn't get there first!

Idea by: Philip Van Slooten,
School of Physical Education,
University of Illinois, Chicago, Ill.

## A GUIDE TO MOVEMENT EXPLORATION

☆ ☆ ☆ ☆ ☆ ☆ ☆ ☆

The "sound mind in a sound body" philosophy is getting new attention with the emulation of British open school practices. For some time researchers have seen a relationship between sensory-motor experiences and perceptual development. And the British "movement exploration" programs, aimed at sensory-motor development and self-awareness, seem to provide a positive foundation for the academic side of education.

The movement exploration approach to physical education is concerned with body movement in response to problems or challenges. (If the word "challenge" seems too strong, just try skipping backward sometime.) All the children in a class can be working on a challenge at the same time. No waiting for turns. You get the most child-miles out of every minute.

A GUIDE TO MOVEMENT EXPLORATION is a concise and useful treatment of the subject. While introductory material clarifies goals and takes into consideration matters of safety and discipline, the largest portion of the 74 pages is devoted to actual questions and challenges and sample lesson plans for kindergarten through grade six on a weekly and yearly basis. The questions and challenges cover such areas as locomotion activities, using apparatus, and rhythmic themes. Suggestions for an activity are brief, often just naming the action. Some plans include references to specific pages in the books from a reading list in the appendix.

The appendix also describes and illustrates apparatus items and layouts for obstacle courses. Charts relate development of particular motor skills to specific pieces of equipment.

The book is compact (digest size, softcover) and content is to the point. Though treatment of the subject is not exhaustive, it has proved helpful to many teachers — as evidenced by the fact that it's in its 20th printing.

Physical illiterates — and others — arise. Your class is ready to move.

Order from: Peek Publications, P.O. Box 11065, Palo Alto, CA 94306. Grade level: Teachers of grades K – 6. Cost: $2.50. No charge for postage and handling on prepaid orders.

## INEXPENSIVE EQUIPMENT FOR GAMES, PLAY, AND PHYSICAL ACTIVITY

☆ ☆ ☆ ☆ ☆ ☆ ☆ ☆ ☆

This 63-page paperback by Charles B. Corbin offers about three dozen ideas for turning throwaway items into low-cost play and physical education equipment. Descriptions for each type of equipment include a list of needed materials, construction instructions, activities and, in many cases, teaching suggestions.

What can you do with an empty bleach bottle? Simply cut out the bottom, tape the rough edges, and you've got a "bleach-bottle ball scoop." Now you're set to have a Whiffle Ball catch, or play scoop and throw — a large group game whose rules are described in the text. So the next time you're greeted by an empty physical education supply closet, don't despair; just sit down with your class and construct your own equipment.

Order from: Wm. C. Brown Company Publishers, 2460 Kerper Blvd., Dubuque, IA 52001. Grade level: Teachers of all grades. Cost: $2.95 plus $.50 postage and handling. Payment must accompany order.

## BE A FROG, A BIRD, OR A TREE
### by Rachel Carr

Children and their teachers will want to dive right into this introduction to yoga. Carr's enthusiasm for her subject shines through the book, which offers practical ways for kids to express themselves physically while loosening their limbs. Photographs show just what a "rocking horse" or "bird" should look like. An added bonus is Carr's description of her success with language- and hearing-impaired children.

DOUBLEDAY, $5.95 (list), $4.46 (school price). Ages 3 – 10. See page 151 for ordering information.

# TIPS FOR AN ALTERNATIVE RECESS

by Stuart Miller

### INFINITY BALL

A variation on volleyball. Ball, net and two teams as usual, but the teams can be mixed as to age, sex and physical prowess without anyone risking failure. The object of both teams is to keep the ball in the air, each team hitting the ball three times on its side of the net and on the third hit, sending it across the net in a way that sets up the other team to do the same. If the ball drops, blame is shared equally between the team that missed it and the team that delivered it. Infinity Ball was played at the New Games Tournament, sponsored by Stewart Brand, the originator of THE WHOLE EARTH CATALOGUE. Spectators remarked on the cheerfulness and energy of the mixed teams, and with no losers, the lack of grimness.

### BEANBAG RELAY

A way of helping younger children improve their coordination — again, without winners or losers. After two teams have lined up, a person from each runs out. One has a beanbag, which he throws to the member of the other team. They throw it back and forth four times and then run back to their respective teams. The rest go in turn. The goal is simply to complete the exercise; no score is kept. Variation: members from each team hop, jump or skip out and back, trying to finish at exactly the same time.

### RELAXATION EXERCISE

Have the pupils lie down with closed eyes. In a soothing voice, ask them to be silent and let a few moments pass so their breathing can become regular. Then ask each student to pay attention to his/her right foot. Ask him to hold the foot tense for ten seconds, then relax. (It's OK for each student to hold his breath as he tenses, but remind him to breathe as he relaxes.) Ask the students to repeat the process with the left foot. Continue the process all the way up the body, including the eyes, ears and top of the head. At the end, give students time to enjoy the experience of having their bodies completely relaxed.

### CHOOSE A COLOR

This is a standard creative drama exercise, but it can be used just as well in a gym period. Have each child silently choose a color. With eyes closed, have them imagine coming close to the color — in whatever form it takes for them. Then have each child enact the color in free, creative movement. Usually, children see that each child's movement is unique — even when the colors chosen are the same.

### IMAGINATION TRAINING

Children are asked to perform a task — running down the field or perhaps doing a gymnastic maneuver. Then they are asked to sit or lie quietly, eyes closed, and visualize themselves doing the task perfectly. Then they perform the task again. The results usually are better the second time.

### RESOURCES

▶ For information about movement education consultants who give classes and workshops in your area, write: Margie R. Hanson, Consultant in Elementary Physical Education, American Alliance for Health, Physical Education and Recreation, 1201 16th St., N.W., Washington, DC 20036.

▶ For information about new sports, games and activities, write: Mike Spino, Director, The Sports Center, Esalen Institute, 1793 Union St., San Francisco, CA 94123. The Sports Center features workshops and courses in subjects ranging from the sociopolitical implications of sports to sensory awareness, aikido and Rolfing.

▶ For a useful framework for reconceptualizing awareness of the whole person, read Roberto Assagioli's books PSYCHOSYNTHESIS: A MANUAL OF PRINCIPLES AND TECHNIQUES (Viking, 1971, $2.75 paperback) and THE ACT OF WILL (Viking, 1973, $10).

▶ For information on lectures, seminars and workshops in the psychosynthesis approach and for other readings, write: Psychosynthesis Institute, 576 Everett, Palo Alto, CA 94301 or Psychosynthesis Research Foundation, Room 1902, 40 East 49th St., New York, NY 10017.

Stuart Miller is an educator and director of the Institute for the Study of Humanistic Medicine.

# SCIENCE

## BUTTERFLY GARDEN

☆ ☆ ☆ ☆ ☆ ☆ ☆ ☆ ☆ ☆

Explaining to a child that a caterpillar changes into a butterfly is one thing; showing him is another. But showing isn't always possible, especially if you happen to be exploring insects during the cold months. This garden kit, however, will enable you and your students to watch the metamorphosis of a butterfly, from larva to adult, no matter what the time of year.

The kit contains an easily assembled display box – a colorful cardboard cube with cellophane windows for viewing the mature butterflies – and the materials for feeding them. It also includes a coupon with which to send for the caterpillars at your convenience. Between three and five caterpillars should arrive within ten days.

The tiny caterpillars come in a transparent plastic container complete with food. Within a week or two they grow to well over an inch, attach themselves to the top of the plastic container and spin their cocoons. After another week or ten days they emerge as butterflies. Either late in the pupal stage (cocoon) or early in the adult stage (butterfly), they can be placed in the display box for observation and feeding.

It is possible to purchase the larva culture and the display box either independently or as a unit. If the caterpillars are purchased separately, the mature butterflies can be housed in an empty aquarium and fed from a paper-towel wick placed in a bottle of sugar water. Also available is a "Butterfly Garden School Kit," which has enough materials for 18 students to independently raise their own butterflies.

Order from: Nasco West, P.O. Box 3837, Modesto, CA 95352. Grade level: Primary – high school. Cost: $6.75, display box with larva culture; $4, coupon for larva culture only; $3.35, display box only; $18, school kit.

## 118 SCIENCE

## PIGS!

☆ ☆ ☆ ☆ ☆ ☆ ☆ ☆ ☆

You may not be able to make a silk purse out of a sow's ear, but you can create one magnificent teaching unit out of Churchill Films' prize-winner PIGS!

The 11-minute color film shows pigs "at home," and if you ever want to discuss the idea of doing your own thing, here is the place to start. There is rooting, eating, mud-rolling and grunting. (You'll never again believe that pigs go "oink.")

The film grips 3-year-olds and 80-year-olds with the same force. PIGS! is accompanied by a delightful musical score and has no narration. All discussion is generated from what students observe and feel. It has started debates on such topics as: Who's dirtier—people or pigs? And, Why do people use animal names for put-downs? Some observers see the film as a metaphor for our society. Others insist that the lesson is "Don't eat ham."

Whether to teach observation skills or to start a discussion among teachers, parents and children at a home-and-school meeting, PIGS! is highly recommended.

Order from: Churchill Films, 662 N. Robertson Blvd., Los Angeles, CA 90069. Grade level: Primary–high school. Cost: $15, rental; $140, purchase.

## CITY ROCKS CITY BLOCKS AND THE MOON

**Written and photographed by Edward Gallob**

This book is a rich storehouse of information about exploring urban geology, a fond pursuit of the photographer-author. The crisp black-and-white photographs introduce the reader to such city rocks as sandstone, marble and slate, and are a compelling invitation to go out into the streets to observe and collect.

SCRIBNER'S, $6.95. Ages 6–9.
See page 151 for ordering information.

## TEACHING SCIENCE WITH GARBAGE

☆ ☆ ☆ ☆ ☆ ☆ ☆ ☆ ☆

For most of us, garbage is an unpleasant fact of life, something we would prefer not to notice or think about. We treat garbage as if it were the final scene in the drama of consumption. Because we fail to realize that, utilized properly, garbage can return precious substance to nature, we use it instead to muck up our air, water and land.

What to do about it? Talk is cheap but it seldom changes attitudes. We've got to do some hands-on learning—for ourselves and with our students. TEACHING SCIENCE WITH GARBAGE by Albert and Vivian Schatz can help do just that. This 60-page "interdisciplinary approach to environmental education" is packed with dirt-cheap experiments requiring not much more than leftovers from lunch and a few elixirs found in almost everyone's medicine cabinet or kitchen shelf.

The well-illustrated activities are open ended. You don't follow the inductive method to a "right" answer. Rather, you and your students will have to experiment, watch carefully and puzzle over the results.

In addition to the several dozen experiments and projects, the book provides a historical perspective on garbage with essays like "George Washington—Compost Scientist" and "Did Composts Provide Ancient Man With Fire?"

Experiments include: "Making A Mold Garden" and "Making A Water-Logged Landfill."

The booklet may not teach you and yours to love garbage, but it should give you a better understanding of its role in the cycle of life.

Order from: Rodale Press, 33 East Minor St., Emmaus, PA 18049. Grade level: Teachers of all grades. Cost: $4.95 (list); $3.96 (school price). Add $.21 postage and handling.

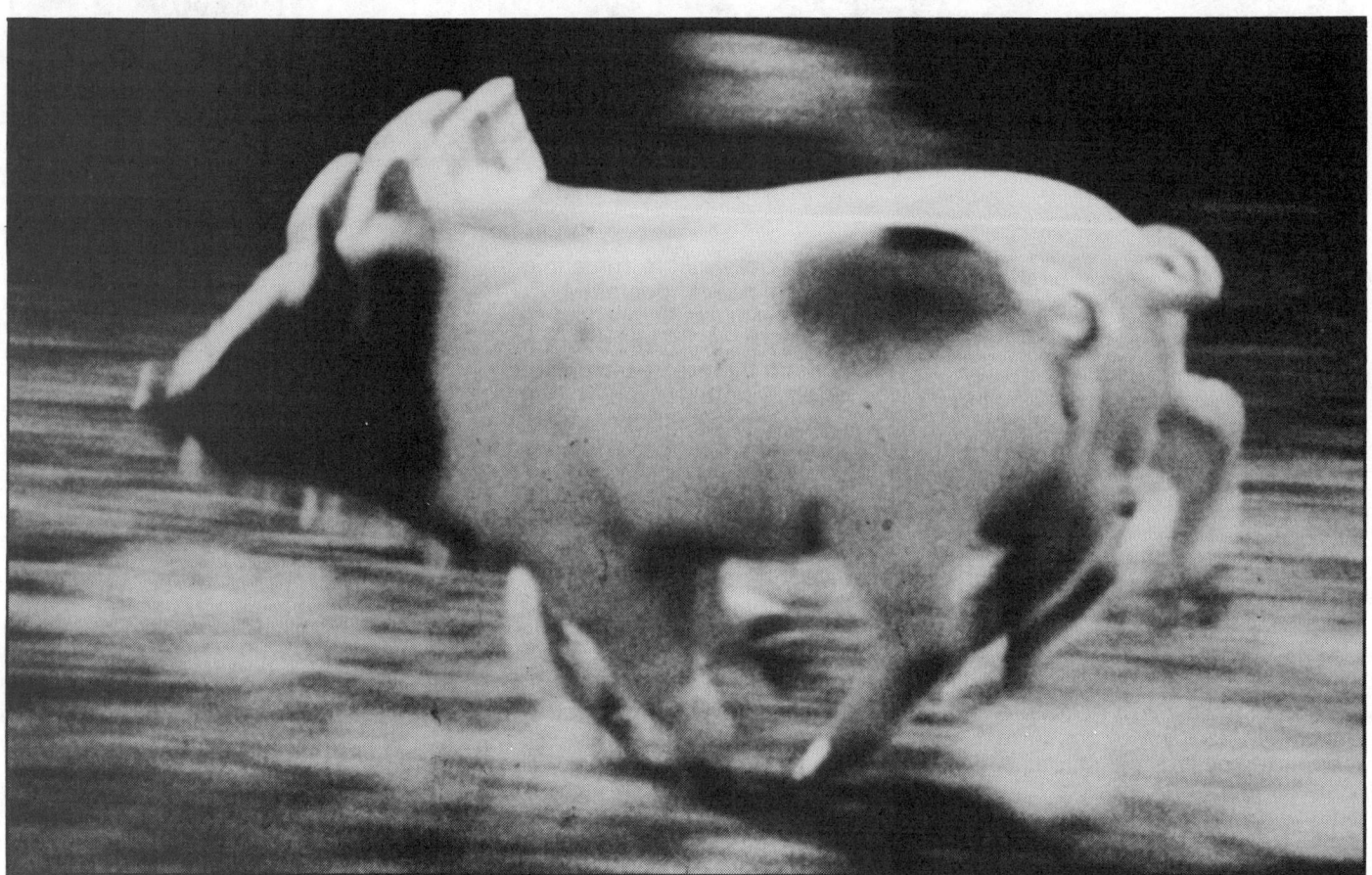

# Selecting an Elementary Science Program

by Sigmund Abeles

ESS, SCIS, SAPA, CIS—these may be familiar acronyms if you're struggling in the soup of selecting a new science program for your school. Or perhaps you're just dipping an experimental spoon in the pot and feel you need some help. Small wonder: Choosing the right program can be a real chore.

You might find the following questions helpful as you go about evaluating and comparing programs:

1. *What kind of content coverage does the program provide? Is it the kind of coverage you want?*

Programs will vary in the ways they treat and the emphasis they give the areas of biological, physical and earth sciences. You'll want to check to see if the content suits your particular needs.

2. *Which program format—the textbook approach or the non-textbook approach—seems most workable?*

A number of new science programs do not use a basic text. If you're well into the selection process, you'll recognize Elementary Science Study (ESS), Science—A Process Approach (SAPA) and Science Curriculum Improvement Study (SCIS) as representative of this approach. These programs are designed around activities, materials and equipment. The organization of these programs varies from the tightly structured type to those providing the sparest guidelines for maximum flexibility.

Textbook programs also provide for the growing emphasis on student involvement. These programs vary in approach and the degree of activity orientation.

A major consideration is whether or not you will be comfortable working with a particular program. Student appeal is critically important, but not exclusively so.

3. *What kinds of materials do the programs provide and how much do they cost?*

Non-textbook programs usually consist of kits or materials stored in cardboard cabinets, plus teacher guide materials. Most of the recent vintage textbook programs consist of a text and teacher's guide, plus a range of materials to be used in carrying out the suggested activities. Additional materials such as films, filmstrips, tests and supplementary readers may be available as well.

For some programs you will have to purchase materials yourself. For others the equipment is furnished down to the last pin and balloon. In reviewing a program, check to see if the suggested activity materials are provided. The availability of equipment—or ease of acquiring it—may be an important consideration in your choice of a program.

Costs of initiating programs range from as little as $50 to over $1,000 for a class of 30. The structure of the program, amounts of equipment provided, as well as other factors, determine the differences in price.

Another consideration: When analyzing finances, you need to look not only at initial costs but also at the costs of upkeep—some materials are consumable.

4. *Is special in-service training needed?*

Most programs require some kind of orientation. In the case of non-textbook programs, an ongoing inservice program is particularly important. Program publishers often provide for in-service programs. Or you may want to contact other districts using the same program. Science education personnel at colleges and state education departments are other possible sources of help in setting up in-service programs.

5. *What facilities are needed?*

Most programs require no special facilities or room arrangements, but you'll need to plan for ample storage space, particularly for the laboratory-kit type programs. Close proximity of utilities, especially water, is a definite plus.

Selecting a science program requires a good amount of time, effort and money. If you are involved in such a task, considering the questions above can be a help. Then, armed with your answers, you can take appropriate action at the next level. Happy hunting!

Sigmund Abeles is a science consultant, Connecticut State Department of Education.

## 120 SCIENCE

## HOME-GRO MUSHROOM GARDEN

☆ ☆ ☆ ☆ ☆ ☆ ☆ ☆ ☆

Beyond what we see on the grocer's shelf, most of us know little about mushrooms. Using the HOME-GRO MUSHROOM GARDEN, students won't be able to solve all the mysteries of mushrooms, but they will be able to plant a crop from which several harvests can be made.

The garden kit comes with all the requisites for growing mushrooms: a plastic pot, compost containing spores, soil, ventilation collar and top, sprinkling jar, detailed growing and harvesting instructions, and a booklet of mushroom recipes.

The mushrooms available for harvesting a month or so after planting are, happily, of the edible variety.

Order from: Edmund Scientific Co., 380 Edscorp Bldg., Barrington, NJ 08007. Grade level: K–12. Cost: $5.95. Payment must accompany order.

## CITY LEAVES CITY TREES
### by Edward Gallob

Winner of the Childrens Science Book Award of The New York Academy of Science, this book of photos and photograms will help children learn more about the trees around them. It will also serve as an easy-to-use tree-identification guide. By bringing in a leaf and matching it with one in the book, readers will both learn the name of the tree and see a picture of it.

SCRIBNER'S, $6.95. Ages 7–13.
See page 151 for ordering information.

## GRASS ON THE HALF-SHELL

This grass-growing project, in addition to being a high-interest activity for young children, helps develop new understanding about plants and their growth.

For materials you'll need old kitchen sponges, grass seed containing a high content of fast-germinating rye, some egg-shell halves, and felt pens, food coloring, paint or commercial dye.

After the shells have been colored, a piece of soaked sponge should be cut and fitted to go inside. Then sprinkle one-half to one teaspoon of grass seed on top of the sponge. Each child should spoon water in his egg shell daily, making sure the seed does not dry out.

Within four days the first green shoots spring up from their sponge planting, and in seven to ten days the grass is so thick and luxurious it can be trimmed with scissors. When the grass reaches the desired height, add straw flowers or other decorations.

As the grass grows, the kids can lift the sponge and see the grass roots growing through it. They will also discover that the grass grows toward light, and it should, therefore, be turned daily.

Idea by: Necy E. Hales,
Moppets Pre-School, Menlo Park, Calif.

# SCIENCE

## MICROSCOPE
☆ ☆ ☆ ☆ ☆ ☆ ☆ ☆

No need to feel on edge when the kids are using one of these microscopes — they're inexpensive, extremely durable and easy to operate. Made of hard plastic, they come in two different powers, 30x and 50x.

They can be used for indoor or outdoor activities. The slide stage has a tiny hole that will hold a drop of pond water. An adjustable mirror reflects natural or electric light indoors.

Each microscope comes with a compound viewing attachment that can raise the power to approximately three times the original magnification. A net bag is also included for carrying and storing the microscope.

Order from: The Workshop for Learning Things, 5 Bridge St., Watertown, MA 02172. Grade level: All grades. Cost: $10.95 plus $1 postage and handling. Payment must accompany orders under $20.

---

### FABULOUS FREEBEE
### SOCKEYE ODYSSEY

Every year, in the North Pacific Ocean, an incredible event takes place: the sockeye salmon begin their spawning runs of up to 2,000 miles, leaving the ocean to return to the small streams where they were born.

This 14-minute film, produced by the National Oceanic and Atmospheric Administration and Screenscope, Inc., documents in beautiful color the various stages of the journey and points out some of the efforts being made by the government to preserve the species.

It highlights the hazards faced by the salmon at every stage of their lives, from egg through adult, and details the remarkable physical changes that take place during the spawning run.

The free-loan film is a natural for science and ecology classes, but language arts and social studies teachers will also find it useful for creative writing and geography studies.

Order from: Motion Picture Service, U.S. Dept. of Commerce-NOAA, 12231 Wilkins Ave., Rockville, MD 20852. Grade level: 4–high school. (User must pay return postage.)

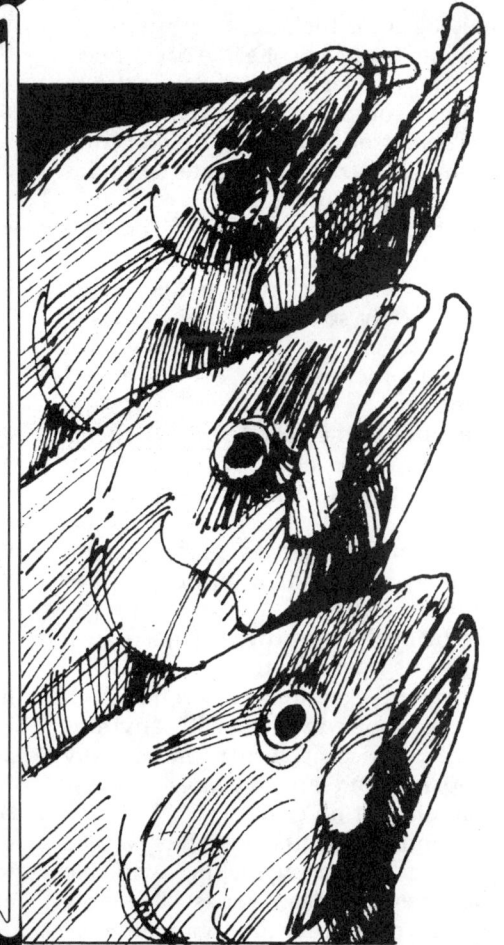

---

## ZOOMING IN: Photographic Discoveries Under the Microscope
**by Barbara J. Wolberg**
**Photographs by Dr. Lewis R. Wolberg**

Marine life, human cells, plants, animals, crystal formations and other fascinating specimens are examined in this collection of black-and-white photographs taken through a microscope. Viewed and discussed at the outset, these photos can make later use of the microscope more exciting. For young geniuses, Wolberg's book offers a careful explanation of how such photographs are taken.

HARCOURT, $7.75 (list), $6.20 (school price). Ages 10–14. See page 151 for ordering information.

## BODIES
**by Barbara Brenner. Photographs by George Ancona**

One thing most young children would like to know more about is bodies — theirs and other people's. This picture book deals with how bodies work, how they grow and how the bodies of different people are alike and different.

DUTTON, $5.95. Ages 4–8.
See page 151 for ordering information.

# The Pollution of Environmental Education

by Odvard Egil Dyrli

Seldom has an educational movement received as much attention as has been given the environment. Everyone's message has been that education is the answer—the government, professional associations, the media, commercial organizations and the general public. Thus, students and teachers have found themselves suffocating under carloads of leaflets, buttons, pamphlets, posters, stickers, club membership cards, kits, records, films, filmstrips, activity collections, newsletters, reports and guides, each dispensing its own brand of propaganda, and all in the name of environmental education.

Too many of these materials have no reason for being in a classroom, except, perhaps, as humorous or tragic examples of thoughtlessness. Such shortcomings frequently spring either from the fact that those who designed the materials had little sense of what the preparation of materials for children should involve, or from the equally disturbing fact that their view of teaching was decidedly dated. Far more objectionable, though, is the deliberate attempt by certain groups to use curriculum materials to present one-sided and inaccurate commercial messages for the sole purpose of improving the image of a line of products generally regarded as detrimental to the environment.

The current crop of slick, well-presented "curriculum materials" includes the following:
- a cute, cartoon-illustrated booklet from a detergent association that implies that phosphates in detergents aren't really so bad;
- an article on the controversial Alaska pipeline, paid for by an oil company;
- a guide to the use of pesticides, created by an association representing manufacturers of agricultural chemicals;
- an environmental game, given away by a major distributor of nonreturnable bottles.

Obviously, it is unwise to make such materials available to students without careful examination, even though they purportedly deal with environmental concerns, are professionally prepared and are available in class quantities at no cost.

Commercial publishers have added to the plethora by making available their new, revised series. But how new are they? Time and again we meet the standard old elementary life/science repertoire with a few social studies refrains added for variety. The word "environment" is interjected in as many places as possible, and such things as field reports are retitled "environmental resource inventories."

Aggravating the situation are rhetoric, slogans and jargon, all rapidly filling the environmental educationalist's catch basin. When elementary school children are hammered too long and too loudly to stop pollution and the deterioration of the environment, insensitivity will inescapably be the result. How long can a child be expected to maintain an emotional high over such reiterated warnings as "Time is running out," "Our very lives depend on it," "Earth is the only world we have"? I, for one, am sick of hearing "spaceship earth," "environmental encounters" and "environmental literacy" over and over again.

Other programs enter the environmental education arena under less than ideal circumstances. A director of a nationally known project, for example, readily admits that his group adopted an environmental education emphasis simply because that was what was being funded at the time. In similar fashion, "model programs" have developed and died throughout the country, having served primarily to springboard individuals into prominence as environmental curriculum consultants and specialists. Nor should we forget the countless committees at national, state, regional and local levels that earnestly set out to "define the issues," then slid quietly out of existence.

Some of the stars of environmental show biz have, of course, thrived. They have traveled widely, lived well and seen their names in print in reports of conference proceedings. Selected ground-floor enthusiasts and a number of the better-known circuit riders have been tapped for prestigious state committees and regional workshops on "the problem." And others have turned solid profits as consultants to school systems.

What will tomorrow bring? We now have materials so varied that environmental education is approached from almost every conceivable angle, yet we also have dampened spirits. But as one fad fades, another inevitably grows in its place. New campaigns to refocus attention on environmental education are always being drafted.

Rather than add to the surfeit by appending the usual list of recommended references, let me suggest a single and somewhat unusual "non-professional" paperback oriented toward action: *The User's Guide to the Protection of the Environment* by Paul Swatek (Friends of the Earth/Balantine Books, 1970). Read it; underline it; reread your underlinings. You will be provided with a strong set of criteria against which you and your students can devise and create a curriculum that meets your own set of unique needs.

Odvard Egil Dyrli is professor of education, University of Connecticut, Storrs.

# AN ECOSYSTEM OF YOUR OWN

Ecology, like a lot of other good things in life, starts best close to home. For teachers and students, this means at school.

Many schools already are devoting time to environmental issues and encouraging children to engage in recycling projects. But what may have been overlooked is that the school itself is a wonderfully complex ecosystem which can provide a unique opportunity for making environmental education real and immediate.

All sorts of raw materials, goods and services flow into a school. Numerous products, by-products and wastes flow out of it. Here are some of the elements of that traffic.

### Paper

Someone once wrote that the world will end not with a bang but with a rustle of paper. Mankind's consumption of paper and paper products is staggering; schools are among the biggest users. From the offices of the superintendents in three communities came these supporting statistics:

| City | Tons of paper used yearly | Number of students |
| --- | --- | --- |
| Atlanta, Ga. | 900 | 112,488 |
| Philadelphia, Pa. | 926 | 290,000 |
| Los Gatos, Calif. | 26.8 | 3,672 |

Using these data, children can calculate the average weight of paper consumed per pupil per year. By writing their own school district office, they can get the figures for a comparison study.

Some questions come to mind: How is all this paper used? How might other materials be substituted for paper? Does the system ever reuse any of the paper? Can the class suggest ways for doing so? (Here's a chance for some meaningful letter-writing practice.)

Students might collect and weigh the waste paper from different classrooms. How does the quantity vary from room to room and grade to grade? If you know teachers in neighboring or distant schools, you might enlarge the scope of your research.

What would happen if your school's paper supply were drastically reduced or eliminated? What paper-using activities would have top priority? Like adults, children take paper pretty much for granted. To recognize how important paper is, students might try a paperless day.

### The Building

The right questions can turn your school into the star of an unusual earth science unit.

How old is the building? What natural and man-made materials were used in its construction? Were the gravel and sand used to make the concrete obtained from local quarries? What about the clay that went into the bricks? Are these local sources still producing materials? This kind of information is often available from local museums, geology clubs or state geological offices. Such groups might also help you to arrange field trips to the quarries, thus enabling students to explore firsthand the natural history of the pits and rock formations. A logical follow-up would be visits to factories which made bricks, cinder blocks and other items used in the building.

### Utilities

How much water is used by the school each year? What's it used for and where does it go? How much energy is required to heat and light the school? What kind of pollution results from the production and use of that energy? How does the school's energy consumption today compare with that of five or ten years ago? How does the school comply with federal, state and local laws designed to protect the environment?

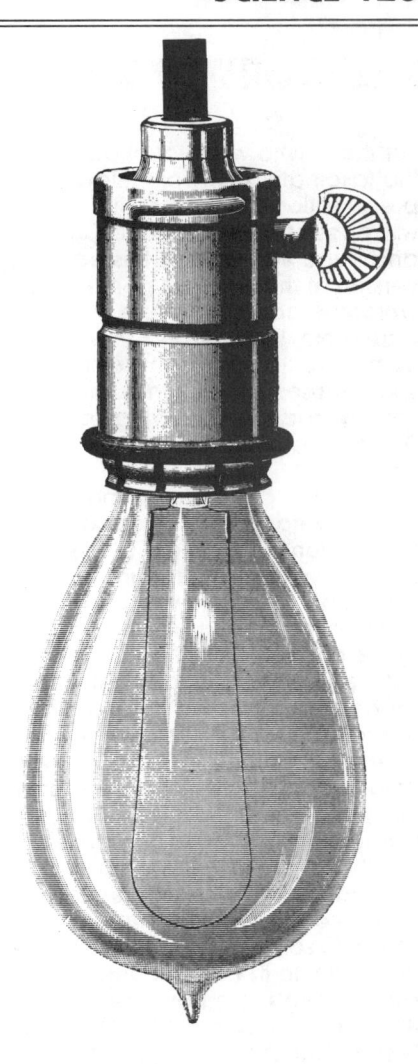

### Summary

Questions like these will help your students understand, in a very concrete way, how their school is part of the total environment and how it affects — and is affected by — that environment. Students will directly confront the problems of population density, utilization of resources, energy consumption and waste disposal. And most important, they will be coming to grips with the Four Laws of Ecology as set forth in Barry Commoner's book THE CLOSING CIRCLE:

1. Everything is connected to everything else.
2. Everything must go somewhere.
3. Nature knows best.
4. There is no such thing as a free lunch.

Idea by: Jean Oak Kriebs, College of Education, the University of Illinois, Chicago, Ill. and Albert Schatz, Temple University, Philadelphia, Pa.

# 124 SCIENCE

## THE STORY OF SOLO
☆ ☆ ☆ ☆ ☆ ☆ ☆ ☆

For those who were touched by the fascinating network television presentation of MISS GOODALL AND THE WILD DOGS OF AFRICA by Jane Goodall and Hugo van Lawick, this edited version of that film will come as a welcome addition for use in the classroom. In color and shortened from 52 to 20 minutes, THE STORY OF SOLO focuses on Solo, the cute, spunky and lone surviving pup of Angel, one of the females in the pack.

Forced to compete for food with pups several weeks his senior and nearly done in by them at the outset, Solo proves to be a tough and self-reliant little fellow.

When the entire pack has to move on to new hunting grounds, Solo, still too young to travel, falls far behind and is left to fend for himself or die. But van Lawick intervenes at this point and delivers Solo to camp, where he is fed until his strength returns. Finally, Solo is released and goes off with another pack of wild dogs.

Because it is a heavily edited version of a longer film, THE STORY OF SOLO has some flaws. Several scenes important to the development of the mother dog's role have been cut. And the circumstances that cause Solo to become the lone survivor of Angel's litter are handled too hurriedly. In addition, some of the vocabulary used by narrators Goodall, van Lawick and actor Hal Holbrook might be a bit difficult for many elementary students. Nevertheless, teachers will find this film particularly useful for science and ecology studies and as a springboard for creative writing and other language activities.

Order from: Films Inc., 733 Greenbay Rd., Wilmette, IL 60091. Grade level: 3–high school. Cost: $20, rental; $275, purchase. Add $2 for postage and handling.

## FABULOUS FREEBEE
### CONSERVATION EDUCATION PUBLICATIONS

"Recycling," a reprint from RANGER RICK'S NATURE MAGAZINE, includes a chart of the life cycle of a car, plus ideas for the classroom on recycling projects. A reprint from NATIONAL WILDLIFE magazine, the annual "National Wildlife Federation EQ Index," rates the environmental quality of the nation each year and lists such milestones as "whooping cranes at new high." These are but two of a whole bag of free pamphlets available from the National Wildlife Federation. Not all of the materials deal with wildlife, but all of them are concerned with ecology.

For more information on these and other free materials, write for the brochure CONSERVATION EDUCATION PUBLICATIONS.

Order from: National Wildlife Federation, Educational Services Dept. RU76, 1412 16th St., N. W., Washington, DC 20036. Grade level: Teachers of all grades.

## PETS-'N-CARE
☆ ☆ ☆ ☆ ☆ ☆ ☆ ☆

Children and animals have a natural affinity for each other, the American Humane Association notes in its PETS-'N-CARE booklet. And since this is true, activities about animals have a built-in motivational factor.

The PETS-'N-CARE booklet offers several pages of activities — some long-term continuing projects, others designed around seasonal themes or specific curriculum areas. Some activities concern humane treatment of pets, economic significance of animals, the roles of animals in the balance of nature. Pets, wild animals and even animals in fiction are featured.

The booklet also provides a short history of the American Humane Association and, for those interested, tells the background of Be Kind to Animals Week — which falls the first full week in May. A catalog of low-cost supplementary educational materials available from AHA completes the booklet.

PETS-'N-CARE can help you make the most of the appeal that animals have for most children.

Order from: The American Humane Association, P.O. Box 1266, Denver, CO 80201. Grade level: Teachers of grades K–6. Cost: $.25 per copy. Also available: An INTRODUCTORY EDUCATION KIT, containing a variety of samples of publications available from The American Humane Association, is offered free of charge.

# WHAT'S IN A LABEL?

Nonfat dry milk, sucrose, corn syrup solids, artificial flavor, lactose, lecithin, carrageenan, magnesium oxide, ascorbic acid . . .

How much do your students know about the mystery foods they buy and eat? Their awareness can be sharpened by some projects.

1. After students have watched at least two TV commercials promoting food, ask them to use their judgment as to what seem to be the facts of the message and what is most likely irrelevant or exaggerated.

2. Ask each student to save and bring in an ingredients list from a food package. Be sure all brand-name and food-name identification is removed. Have several lists read aloud and have the rest of the class guess what the product is. When students have had the opportunity to guess a few, number the lists and mount them on a piece of tagboard with the answer key nearby. New lists may be added periodically.

Students with a will to win will discover that the ingredients are listed in order according to their proportion in the food item. Besides giving a clue to the item's identification, this fact can be an important discussion starter. What vegetables are predominant in mixed vegetables? Is beef the main ingredient of beef stew?

The list should also spark other questions: What is carrageenan? What does it do? What ingredients are basic in a particular food product and which are additives? Why are preservatives used?

Hopefully, these projects can promote further inquiry into what food is and what it does.

Idea by: Margaret D. Jones,
Valley Springs Elementary School,
Valley Springs, Calif.

# SCIENCE EXPERIMENTS YOU CAN EAT

☆ ☆ ☆ ☆ ☆ ☆ ☆ ☆

Where would you expect to find a stabilized suspension, immiscible liquids and denatured protein? In a kitchen – a scientist's paradise. Beat oil into a batch of homemade mayonnaise, shake up a bottle of salad dressing, or use vinegar to sour milk, and you're dealing with basic scientific phenomena. Such activities can be carried out in the classroom with great success and satisfaction – particularly in the clean-up phase, when you get to eat your experiments. (You put the dressing on something and the sour milk in something.)

SCIENCE EXPERIMENTS YOU CAN EAT was written by junior high science teacher and writer Vicki Cobb. She points out that a kitchen is an ideal laboratory. She notes sources of heat, water, cooling equipment, measuring instruments and a wealth of chemically interesting substances.

These substances are grouped into chapters labeled "Solutions," "Proteins," "Enzymes" and the like. Each chapter begins on a scientific note and goes on to detail several activities with common food substances demonstrating the principles described. Making muffins is a study of gluten; a fruit salad becomes a way of observing oxidation; pretzel making shows yeast-action inhibition.

The materials, procedures and guides to observation for each activity are clearly stated, with safety precautions getting appropriate emphasis. New vocabulary is carefully developed, and a sense of inquiry and discovery built in. Illustrations serve explanatory functions and also inject a note of whimsical fun.

The book may be used by older students for independent investigations at school or as homework. Teachers of younger children may want to use the book as a resource for group activities or for demonstrations leading to independent follow-up.

SCIENCE EXPERIMENTS YOU CAN EAT is digest sized, with 127 pages, and is available in either paperback or hardcover. It's a book that produces a host of eager, enlightened and well-fed scientists. Let us know how your yogurt turns out.

Order from: J.B. Lippincott Co.,
E. Washington Square, Philadelphia, PA 19105.
Grade level: Intermediate–junior high.
Cost: $2.50, paperback. Add $.30 for postage and handling. Payment must accompany order.

# Obis: The Science Un-Curriculum

by Alan J. McCormack

Imagine this: with paint and palette, you engage in a pleasurable outdoor activity that seems at the outset to be an art project. Twenty minutes later, you find yourself discovering ideas about animal adaptations. Or imagine being part of a group making "sun print" photographs with simple materials. In short order, you find yourself using the techniques you have just learned to piece together the links of a food chain in a nearby vacant lot. Ecology plus art and ecology plus photography both equal ecology made fun.

This free-swinging style characterizes materials of the first "un-curriculum" funded by the National Science Foundation—Outdoor Biology Instructional Strategies (OBIS).

Why "un-curriculum"? Because OBIS activities are planned for the programs of community-sponsored youth organizations such as Scouts, recreation-center clubs, summer camps and nature-center groups, rather than for the conventional school science curriculum. Many teachers, however, will find the materials suited for class use.

OBIS, designed for youngsters 10 to 15, is concerned with promoting the understanding of ecological relationships. A main goal of the project is to provide for outdoor biology learning experiences that can be adapted to virtually *all* environments. Because so much of the world is now man-altered, man-managed environments have been chosen as study sites, rather than classic climax ecosystems. Thus OBIS activities focus on the surroundings where children *are*, using lawns, parks, vacant lots and backyards as study sites. And, *all* OBIS experiences "happen" at out-of-doors locations.

**Universally Applicable.** Though activities introduce environmental ideas in ways that are palatable and exciting to youngsters, OBIS is much more than mere outdoor fun and games. Underlying all the materials is the assumption that basic understandings of ecosystems, populations, communities and food chains are essential in making intelligent management decisions about the environment. The techniques useful for the study of man-managed ecosystems are universally applicable where there is life. Thus, OBIS represents a broader view of environmental concerns than that of programs focusing on the "tin-can ecology" of pollution or recycling.

OBIS also departs from the curriculum-development procedure of determining a specific sequence of learning activities leading to an isolated concept. Instead, the OBIS staff is identifying and trying out a variety of alternative strategies and techniques for environmental study. Assuming that no single learning pathway can be either interesting or applicable to all youngsters in all locales, OBIS plans flexible units involving multiple learning entrance and exit points.

**Sample Activities.** Let's look at two sample OBIS activities: *Invent-a-Plant* and *Who Goes There? Invent-a-Plant*, like many OBIS experiences, is developed around an engaging overall challenge: "Invent a model of a plant that is well-adapted to survival in a particular habitat." Kids first inspect plants in contrasting habitats to determine survival problems and how plants are adapted to meet them.

Then, using wire and Fantasy Film (a liquid plastic commonly used in craft projects), participants construct "plants" designed to meet specific survival problems posed on individual "action cards." Some examples: Invent a plant capable of surviving in a hot, dry roadside area; invent a plant that can withstand high winds; invent a plant to survive on the floor of a very dense forest. When the "plants" are completed, the ensuing group discussion is likely to develop many important concepts of biological adaptation. And in the process, kids have enjoyed a pleasurable craft project.

*Who Goes There?* focuses on nocturnal animals. Most small mammals, except for squirrels and chipmunks, are active primarily at night. Though we may find evidence of their presence (footprints or chomped-on cookies), most people never actually see these small creatures or learn much about their habits. To meet these difficulties, OBIS suggests a *Who Goes There?* mammal hunt. A nontoxic fluorescent tracing powder is mixed with bird seed or other bait and placed at a study site. Many small mammals will come to the bait station and feed—field mice, perhaps, in a fallow farm field; possibly rats in an urban area. The harmless powder passes through digestive processes unchanged. Result? A trail of urine, feces and footprints will fluoresce at night when exposed to a portable black light, or sparkle during daylight hours under a bright Day-Glo type powder.

Forty-eight other OBIS activities are now available in trial edition. Another twenty-eight are currently in production. A few more examples:

*Terrestrial Hi-Lo Hunt*: In any chosen study site, participants find the warmest, coldest, brightest, darkest, wettest, and driest places. Then they check distributions of plant and animal populations and relate these to environmental "highs" and "lows."

*Seed Dispersal*: Given a pea seed and a box of diverse materials (junk!), kids are asked to modify the seed for dispersal by wind, water, animals and mechanical propulsion.

*Sound Off!*: Kids learn about animal sound communications through a game in which blindfolded partners find each other using only specified sound signals and their sense of hearing.

A note to OBIS at the Lawrence Hall of Science, University of California at Berkeley, Berkeley, CA 94720, will bring more information about materials and activities.

Alan J. McCormack, former OBIS project coordinator, teaches at the University of British Columbia, Vancouver, BC.

## ADVENTURES WITH A CARDBOARD TUBE: First Science Experiments

☆ ☆ ☆ ☆ ☆ ☆ ☆ ☆

If you've always thought that there must be some use for the cardboard tube that appers when a roll of paper towels is finished (besides the standard art projects), you were right. Harry Milgrom, author of this book for young children, uses lively illustrations and simple text to demonstrate more than a dozen different basic science experiments primary children can try with cardboard tubes.

The experiments are usually one step and easy to do. Most are open-ended enough (what do you expect from a tube?) to be developed further by creative teachers or kids. In carrying out the experiments, children become involved in many of the important scientific processes—observing, comparing, hypothesizing—as they work with concepts of shape, friction, weight, light, sound and balance.

Order from: E.P. Dutton & Co., Inc., 201 Park Ave. South, New York, NY 10003. Grade level: Primary. Cost: $6.50 (list); $5.20 (school price). No postage and handling on prepaid orders. Orders less than $25 must be prepaid.

## MAKING SMALL THINGS LOOK BIGGER

☆ ☆ ☆ ☆ ☆ ☆ ☆ ☆

An investigation and project booklet, MAKING SMALL THINGS LOOK BIGGER helps take the mystery out of magnification and microscopes. Students start with activities involving only the magic of eyesight and discover magnification as a product of perspective. Next they try looking through a water-drop lens. With a plastic hand lens they examine common objects and note properties not observed before. Work with a simple microscope follows. Students check out cells, crystals and insects.

The booklet is composed of 8-1/2-by-11-inch perforated pages. The pages are designed for written responses and drawings. Permission is given for you to copy the pages for the use of your own class.

Though the booklet is intended to serve grades 3 through 12, you will probably find the type a bit small and the response spaces too confining for younger children. If this is the case, the book can serve as a resource from which you may select appropriate investigations and develop your own worksheets.

As the introduction to the book suggests, it is best to work through the activities yourself to become familiar with the techniques and experience the results. In this way you may select the investigations that suit the maturity and abilities of your class. The book does follow a developmental sequence, however, and this should be considered in the process of selecting activities.

MAKING SMALL THINGS LOOK BIGGER won't make bacteriologists out of your class, but it can help them—and you—understand how magnification works.

Order from: Educational Science Consultants, P.O. Box 1674, San Leandro, CA 94577. Grade level: 3–12. Cost: $2.50 plus $.25 postage and handling.

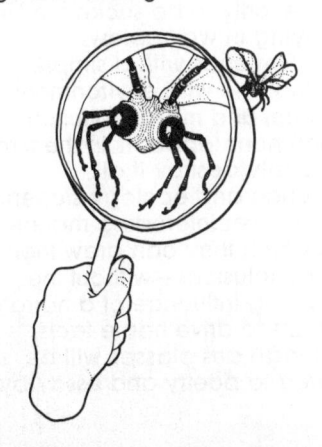

## A STREAM ENVIRONMENT

☆ ☆ ☆ ☆ ☆ ☆ ☆ ☆ ☆

This unusual science film by Hans Halberstadt spends nine minutes, all in stunning color, following a crystal mountain stream from its snow-fed source to a placid valley meadow. Along the way, the varied plants and animals dependent upon the stream's waters are shown.

Uniquely and blessedly, narration is kept to a minimum, and the narrator's occasional statements are counter-pointed visually. When he says, for instance, "This mountain stream begins with the melting of snow and it grows one drop at a time," the camera cuts quickly to rivulets of water gaining size and strength and flowing swiftly over rocks and down slopes. The music quickens in synchronization.

The interrelationship of plants, animals and stream is highlighted through beautiful close-up photography. Mayflies, for example, are first seen as larva attached to rocks under water. Then we see them as adults floating along the surface, only to be sucked in by trout lying in wait below.

The film ends with a simple warning: The wild environment is delicate, and man's pollution—though none appears in the film—can easily destroy it all.

Science and ecology students will discover interesting material from which they can draw their own conclusions—without the distracting influence of a narrator's attempts to drive home facts. Language arts classes will be inspired to poetry and essay by the natural beauty of the stream. A brief but useful discussion guide comes with the film.

Order from: Barr Films, P.O. Box 5667, Pasadena, CA 91107. Grade level: K–12. Cost: Rental — $15 plus $2 postage and handling; purchase — $140 plus $.50 postage and handling.

## ZOO KEEPERS

When a hamster or lizard arrives for show-and-tell, or the class returns from a zoological excursion, you may suddenly become uncomfortably aware of a distinct housing shortage in your room. You can prepare for future animal visitors with one or two easily and inexpensively assembled cages. These cages will be cylindrical, screened all around, standing on a solid metal base and capped with a metal top.

You may have already encountered recipes for homemade cages (such as the pie-plate-and-screen variety) in your travels through teacher publications. But for roomier and sturdier animal accomodations, you might consider using this oil-drain-pan alternative.

For one cage you'll need two oil drain pans (about 16 inches in diameter and 3 inches deep), available at discount and auto supply stores at reasonable cost. You'll also need some easy-to-bend wire (not much) and some hardware cloth. Hardware-cloth screening comes in a variety of meshes and widths. Pick a mesh that suits the sort of critters you've been getting, or make one coarse-mesh cage and one fine-mesh cage. Whatever width you buy, you'll probably need to trim some off in order to have a cage that's not too tall. The length of the screening will be determined by the circumference of the oil drain pan; the screen should be equal to the circumference with a little extra for overlap at the seam.

Roll the screening into a tube and fit it snugly into one of the pans. Secure the seam by twisting wire through the mesh in several places. (Use some more wire or perhaps heavy-duty tape to fasten the pan to the screen if you want to guard against losing the cage bottom accidentally.) The other drain pan is placed over the top of the screening tube. The ends of the cage can be removed for easy feeding and cleaning operations.

Idea by: James Chupa, Horizons School, Twin Falls, Idaho.

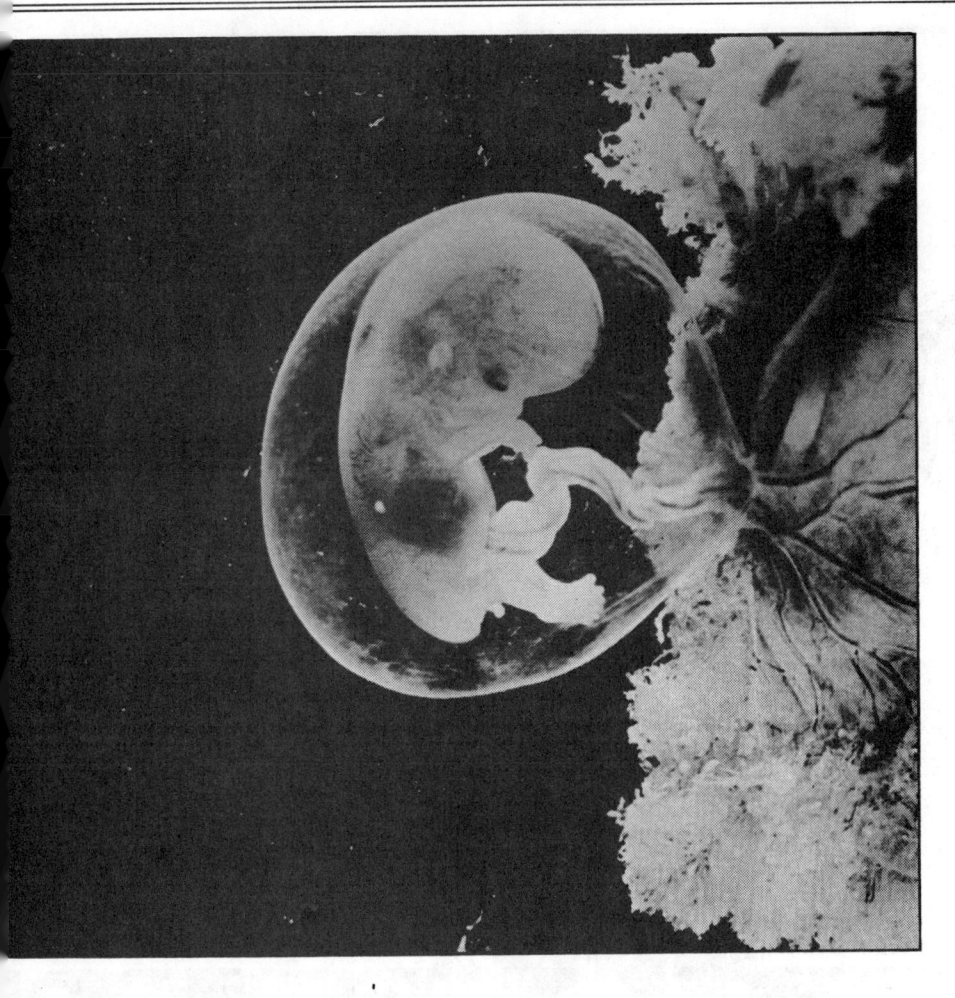

# SCIENCE 129

## MAKING BABIES: An Open Family Book for Parents and Children Together
**by Sara Bonnett Stein. Photographs by Doris Pinney**

Part of a series developed by the Center for Preventive Psychiatry, this book is designed for simultaneous reading by adult (a running text of advice) and child (a simple story with giant type). The photographs include nudes of both sexes, dogs mating, kittens being born and embryos. The text is direct, neither overly romantic nor overly sophisticated. An honest, unself-conscious treatment of the subject.

WALKER, $5.95. Ages 4–8.
See page 151 for ordering information.

## EXAMINING YOUR ENVIRONMENT
☆ ☆ ☆ ☆ ☆ ☆ ☆ ☆

BIRDS, POLLUTION, TREES, MINI-CLIMATES, SNOW AND ICE, RUNNING WATER, ASTRONOMY, ECOLOGY IN YOUR COMMUNITY, MAPPING SMALL PLACES, SMALL CREATURES, THE DANDELION and YOUR SENSES are the titles in this 12-book science series. Around each topic the authors, D. F. Wentworth, J. K. Couchman, J. C. MacBean and A. Stecher, have created unique sets of far-reaching, individualized activities.

In implementing each of the books, the teacher has a great deal of flexibility. Though the books are structured as coherent studies of each subject area, most sections and activities can stand alone.

The format used for BIRDS is typical of the whole series. The book is divided into four major sections — "Live Birds," "Birds' Eggs," "Birds' Nests" and "Dead Birds" — with each unit offering between five and eight major activities and two groups of follow-up exercises.

One activity from the "Birds' Nests" section asks: "What materials are found in a bird's nest?" It suggests that the student take apart an abandoned nest piece by piece. (If the nest is held together with mud, "soak it in a pail of water before taking it apart.") The materials are then sorted, classified, labeled and displayed. In the follow-up section it asks several related questions: How many different types of materials are found in the nest? Which materials are most common? Do all nests contain the same materials? What is the reason birds build nests? In addition, the student is asked to list, among other things, the birds in the area that make nests but do not collect materials to do it.

Developed for use in grades 4 through 8 as a supplement to the regular science course, the books are by no means limited to those specifications. Though primary grade children would find it difficult to read the text, they could, through teacher guidance and the use of the abundant color photographs and illustrations, participate in many of the activities.

If your budget is limited, one copy of each book will suffice. Though these books make fine student texts, teachers can use them as guides.

Order from: Winston Press, 25 Groveland Terrace, Minneapolis, MN 55403.
Grade level: Primary – junior high. Cost: $3.95 per book plus $.50 postage and handling. Payment must accompany orders under $10.

## 130 SCIENCE

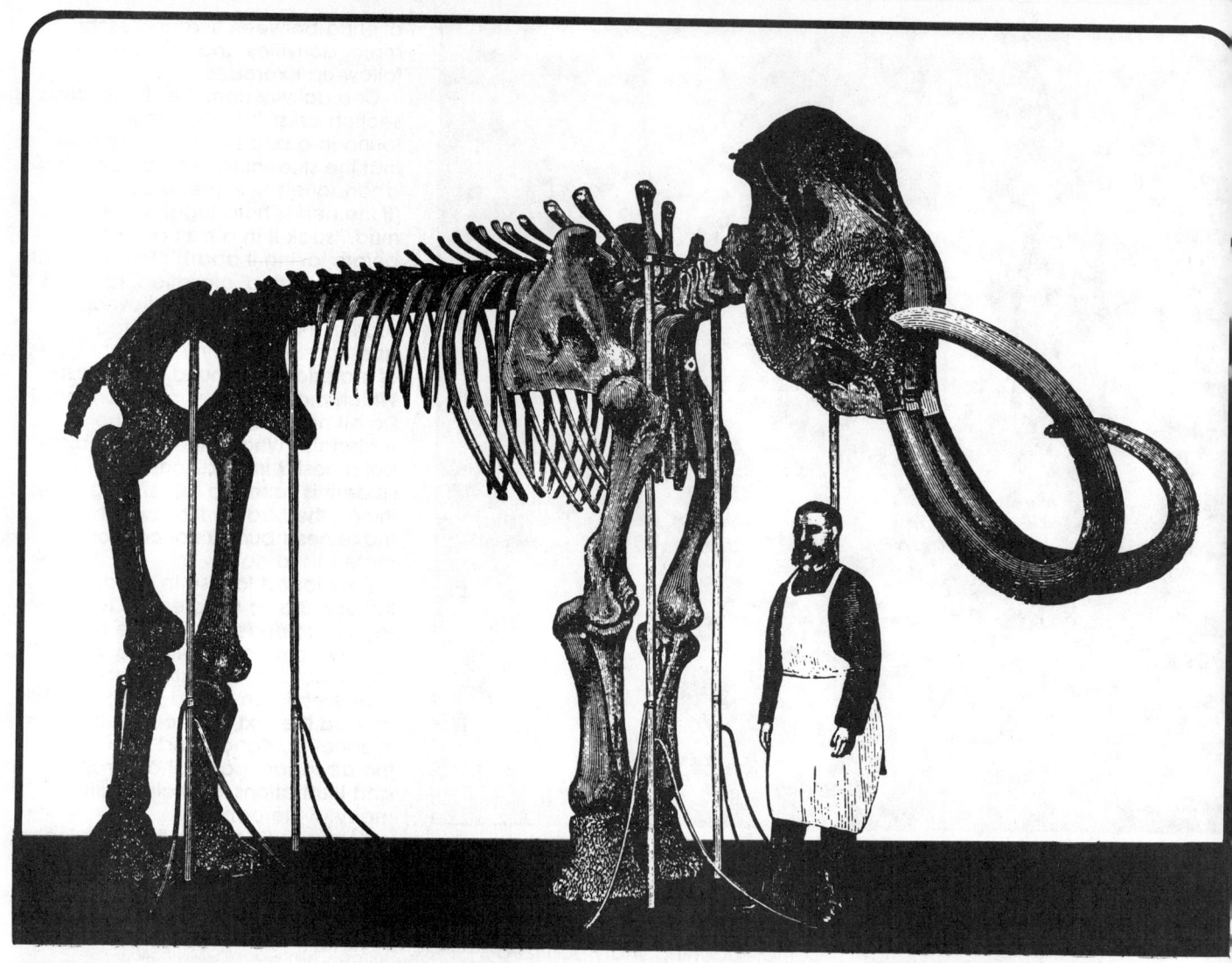

## WISHBONE CONNECTED TO THE...

Recycled leftovers become the not-so-raw materials of this activity, which is part science and part art. Have children begin to collect bones left over from their dinners at home—chicken, lamb, ham, steak, rabbit—the greater the variety the better.

Bones to be brought in to school must be thoroughly cleaned. Children may find that a plastic or nylon-mesh scrubber helps in this process. Then bones should be boiled in vinegar water and allowed to dry. (Some children may try soaking the bones in a bleach-and-water solution. This gives the bones an interesting whitish appearance.)

As bones are brought in, find out what kind of animal and from what part of the body they came from. Observe the sizes and shapes of the various bones; compare chicken bones with ham bones, for instance.

The children then deposit their contributions in the class "boneyard," a large open box, where the bones can become completely dry. The collection of bones should be large enough for each child to select several.

After devising an equitable mode of distribution—some bones will undoubtedly be more popular than others—see that each child has a bone pile to work with. From the bones, the children construct their own creatures—dinosaurs, more than likely.

Have rubber cement, white glue, wire, masking tape and modeling clay ready to connect the bones. An electric drill (teacher operated) can be a big help in making holes in the bones for the insertion of wire connectors.

Your young paleontologists will amaze you and themselves with their creations. And a display of their work, appropriately labeled with mock scientific names, will certainly be in order.

Idea by: Drenda Underwood,
Washington Elementary School, St. Louis, Mo.

## MIRROR CARDS

☆ ☆ ☆ ☆ ☆ ☆ ☆ ☆ ☆

"It was done with mirrors" is the usual disclaimer when one is bamboozled by a magician's sleight-of-hand. This product, however, needs no disclaimer; everything is done with mirrors—from the reconstruction of a bitten-into hot dog to the vibration of a broken comb.

MIRROR CARDS are part of the Elementary Science Study (ESS) program and comprise a set of more than 200 activity cards and four mirrors. They're intended for use in grades one through six. (Don't worry about the mirrors. They're not the kind with the built-in seven-year curse. They're steel.)

The MIRROR CARDS box has 21 different sets of cards that are number-coded for easy sorting and storing. Each set has a title card that gives brief directions. Usually there is a pattern card with a picture or a design. The rest of the cards in the set will have elements of the pattern card design in various arrangements or positions. The activity consists of trying to recreate the model pattern by using the mirror to reflect the part of the design shown on each card.

Beginner sets help younger children understand ways they can manipulate the mirror to change images. They also provide valuable orientation for older students. Later sets are quite challenging and complex, including a number of cards in the "can't match" classifications.

The cards lead children to deal with lines of symmetry and relationships among geometric forms. Activities are also the basis for more complex work with geometric concepts and optics.

Once cards are introduced and the pattern of usage established, individual children may work with MIRROR CARDS on their own. They may also work in small groups, challenging each other with their "can't match" discoveries.

A separate illustrated guide provides information about introducing the cards and suggestions for working with individual sets and helps establish principles of the solution process. MIRROR CARDS' applications to informal geometry investigations and a treatment of the mathematical ideas involved are also included.

Children will exult in their magical powers as they turn bugs into butterflies and see how a triangle can become a diamond. It's all done with mirrors.

Order from: Webster/McGraw-Hill, 1221 Ave. of the Americas, New York, NY 10020. Grade level: 1–6. Cost: $15.99, set of cards with four mirrors; $4.47, teacher's guide.

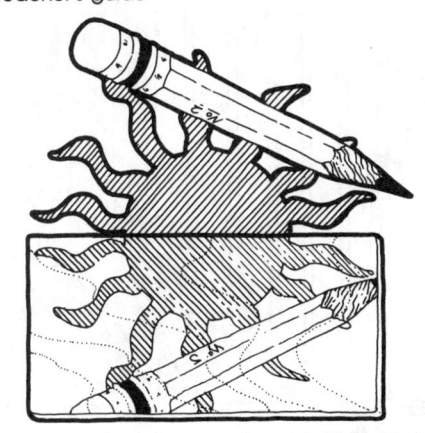

## HOW MUCH NOISE ANNOYS?

The coexistence of noise and people is a recognized fact of modern life. What effect, if any, does noise have on a student's concentration? A noise-pollution project in your classroom may help provide some answers.

Make up a five-minute tape of the noise of your choice. (One possibility might be a portion of a film sound track run in reverse.) The equipment on which the tape is played should have the capability of producing a fairly wide range of volume – including a level that could be subjectively termed "uncomfortably loud."

Next, prepare a word-maze puzzle in which 36 words are hidden. Duplicate enough copies of the maze for each student in the project to have three copies, one for each of three noise "trials."

On a second duplicator sheet, list the 36 puzzle words, divided into three 12-word sets. Head each set with the number of the trial and end each with a box for recording the number of words found in that trial. (You may wish to simply indicate spaces for the words to be written in; then dictate them for each trial separately to avoid the possibility of students locating trial 2 words while in the midst of trial 1.)

On the bottom of this sheet design a graph form for participants to use in recording data from each trial. Include space for some written conclusions.

Trial 1 consists of finding as many of the first 12 words as possible while the noise tape is played at a volume below a normal conversational level. Trial 2 is carried out with noise at a conversational level, and trial 3 at above-normal volume.

Students count up words found for each trial and record the data on their individual graphs. Students may also combine data, compute averages and prepare a large composite graph.

Have the class discuss individual and group results. [Editor's note: Of the experiment results, Mr. Hoek states that scores tend to rise on the second trial (practice effect) "but will plunge significantly when recording is played at a blaring decibel level even though the task and its difficulty remain approximately the same."] What conclusions can be drawn? Are there factors other than noise to be considered? How much do results vary from person to person? And on a different level – how did students feel during the trials? Students may decide they want to try similar trials with other kinds of noise.

Note: Be sure to apprise the neighboring rooms of your intentions to launch noise experiments, or you may get results faster than you'd anticipated.

Idea by: John Hoek,
North Junior High, Portage, Mich.

### FABULOUS FREEBEE
## OUTDOOR CLASSROOMS ON SCHOOL SITES

Prospects for warmer weather may turn thoughts toward outdoor activities. Where can you go and what can you do outdoors around your school?

OUTDOOR CLASSROOMS may be the impetus to a better usage of school grounds. The booklet describes the learning potential of outdoor classrooms. Photographs throughout show students in diverse climatic regions and varied settings engaged in environmental activities. Captions describe their work. Organization plans and procedures for developing outdoor classrooms are outlined, and uses of environmental features are illustrated. Diagrams show plans for outdoor classrooms on both city and suburban or community sites.

The emphasis is on understanding and appreciation of the environment, including active problem solving on a practical, local level.

Order from: U.S. Department of Agriculture, Soil Conservation Service, Information Division, Washington, DC 20250. Single copies available free to teachers. Grade level: Teachers of all grades.

## CENTER FOR SHORT-LIVED PHENOMENA EVENT REPORTS

☆ ☆ ☆ ☆ ☆ ☆ ☆ ☆

The Center for Short-Lived Phenomena, which keeps tabs on volcanic eruptions, oil spills, red tides, "raining" fish and the like, has sent out a call for teachers and students to participate in an on-the-spot international science reporting network. In the past, approximately 35 percent of all events reported professionally by the Center have come from firsthand accounts by students, through their teachers.

A school subscription to the Center brings weekly postcard reports on current short-lived phenomena around the world and makes the school eligible to send in reports. Subscribing schools also receive a handbook telling how to gather information about and write up such events. Subscribers receive reports in the science fields of biology, environmental pollution, geophysics and astrophysics.

Order from: The Center for Short-Lived Phenomena, 185 Alewife Brook Pkwy., Cambridge, MA 02138. Grade level: Intermediate–high school.
Cost: $50 for a one-year subscription.

## FABULOUS FREEBEE
## ECOLOGY REPRINTS

The Ecology Center, a small nonprofit organization in Berkeley, California, is "dedicated to informing the public on environmental problems and ecologically sound alternatives." One of its means of informing people is through a series of free ecology-related reprints — several of which were originally developed by the center's staff.

Each of the reprints includes practical suggestions on gardening or on how to recycle or prevent waste. In addition, one of them, "Recycling Is Only a Start," answers one of the biggest questions about recycled cans, glass, newspaper and corrugated cardboard: Where does it all go when it leaves the recyclers?

The information and activities contained in many of the reprints can be adapted for use in elementary through junior high classrooms. Although some of the information included in several of the reprints pertains primarily to residents in and near Berkeley, most of it is relevant to readers anywhere.

When requesting reprints, be certain to include a stamped, self-addressed, legal-sized envelope; otherwise the request cannot be filled.

(The center also has available a booklet entitled HOW TO START A NEIGHBORHOOD RECYCLING CENTER for 50 cents.)

Order from: The Ecology Center, 2179 Allston Way, Berkeley, CA 94704. Grade level: Teachers of all grades.

## WASTE WATCHERS

Famine is a faraway phenomenon for most American children. High food costs hit closer to home, but few students feel they personally have anything to do with food problems. The experience of many students with regard to food has been one of infinite variety, endless supply — and mindless waste.

Waste is a problem students can do something about. Start in a small way in your own cafeteria. For one meal, have your students collect the portions of bread and cake that are returned on trays. A display of these leftovers with a large caption, "WE WASTE, OTHERS STARVE," could be a disturbing reminder to all. (And the weak-stomached ones should be able to endure the few moments it takes to make the point.)

Step Two is a "public service" advertising campaign carrying the message "Take less; eat more of what you take." Posters with slogans and attention-getting (but tasteful) illustrations can be displayed near the cafeteria. Your class might compose an open letter to students, teachers and parents who prepare box lunches, explaining the goal of your campaign and the actions advocated. You may also wish to initiate dialogue with the cafeteria staff on how to combat waste on trays. Perhaps a review of the size of serving portions and a come-back-for-seconds policy might be possible deterrents.

Motivated by your class, other students may take more seriously their responsibility to use food resources wisely. And those youngsters with malfunctioning appetite gauges may be helped in assessing more realistically the size differential between their eyes and their stomachs.

Idea by: Lillian Flanagan, St. Albans City Elementary School, St. Albans, Vt.

## THE ANIMALS ARE CRYING

☆ ☆ ☆ ☆ ☆ ☆ ☆ ☆

Don't adopt or buy pets or allow a pet to produce offspring if you cannot or will not take care of them. That's the message of this hard-hitting, 28-minute color film — a dynamic lesson in social and humane responsibilities. It is a memorable film experience, the kind that can lock itself permanently into a child's consciousness.

Opening with a scene in which two garbagemen find a litter of live kittens in a trash bag, the film goes on to become a litany of animal abuse. In what is certainly the most powerful scene — and one which not all teachers will choose to show (and those who do should not make student participation mandatory) — a Humane Society director goes from cage to cage putting animals to sleep by injecting them with sodium pentobarbital, "the least cruel way of killing them." The animals receive the shot and quickly die. Then they are laid out on the floor.

The Humane Society director, who clearly loves animals, explains: "I hate this part of the job. It becomes harder and harder putting them to sleep.... I love animals and some days I can't face it. Someone else has to. It may be humane, but whatever way you look at it, you're taking a life."

There is also a very touching sequence in which a conscientious family debates adopting a Doberman puppy and having it spayed. The actual operation, shown in part, proves to be a relatively minor procedure, usually lasting less than 30 minutes. The director explains that most "fixed" animals are actually better pets.

Some of the film is narrated, some is reconstructed from real events, and the rest consists of interviews. An excellent documentary, the film, without being didactic, teaches children to love animals while at the same time preventing the proliferation of unwanted pets.

A 15-minute version, more appropriate for younger audiences, is also available. The sequences on spaying and destroying animals are left out.

Both versions include discussion guides.

Order from: Learning Corporation of America, 1350 Ave. of the Americas, New York, NY 10019. Grade level: 4–high school (long version); K–junior high (short version). Cost: Long version — $30, rental; $370, purchase; short version — $20, rental; $230, purchase.

# ESSENCE I AND II

☆ ☆ ☆ ☆ ☆ ☆ ☆ ☆

Talk of environmental studies fills the air but ESSENCE activity cards can help you bring it all down to earth.

The program consists of two packets, each with visually exciting and highly imaginative assignment cards (78 in ESSENCE I and 171 in ESSENCE II) written for the teacher. The cards tell what to do, how to follow it up, what materials are needed and cautions about special problems that might arise. For instance, a card entitled "Weed Seeds" suggests:

"Go outside and collect as many weed seeds as you can find. Plant them and grow them. (In early fall the vacant lots and sidewalks are full of plants from which kids can get seeds.)"

For follow-up the card continues:

"What can you do to change how the plants grow?

"Design and plant a garden of special and beautiful weeds alongside the school. What reactions do people have to the weed garden?

"What is a weed? How does a plant become a weed?"

This program is built on the belief that students best develop their basic skills in a learning environment where there is trust and openness. To this end, each assignment has been created so that students and teachers will develop new insights into their environment and themselves.

Order from: Addison-Wesley Publishing Co., Innovative Division, 2725 Sand Hill Rd., Menlo Park, CA 94025. Grade level: Teachers of all grades. Cost: $20.94, Essence I; $34.89, Essence II; $1.20, sample cards from both sets.

# OBSERVATION

☆ ☆ ☆ ☆ ☆ ☆ ☆ ☆

Anyone can be a good observer; it's simply a matter of accustoming oneself to "seeing" with all the senses and making comparisons.

Students who read Jeanne Bendick's 71-page book about the skill of critical observation almost certainly will become observers themselves. Bendick makes learning how to observe enjoyable by providing a guide to some of the tools, methods and skills involved, and then going on to give kids sound practice activities.

The book's sections begin with a statement or definition, followed by pertinent questions and activities. "Observing Things Change," for example, starts off by explaining that while some things may change shape, others may change color, speed and so on. Then it asks readers to think for themselves about things that change quickly or slowly. Readers are also asked to think about what has caused obvious or subtle changes in several pairs of pictures. A sampling of titles of other sections includes: "What Is Observation?" "What Is Important?" "Some Important Things for Observers," "Asking Yourself Questions" and "Does Everybody Observe the Same Things?"

OBSERVATION is written for the intermediate grades and is chock-full of single-color illustrations that extend or complement the text.

Order from: Franklin Watts, Inc., 730 Fifth Ave., New York, NY 10019. Grade level: 4–6. Cost: $4.90, plus $.25 postage for the first copy and $.10 each additional copy. Payment must accompany orders under $15.

## ENVIRONMENTAL DISCOVERY UNITS

☆ ☆ ☆ ☆ ☆ ☆ ☆ ☆ ☆

Ever puzzle over ecosystems and food chains? Help is available from the National Wildlife Federation, which has developed more than 20 units for teacher preparation in the field of ecology.

Each unit, contained in its own soft-bound booklet, treats a different topic, providing necessary factual background and outlining procedures for setting up field trips and class activities. Individual and small-group projects are also described. Whenever the text suggests that the students collect data or record observations, the booklet provides pages designed as masters for such worksheets. Questions for discussion, lists of needed equipment and suggestions for further reading round out the contents of each unit.

Topics are quite specific and vary in complexity. Topics for younger children include "Color and Change: Magic Colors in Nature" and "Nature Hunt: Similarities and Differences in the Natural World." Other topics are listed for a wider range of ages—grades 1–6, 2–9 or even 1–12. But since the booklets are teacher resource units, not student materials, it is expected that suggested activities will be adapted to the interests and maturity of particular levels.

To select topics that are appropriate for your class—from "Contour Mapping" and "Stream Profiles" to "The Rise and Fall of a Yeast Community"—inquire about the free brochure that describes all the units.

Order from: National Wildlife Federation, Environmental Discovery Units, 1412 16th St., N.W., Washington, DC 20036. Grade level: Teachers of all grades. Cost: $1.00 or $1.50 per unit, plus $.85 for postage and handling.

## AIR POLLUTION TEST

For most kids air pollution is synonymous with factory or automobile exhaust. Other than that it's something they read about, something other people experience. Here then is a way to truly bring air pollution home to them.

You need microscope slides or plates of glass, petroleum jelly, masking tape and either a magnifying glass or a microscope. Coat one side of a slide with petroleum jelly and hang it or place it (jelly side up) in an exposed area. Particles from the air will collect on the jelly.

Any number of different places can be compared for level of pollution. In the school, for instance, place slides in the classroom, the cafeteria, the main office and the gymnasium. As homework, have the students hang slides in different rooms of the house. For a larger project, place slides around the neighborhood or the city.

In each instance, the experiment should be done under controlled circumstances. First, each of the slides in a comparison should be exposed for the same amount of time: an hour, a day, a week, a month. Also, keep a slide in a closed box or a drawer as a control mechanism for later comparison. And, when placing out an experimental slide, either coat it right at the site or carry it there in a closed box so that it won't pick up particles along the way.

These experiments will raise hundreds of questions, most of which the kids will be able to answer for themselves. Is there greater pollution near factories or parks or schools or the downtown shopping area? Why? How do these levels of pollution compare to that found near a major roadway? Is it possible to determine what the particles are composed of by examining the slides under a magnifying lens? Why does the amount of pollution vary within an area as small as the classroom? Is there more pollution in the cities, the suburbs or rural areas? What is the purpose of the control slide?

These and similar questions should lead your kids into a greater understanding of air pollution.

Idea by: Robert De Blasi, Paramus Public Schools, Paramus, N.J.

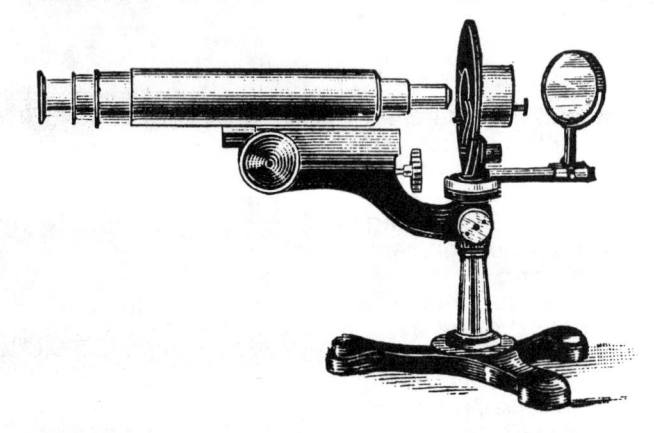

## SCIENCE

# SEEDBED IN A BAG

How does your garden grow? Kids will be able to watch the process for themselves with their own miniature plastic-bag greenhouses.

Materials for these individual seedbeds are: Ziploc plastic bags, paper towels and some large quick-sprouting seeds, e.g., radish seeds, peas, beans. Children may "plant" the gardens by following these steps: (1) In each bag place a damp paper towel. (2) Put some seeds into each bag — various kinds in separate rows or different kinds in different bags — and lock the bags. (3) Arrange the bags on a shelf or in several shallow boxes, and the class is ready for germination observation. (Each bag is marked with the gardener's name and the breed of the seed.) Children watch to see which seeds sprout first and check daily on how they grow.

There's no need to re-water the toweling. If the bags are locked shut, the toweling will stay moist and the seeds will grow in about three weeks.

You won't harvest any crops from your in-the-bag greenhouses, but the children will be able to observe, compare, record and chart processes that are usually mysterious underground phenomena.

Idea by: Julie Hacala, Elwell School, Belleville, Mich.

## FABULOUS FREEBEE
# PUNCH 'N GRO

Each of these seed kits is a little plastic container preplanted with dozens of seeds. By simply punching holes in the soft plastic cover, adding water and turning the cover over to retain moisture and let in sunlight — not unlike a greenhouse in miniature — the plants will begin to germinate. After a period of several weeks, the plants must be transferred to regular soil. More than likely there will be enough plants for each of your students.

Though you can't be sure which free kit you will receive, you might, if you're lucky, get the MIMOSA PUDICA, better known as "the sensitive plant." At the very least you'll receive a flower, vegetable or herb kit.

Teachers should request one kit only on school stationery.

Order from: Northrup, King & Co., Attn: Adele Miller, 1500 Jackson St., N.E., Minneapolis, MN 55413. Grade level: Preschool–high school.

# RIVER, WHERE DO YOU COME FROM?

☆ ☆ ☆ ☆ ☆ ☆ ☆ ☆ ☆

This is a short science film, which, because it is so artistically presented, can also be used as a language arts experiment. It presents the cycle of water in the life of a river; water evaporating from the ocean eventually returns to the ocean in that river. The film, recommended for children in grades three through eight, follows the whole sequence, from clouds precipitating snow and rain in the high mountains to a major flood near the mouth of the river. The film presents the idea of a cycle in an almost poetic manner. The first and last scenes, for example, occur in the same place and have the same mood.

The film is beautifully photographed, the color is lovely, and the scenes range from tranquil to violent.

The soundtrack is a ballad, quite well sung and rich in appropriate scientific vocabulary. This comment notwithstanding, some children who have viewed the film felt that the song was unnecessary and that the photography accompanied by natural sounds might have been better. If you anticipate the same comments from your students, the solution is a simple and obvious one.

Order from: Learning Corporation of America, 1350 Ave. of the Americas, New York, NY 10019. Grade level: 3–8. Cost: $15, rental; $145, purchase.

## 136 SCIENCE

## DROPS, STREAMS AND CONTAINERS: Science Activity Cards

☆ ☆ ☆ ☆ ☆ ☆ ☆ ☆

"How full is full?"
"How small a drop can you make?"
"What things does water sink into?"
The children who work with DROPS, STREAMS AND CONTAINERS (part of Elementary Science Study) will investigate these and other watery matters. With this set of 38 activity cards and accompanying teacher's guide, you can help third and fourth graders explore the features and phenomena of many common liquids.

On each card the text is brief and to the point—a few open-ended questions or a suggested task. Large illustrations—usually photographs—clarify and reinforce procedures to follow.

The children examine drops from different perspectives, stack them, pull them around, drop them, roll them together, look through them and create drop pictures before moving on to streams.

The cards are ideal for individual or small group study areas and need not be taken up in strict sequence. (The first 17 cards deal with drops; the remainder deal with liquids.)

Equipment may be ordered for use with these activity cards, but most of the materials—waxed paper, eyedroppers, straws, cheesecloth, etc.—are common household or schoolroom items and are easily scrounged.

Order from: Webster/McGraw-Hill, 1221 Ave. of the Americas, New York, NY 10020. Grade level: 3–6. Cost: $6.27, teacher's guide and activity cards.

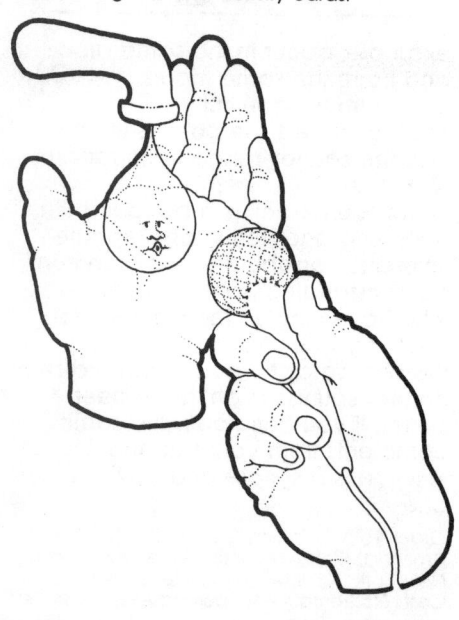

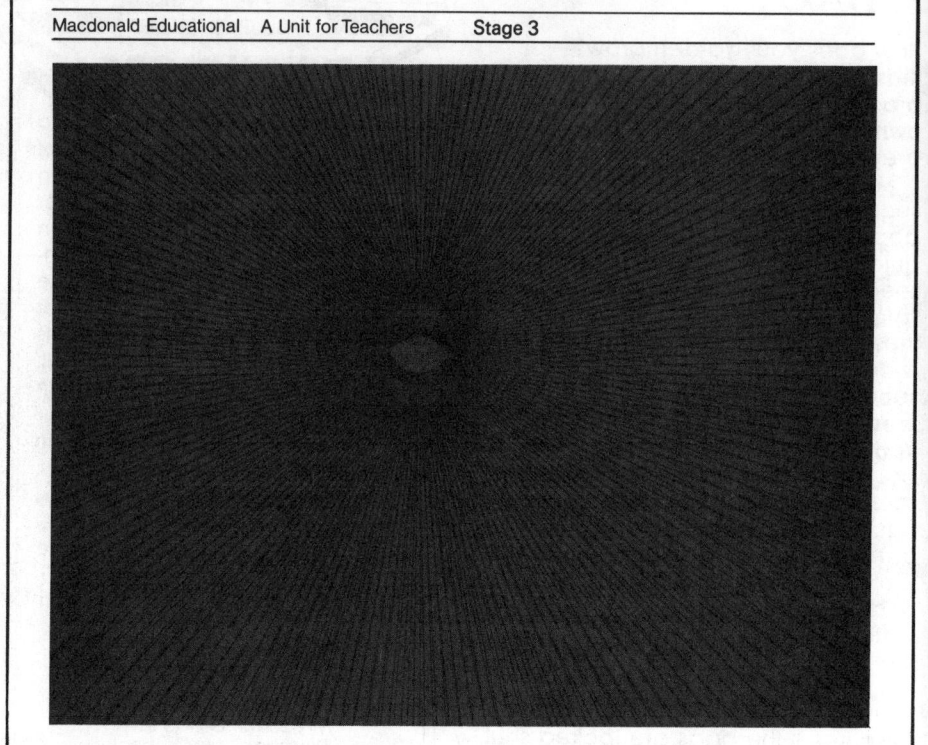

## Science 5/13: Economy Import

by Richard D. Konicek

With the plethora of science programs that make up the alphabet soup we have been sipping for the past decade, it is a pleasure to see a program emerge that doesn't spell a thing! Science 5/13 is its name and, wouldn't you know, it's an import from Great Britain. [Editor's note: Science 5/13 may not spell out anything, but its title still could be a bit confusing. The 5/13 indicates that the program is appropriate for children between the ages of 5 and 13.]

The program, loosely defined, is made up of individual teacher's guides bearing imaginative, simple, yet broad and inviting titles. These include *Early Experiences*—a book of activities for fives and sixes; *Time*—the exploration of time both firsthand and in the historical perspective; *Working with Wood, Stages 1 and 2*—activities with both living and dead wood; *Minibeasts*—keeping and studying small insects, worms, etc., in the classroom; *Science from Toys*—a fascinating booklet on using toys in the classroom; and *Holes, Gaps and Cavities*—a booklet that encourages discovery in all kinds of areas, including electricity, buildings and living things.

Among the other 26 available titles are: *Structures and Forces, Stages 1 and 2*; *Structures and Forces, Stage 3*; *Change, Stages 1 and 2 and Background Information*; *Metals, Stages 1 and 2*; *Metals, Background Information*; and *Working With Wood, Background Information*. The booklets are colorfully illustrated with both drawings and photos, many of, and by, the children they are about.

Developed at the School of Education of the University of Bristol, the materials show definite signs that the authors had a soft spot in their hearts for the teachers and children who work in the open classroom. This is evidenced immediately from the four "educational convictions" that form the background against which the program was developed:

(1) In general, children work best when trying to find answers to the problems they have themselves

chosen to investigate. (2) These problems are best drawn from their own environment and tackled largely by practical investigations. (3) Teachers should be responsible for thinking out and putting into practice the work of their own classes. (4) In order to do so they should be able to find the help where they need it.

The program designers subscribe to Piaget's position that children progress through logical development stages and that the time spent in any stage varies with each child. Work that is based on logical thought processes is best deferred until children have developed some ability for abstract thought. The developers further believe that it is possible for children to work together each at his own pace and level, if led by suitable objectives. Desirable attitudes concerning science and inquiry can be gained by using the subject matter of science even though that subject is not structured by the teacher.

Science 5/13 states as its broad general aim: "developing an inquiring mind and a scientific approach to problems." This aim is broken down into eight specific and practical objectives. Then, these objectives are further isolated into specific observable behaviors that can be expected at each level. The objectives are not so specific as those found in Science—A Process Approach, nor so general as to be meaningless. They are just specific enough to indicate the desired outcome, but not to prescribe the means for reaching that outcome. Nor are the objectives confined to science. Aesthetics, language arts, social studies and math are also included. Imaginative and creative "flow charts" designed to integrate all subjects within the program are provided in abundance. The teacher is thus aided in helping the children to be aware of the potential elements of knowledge inherent in the activities they normally pursue every day.

Because of the program's concern with objectives, the most important introductory reading for a teacher planning to use the units is a manual entitled *With Objectives in Mind*. Here is a lucid, thorough statement of philosophy, devoid of "pedagese" and clichés—written leanly and full of charming British idioms. It moves nicely through the concepts necessary for understanding the program. What kind of science is *right* for children? What do we want children to *achieve* through science? How can we help them achieve their *own* potential? There are chapters on the development of children, the contribution of science to early education, the selection of objectives for children learning science, and a discussion of the units themselves.

Even though objectives are stressed, readers are warned that objectives must not intervene between teacher and pupil; they must be present in the teacher's mind, but not so far in the forefront that she concentrates on them rather than on the children and the way in which their needs can be met.

The program is not without its shortcomings though. Some of the objectives have questionable value, and others are difficult to use because of their lack of specificity. The numbers of objectives, too, might seem overwhelming. One needs also to translate from the British in idiom as well as in materials. However, it does not take long to realize that a cotton reel is a thread spool or that a washing-up liquid bottle is a dishwashing liquid bottle.

A note to Purnell Educational, 850 Seventh Ave., New York, NY 10019, will bring a colorful brochure and price list by return mail. Science 5/13 is certainly worth a look!

Richard D. Konicek is associate professor of education, University of Massachusetts, Amherst.

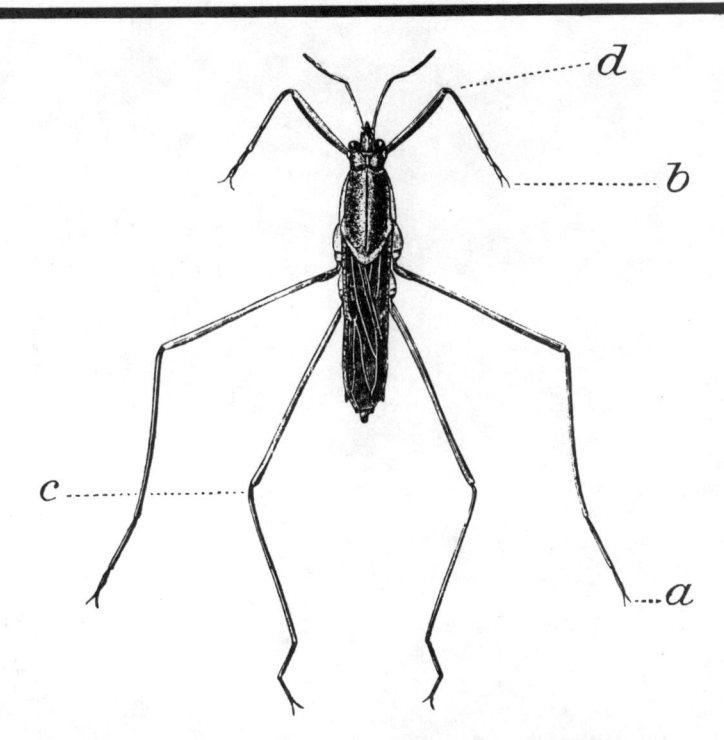

## THE BUG HOUSE
☆ ☆ ☆ ☆ ☆ ☆ ☆ ☆

To your classroom collection of gerbil cages, rabbit hutches and aquariums, add THE BUG HOUSE. Made primarily of fine wire mesh set in a solid plaster-of-paris and metal base, the cylindrical BUG HOUSE is capable of housing all sorts of bugs, from arachnids to insects, in all sizes and shapes (though a praying mantis would be slightly cramped inside).

The five-by-three-inch BUG HOUSE is not as aesthetically interesting as your typical, decorative cricket cage, but its fine mesh construction accommodates much smaller bugs. In addition, THE BUG HOUSE allows full light and air to enter. It is a good observation chamber, and it is certainly safer than the old, familiar bug container, the glass-jar-with-holes-poked-through-the-top.

Making use of THE BUG HOUSE presents no technical problems. Kids can collect whatever species of bugs they prefer by removing the slip-on metal top, easing their new-found pet(s) inside and replacing the top. Leaves can be placed inside for food and shelter either before or after the bugs arrive.

With all this luxury, what bug wouldn't be happy to call THE BUG HOUSE home?

Order from: Lakeshore Curriculum Materials, 1144 Montague, San Leandro, CA. 94577. Grade level: K–6. Cost: $2.00 each plus $.75 postage and handling. Payment must accompany order.

# KIDS' LEISURE READING

# KIDS' LEISURE READING 139

## ONCE UPON A TIME: THE FAIRY-TALE WORLD OF ARTHUR RACKHAM
**Edited by Margery Darell**

Many of today's children have grown up without knowing Arthur Rackham, the noted English illustrator of the Edwardian period. Viking has reprinted his illustrations with such classic texts as "Rip Van Winkle" and seven fairy tales by the Brothers Grimm.
VIKING, $14.95 (list), $13.46 (school price). Ages 9–12.

## GEORGE AND MARTHA
**Written and illustrated by James Marshall**

These two hippopotamus friends may look a bit like Babar and Celeste (all that clothed bulk does it), but their antic emotional honesty is in a class all its own. Marshall's truly original point of view is seen also in his book YUMMERS! (Houghton Mifflin), starring Emily the pig and Eugene the turtle. But if you can only choose one, opt for GEORGE AND MARTHA.
HOUGHTON, $.95, paperback. Ages 4–8.

## THE CHICK AND THE DUCKLING
**by A. Sutayev, adapted from the Russian by Mirra Ginsburg Illustrated by Jose and Ariane Aruego**

Everything the duckling does, the chick does, too — until they both run into the water and only one can swim. This gentle, easy-to-read tale is perfectly complemented by the illustrations of a fresh new world.
MACMILLAN, $5.95. Ages 3–6.

## THE FUNNY LITTLE WOMAN
**by Arlene Mosel Illustrated by Blair Lent**

A retelling of Lafcadio Hearne's tale about a Japanese woman who chases a rice dumpling down a hole and finds herself in the nether world where live the wicked "oni". A good read-aloud book with lots of suspense but nothing too frightening for young children. Blair Lent's pictures of the worlds below and above are delightful.
DUTTON, $5.95. Ages 4–8.

## MISS JASTER'S GARDEN
**Written and illustrated by Neils M. Bodecker**

A large book, with excellent illustrations, a whimsical story, and a very small price tag. It's all about Miss Jaster, who lives by the sea at Sandgate, England. It's also about her garden and Hedgie, a hedgehog that becomes a flowerhog when seeds inadvertently sprinkled on his back begin to sprout. A good read-aloud book.
GOLDEN PRESS, $3.95. Ages 5–9.

*Illustration from The Impossible People*

## THE IMPOSSIBLE PEOPLE: A History Natural and Unnatural of Beings Terrible and Wonderful
**by Georgess McHargue Illustrated by Frank Bozzo**

Witches, pixies, brownies, fairies, giants, goblins, satyrs and merfolk. All of these and more are described in this well-researched catalog of imaginary beings. Or were they all imaginary?
HOLT, $6.95. Dell/Yearling, $1.25, paperback. Ages 10–14.

## MUFFEL AND PLUMS
**by Lilo Fromm**

Two beguiling characters, Muffel the lion and Plums the rabbit, romp through antic adventures without a word of text. Preschool children can use the comic-booklike illustrations to "read" by themselves.
MACMILLAN, $4.95. Ages 4–8.

## TOMFOOLERY
**by Alvin Schwartz Illustrated by Glen Rounds**

Students can produce their own "Laugh-In" or "Zoom" using the "trickery and foolery with words" from American folklore collected by Alvin Schwartz. Just enough silly business to delight kids.
LIPPINCOTT, $1.95, paperback. Ages 7–13.

## THE DEVIL'S STORYBOOK
**by Natalie Babbitt**

The devil has left his brimstone home to go walking in the world, messing with mortals as he goes. These ten original stories by Babbitt, author of KNEE-KNOCK RISE, are both masterfully written and true to the folk idiom. Old Scratch's multifaceted personality makes him by turn egotistical, insecure, sly and naive. He is tricked as often, truth to tell, as he tricks. And how dull the world would be without him.
FARRAR, $4.95 (list), $4.55 (school price). Ages 8–12.

## 140 KIDS' LEISURE READING

### HOW TOM BEAT CAPTAIN NAJORK AND HIS HIRED SPORTSMEN
**by Russell Hoban**
**Illustrated by Quentin Blake**

Tom's verrry British Aunt Fidget Wonkham-Strong (who wears an iron hat and forces Tom to eat his cabbage and potato sog) cannot tolerate Tom's easy-does-it attitude. But all that experience in fooling around helps Tom win the day, escape and find a new aunt—Bundlejoy Cosysweet. This tangy confection about the merits of hanging loose is a distinctly different cup of tea from what Hoban, the author of the FRANCES books, usually serves. But like its hero, this book is a winner.

ATHENEUM, $7.95. Ages 5–9.

Illustration from *How Tom Beat Captain Najork and His Hired Sportsmen*

### MOM, THE WOLF MAN AND ME
**by Norma Klein**

Klein is a marvelous writer, always right-on in her characterizations of children about to become adolescents. Brett, the almost-12 narrator, tells the story of her life in a decidedly offbeat family, consisting of her mom, who never married her father, herself and, occasionally, her mother's new boyfriend (the wolf man), who spends the night sometimes. The possibility that her mother might get married and change their life-style is the big crisis in Brett's life. A great book for sophisticated young teens anywhere (not just in New York City) and 21-year-olds in the Bible Belt.

AVON, $.95, paperback. Ages 12 and up.

Illustration from *King Grisly-Beard*

### KING GRISLY-BEARD: A Tale From the Brothers Grimm
**Pictures by Maurice Sendak**
**Translated by Edgar Taylor**

A retold fairy tale that is not at all grim, with delightful comic-booklike illustrations. It stars two children who act out the parts of King Grisly-Beard and his bride. Readers may very well want to play the parts themselves. The story lends itself well to being read aloud. It's all about a selfish, impolite and spoiled princess who learns humility and lives happily ever after.

FARRAR, $2.95 (list), $2.65 (school price). Ages 4–8.

### A PROUD TASTE FOR SCARLET AND MINIVER
**Written and Illustrated by E. L. Konigsburg**

The author of the 1968 Newbery Award winner has written a tale of Eleanor of Aquitaine, part fact, part fantasy. Eleanor, awaiting the arrival in Heaven of her husband, Henry II, passes the time reminiscing with Abbot Suger, Matilda-Empress (Henry's mother) and William the Marshall, who each tell part of Eleanor's story.

ATHENEUM, $6.95. Ages 10–14.

### THE MUSHROOM CENTER DISASTER
**by N. M. Bodecker**
**Illustrated by Erik Blegvad**

A beetle visiting the Mushroom Center is transformed into an emergency planner when disaster—littering picnickers—hits the little burg. This is a cozy tale of life among the snails, fireflies and ladybugs. Its precise details (discarded drinking straws become part of the new waterworks) are brought to life in Blegvad's line drawings. For lovers of the miniscule.

ATHENEUM, $5.25. Ages 7–9.

## SING SONG SCUPPERNONG
**Compiled by Jeanne B. Hardendorff**
**Illustrated by Jacqueline Chwast**

Readers from Tennessee and Mississippi, the childhood home of the compiler, may find these 16 nonsense songs familiar, but most others will find pieces like "The Whizz-Fish Song" hilariously new and great fun to sing.
HOLT, $5.95. All ages.

## HURRY THE CROSSING
**by Alan Venable**

Mfupi, a Tanzanian boy, learns about life through a series of encounters with such characters as a tattooed wood-carver and a fisherman who'd rather tell tall tales than fish. A lively and moving glimpse of life in this African nation. Includes a nice sprinkling of Swahili for extra authenticity.
LIPPINCOTT, $4.95. Ages 9–14.

## OMOTEJI'S BABY BROTHER
**by Mary-Joan Gerson**
**Illustrated by Elzia Moon**

The naming ceremony for the new brother of Omoteji, a Yoruba from Nigeria, is the subject of this informative picture book. Like siblings everywhere, Omoteji is at first jealous of the newcomer but overcomes it by thinking about his own special gift to the baby.
WALCK, $6.95. Ages 4–8.

## LONGHOUSE WINTER
**Adapted by Hettie Jones**
**Illustrated by Nicholas Gaetano**

A masterfully designed book with glorious geometric illustrations which complement the Iroquois legends retold by Hettie Jones. These four tales of transformation were told by the five-league Iroquois nation (the Longhouse) only in the winter.
HOLT, $5.95. Ages 8–12.

## THE FRIENDS
**by Rosa Guy**

Phyllisia Cathy is a young girl from the West Indies who suddenly finds herself (as Rosa Guy once did) in the hostile world of New York City's Harlem. Her father insists that her family is better than the American riffraff, and Phyl must decide between obeying his wishes or continuing her friendship with a very poor but kind girl. The dialogue is appropriately powerful.
HOLT, $5.95. Ages 12 and up.

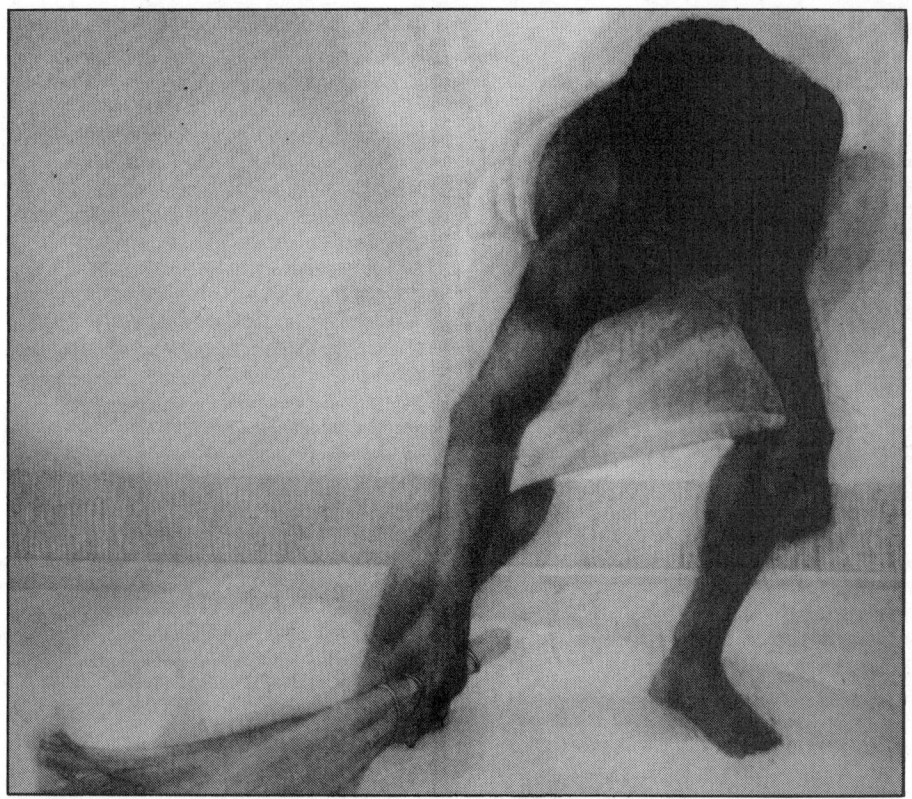

*Illustration from* Jambo Means Hello

## JAMBO MEANS HELLO: Swahili Alphabet Book
**by Muriel Feelings**
**Illustrated by Tom Feelings**

A fascinating look at East African life from the team that produced the much-acclaimed MOJA MEANS ONE: SWAHILI COUNTING BOOK. This African ABC presents a Swahili word and definition for each letter of the alphabet (except q and x). The exuberance and grace of the people and their sense of community are here captured by Feelings' skilled charcoal drawings.
DIAL, $5.95 (list), $4.76 (school price). Ages 6–8.

## SONGS AND STORIES FROM UGANDA
**by W. Moses Serwadda**
**Transcribed and edited by Hewitt Pantaleoni. Illustrated by Leo and Diane Dillon**

Here is an abundance of authentic African folklore written by an African. Serwadda, a musician and scholar from Uganda, learned many of the stories from his grandmother and the songs from his grandfather's group of musicians. An English translation is provided, along with phonetic spelling of the Ugandan lyrics. One caveat from editor Pantaleoni: Please don't sing these African songs in English.
CROWELL, $6.50 (list), $5 (school price). All ages.

## THE TRUTH ABOUT MARY ROSE
**by Marilyn Sachs**

A sensitive novel about the second Mary Rose. She idolizes her aunt and namesake, who died in a fire as a young girl. Whether she did or didn't die a heroine is what the story's all about. Deft portraits of very contemporary characters (her mother is a dentist; her artist father cooks rice pudding) makes this an outstanding book.
DOUBLEDAY, $4.95 (list), $3.71 (school price). Ages 9–12.

# 142 KIDS' LEISURE READING

### WITH A DEEP SEA SMILE
**by Virginia A. Tashjian**
**Illustrated by Rosemary Wells**

Tashjian happily invites children to get moving—sing along, set out, answer riddles, do finger plays—while listening to the book's short poems and funny stories. The well-chosen selections are enlivened and stitched together by Wells' captivating illustrations.

LITTLE, $5.95 (list), $4.76 (school price). All ages.

### THE GIRL WHO CRIED FLOWERS AND OTHER TALES
**by Jane Yolen**
**Illustrated by David Palladini**

Six new and lush fairy tales by Yolen, meant to be clutched to the hearts of all incurable romantics. Palladini's Art Nouveau-esque illustrations in full color are entrancing.

CROWELL, $5.95 (list), $4.28 (school price). Ages 10 and up.

*Illustration from* The Great Brain Reforms

### THE GREAT BRAIN REFORMS
**by John Fitzgerald**
**Illustrated by Mercer Mayer**

The young con-artist finally gets his just deserts in this book in the "Great Brain" series. Tom, the narrator's older brother, can talk anybody out of anything. He's just as mischievous as Mark Twain's Tom, though at times not as likable. His myriad schemes are fascinating.

DIAL, $5.95 (list), $4.76 (school price). Ages 9-12.

### DINKY HOCKER SHOOTS SMACK
**by M. E. Kerr**

Dinky isn't really a heroin addict, but she is addicted to food. Like many adolescents, she has a problem with weight and a problem with identity. And her social worker mother spends more time with drug addicts than she does with Dinky.

This first-rate book is as witty and offbeat as its memorable 14-year-old heroine.

DELL/LAUREL-LEAF, $.95, paperback. Ages 12 and up.

### DON'T COUNT YOUR CHICKENS
**by Ingri and Edgar Parin d'Aulaire**

What happens when the old woman does count her chickens before they hatch? The illustrations are stone lithographs and have a fine country feel about them.

DOUBLEDAY, $5.95 (list), $4.46 (school price). Ages 4-8.

### MUD PIES AND OTHER RECIPES
**by Marjorie Winslow**
**Illustrated by Erik Blegvad**

How to make such delicacies as Roast Rocks, Dandelion Souffle and Leaves En Brochette. This cookbook for dolls is full of such one-of-a-kind gourmet delights.

MACMILLAN/COLLIER, $.95, paperback. Ages 4-8.

### BEAR'S PICTURE
**by Manus Pinkwater**

A whimsical tale with marvelous use of color. It tells about a bear who keeps right on painting his own vision (complete with swirls, dashes and squibbles) despite a running commentary by two very proper gentlemen who don't believe bears can paint pictures.

HOLT OWLET, $1.45, paperback. Ages 4-8.

### YOU'RE THE SCAREDY-CAT
**by Mercer Mayer**

A good book for beginning readers, especially those who might be fascinated with the notion of pink-nosed, green-garbage-can monsters that carry off small boys in the night. This tale of two brothers camping out in their own backyard gives Mayer ample opportunity to indulge his talent for the humorously grotesque.

PARENTS' MAGAZINE PRESS, $5.50. Ages 4-8.

### MINE'S THE BEST
**by Crosby Bonsall**

Two small boys arguing over who has the best beach toy (of course, the two toys are identical) provide the focus of this simple but hilarious, easy but involving reader. An "Early I CAN READ Book."

HARPER, $3.95 (list), $3.55 (school price). Ages 3-7.

### THE WAYFARER'S TREE
**by Anne Colver and Stewart Graff**

Henry David Thoreau tutors Joel, a boy from New York City, and involves him in nature study when Joel isn't playing with Emerson's children or going ice skating with Louisa May Alcott. A warm and involving glimpse of 19th century life.

DUTTON, $5.50. Ages 8-11.

## Magazines For Children

### CRICKET: The Magazine for Children

A magazine that treats children's literature seriously, CRICKET publishes poetry, fiction and nonfiction of a uniformly high caliber by authors ranging from Sendak to Shakespeare. Senior editor Clifton Fadiman and art director Trina Schart Hayman enliven the pages of each issue with a tiny cricket and ladybug who kibitz about the magazine's material. CRICKET clearly outjumps its competition.

Order from: CRICKET, Walnut Lane, Boulder, CO 80301. Cost: 6 issues per year, $5.97. Ages 6-12.

# KIDS' LEISURE READING

*Illustration from Knee-Knock Rise*

## KNEE-KNOCK RISE
**Written and illustrated by Natalie Babbitt**

Set in a timeless world of village fairs, cart rides and the legendary Megrimum who lives among the mists of Knee-Knock Rise, this sensitive adventure story shows the magic touch of a master writer. A Newbery Honor Book.

AVON, $.95, paperback. Ages 8–12.

## THE COOL RIDE IN THE SKY
**Told by Diane Wolkstein**
**Illustrated by Paul Galdone**

This black folk tale was first made popular as a song. Remember Nat King Cole's "Straighten Up and Fly Right"? Storytellers of all ages will find rich material in this story of the monkey who outwits the buzzard with cunning and humor.

KNOPF, $5.69. Ages 4–8.

## TO MARKET! TO MARKET!
**Illustrated by Peter Spier**

Children will be fascinated with the highly detailed pictures of life in 19th-century America, accompanied by familiar rhymes. The book is also an excellent resource for history lessons.

DOUBLEDAY, $4.95 (list), $3.71 (school price). Ages 4–8.

## A MAGIC EYE FOR IDA
**Written and illustrated by Kay Chorao**

Thinking that all she needs to bring her happiness is a dolly-wetsy-bye, Ida learns otherwise when she runs away from home and meets Madame Julia, a frenetic but very wise gypsy.

SEABURY, $5.50 (list), $4.95 (school price). Ages 5–8.

## DREAMLAND LAKE
**by Richard Peck**

Two boys not quite yet adolescents discover the body of a tramp in the woods and begin to deal with death. This first-person account told by a 13-year-old boy has the element of mystery that can capture the interest of most young readers.

HOLT, $5.95. Ages 9–13.

## STONE SOUP: A Journal of Children's Literature

STONE SOUP, dedicated to publishing children's writing in its original, unedited form, along with the best of children's art, is as uninhibited as kids themselves. Consider this powerful image by three-year-old Emmett Dacey.

> Why the Sunset Is That Color
> a bat squirted red food-coloring out of his penis into the sky.

The intentions of William Rubel, the young editor/founder of STONE SOUP are admirable. He has managed, with little capital, to put together a fine compilation of prose, poetry, art and book reviews by kids.

Order from: STONE SOUP, Dept. 17, Box 83, Santa Cruz, CA 95063. Cost: 5 issues per year, $5.50. Ages 6–12.

## EBONY JR!

The first national magazine for black children, EBONY JR!, is the product of collaboration between the publishers of EBONY magazine and the new magazine's managing editor, Constance Van Brunt Johnson, a reading specialist. The magazine emphasizes discovery both of self and the joy of reading. Games, cartoons, recipes, African history, reader contributions, crafts and other features all contribute to those discoveries.

Order from: EBONY JR!, 820 S. Michigan Ave., Chicago, Il 60605. Cost: 10 issues per year, $4.50. Ages 6–12.

## THE ELECTRIC COMPANY MAGAZINE

City Cat and Fargo North Decoder are a couple of the comic-strip superheroes found in the pages of this publication from Children's Television Workshop. The magazine is not a mere rehash of the show but includes contributions from kids, fresh features and inventive word games, all of which involve students in reading. It's just as silly and savvy as its seven-year-old audience and is practical without being uptight.

Order from: THE ELECTRIC COMPANY MAGAZINE, Dept. L, P.O. Box C-19, Birmingham, AL 35201. Cost: 10 issues per year, $5. For beginning readers and those needing beginning remedial reading.

## 144 KIDS' LEISURE READING

*Illustration from*
*The Best Christmas Pageant Ever*

### THE BEST CHRISTMAS PAGEANT EVER
**by Barbara Robinson**
**Illustrated by Judith Gwyn Brown**

The Herdman kids are the bane of their Sunday School. Naturally, when they're assigned roles in the Christmas pageant, they come up with a distinctly unusual interpretation of the Christmas story. A nice, unsentimental treatment.

AVON, $1.25, paperback. Ages 8–10.

### HILDILID'S NIGHT
**by Cheli Durán Ryan**
**Illustrated by Arnold Lobel**

Hildilid is a roly-poly peasant lady who lives with her wolfhound in a thatched hut high in the hills of Hexham. Her story, a natural for read-aloud sessions, moves rhythmically along as she tries to chase away the night by sweeping it, boiling it and applying other home remedies that, alas, don't work. Lobel's scratchy black-and-white drawings captured a Caldecott Honor Book citation.

MACMILLAN/COLLIER, $.95, paperback. Ages 4–8.

### THE UNDERGROUND CATS
**by Susan Bennett**

Bennett retells and illustrates an old Italian tale in which the heroine, a Cinderella-like sweetheart (with a suitably vindictive stepmother and slothful stepsister), finds an underground cache of cats when she pulls up a cauliflower one day. Because she is helpful and considerate, these extraordinary felines present her with marvelous clothes and jewels and, as a final touch, a star for her forehead. When the selfish stepsister tries to reap the same rewards, the cats leave her in rags and with a sour pudding dripping down her face. Her just dessert?

MACMILLAN, $5.95. Ages 4–8.

### THE MIDNIGHT ADVENTURES OF KELLY, DOT AND ESMERALDA
**by John S. Goodall**

A wordless tale by the author of the celebrated Paddy Pork books. This one is in marvelous watercolor and entices the young reader with a gentle adventure of three toys — Kelly the koala bear, a doll named Dot, and the demure mouse Esmeralda — who climb into a painting on the wall and thence to a dangerous encounter with a cat at the village fair.

ATHENEUM, $4.95. Ages 4–7.

### ONE FINE DAY
**by Nonny Hogroglan**

The fox is outfoxed by the old woman, who cuts off his tail and starts an escalating adventure. Drawings and story are as warm and elemental as the big yellow ball of a sun decorating every page of this Armenian folk tale. Winner of the Caldecott Medal.

MACMILLAN/COLLIER, $1.25, paperback. Ages 3–6.

### THE HUNDRED DRESSES
**by Eleanor Estes**
**Illustrated by Louis Slobodkin**

A new generation of young readers can weep over the bittersweet saga of Wanda Petronski, who has only one faded dress to wear to school each day but insists she has 100 dresses at home. First published in 1944, this obviously is a book that has endured.

HARCOURT/VOYAGER. Paperback: $1.50 (list), $1.20 (school price). Ages 6–10.

### BENJAMIN AND TULIP
**by Rosemary Wells**

Benjamin's Aunt Fern calls Tulip "that sweet little girl," but each time Benjamin passes Tulip's house, she says, "I'm going to beat you up" and proceeds to do it. Never fear, things do work out in the end.

DIAL, $4.95 (list), $3.96 (school price). Ages 3–7.

# KIDS' LEISURE READING 145

## NUMBER 24
**by Guy Billout**

This wordless fantasy is brought to life by Guy Billout's compelling illustrations, which have been admirably packaged in quality paperback form by Harlin Quist. The passive protagonist, waiting patiently for the number 24 bus, finds instead a ship, an airplane, even marching soldiers and a tank. A dream of a book.
DIAL/DELACORTE. Paperback: $1.50 (list), $1.20 (school price). All ages.

## IF I WERE A CRICKET
**by Kazue Mizumura**

The author of IF I WERE A MOTHER captures the feeling of wonder that is usually unique with small children. Words like "sparkling," "shiny," "shimmering" are sprinkled through her prose, and her gentle, luminous illustrations of ladybugs, snails and other small creatures fit the text perfectly. Young writers can use the "If I Were..." concept as a model for their own writing.
CROWELL, $6.95 (list), $5 (school price). Ages 3 and up.

## A LONG WAY FROM VERONA
**by Jane Gardam**

An independent English schoolgirl's personal account of trying to be herself and the obstacles put in her path by her very proper teachers. Set during World War II, this novel is a rare find, funny and real without being "relevant."
MACMILLAN/COLLIER, $1.25, paperback. Ages 12 and up.

## THE BORROWERS ALOFT
**by Mary Norton**

Homily, Pod and their 15-year-old daughter, Arrietty, are a family of miniature people living in late-Victorian England. They're off again on another suspenseful adventure in this, the fourth and last of a series. They're kidnapped by a greedy couple who plan to exhibit them. Resourcefulness and a balloon save the day.
HARCOURT/VOYAGER. Paperback: $1.35 (list), $1.08 (school price). Ages 8–12.

*Illustration from The Midnight Adventures of Kelly, Dot and Esmeralda*

*Illustration from Book of Bears*

## BOOK OF BEARS
**by Michael Bond**

The creator of Paddington Bear presents a unique all-bear collection for bruin lovers. There are a British comic-strip bear named Rupert; Winnie the Pooh, of course; and lots of Russian bears, including Michael Ivanovitch, Nastasia Petrovna and Mishutka, three bears who find a strange little girl in their house in Tolstoy's retelling of an old folk tale.
PENGUIN/PUFFIN. Paperback: $1.95 (list), $1.75 (school price). Ages 5 and up.

## THE EASY HOW-TO BOOK
**by Seymour Reit**
**Illustrated by William Dugan**

Offerings include how to read a thermometer, peel an egg, get a swing started when you're all by yourself, and 50 other entries of pertinence to kids who would really rather do it themselves.
GOLDEN PRESS, $5.95. Ages 5–9.

# 146 KIDS' LEISURE READING

*Illustration from The Juniper Tree and Other Tales From Grimm*

## THE JUNIPER TREE AND OTHER TALES FROM GRIMM
**Selected by Lore Segal and Maurice Sendak**
**Translated by Lore Segal, with four tales translated by Randall Jarrell**
**Illustrated by Maurice Sendak**

Sendak, who first considered illustrating the Grimm brothers' tales ten years ago, surpasses all that he has done before in this two-volume boxed set, a delight to see and touch. Segal's translations, faithful to the originals, manage to combine the straightforward and the magical, a very difficult feat.

FARRAR, $15 (list); $13.50 (school price). Paperback (one volume), $4.95 (list); $4.55 (school price). All ages — from read aloud to read alone.

## LEO THE LATE BLOOMER
**by Robert Kraus**
**Illustrated by Jose Aruego**

Like most young creatures, Leo the toddling tiger needs time to become civilized, that is, to learn such important things as reading and writing and eating right. Kraus and Aruego combine to create a kaleidoscopic delight.

YOUNG READERS PRESS/SIMON & SCHUSTER. Paperback: $1.50 (list), $1.20 (school price). Ages 3–6.

## THE GENIE OF SUTTON PLACE
**by George Selden**

Readers get both a spell-binding tale of the occult and an action-packed dog story in this hilarious novel. The hero, Tim, summons a genie to save his dog from the pound. The only rescue method available, it seems, is to turn the dog into a man. Sam-the-man-dog provides the book's fun. This zany story is by the author of the critically acclaimed THE CRICKET IN TIMES SQUARE.

FARRAR, $5.95 (list), $5.35 (school price). Dell/Yearling, $.95, paperback. Ages 9–13.

## THE GIRL WHO LOVED THE WIND
**by Jane Yolen**
**Illustrated by Ed Young**

An intriguing tale of a Persian princess, sheltered from sorrow by her father, who hears of another world in the songs of the wind. The illustrations, very reminiscent of Persian miniatures, are as exotic and poetic as the story itself.

CROWELL, $4.50 (list), $3.24 (school price). Ages 4–8.

## THE TIGER'S BONES AND OTHER PLAYS FOR CHILDREN
**by Ted Hughes**
**Illustrated by Alan E. Cober**

Hughes, the noted British poet, wrote these plays originally for radio. They are quite adaptable to classroom performance or may simply be read aloud. The folk tale, the fable, the myth are all represented in the five plays, illustrated with a nice eccentric touch by Cober.

VIKING, $5.95 (list), $5.35 (school price). Ages 10–14.

## THE SON OF SOMEONE FAMOUS
**by M. E. Kerr**

Brenda Belle Blossom's mother is worried about the femininity of her wise-cracking daughter; Adam Blessing's very famous father does not concern himself enough with his son. The relationship of parents with their teenage children is a recurring theme in the novels of Kerr, whose forte is treating sensitively and humorously the growing pains of adolescents.

HARPER, $4.95 (list), $4.45 (school price). Ages 12 and up.

## JULIE OF THE WOLVES
**by Jean Craighead George**

The powerful story of the journey of a young Eskimo girl (Miyax/Julie) through the arctic wilderness. As she learns to cope with the environment, which grows less hostile as her journey continues, she seems to understand the value of her own heritage. Through her eyes, the reader gains a new respect for that much maligned animal — the wolf.

HARPER, $4.95 (list), $4.45 (school price). Paperback: $1.25 (list), $1.12 (school price). Ages 12 and up.

# KIDS' LEISURE READING 147

*Illustration from Timothy the Terror*

### TIMOTHY THE TERROR
**by Ruth Cavin**
**Illustrated by Jean-Jacques Loup**

Timothy, a much put-upon preschooler, narrates the spunky story of his transformation from a pussycat to the "biggest mos' fierce tiger ever was." Marvelous illustrations match the prose, written in Black English.

DIAL/DELACORTE.
Paperback: $1.50 (list),
$1.20 (school price). Ages 4 – 8.

### FLOATING CLOUDS, FLOATING DREAMS: Favorite Asian Folktales
**Edited by I. K. Junne**

Folktales from all over the Orient (Burma, Cambodia, China, India, Japan, Korea, Laos, Persia, Thailand, Tibet and Vietnam), exotically alive with princesses, ogres, merchants and greedy old men and women. These very same characters, in fact, may well have been the prototypes for tales we now think of as European. I. K. Junne is a Korean-born art historian and folklorist.

DOUBLEDAY, $4.95 (list),
$3.71 (school price).
Ages 10 and up.

### THE CHECKER PLAYERS
**by Alan Venable**
**Illustrated by Byron Barton**

This first book by Venable introduces a fascinating pair: the fastidious carpenter, a bear, and the somewhat messy but very ingenious tinker, an alligator. Despite their differences, they manage to enjoy checkers and each other. Readers will enjoy them, too.

LIPPINCOTT, $5.50. Ages 4 – 7.

### THE BOY WHO DIDN'T BELIEVE IN SPRING
**by Lucille Clifton**
**Illustrated by Brinton Turkle**

King Shabazz, a cool, sunglass-wearing seven-year-old, drags his friend, Tony Polito, with him on an authentically urban adventure in search of Spring. The reality of the dialogue helps to make it one of the best children's books about a black.

DUTTON, $5.95. Ages 4 – 7.

### EYE WINKER, TOM TINKER, CHIN CHOPPER: A Collection of Musical Fingerplays
**by Tom Glazer**
**Illustrated by Ron Himmler**

What teacher of young children wouldn't like a book like this one, chock-full of songs for fingerplay? Each of the 50 songs is accompanied by guitar chords as well as piano arrangements. The illustrations, in a Victorian mode, are enchanting.

DOUBLEDAY, $5.95 (list), 4.46 (school price).
Ages 4 – 8.

### THE KNEE-HIGH MAN AND OTHER TALES
**by Julius Lester**
**Illustrated by Ralph Pinto**

These tales are drawn from memories of stories told by the author's father, which in turn were drawn from the oral heritage of black America.

DIAL, $5.95 (list), $4.76 (school price).
Ages 4 – 8.

*Illustration from The Checker Players*

# 148 KIDS' LEISURE READING

## ALEXANDER AND THE TERRIBLE, HORRIBLE, NO GOOD, VERY BAD DAY
**by Judith Viorst**
**Illustrated by Ray Cruz**

Adults have days when nothing goes right, and so do little boys like Alexander. Days when he might as well give up and move to Australia. A marvelously unsaccharine story for young children with a title and illustrations to match.
ATHENEUM, $6.95. Ages 5–9.

## CINDERELLA, OR THE LITTLE GLASS SLIPPER
**by Charles Perrault**
**Translated, adapted and illustrated by Errol Le Cain**

This import is a smashing version of the old story, retold and illustrated by a young British genius, Errol Le Cain. The elegance of his touch is particularly effective in the magical transformation sequences (lizards into footmen, mice into horses). Cinderella is a touchingly humble and forgiving heroine.
BRADBURY, $5.95 (list), $4.46 (school price). Ages 4–8.

## PIPPEN AND ROBBER CRUMBLECROACK'S BIG BABY
**Written and illustrated by Margriet Heymans**

Pippen — half puppet, half boy — is a most appealing character. His adventures in the countryside are adapted from a puppet play performed in Holland by Clown Wondi. With cunning and wit, the lad is able to outfox a band of suitably scruffy robbers.
ADDISON-WESLEY, $5.50 (list), $4.13 (school price). Ages 3–8.

## THE WOLF WHO HAD A WONDERFUL DREAM: A French Folktale
**by Anne Rockwell**

A fresh reworking of the three-little-pigs-meet-the-big-bad-wolf tale, accompanied by lively watercolor illustrations. The wolf's dream of a gourmet feast of three juicy piglets is punctured by a quick-thinking mama pig. We leave the starving animal (converted to vegetarianism?) dreaming of apples, bread and Camembert.
CROWELL, $4.50 (list), $3.24 (school price). Ages 4–8.

## THE POOH PARTY BOOK
**by Virginia H. Ellison**
**Illustrated by Ernest H. Shepard**

Five special Pooh parties, with ideas for decorations, invitations and activities inspired by A. A. Milne's books. Recipes have names like "Piglet Underneath Cake" and "Violet Honey Sauce." A must for Pooh fans.
DELL/YEARLING, $1.25, paperback. All ages.

*Illustration from Alexander and the Terrible, Horrible, No Good, Very Bad Day*

*Illustration from Ishi, Last of His Tribe*

In the age of McLuhan, why bother to turn children on to books? Simply because when children learn to love books, very special things happen.

There is, of course, that unique privacy, that sense of being in personal control when you read. Books, like climbing trees, can be scary, but the child controls the fear faucet. Sometimes, experimenting, the child goes beyond where he is comfortable alone; frightened, he can slam the book shut for a while, open it later for another peek, and finally, plunge fully into it again.

But which books? Which mysteries? Adults, of course, write most children's books, and that is unfortunate, for few adults can get in touch with the primal flows of childhood, let alone express them artistically. Thus it is that much of children's literature drifts into the indulgence of nostalgia. Fortunately, some children's books do tap what lies deep within each of us. They are the ones that bring us our myths.

It is an ancient process, this sharing of symbols, this telling of stories that touch on mythical themes and provide windows into the ineffable and identify the great concerns. Of all the thousands of books, only a handful really have this power. But, oh, that handful! They are very good indeed.

The books recommended here have done those things for children in our experience. Invariably, they touch special places in their readers. The

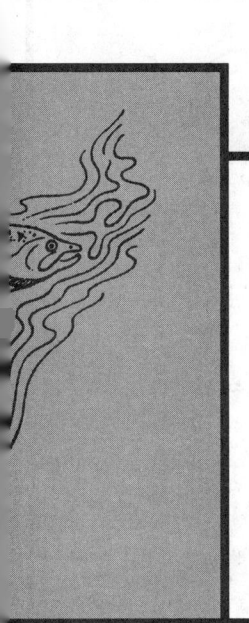

# CHILDREN & BOOKS
## THE ETERNAL MAGIC

by Salli Rasberry and Robert Greenway

*Illustration from Velveteen Rabbit*

age recommendations apply when children are reading to themselves. Almost every book here can be read aloud to children of any age.

### Books That Reach Deep Into the Inner Being

*The Mother Deer* by Edith Thacher Hurd, illustrated by Clement Hurd (Little, Brown, ages 6 to 8). One year in the life of a mother deer . . . the effects of the environment . . . changing seasons . . . the meaning of life in different forms . . . incredible images.

*The Winner* by Kjell Ringi (Harper & Row, ages 3 to 6). A classic that uses words only in its gentle address "To all neighbors," and that clearly identifies, even for the smallest children, the tragic results of failing to cooperate.

*The Nest* by Constantine Georgiou, illustrated by Bethany Tudor (Harvey House, ages 4 to 7). The way a mother robin builds a nest, a process not so far removed from what more and more folks are doing—actually building their own shelters rather than accepting standardized tract housing.

*The Biggest Bear* by Lynd Ward (Houghton Mifflin, ages 5 to 8). Disaster and bears and big scares. Johnny wants a cub, and to the dismay of his parents, a small bear arrives to capture their son's heart.

*The Yearling* by Marjorie Rawlings (Scribner's, ages 10 and up). The sad tale of a 12-year-old boy and the fawn he tames and loses. It mirrors real life in that not all the action has happy endings.

### Books That Deal With the Confusions of Childhood

*Bubbles* by Eloise Greenfield, illustrated by Eric Marlow (Drum & Spear, ages 4 to 8). A boy learns to read and runs home to share his excitement with his mom, only to find her too busy to listen. He feels sorry for himself until he gets involved with comforting his baby sister. Very tender and loving.

*The Bear's House* by Marilyn Sachs (Doubleday, ages 9 to 12). A somber book about the life of a lonely little girl whose daddy deserts the family, leaving his despondent wife unable to care for herself or the house full of children. Fran Ellen's only warmth comes from her baby sister. When her sister becomes ill, Fran Ellen retreats. Partly because its ending is ambiguous, the book opens some deep communication channels.

*Lisa Bright and Dark* by John Neufeld (S. G. Phillips, ages 10 and up). Lisa is violent yet gentle, open yet closed; at 16, she's a very confused girl. A very compassionate and believable tale of how a child's own friends help her to deal with insanity.

*The Planet of Junior Brown* by Virginia Hamilton (Macmillan, ages 10 and up). A memorable story of inner strength and friendship, it tells of Junior Brown, a very over-weight musical prodigy, and his friend Buddy Clark, who has no one who cares.

### Books That Deal Honestly With Current Realities

*The Seven Stone* by Mary Francis Shura (Holiday House, ages 10 and up). Magic stones mixed up with cultural conflicts as, hang on, a hippie child comes into a public school.

*The Soul Brothers and Sister Lou* by Kristin Hunter (Scribner's or Avon [paperback], ages 10 and up). The heart, soul and music of a beautiful black girl growing up in a Northern ghetto.

*Crimson Moccasins* by Wayne Doughty, (Harper & Row, ages 10 and up). An extremely moving story of what happens to the son of an Indian chief when he finds out he is really white.

*Picture Stories in Color* by collective authors (China Books & Periodicals [2929 24th St., San Francisco, CA 94110], ages 4 to 8). A lovely series of books imported from China. Though they have been put down by some reviewers as doctrinaire, these books are a delight for younger children, providing insight into the values, goals and dreams of the Chinese.

### Books of Adventure

*Snail and Caterpillar* by H. Piers (McGraw-Hill, ages 3 to 8). Crossing cultures in order to help each other, the snail and the caterpillar work their way out of a very scary dilemma.

# 150 KIDS' LEISURE READING

Illustration from *The Little Prince*

Illustration from *Just So Stories*

*Just So Stories* by Rudyard Kipling (originally published in 1902, various editions, ages 8 and up). Remember these fables? They raise marvelous issues about reality by using the style of ancient myths as the basis for "just so" stories—about how camels got their humps, how leopards got their spots and, subliminally, how humans got their ideas.

**Seed Gift Books**

*Listen, Children, Listen: An Anthology of Poems for the Very Young*, edited by Myra Cohn Livingston, illustrated by Trina Nyman (Harcourt Brace Jovanovich, ages 4 and up). An exquisite gift of sound, beauty and insight, not just for the very young but for children of all ages, races and persuasions.

*The Carrot Seed* by Ruth Krauss (Harper & Row, Scholastic Book Service [paperback], ages 4 to 7). A boy plants a seed that everyone says won't come up. He persists, loving his little seed in the ground, and the carrot grows, just as he knew it would.

*Velveteen Rabbit* by Margery Williams (Doubleday, ages 8 and up). Remember your favorite stuffed animal? This is a story of a rabbit and his favorite boy and what happens to well-loved toys.

**Our Families' All-Time Favorites**

*These books seem to transcend categories; they take us to that magical meeting ground where children and adults dance together.*

*James and the Giant Peach* by Roald Dahl (Knopf, ages 6 to 10). High fantasy and adventure involving sharks and caterpillars and sea gulls and James and his incredible peach. The drawings are magnificent.

*Ishi, Last of His Tribe* by Theodora Kroeber (Parnassus Press or Bantam [paperback], ages 9 and up). The last of his tribe, Ishi ended up as a living display in a museum. This story, based on actual anthropological records, made us weep, not only for Ishi and his tribe as its numbers dwindled and its plight worsened, but for ourselves, the white man, *Saldu*. For we realized that we were the enemy, and that we are part of the continuing crime.

*Indian Tales* by Jaime De Angulo (Hill & Wang, ages 10 and up). Jaime De Angulo, a remarkable man, lived with the Pit River Indians for many years and shares with us stories of "fox boy," "coyote old man" and "antelope woman." The book captures the Indian spirit and is wonderful to read aloud or to calm and refocus ourselves at the end of the day.

*The Little Prince* by Antoine de Saint-Exupery (Harcourt Brace, ages 8 and up). The classic myth of the lonely, the hero, the wise child, the unseeing adult; a story also of pride and of learning what is important in life. The watercolors are like happy music.

*High Wind in Jamaica* by Richard Hughes (Harper & Row, ages 12 and up). For us, this has been a magic and terrifying read-aloud book summer after summer. Our children sigh with recognition, murmuring, "Yes, that's really how it is." Full of pirates, serious adventure and some grimly violent episodes, we recommend it be read with adults around who can deal with the strong emotions it taps.

*The Chronicles of Narnia* by C. S. Lewis (Macmillan, ages 10 and up). A fantasy trip to a world where trees and animals and dwarfs and magic lions are given a special place close to the hearts of us all. Our children now stop at puddles and other strange places resembling the doorways to Narnia and, with faraway looks in their eyes and awe in their voices, say, "Through there lies Narnia."

*Island of the Blue Dolphins* by Scott O'Dell (Houghton Mifflin or Dell [paperback], ages 9 to 14). A true story that mesmerizes and moves, this book is about a young Indian girl living alone on an island for 18 years, making everything she needs to survive. Perhaps the finest book to give to any child who is exploring country living and survival.

*A Wrinkle in Time* by Madeleine L'Engle (Farrar, Straus & Giroux or Dell [paperback], ages 10 to 13). A fine science-fiction story that transcends time and space, with a mother and father who are both great scientists, and children who risk everything to save their father.

Salli Rasberry and Robert Greenway are coauthors of RASBERRY EXERCISES (Freestone), one of the first manuals on how to establish and run free schools.

# Ordering Information

ADDISON-WESLEY. Order from: Addison-Wesley Publishing Co., Reading, MA 01867. Attn.: Dorothy Williams. Add $.40 postage and handling on billed orders.

ATHENEUM. Order from: Sales Dept., Atheneum Publishers, 122 East 42nd St., New York, NY 10017. Add $.50 per book postage and handling. Payment must accompany order.

AVON. Order from: Education Dept., Avon Books, 959 Eighth Ave., New York, NY 10019. Add $.35 postage and handling for first book, $.70 for any number more than one. Payment must accompany order.

BANTAM. Order from: Bantam Books/Learning Ventures, 666 Fifth Ave., New York, NY 10019. Add $1.50 postage and handling on orders of less than 25 books. Orders under $15 must be accompanied by payment.

BRADBURY. Order from: Miriam Karp, Library and Education Dept., E.P. Dutton & Co., 201 Park Ave. South, New York, NY 10003. Payment must accompany order.

CROWELL. Order from: Dept. SS, Thomas Y. Crowell Co., 666 Fifth Ave., New York, NY 10019. Payment must accompany order.

DELL/LAUREL-LEAF. Order from: Ms. Edith Mayer, Dial/Delacorte Press, Box 2000, Pinebrook, NJ 07058. Add $.40 per book postage and handling. Payment must accompany orders from individuals. School purchase orders will be billed.

DELL/YEARLING. See DELL/LAUREL-LEAF.

DIAL. See DELL/LAUREL-LEAF.

DIAL/DELACORTE. See DELL/LAUREL-LEAF.

DOUBLEDAY. Order from: Doubleday & Co., School and Library Division, 501 Franklin Avenue, Garden City, Long Island, New York 11530. Add $.25 per book postage and handling. Payment must accompany order.

DUTTON. See BRADBURY.

FARRAR. Order from: Farrar, Straus and Giroux, 19 Union Square West, New York, NY 10003. Add $.40 per order. Payment must accompany order.

GOLDEN PRESS. Order from: Education Division, Western Publishing Co., 150 Parish Dr., Wayne, NJ 07470. Orders under $30 must be prepaid.

HARPER. Order from: Harper & Row, Publishers, Keystone Industrial Park, Scranton, PA 18512. Add $.50 per book postage and handling.

HARCOURT. Order from: Harcourt Brace Jovanovich, 757 Third Ave., New York, NY 10017. Add 5 percent to order for postage and handling.

HARCOURT/VOYAGER. See HARCOURT.

HOLT. Order from: Holt, Rinehart and Winston, 383 Madison Ave., New York, NY 10017. Add 5 percent to order for postage and handling.

HOLT OWLET. See HOLT.

HOUGHTON. Order from: Trade Division, Houghton Mifflin Co., 2 Park St., Boston MA 02107. Add $.85 per book postage and handling. Payment must accompany orders from individuals. School purchase orders will be billed.

KNOPF. Order from: Random House, Inc., Westminster Distribution Center, Westminster, MD 21157. Add $.75 postage and handling. Payment must accompany order.

LIPPINCOTT. Order from: J.B. Lippincott Co., East Washington Square, Philadelphia, PA 19105. Add $.30 per book postage and handling. Payment must accompany order.

LITTLE. Order from: Little, Brown and Co., 200 West St., Waltham, MA 02154. Payment must accompany orders from individuals. School purchase orders will be billed. No postage and handling when payment accompanies order.

MACMILLAN. Order from: Macmillan Publishing Co., Front and Brown Sts., Riverside, NJ 08075. Add $.50 per book postage and handling. Payment must accompany order.

MACMILLAN/COLLIER. See MACMILLAN.

McGRAW-HILL. Order from: McGraw-Hill Book Co., Hightstown Distribution Center, Hightstown Rd., Hightstown, NJ 08520. Add $.75 postage and handling. Payment must accompany order.

PARENTS' MAGAZINE PRESS. Order from: Sales Dept., Parents' Magazine Press, 52 Vanderbilt Ave., New York, NY 10017. Add $.30 per book postage and handling. Payment must accompany order.

PENGUIN. Order from: Educational Sales, Dept. BK, Viking/Penguin, 625 Madison Ave., New York, NY 10022. Payment must accompany order.

PENGUIN/PUFFIN. See PENGUIN.

SEABURY. Order from: Order Dept., The Seabury Press, 815 2nd Ave., New York, NY 10017. Add $.40 per book postage and handling. Payment must accompany orders from individuals. School purchase orders will be billed.

SCRIBNER'S. Order from: Charles Scribner's Sons, Vreeland Ave., Totowa, NJ 07512. Add $.50 per book postage and handling.

STACKPOLE. Order from: Stackpole Books, Cameron and Kelker Sts., Harrisburg, PA 17105. Payment must accompany orders from individuals.

VIKING. See PENGUIN.

WALCK. Order from: David McKay Co., 750 Third Ave., New York, NY 10017. Payment must accompany order.

WALKER. Order from: Walker & Co., 720 Fifth Ave., New York, NY 10019. Add $.50 per book postage and handling.

WHITMAN. Order from: Order Dept., Albert Whitman & Co., 560 W. Lake St., Chicago, IL 60606. Payment must accompany order.

YOUNG READERS PRESS/SIMON & SCHUSTER. Order from: Simon & Schuster, 1 West 39th St., New York, NY 10018. Add $.50 per book postage and handling.

# KIDS HAVE FEELINGS, TOO

# A HANDBOOK OF PERSONAL GROWTH ACTIVITIES FOR CLASSROOM USE

☆ ☆ ☆ ☆ ☆ ☆ ☆ ☆

More and more teachers are beginning to realize that increased awareness of personal feelings, attitudes and emotions is a critical part of any child's education and that it may indeed be one of the keys to better cognitive skill development.

A HANDBOOK OF PERSONAL GROWTH ACTIVITIES FOR CLASSROOM USE, by Robert C. and Isabel L. Hawley, offers an excellent selection of activities — 94 in all — designed to develop a sense of personal awareness in each individual and a sense of community among members of a group or class. All activities have been created for use with groups of 20 to 30 students.

The Hawleys are experienced teachers, and their presentation of teaching ideas shows thoughtful concern for ease of use. For each activity they give straightforward directions and, when necessary, a list of needed materials.

The activities are grouped into chapters by topics: "Teaching for Personal Growth," "Identifying Student Concerns," "Developing Open Communication in the Classroom," "Identity," "Interpersonal Relationships," "Nonverbal and Sensory Awareness Activities" and "Teaching Content Through Personal Growth Activities." "High Tension Wire," an activity from the last chapter, is a good example of how the activities get students to support one another. Working in groups, they help each other learn basic curriculum material with the objective of getting over the "high tension wire" — the final test.

Since the focus is on personal growth, the authors strongly believe that for every activity the individual student has the right to "pass" — to withhold his thoughts and ideas — for whatever personal reason he may have. In addition to encouraging personal growth, most of the activities simultaneously develop cognitive skills by requiring students to process information.

Occasional activities involve situations that seem to have been developed specifically for students in junior high and above. But even those activities can be adapted by teachers for use in the intermediate grades.

Divided into ten major sections, the 8-1/2-by-11-inch spiral-bound book includes a "credo," some general guidelines for using the activities, the activities and a bibliography of suggested readings.

Order from: ERA Press, Box 767, Amherst, MA 01002. Grade level: Teachers of intermediate – high school. Cost: $4.95 plus $.50 postage and handling. Payment must accompany orders from individuals.

# GREENHOUSE

☆ ☆ ☆ ☆ ☆ ☆ ☆ ☆

A boy's senseless act — the breaking of windows in a greenhouse — launches this 11-minute color film into a sensitive, effective exploration of vandalism and values.

The film begins with an old man closing up his greenhouse at night to the placid chirping of crickets. After he retires, a smashing of glass abruptly disrupts the silence. The young vandal is caught and agrees to work off his debt by working in the greenhouse.

At first the boy dislikes both the work and the old man, but gradually he gains an appreciation for both. When once again the greenhouse is vandalized, everything becomes clear to the boy. Now just as attached to the greenhouse and the beauty it represents as the old man, the boy realizes how very foolish he had once been and how he must have hurt the old man when he broke the windows. This time they work as partners to repair the damage.

Narrated from the boy's point of view, the film successfully shows how the boy grows to understand and empathize with the old man's attitude toward the greenhouse. The color photography, sound track and acting are all excellent. The film makes a fine starting point for discussion or writing activities that probe the development of human values.

Order from: Barr Films, P.O. Box 5667, Pasadena, CA 91107. Grade level: K–high school. Cost: $15 plus $2 postage and handling, rental; $160 plus $.50 postage and handling, purchase. Payment must accompany orders by individuals. School purchase orders will be billed.

# THIS IS ME

A Kleenex carnation, a clipping of baseball box scores, a photo of a beaming bald-headed baby, a drawing of a horse at full gallop with mane and tail streaming, and the foil from a chocolate kiss — a self-portrait of Mona. Each item represents something of herself — things especially dear, especially exciting, especially a part of her.

Collecting and composing a collage of such items can be a means of developing self-awareness, a feeling of one's own uniqueness and self-worth.

Have children collect magazine pictures, photographs, drawings, small objects, clippings or other items that tell about themselves and things they enjoy. Though the idea may be introduced to the group and possibilities for items discussed, the project itself is a personal one with each individual deciding what best represents his world.

Each child arranges his collection on a large piece of construction paper or tagboard. After the items are glued down, collage fashion, each child has a display of his interests and personal history. Some children may wish to share with the class just what the items represent.

Through this project you will learn more about each child, while classmates may discover mutual interests. And each child can take quiet pride in the collage collection that declares, "This is me!"

Idea by: Marsha Adler, Parker Elementary School, Royal Oak, Mich.

# 154 KIDS HAVE FEELINGS, TOO

## AFTER THE FIRST
☆ ☆ ☆ ☆ ☆ ☆ ☆ ☆ ☆

Killing and violence are subtly and sensitively explored in this 14-minute color film. AFTER THE FIRST explores the feelings and emotions of a 12-year-old boy up to the point and immediately after he kills a rabbit on a first hunting trip with his father.

At first the boy excitedly looks forward to the trip and the kill, but as the day wears on, reservations build up. Then the moment of kill arrives. He makes ready, then hesitates. All the thoughts of the morning's conversations – radio mention of enemy dead, his father in the war, instructions on how to use a gun – come rushing back to him. His father prods him on, and the trigger is pulled. Whether he would have done it of his own accord is never clear.

After the kill, the boy picks up the rabbit, returns it to his father who had earlier shot one himself and asks, "Is two enough?" This beautifully photographed and finely acted film, created originally for parochial school audiences, ends with the father trying to console the boy by saying, "Come on, you'll see. After the first time, it gets easier."

An apparent cycle has unfolded: the site of the hunt is where the father had first been taken hunting by the boy's grandfather. The father had then gone on to war, where he may have killed people ("You never know for sure"). And now the boy has killed for the first time.

Viewers are left to question whether at some time in his life the boy will also be called upon for – and capable of – killing humans. A useful little teaching guide suggests follow-up discussion topics and activities in values clarification, language arts and social studies.

Order from: TeleKETICS, 1229 S. Santee St., Los Angeles, CA 90015. Grade level: 4–high school. Cost: $17 plus $1 postage and handling, rental; $185 plus $1 postage and handling, purchase.

# GETTING ALONG

☆ ☆ ☆ ☆ ☆ ☆ ☆ ☆

Materials created to teach kids about feelings too often approach the subject by telling them how to feel. They preach rather than question. The five GETTING ALONG filmstrips — part of Scholastic's Kindle series for the preprimary and primary levels — manage to concentrate on asking why rather than telling how. And they do so without imposing too many values.

Each of the full-color filmstrips is accompanied by either a record or a cassette. The titles — "It's Mine!" "Sticks 'n Stones," "Will You Be My Friend?" "Smiles Don't Just Happen" and "I Don't Care, Anyhow!" — deal with the topics of selfishness, love, hate, jealousy and anger.

Typical of the series' approach is the filmstrip "It's Mine!" It begins with two boys arguing over a baseball bat and goes on to ask questions like: "Do you have something that belongs only to you?" "Is it easy to share with someone else?" "Is there something you can give away and still have, like the measles?" and "Can you share the way you feel with others?"

Along with the questions presented throughout the filmstrip, there is a teaching guide that presents follow-up questions and activities for each filmstrip.

Order from: Scholastic Book Services, 904 Sylvan Ave., Englewood Cliffs, NJ 07632. Grade level: Preschool–3. Cost: $69.50, record or cassette. Add 6 percent postage and handling on billed orders.

# IMPROVING STUDENT SELF-IMAGE

"I think you are a good friend and very honest," Suzy tells Lisa. Compliments are the serious business of Monthly Positive Sessions. It takes practice to say something nice about someone — to that person directly. Being critical in a negative way seems to be no problem for most junior high students. And at first a student may tend to talk about rather than to someone. Suzy may need to be reminded to tell Lisa directly, and Lisa should really listen, not respond.

Kids can be pretty superficial. If all Joe can say to Tom is that he likes his minibike, let him. As kids touch other areas, they will learn from each other.

Finish up by discussing how students felt giving and receiving compliments. Sharing and feedback are part of this learning process.

Skills gained from the Monthly Positive Sessions should help in the honoring of a Student of the Week.

1. The students' names are placed in a box and one name is drawn to become Student of the Week.
2. S.O.T.W. may leave the room (optional) while the rest of the class states things they like about that student. Be patient, encouraging. Stress that everyone has many good qualities. Also, the fact that each person's turn will be coming up tends to be an incentive. Six or eight statements should be listed. (Try to keep the lists about equal in length.)
3. Have the S.O.T.W. bring in a picture of himself, or take one with a Polaroid camera.
4. Post the S.O.T.W.'s picture, name and list of good qualities on the bulletin board. You may change this bulletin board each week, or you may wish to make a cumulative bulletin board of the S.O.T.W.s.

To assure all class members recognition within a shorter period of time, you may want to have three Students of the Week at a time.

Monthly Positive Sessions and Student of the Week have proved to be simple and effective ways of improving students' self-image. And the kids really seem to like it.

Idea by: Astrid Collins, Markham Junior High School, San Jose, Calif.

# CROSSROADS

☆ ☆ ☆ ☆ ☆ ☆ ☆ ☆

The five filmstrips in this set, subtitled "Stories About Values and Decisions," depict moral problems and offer several alternative solutions. Each story is realistically narrated by the youngster who must make the decision. At the point a problem arises, the narrative stops and viewers are asked to consider what they would do in a similar situation. Then, one by one, the filmstrip presents four or five different outcomes, providing opportunities between each outcome for viewers to discuss their reactions. A teacher's guide suggests questions for consideration during the pauses.

The titles of the filmstrips suggest the moral dilemmas they present: "Generosity," "Honesty," "Guilt," "Hostility" and "Integrity." Some of the themes overlap; the decision called for in "Honesty," for example, is no less a question of guilt. In that filmstrip, a woman mistakenly overpays a boy collecting for his paper route. Since she is unaware of her oversight, it is up to the boy to decide what to do. The solutions vary from keeping the money for a new bicycle light to returning it immediately. Other alternatives fall between these two extremes.

The effectiveness of the filmstrips is due in part to the realistic problems and solutions they present — the kinds of situations kids actually face. But the strips possess several minor weaknesses. "Integrity," for one, loses some of its forcefulness because the narrator speaks too quickly. Another, "Guilt," offers solutions that vary only slightly, though students should be able to make distinctions. A more general weakness is that in each filmstrip the decision considered traditionally "correct" is presented last. If kids pick up on this pattern, it may tend to affect their responses.

Despite these minor flaws, the filmstrips make excellent discussion and writing starters about important personal issues.

Order from: United Learning, 6633 W. Howard St., Niles, IL 60648. Grade level: 4–7. Cost: $65.50 plus postage for filmstrips with cassettes.

## Video and Values

by Jack C. Morgan

Shifty eyes versus steady gaze, pleasant request versus harsh order, glowering visage versus clean-cut looks — telling the good guys from the bad is an easy matter in many TV shows. TV simplifies the real world, thus making value judgments easy to make and consistent with standard stereotypes. Even in those programs involving more complex values—the classic Robin Hood theme of robbing the rich to give to the poor, or the quandary of the young physician who feels morally bound to disregard the advice of a superior in trying to save a patient's life—the final scenes must resolve things within the bounds of the accepted value system. Values in short, are an integral part of the hidden and not-so-hidden curriculum of TV viewing.

**Values Analysis.** In TV, as in written literature, stories deal with conflicts and their resolutions. Some end happily, some not, but whatever the ending, if television is to remain solvent, it must appeal to the widest possible audience, must base its stories on the most commonly held values. Thus TV offers a values definition for student study.

Children can look for the human qualities in TV stories, seeking answers to questions such as: (1) What problem occurred? (2) Why was it a problem? (3) How was the problem resolved? (4) What qualities seemed important in the principal characters?

Have children try to put themselves into the story situation, and ask them to guess at their own actions and reactions. They can also create, discuss and possibly act out alternative endings for the story.

Suggest that the children share their own experiences in resolving conflicts. They may wish to discuss whether a given television conflict resolution is realistic in terms of their own experiences.

**Moral Lessons.** At the simplest values level, some programs communicate either implicit or explicit moral lessons to children who watch them. Though such stories probably won't conclude with the moral intoned in a solemn voice-over, the lesson that is there shouldn't be hard for children to find. Some of the programs featuring families and some of the Saturday morning cartoon shows are likely locations to begin looking for lessons. Older children might be asked to watch particular shows and write a sentence or two about the lessons being offered. These interpretations can later be discussed in class.

Try collecting a number of sayings: "Look before you leap," "Little strokes fell great oaks," "A stitch in time . . ." (Thumbing through Bartlett's *Familiar Quotations* may help.) Write them on the board and discuss their meanings; encourage the children to suggest a wide range of possible applications. Then have the students watch for TV stories that illustrate such sayings. Older students might want to try coining their own wise sayings in order to express the "moral" of stories they've watched.

**Commercials.** TV advertising topics and techniques can also be inspected for their treatment of values. Commercials, with their capsule stories and catchy phrases, are highly attractive to young children. Ask children to identify key words emphasized in the commercial. Are the words also shown on the screen? Are the words repeated? Which words are used the most? Examples might include *fresh, natural, pleasure, beauty, best* and *most.* Make a list of these words; explore their meanings and the feelings children have about them. Discuss why they are used.

*Social acceptance, thriftiness, cleanliness, fun, good health* and *attractiveness* are values that are emphasized in TV ads. To what extent are these values desirable and realistic? To what extent do we accept these values on our own? Children, keying on value-charged words and phrases, might write their own 30-second commercials for pencils, candy or toys.

**What America Wants.** Beyond the stories and their sponsors, TV programming as a package carries a hidden curriculum that teaches youngsters the value priorities of adult Americans. Have children imagine themselves as visitors to America, completely unfamiliar with the ways of our culture (highly unlikely, but try it). Invested with their new outlook, children may be able to take up a basic question: What does TV tell about what Americans value?

Discuss what your "visitors" conclude from some of the following: a show in which people compete hysterically for large cash prizes; a story in which a child is remorseful after cheating on an exam; a news program covering war, assault, disaster, scandal; a three-hour baseball game; a documentary about an endangered species. What is it, you might want to ask, that Americans find entertaining, exciting, funny? What do Americans consider newsworthy? What qualities, conditions or material items do they seem to prize? Older children might try formulating descriptions of the "typical American" drawn from the images, impressions, interests and values depicted on TV.

Values are a part of us. Much of what we do is influenced by our collective values. As a mass medium, television provides one of the best common resources for helping a child analyze values—a first step towards developing his own value system.

Jack C. Morgan is professor of education, University of Louisville, Belknap Campus, Kentucky.

---

*"Intellect is but a speck on the sea of emotion."*

— Psychologist G. S. Hall (1846–1924)

## SEARCHING FOR VALUES

☆ ☆ ☆ ☆ ☆ ☆ ☆ ☆

A remarkable series which brings into focus the many dimensions of human behavior, SEARCHING FOR VALUES consists of 15 films (each 13 to 15 minutes in length) edited from Columbia Pictures' feature films. One of the best is "Loneliness . . . and Loving," edited from the motion picture FIVE EASY PIECES. Technically, it is a thoroughly professional job, the editing so skillfully done that the main theme — an individual's search for meaningful relationships — is always clearly presented even though the film stops before any final solution to the problem has been offered. Indeed, its resolution necessitates thought and discussion on the part of the class.

Another film in the series, "Love to Kill," edited from BLESS THE BEASTS AND THE CHILDREN, raises endless questions about attitudes toward hunting and killing for pleasure. Characteristic of every film in the series, it leads to open-ended and provocative discussions. At a time when teachers are looking for relevant materials, this original concept should prove popular.

Order from: Learning Corporation of America, 1350 Ave. of the Americas, New York, NY 10019. Grade level: Junior high–high school. Cost: $25 per film, rental; $270 per film, purchase.

## CLARIFYING VALUES THROUGH SUBJECT MATTER

☆ ☆ ☆ ☆ ☆ ☆ ☆ ☆

"How are rocks formed?" That's a "facts" question right out of the earth science book.

"Should oil companies receive a depletion allowance? Give reasons for your answer." That's a "values" question right out of a student's own feelings and opinions. His answer is drawn from his own frame of reference and reflects what he himself values.

CLARIFYING VALUES THROUGH SUBJECT MATTER is a resource that helps to bring the concern for values into the context of the classroom. The authors, Merrill Harmin, Howard Kirschenbaum and Sidney Simon, have already contributed many important books in the area of values. But in this paperback they bring their philosophies to bear on the daily task of the teacher, who must deal in curriculum as well as children.

The book discusses teaching on three levels: facts, concepts and values. It illustrates movement through these three levels with special emphasis on guidelines for values-level teaching.

The major portion of the book is devoted to examples of three-level questioning and activities drawn from 20 subject-matter areas. The

# 158 KIDS HAVE FEELINGS, TOO

subjects range from bookkeeping to grammar. Values questions are equally diverse. In each subject area questions involve the learner personally in choice-making, prizing and acting.

This is not the usual kind of how-to book. It offers help in building values clarification into your teaching, whatever your subject matter.

Order from: Order Dept., Winston Press, 25 Groveland Terrace, Minneapolis, MN 55403. Grade level: Teachers of all grades. Cost: $2.95 plus $.50 postage and handling. Payment must accompany orders under $10.

## WE SEE!

Understanding and being sensitive toward others is a vital part of the effective human being, but developing such qualities is a complex process. To feel as someone else feels is never easy, and it is especially hard to identify with a person whose situation is very different from one's own.

Literature, with its best devices activated, treats problems of many individuals, including the problems of the physically handicapped. Identification through creative reading is a step toward understanding. But a further, more poignant sense of understanding can come through an activity that re-creates experience.

"Blind for an hour" is not a new idea, but a variation of it, and the introduction of videotape may bring a breakthrough in appreciating the problems of the sightless.

The setting for this experience is an unfamiliar classroom to which blindfolded students are led, one by one. The seats are scattered about the room—some face the back wall, some are isolated from the others—and as each student is seated, he has no idea which way he is facing.

The next part of the experience is listening to the rock opera TOMMY, the story of a blind teen-ager. Following this, each student is approached individually to react to the story's message. The student is asked to go to the chalkboard and write how the story made him feel. When this is finished, he is to return to his seat. Simple enough, if you can see where you're going and what you're doing. But the blindfolds are to stay in place.

The students, two or three at a time, set out to fulfill their tasks. Videotape can enrich the experience by recording their wanderings and searchings, their impatience and their embarrassment. And if the chalk falls, the student must find it, on his hands and knees.

The thoughts and feelings—frustration, humiliation, despair—experienced by the handicapped come out in the discussion that follows. The videotape is a faithful and uncomfortable reminder of the students' trials.

An experience such as this one remains a strong and disturbing memory that may help build sensitivity and respect for the feelings of others.

Idea by: Tom Vernier,
Mascoutah High School, Mascoutah, Ill.

## KEVIN

☆ ☆ ☆ ☆ ☆ ☆ ☆ ☆ ☆ ☆

This is a moving, sensitively filmed, 16-minute documentary about a blind child and his perceptions of life. It shows him out of doors alone, wandering about investigating his surroundings. The stream-of-consciousness script as well as the action convey a feeling of groping and questioning. The words beautifully portray how much this child's ideas of the world are dependent upon things that he experiences vicariously through his sighted friends.

The black-and-white film is an excellent means of sensitizing children to the importance of their senses in understanding the world they live in. It is also a beautiful artistic experience in its own right.

Order from: Churchill Films, 662 N. Robertson Blvd., Los Angeles, CA 90069. Grade level: 2–junior high. Cost: $18, rental; $120, purchase.

## ON THE OTHER HAND . . .

While students are learning that some questions can be answered simply "yes," "no," "the Nile" or "a right angle," they perhaps need reminding that questions and answers don't always come in neat pairs. Many decisions

# KIDS HAVE FEELINGS, TOO

are choices between two rights or among a number of quite distasteful alternatives.

To give students a taste of the difficulties and frustrations in this kind of decision making, pose a problem of crisis proportions with no clear-cut solution:

> "You are the chief surgeon at a big hospital. You must make a decision about four patients in need of a heart transplant. There is just one donor. Assuming all the patients could receive this heart, which one would you choose? (1) a famous brain surgeon at the height of his career; (2) a 12-year-old musician; (3) a 40-year-old lawyer; (4) an expectant mother."

The class may be divided into small groups to discuss the case. After 20 to 25 minutes of discussion, bring the class together to share ideas and grounds for decisions. Their arguments and judgments may be surprising.

Such decision-making forums can lead to other activities. Students may wish to investigate the difficult decisions involved in such fields as environment, city planning, economics, foreign relations. Sensitivity to the agonizing decisions faced daily in many walks of life can be the result of this project.

Idea by: Herb Bacon, Pedricktown Elementary School, Pedricktown, N.J.

## PEOPLE PROJECTS

☆ ☆ ☆ ☆ ☆ ☆ ☆ ☆

Once a theory is accepted, practical suggestions for implementation never seem to come quickly enough. Such has been the case in the relatively new fields of affective education and values clarification. One fine addition to materials in these areas is PEOPLE PROJECTS.

Written by Merrill Harmin, the projects are designed to develop "language and thinking skills, human relationship skills, and emotional and value maturity." They take the form of large (10-by-13 inches) student activity cards with interest-grabbing four-color illustrations — three sets of 40 cards each. Set A roughly corresponds with the 9-to-11 age group, Set B with ages 10 to 12 and Set C with ages 11 to 13, but teachers might try using higher- or lower-level sets with their classes, depending on the maturity of the students.

The problem-solving activities demand student interaction (sometimes confrontation) in a variety of forms, including acting, discussion and nonverbal communication. Some of the more powerful projects involve discussions of rarely shared feelings. "Which is Worse?" asks kids to discuss unpleasant situations — like being the last one picked for a team or getting no votes in an election. But the activity ends on a positive note as participants tell about the happiest things that can happen to them. One project explores "Loneliness." Another invites reaction to a newspaper article in which "A Teacher Hits a Student."

Not all of the cards are so intense. Some of the milder ones ask: "Brainstorming: Are Two Heads Better Than One?" and "What Would It Be Like to Live in a Jungle?"

A few of the projects are not entirely satisfying: Figuring out "Secret Codes," though calling for student interaction, is a somewhat tired activity.

Though all of the activities can be easily implemented by the kids working independently, some would be best served if the teacher works with the kids or is at least close by. Teachers can choose to integrate the cards into language arts or social studies classes or use them as they are.

An in-depth but quick-to-read teacher's manual describes the purposes of the projects, how to orient students, different ways of getting started, methods of evaluating students and means of evaluating the effectiveness of the projects.

Order from: Addison-Wesley Publishing Co., 2725 Sand Hill Road, Menlo Park, CA 94025. Grade level: 4–9. Cost: $22.32 per set, plus $.30 postage and handling.

# KIDS HAVE FEELINGS, TOO

## AFFECTIVE EFFLUENCE

"It has come to the attention of the authors that an affect is more effective than a defect. The prepotent overarching effectiveness of affect is becoming more effective in affecting educational affect in classroom situations, and the effects of this overarching precept will surely effect a change in educationalists' respect for the effective use of affect.

"The infectious nature of the injection of 'affect' and 'effect' into intellectually inflected discourse has never been inspected. The dejection of those not infected with an effective affect may even cause defection from intellectual collection. The detection of this defection may be intricate and impracticable to effect, resulting in a perplexing pickle. In short, the neglect of effective research on the effects of affect effectiveness effects an introspective affect reflecting this neglect."

— Alton O. Roberts and Pamela A. Miller, instructors, College of Education, University of Vermont.

## THE GIVING TREE

THE GIVING TREE is the title of a story about friendship for "children of all ages" written by Shel Silverstein (Harper & Row, 1964). It is the kind of story that can get teen-agers thinking about what friends mean to each other — the need for giving and receiving.

Teen-agers can do much for each other by simply listening, trying to understand and showing they care. But "real sincerity" can be verbally elusive, and sometimes it is easier for young people to express their thoughts to others in writing.

Perhaps your students will react favorably to the idea of having their own "giving tree." A tree limb with a number of smaller branches can be set up in a large sand-filled coffee can. Hang an envelope for each student on the branches. Notes in a positive vein — supportive, expressing understanding, offering help — can be written and slipped into an envelope at any time. The sender may remain anonymous.

A giving tree can serve as an intermediary, letting students give to each other without risk.

Idea by: Sister Margaret McNamara, St. Agnes School, Chicago, Ill.

## BUILDING POSITIVE SELF-CONCEPTS

### by Donald W. Felker

Children who enter school handicapped by low self-esteem can be helped by the teacher who makes learning a positive experience, says the author. This clearly written book offers five practical ways to build positive self-concepts in children, perhaps the most important of which are realistic goal setting and being able to praise self and others.

Order from: Burgess Publishing Co., 7108 Ohms La., Minneapolis, MN 55435. Grade level: Teachers of primary–high school. Cost: $3.25.

## anti social

"If one wants children to express their feelings in writing, one must be prepared to receive feelings which are considered antisocial as well as acceptable. One must be willing to wade through a great deal of kaka and to have faith that something more interesting will emerge when the scatology has run its course. One must convince the children that the freedom to express their innermost thought[s] is meant in earnest."

— Poet Phillip Lopate, in Teachers & Writers Collaborative Newsletter, vol. 5, issue 2.

## PRELUDES TO GROWTH: AN EXPERIENTIAL APPROACH

### by Richard Katz

Unlike so many books about affective/humanistic education, this one doesn't try to establish general educational goals, objectives and performance criteria for lessons about self-awareness, feelings and personal relationships. It presents instead nitty-gritty, sense-making activities that excite and involve the reader. Both Esalen and Outward Bound have influenced Katz, and while he offers a few ho-hum activities (the old blindfolding routine), the book as a whole is fresh and doable. So much so, in fact, that while the activities are intended for teachers in training or practicing teachers interested in their own growth, they can be easily adapted for the elementary classroom.

Order from: The Free Press, 866 Third Ave., New York, NY 10022. Grade level: Teachers of primary–high school. Cost: $4.95.

# HELPING NEW KIDS FEEL AT HOME

BY MARY GRISHAVER AND BRUCE RASKIN

Every year it happens: you, as a teacher, face children you've never set eyes on before. You've learned to deal with the anxieties that can produce, especially if you've been teaching for a number of years. After all, you know the school and its procedures, and as an adult, you've developed the skills to meet new situations. But many of the children you face each fall are much less confident than you. Their lack of experience in dealing with change leaves them vulnerable and uncomfortable in unfamiliar surroundings. Kids who have done no more than change teachers or classes within a school often have a difficult time, and kids new to a school and a community find the transition even harder.

In our mobile society, some six million children move to a new community each year. If these kids are to learn to cope with moving, they are likely to need more than the help of their parents, who may be unprepared themselves or too burdened with their own adjustments to give the necessary support to their children. Kids, therefore, need the help of the teachers and students in their new school.

The transition is easiest for kids who are in a classroom where the students and teacher get along well, respect each other and themselves, and feel they are part of a learning community. Developing this kind of atmosphere is no easy job, especially at the start of the new school year. No single method will establish an ideal environment, but the process of making new students in your class feel at home can be helped by these practical suggestions:

## 1 PICTURE BOX

This is a nonthreatening and enjoyable way to get to know a child. Ask the new child if she would like to sort through a box of pictures with you to find a selection that will help her make up a story. Children looking through the box usually talk freely about themselves. The interest you show and the responses you give to her comments will help lay the groundwork for mutual trust. It will also give you some indications about her personality and capabilities.

Once she selects the pictures, have her write a story or dictate one to you. If you think that sharing the story with the rest of the class will focus positive attention on the new student, ask her if she would like to read it to the class or if she will permit you to read it. And if she doesn't want it to be read, see if she would mind having it posted.

## 2 SELECT-A-FRIEND

Once you know something about the child personally, you will want to see how she relates to her peers and what type of child she likes best. Find out if she would like to work with you and another student of her own choosing on a special, pleasant project—cook-

## 3 PARENT INVOLVEMENT

To add both to the new child's sense of belonging and your sense of the child, encourage her parents to participate in some way in school activities. One way is to initiate a party or picnic that parents, including the new child's, can help organize. By planning the event themselves, parents will have a chance to communicate directly with one another instead of through you. Usually when parents begin to feel accepted in the community, so do their children.

At the party or at individual or group conferences with the parents of new children, try to find out as much as possible about each new student. Parents are usually happy to talk about their children and reassured to learn that you want to treat kids as individuals. Knowing something about the student—she is the youngest sibling or is afraid to try new math concepts—will help you deal more effectively with her. These conferences can lay the foundation for effective cooperation between home and school.

## 4 CREATIVE ACTIVITIES

If you find that the new student isn't at ease during regular academic activities and you haven't yet introduced creative expression, now is a good time. Dance, drama, music, art or poetry may uncover talents which you can use as another bridge between her and the class.

## 5 THIS IS US

Making a "This Is Us" booklet of the names, addresses and phone numbers of both you and the students is a good way for everyone to become acquainted. The booklet should be updated throughout the year to include changing information about both old and new students. The booklet can be produced through one or both of the following activities:

*Pairs.* Pair students off and encourage them to exchange names and bits of information about themselves. If you have an odd number of students, include yourself in the activity. Each pair then meets with another pair, and the partners introduce each other as fully as possible. Then the foursome meets with another foursome and repeats the procedure. (Variation: After two pairs have exchanged information, organize the kids into new pairs.) When the game is finished, have the information written up and mimeographed as your "This Is Us" booklet. Make enough copies for the entire class.

*Questions.* To solicit information beyond what the students might come up with themselves, write questions on the board and then pair the children up to discuss them. During the discussion each member of the pair takes notes on the other's answers. These notes can be used in a class discussion and in compiling the "This Is Us" booklet. A few suggested questions: "What is the funniest experience you have ever had? the saddest?" "What was your strangest dream?" "Who in your life has had the most influence on you?" "Who was your favorite teacher? why?" "Where is the best place you have ever been?"

## 6 CLASS INTERVIEW

A technique for focusing on an individual in helping others get to know her is the class interview. In one type of interview, the whole class prepares questions from which a panel of five reporters selects several to ask the new student. The new child has the option of choosing a host who will introduce her before and sit next to her during the interview. As an alternative to the class interview, you can reverse the procedure and have the new child play the role of roving reporter. Given note pad and pencil or tape recorder and a couple of weeks to collect information, your young Barbara Walters can go about interviewing each of her new classmates. The activity finale can take a "Guess who I'm describing?" form—the interviewer reveals information gathered in the interview without revealing the student's name. Each class member tries to identify the mystery student.

## 7 HOME-SCHOOL MAP

Develop a map, with the kids if possible, clearly indicating home locations in relationships to the school and to each other. Bus routes and transportation methods between various locations can be penciled in during a map study discussion. Neighborhood, class-time or after-school walks can yield a feeling of familiarity and solidarity in and outside the classroom. When new students arrive during the year, take out the map for updating.

## 8 BIG SIBLINGS

Organize a Big Siblings Club for your school. Ask help from older kids and faculty advisors in planning ways to make new, younger students feel at home in the school. One way is to match up a Big Sibling with one or more younger students who live near each other or who are in the same homeroom. Kick off the program with a party for the entire group by inviting other teachers, the principal and parents.

Big Siblings can also be used as peer counselors. Trained by counselors in the school, the Big Siblings should be prepared to listen well and talk straight to the kids who come to them for advice or a friendly ear.

## 9 SPONSORS

Within your class, form a group of kids who are thoroughly familiar with the school and the community. Let them plan ways to make new members of the class feel welcome. The sponsors

# 60 Activities That Develop Student Independence

### BY KENNETH AND RITA DUNN

Many teachers who have begun to individualize have been disappointed and frustrated by an apparent lack of success. The failures have been especially disappointing to those able instructors who identified a method that they believed to be appropriate, discussed plans for varying instruction with their students, established some rules for functioning in the new environment and then proceeded to introduce the changeover. To their dismay, new kinds of problems with their students arose. Their charges appeared to take advantage of the informality of the setting, and discipline sometimes seemed to break down, particularly with those students who previously had been unmotivated or nonconformist.

The goal of independent study is a reachable one only if students have the appropriate attitudes and skills. This cannot be achieved overnight; it is evolutionary and demands repeated evaluation. Because one of the best ways to learn is "by doing," students first should be encouraged to achieve limited objectives on their own. Some may be hesitant and others will be fearful, but eventually most, if not all, will begin to feel the wonderful sense of independence, responsibility and accomplishment that accompanies success. "Nothing succeeds like success" will come to have real meaning for students who were previously unmotivated or apathetic.

What follows is a list of 60 activity and reporting alternatives that may be used to develop options for all students. Teachers will want to identify those activities that would be motivating for their youngsters, adapt and rewrite them so they're appropriate for the specific unit or topic being studied, and use them as part of an individualized assignment contract, prescription or "free choice" activity list. They may also be used as learning station "task cards" or placed at interest centers, little theaters or other instructional areas to task-orient the learner and to help him become an independent and responsible student.

## ACTIVITY AND REPORTING ALTERNATIVES

**1.** Make a miniature stage setting with pipe-cleaner figures to describe part of the information you learned about your topic. Display the stage setting and figures and give a two-minute talk explaining what they represent and why you selected them.

**2.** Make a poster "advertising" the most interesting information you have learned. Display the poster and give a two-minute talk explaining why you found the information interesting.

**3.** Design costumes for people or characters you have learned about. Describe to a group of classmates how you decided what the costumes should be, how you made them, and the people who would have worn them. You could also hold a fashion show with the help of friends.

**4.** Prepare a travel lecture related to your topic. Give the lecture before a small group of classmates. You may also tape-record it for others who are working on the same topic.

**5.** Make a "movie" by drawing a series of pictures on a long sheet of paper fastened to two rollers. Write a script and show your movie to one or more small groups of classmates.

**6.** Describe in writing or on tape an interesting person or character that you learned about and dramatize something he or she did. Ask a few classmates to tell you what they think of the human being you portrayed.

**7.** Write or tell a different ending to one of the events you read about. After sharing your thoughts with a classmate or two, ask them to think of other ways the event could have ended.

**8.** Pantomime some information you found very interesting. Let a few classmates try to guess what you are pantomiming.

**9.** Write and mail a letter to a friend recommending that he study this topic too, and explain why.

**10.** Construct puppets and use them in a presentation that explains an interesting part of the information you learned. Have a friend photograph your presentation. Display the pictures and the puppets.

**11.** Make a map or chart representing information you have gathered. Display the map or chart and answer questions about it.

**12.** Dress as one of the people you studied. Answer questions in an "interview."

**13.** Broadcast a "book review" of your topic, as if you were a critic. Tape-record the review and permit others to listen and tell you if they would now like to read the book, and why.

**14.** Outline a biography of one of the authors you read and tell about his writing on tape, in writing or orally. Give your report to a small group of students.

# 172 POTPOURRI

**15.** Make a clay, soap or wood model to illustrate a phase of the information you learned. Display the model and answer questions as a museum guide might.

**16.** Construct a diorama to illustrate an important piece of information. Display the diorama and answer questions as an artist might.

**17.** Dress paper dolls as people or characters in your topic. Give a two-minute talk about the doll characters.

**18.** Make a mural to illustrate the information you consider interesting. Display the mural and answer questions which may arise.

**19.** Build a sand-table setting to represent a part of your topic. Explain the setting to other students. Ask them to evaluate your effort in a few short sentences.

**20.** Rewrite an important piece of information, simplifying the vocabulary for younger children. Develop a project with the children around the information.

**21.** Make a time line, listing important dates and events in sequence. Display the time line and be prepared to answer questions.

**22.** Write a song including information you learned. Sing the song in person or on tape for a small group of students.

**23.** Make up a crossword puzzle and let other students try to complete it. Check and return their answers to them.

**24.** Make up a game that uses information from your topic. Play the game with other members of your class.

**25.** Direct and participate in a play and/or choral speaking about your topic. Present the dra-

# POTPOURRI 173

matic or choral creation to a small group of classmates.

**26.** Write a script for a radio or television program; produce and participate in this program. Present the program for a group of classmates.

**27.** Develop and present commentaries for a silent movie, a filmstrip or a slide showing. Use your own photographs or slides, if possible.

**28.** With others, plan and then participate in a debate or panel discussion on challenging aspects of your topic.

**29.** Conduct for your classmates an interview on your topic with an adult or students from upper classes. Ask specific questions.

**30.** Prepare and make appeals before another class on behalf of school or community drives that can be related to your topic. Contribute whatever monies or goods you receive to the proper agency.

**31.** Write a news story, an editorial, a special column or an advertisement for the school or class newspaper explaining your views concerning any one aspect of your topic. Mount and display your writing. Ask three students to write "letters to the editor" praising or chastising you as a reporter.

**32.** Correspond with hospitalized children (particularly at holiday seasons). Share interesting information about your topic.

**33.** Design and then display an unusual invitation to a class party or program centered around information on your topic.

**34.** Write a letter to an imaginary friend about fictitious travels concerned with your topic. Mount and display the letter.

**35.** Take a character from a story such as *Robin Hood* or *Cinderella* and rewrite the story in a setting suitable to your topic. Mount and display the story.

**36.** Write and then display an imaginary letter from one story character to another. Tell about something that might have happened had they both lived at the time and place of your topic.

**37.** Make up and tell "tall tales" about your topic. Either write or tape-record at least two of the tales you create. Illustrate them and permit others to react to them.

**38.** Convert a story you have written into a short play on your topic. Ask a few of your classmates to take parts in the play. Tape-record it and present it as a radio program to a group of younger children.

**39.** Keep a make-believe diary about your memorable experiences as you lived through the period concerned with your topic. Read a portion of your diary to some of your classmates. See whether they can identify the period concerned with the topic. Add the diary to the resource alternatives available for other people who are studying the topic.

**40.** Write stories about different phases of your life as they might have happened had you lived in your topic time and place. "Important Happenings During My Life,"

"Important People in My Life," "My Library" (kinds of books I like and why) or "The Most Exciting Thing That Ever Happened to Me" might be some choices. Combine the stories into a book entitled "My Autobiography" and show it to your teacher, parents and a group of classmates. Add your book to the resource alternatives available for study of your topic.

**41.** Make a magazine for the classroom by compiling voluntary artwork and composition contributions on your topic. "Publish" the magazine and distribute it among your classmates.

**42.** Develop for classroom display collections of colloquialisms or "regional" expressions related to your topic.

**43.** Collect folklore such as rope-jumping rhymes, counting-out rhymes, legends or folk songs related to your topic. Write (or type) them neatly and combine them into a book of resource materials. List yourself as editor. Use proper credits. If you are uncertain about the format, ask the librarian to show you samples of edited books.

**44.** Make a collection of myths, legends, interesting mottoes and proverbs on your topic. Cover the collection with an attractive jacket and display the booklet as a resource alternative.

**45.** Try to find original manuscripts, old page proofs, first editions of books, book jackets, taped interviews with authors or other interesting persons in the community, autographs of authors or any other documentation related to your topic. If the material cannot be brought to school, organize a small group trip to visit the place where you found the items.

**46.** Document some original research you've found on your topic using bibliographies, footnotes and quotations.

**47.** Search the library card catalog and periodical index and list all the books and articles concerned with your topic. Add the list to the resource alternatives for your topic.

**48.** Make constructive evaluations of a TV program related to your topic. Mount the evaluation on a sheet of construction paper and display it. Discuss your thoughts with someone else in your group who saw the program.

**49.** Make a comparison between getting information by listening or by reading. Compare the devices used in the two media. Which do you like better and why? Write your answers. Compare your findings with those of another student who selected the same activity alternative. Discuss your reasons for selecting one method as being more interesting than the other.

**50.** Study the speeches and written work of a particular public figure, determine his motives and find possible hidden objectives, if any. List any clues which indicate the author's real beliefs.

**51.** View a television program of your choice. Check the facts presented in written materials with those on the program. Put your conclusions into written form and share them with your teacher and two other classmates who have seen the same program.

**52.** Analyze the point of view of an author of a particular book. Read about the author in order to explain why he believes what he does. Tell at least three other classmates something you learned about the author which might account for his point of view in writing the book.

**53.** Write an article persuading people to your point of view by using biased words and appropriate propaganda devices. Analyze words with similar meanings to differentiate shades of meaning. List at least 20 such words.

**54.** Organize a file box for new words, arranging them under headings such as "Descriptive Words" or "Words With More Than One Meaning." Compile a list of words overused in class discussions, such as: *fantastic, man, great, cool, uptight, pretty* and *touch*. Find substitutes for these words and make a compilation for class references. Add the file box to the resource alternatives for your topic if they are appropriate.

**55.** Compile a reading notebook containing excerpts which are unusually expressive and make use of similes, metaphors or alliterations. Use the figures of speech to describe some aspect of your topic.

**56.** Describe a character in a story. Describe how the author developed the character and influenced the sentiments of the reader. Through a written, taped or oral report, share your thoughts with at least two or three classmates. Ask for their reactions to your findings.

**57.** Attempt to understand the behavior of characters in a book by analyzing possible causes. Evaluate the choices made by characters and think through possible alternatives. Write a short (one or two sentence) description of the character. Write a short description of the character's behavior. Write three possible alternative behaviors the character might have shown.

**58.** Compare the illustrations in different editions of fairy tales or in various types of books. Draw alternative illustrations for three stories you've read.

**59.** Catalog your own books and records or the books and records in the classroom library. (Topic, value, reading levels, etc.).

Plan a personal library. List the books and records related to your topic that you'd like to own. Display the list attractively mounted and suggest that others obtain the books or records which you liked best.

**60.** Form a poetry club. Members can bring favorite poems to discuss or compose poems based on their topics. Have the club members present a series of recitations.

In carrying out the above activities, students should be free to learn through a wide variety of multimedia resources—tapes, films, filmstrips, transparencies, books, games, records. Experience with these materials will increase the pleasure of learning and often lead to the discovery of additional options for building independence and responsibility.

Rita Dunn is professor of education, St. John's University, Jamaica, N.Y.
Kenneth Dunn is superintendent of schools, Hewlett-Woodmere, N.Y.

## 10

### I'M UNIQUE

The activities already suggested are good starting points for integrating the new child. To assure even greater acceptance, communication must be extended beyond introductory exercises. Now that you and the class know about each other, find a way to focus positively on something you have learned about the new child and to which the other children can relate. For instance, if the child is from another part of your state or the country, she could tell about the things that are unique to that area. Activities and discussions involving differences may arise from such a presentation. In addition, if a new student has a special skill or talent—being expert at making paper airplanes or doing long division—find a way to share her abilities with the class.

### Special Problems

Some new-kid problems don't surface during regular class time. If you're willing to share part of your lunch, recess or planning time with the class, you're likely to uncover some of these hidden problems. By discovering and dealing with them early, you'll save time and energy in the long run.

More readily identifiable problems, such as hostility, rejection or ostracism of newcomers, can be dealt with through role play or problem-solving discussions. Exercise your own judgment as to whether the entire class or only those students most closely involved should participate. You can assign parts in such a way that students find themselves in unaccustomed roles. If ostracism is a problem, try this role-playing situation: Have four shy children pretend they are involved in a game with which they are familiar. Have a new child, played by a class leader, pretend she wants to join the game but is shy and does not know all the rules. Tell all the participants that the "new kid," though afraid of rejection, wants to play the game, but the other four children are reluctant to let her in. Then have them spontaneously act out the drama. A discussion of how it feels to be new, to be rejected and to reject follows naturally from the role play.

Sharing your own feelings and interpretations is also effective. One way is to describe how you felt when you were rejected or felt alone. You can use yourself as a model as soon as a problem arises or later, during a class or group meeting. By telling how you dealt with a situation, you may enlarge each child's repertoire of coping mechanisms. Children are often relieved to learn that adults have suffered just as they have. Moreover, being in touch with your own feelings of rejection will probably enable you to be more spontaneous and empathetic in helping the new child.

### Clarification and Feedback

You will regularly want to assess how well new children are adapting. The best guideline is your own observations. But other measures can help. Though a child may appear to be adjusting well in school, she may be having problems at home. For example, a child who gets along well with classmates at school may act depressed at home because her friendships don't extend beyond the classroom. The best way to obtain this kind of information is through conferences with both students and parents after the initial adjustment to the school has passed. You can alleviate the problem of kids being lonely at home by giving parents class enrollment lists with telephone numbers and addresses. Parents can then help their kids get in touch with classmates outside the school.

### Moving Away

Some of the problems with new students might have been prevented or ameliorated had the students been better prepared before moving. If you know in advance that one of your students is going to leave, you can help reduce her anxieties. She can be given an individual or group study project to find out about the area to which she will be moving. Another step is to hold a group discussion about how it feels to move, drawing especially upon those students who have recently made moves themselves. Before the child leaves, the class can think of ways to keep in touch—through class letters or cassette messages. The kids might develop this into a pen-pal exchange after the student is established in her new school. The possibility of visits should also be explored.

Moving is almost always a wrench for kids, and no panacea for the pain exists. But teachers can be instrumental in making such adjustments easier. Classroom activities help make the new student more comfortable, but what ultimately makes her feel she belongs is knowing that you and her classmates accept her as a unique individual.

*Mary Grishaver is a school counselor in Modesto, California.*
*Bruce Raskin is a staff writer of LEARNING.*

# POTPOURRI

# CALENDAR BINGO

Don't throw out those old calendars. The calendar is one of the first table-forms that primaries experience. A variety of opportunities to work with calendars can help youngsters gain facility in using the format, recognizing the days of the week and understanding number series. So, if you don't teach primaries yourself, you might cart some of the old calendars around to someone who does and share this calendar-bingo activity.

Make bingo cards by mounting each month on heavy cardboard. (Laminating the cards will give them longer life.) Each bingo card will have 35 squares or cells — 7 columns for days times 5 rows for weeks. Months with 31 days will have 4 blank squares, coming at the beginning and/or end of the month; 30-day months will have 5 blanks. And, of course, February, the maverick month, will have 7 blanks.

Mark some days as "free" squares, which children may cover immediately before the calling begins. Indicate free squares with a wash of color—rather than blocking out numerals—to avoid interrupting the number series. Cards of the same month can be made different from each other if care is taken to mark different free squares on each.

Markers for covering squares can be cut from laminated sheets of construction paper, scraps of tagboard, etc. They'll be needed in considerable quantities.

For the "calling" part of the game, prepare two decks of cards. One deck is for days of the week. One word is to appear on each card. Go through the seven days, shuffle the deck, turn it over and go through the days again. The other deck of cards will have the ordinals 1st through 31st, plus a few blank cards. If you use enough cards to go through the ordinals twice before turning the deck, you'll reduce the predictability of the calling somewhat—you won't always have to go through all 31 days before a day "comes up" for a second time. Use both sides of the cards, shuffling thoroughly before turning the deck.

For each play, the caller (or callers) draws one day card and one date card. To keep a record of what's been called, prepare a grid chart marked with the day across the top and the numerals 1 through 31 listed below each day. Mark the appropriate square for each play. (Laminating the chart has its obvious advantages.)

With a few modifications, calendar bingo is played just like regular bingo. A completely covered column or row wins a game. Modifications: (1) no diagonals; (2) squares marked with two dates, e.g. 23/30, can be counted as covered if either of the two dates is called.

Idea by: Harriet J. Blomberg, Park Row School, Mansfield, Mass.

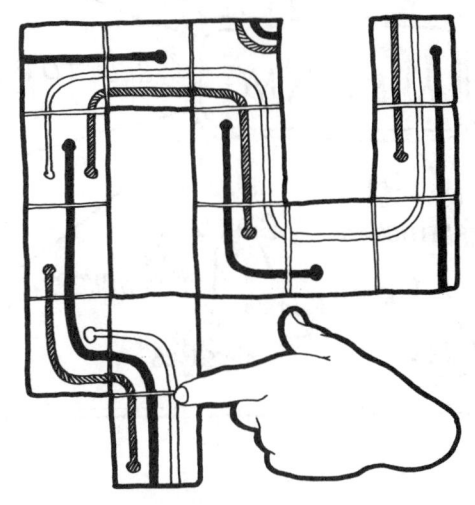

## CONNECT

☆ ☆ ☆ ☆ ☆ ☆ ☆ ☆ ☆

CONNECT is a game without words, letters or numbers. The challenge of play can be in simple visual matching, or in the strategy of anticipating future moves and predicting the moves of others.

CONNECT involves a principle of play similar to that of dominoes — construction of paths by matching elements on the playing pieces. In CONNECT, the matching is of colored tracks rather than dots.

Each playing piece has a part of a track or tracks. The tracks are always red, blue or black, and a piece has one, two or three track lines on it. Some lines are straight, some are curved; some are beginning points, some are end points. On some pieces the tracks divide, adding to the complexity and possibilities for strategy.

The rules folder suggests two to ten players. It also makes an interesting construction activity for one.

And if you shudder at the thought of 140 playing pieces floating around, you'll be glad to know that: (1) there is a 12-compartment tray inside the box for storage; (2) even if one or two pieces are mislaid, the game can still be played quite satisfactorily.

This is an English import and directions are provided in French, German and Spanish. English, too.

Order from: Selective Educational Equipment, 3 Bridge St., Newton, MA 02195. Grade level: Preschool – 5. Cost: $4.85. Add 5 percent on billed orders. Orders under $20 must be prepaid.

## AN ACTIVITIES HANDBOOK FOR TEACHERS OF YOUNG CHILDREN

☆ ☆ ☆ ☆ ☆ ☆ ☆ ☆ ☆

Doreen Coft and Robert Hess have put together a rich compendium of early childhood activities, all of which have proved successful in actual classroom use. The lessons cover a variety of curriculum areas—science, math, language, arts and cooking. All the lessons are based on principles set forth in an accompanying text, TEACHERS OF YOUNG CHILDREN. Both teachers and children should find learning enjoyable as they participate in such imaginative exercises as making a rainbow (science) or making a "feeling" picture (art).

A particularly delightful section of the book is the one on cooking. Children love to cook and the things they learn from it range from geography to philosophy. The popcorn recipe even gives the scientific explanation for the popping.

The authors have included an intelligently selected and annotated bibliography with each section. Another helpful thing about the book: It calls for inexpensive and readily available equipment.

Order from: Houghton Mifflin Co., Dept. M-L, One Beacon St., Boston, MA 02107. Grade level: Teachers of preschool–primary. Cost: $5.80 plus 8 percent postage and handling. Payment must accompany order.

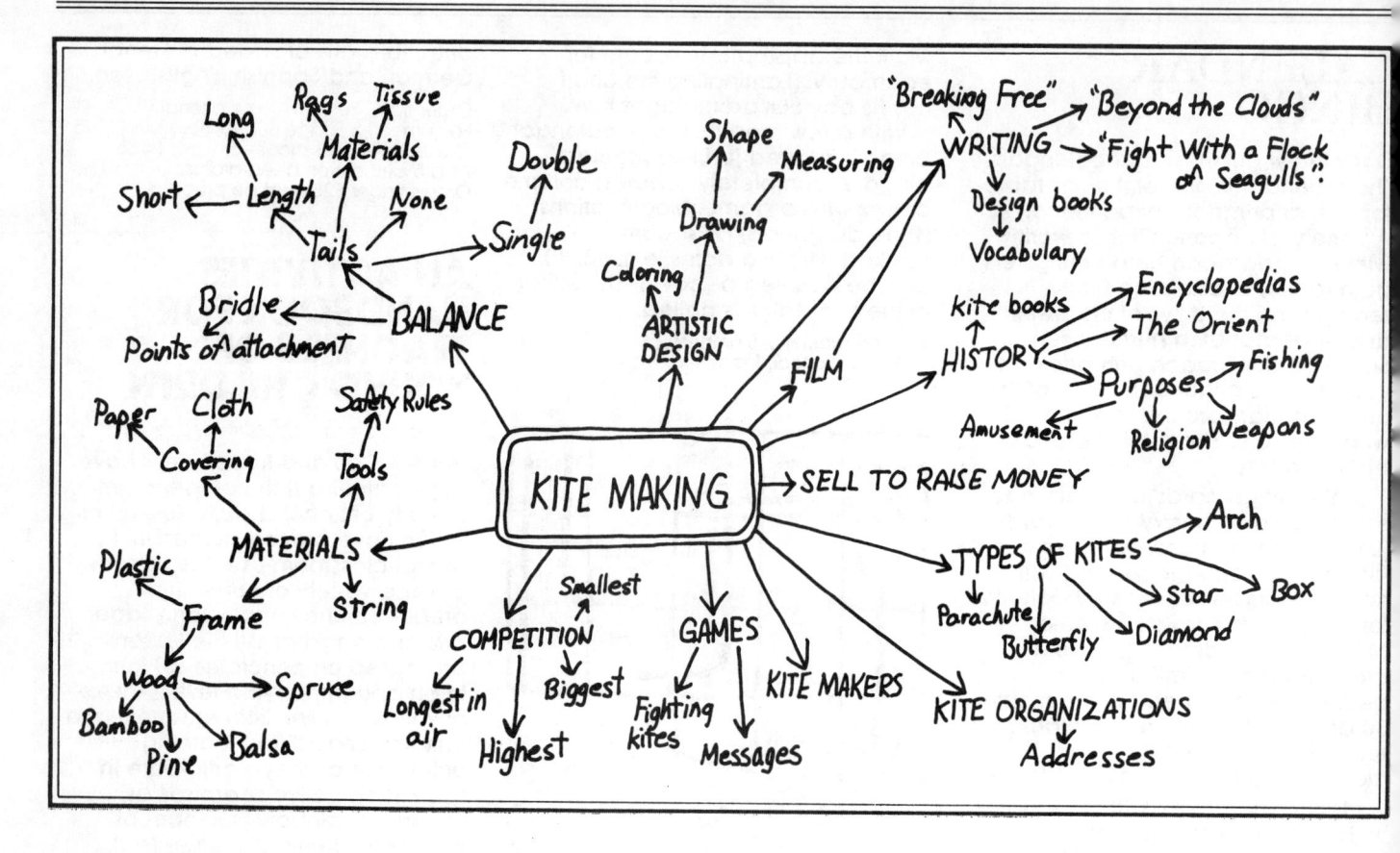

## Let the Kids Spin Their Own Curriculum

by Bruce Raskin

Hardly a week goes by that we aren't admonished by one "expert" or another for not "involving the kids in curricular planning." "Great advice," we mumble to ourselves. But when children are asked what they'd like to do in class, their minds go blank, or they suggest the overworked activities that have already occupied their time day in and day out.

None of this, of course, is very surprising; kids have been highly conditioned to do only what they're told. But give them the skills they need to help develop curriculum, and they can make valuable contributions at every step along the way.

How, then, can kids be involved in the real nitty-gritty of planning curriculum?

Here's a hypothetical example: It's only weeks before summer vacation; your kids are in the classroom, but their minds are outside, dancing with visions of kites, baseball, jump rope and bikes. You ask them what they'd like to study in class and get the same tired suggestions. Realizing that sometimes skills are best developed in the most unlikely ways, you decide to take the plunge. "How about kite flying as our next unit of study?" you ask. "Great," the class responds, "but what will we do?" Now you have a choice: either sit down and develop the lessons yourself, or show your pedagogy is where your mouth is and work the unit out with the kids. Assuming your choice is the latter, how do you proceed? For the moment, since you're probably reading this by yourself, grab a pencil and a sheet of paper and list all the ideas and activities you can think of associated with kite flying.

Fill the page? If you're like most of us, you started off like gang busters, then quickly petered out. No need to worry. You don't have to be an aeronautics expert to develop superb lesson plans around kite flying. There's a simple technique, useful in all subject areas and at all grade levels, for helping you move on. What's more, the method is perfect for bringing in the kids since it works best as a group process. Called "webbing," this technique helps you to build a network of ideas and activities. On paper, a web looks like a computer programmer's "flow chart," one item flowing graphically into another.

To create a web, take a single experience, word, phrase, topic—a single anything—and start brainstorming. Let your mind explore the idea freely, wandering in and out of its core. All the time you're jotting down your thoughts—not in a tight list form, but in an expanding web, tracing the flow of ideas by drawing a line from one thought to the next. If you get too far off the starting point, come back to it. Keep thinking about all of its ramifications, all of its connections.

Now try this: In the center of another sheet of paper, write the word "kite" and circle it. Then connect to it anything that is related. To develop the connections, ask yourself, "Who? what? why? when? where? and how?" What is a kite? What is it made of? What are its different parts? When were kites first used? What were they used for? What are the different types of kites? What kinds of activities can kids do with kites? How do kites fly?

When is the best time to fly kites? In which countries are kites most popular? Are there any books, films, poems or stories about kites? Are there any famous kite flyers? Why were they famous? What did they do? Can the class do some of the same things?

Next step, of course, is to try to answer some of the questions. As you find answers, weave them into your web. Webster tells us that a kite is "a light frame, usually of wood, covered with paper or cloth, to be flown in the wind at the end of a string." And everyone knows Ben Franklin discovered electricity with a kite and a key. The different parts of a kite? Well, there's a tail and a, uh, . . . And, of course, the wind makes a kite fly.

But none of us can answer all the questions. Nor, working alone, can we pose nearly all the questions. So bring in reinforcements. Have the kids brainstorm with you. Extend the web by researching through some related books. A quick skimming will unleash a windfall of new ideas and activities.

Once you've created a web, the final step is to translate it into a usable curriculum. Whether you work alone or with the class, there should be sufficient material within the web to create projects, activity cards, contracts, student booklets or whatever. Some of the items in the web will already be in the form of activities; others will have to be reworked.

In class tomorrow, if you or your kids have an idea you would like to expand, try webbing it. Applied to any curriculum problem, it can be a valuable tool and a useful skill. But most of all, it can help bring kids into the curriculum planning process.

Bruce Raskin is a staff writer of LEARNING.

## THE MIND BENDERS

☆ ☆ ☆ ☆ ☆ ☆ ☆ ☆ ☆

Do you accept the McLuhanesque idea that we are caught in a daily, overwhelming barrage of messages from the mass media? Do you suspect that those who understand the basic workings of perception have the power to manipulate and ultimately to dominate us?

If your answer is yes, then you probably already have been looking for some kind of antidote for your students and yourself. THE MIND BENDERS, a 96-page softback of activities and ideas dealing with communications, may be just what you need. And even if you don't think that we're nearing the mind-control world of 1984, you probably will find this book — which the authors call a "think thing" — a rich source of language and social studies projects.

The first section of the book gets at basic perceptual processes. Chapter one starts off with the question, "How good is your visual perception?" An intriguing visual-perception test helps you find out. Next comes a mind-set test featuring dazzling optical illusions. Follow-up questions relate the visual experiences to issues such as attitudes, opinions and prejudice.

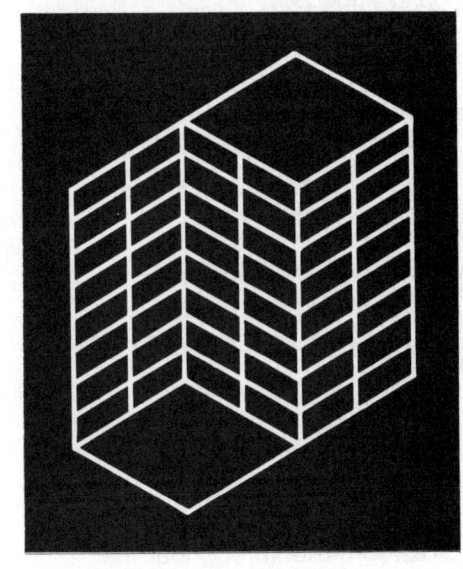

The final five chapters focus on specific media: "Advertising — Behind the Big Sell"; "Radio — The Sound of Now"; "Films — Get the Picture, Man?"; "Print — It's Not All Black and White"; and "Music — There's More Than Meets the Ear."

For each topic there are numerous concrete activities suited to classroom or at-home work. In the advertising chapter, for example, there is an evaluation form which students can use to study ads for autos, patent medicines, cigarettes and soft drinks. The analysis helps the students raise questions about the psychology of persuasion, music, association, fantasy and humor. The print chapter includes an association test for determining "colored language."

While most of the material is suited for the upper elementary grades (5–8), there are ideas and activities that can be adapted to even the youngest schoolchildren.

Order from: Friendship Press Distribution Office, P.O. Box 37844, Cincinnatti, OH 45237. Grade level: Teachers of grades 5–8. Cost: $1.95 plus $.30 postage and handling. Payment must accompany orders for less than $20.

## TRAVEL + A LOG = LEARNING

When a student takes time off from school to accompany his parents on a vacation trip, he need not experience, academically speaking, "lost days." There are many ways to turn the trip into a special kind of learning opportunity. One way that has worked especially well in the middle grades is to encourage the student to keep a travel log.

Though the content of the log will vary with the student's age, interests and abilities, as well as the trip destination, these suggestions should be helpful in most circumstances:
▶ Keep a diary of trip activities.
▶ Maintain a record of expenses. Include what is spent for transportation, food, lodging and all other items.
▶ Chart the route of the trip on a map. Note the places that are visited and keep a mileage chart.
▶ Interview different people along the way and write a summary of the interviews in the log.
▶ Draw a sketch impression of the places visited.
▶ Collect postcards and souvenirs along the way.
▶ Make a list and drawings of the different types of plants and animals observed during the trip.
▶ Construct a day-to-day temperature graph. Record the high and low temperatures for each day. Which day showed the greatest range?
▶ Time the trip going and returning. What was the variation and why?
▶ Describe the colors observed along the way. Tell about something that goes with each color.
▶ Describe how the visit to the person or place was different from a previous visit.

This kind of log can be an exciting experience for the traveling student as well as his classmates.

Idea by: James T. Howden, James Leitch-Warmsprings Elementary School Complex, Fremont, Calif.

## CHANGE FOR CHILDREN: Ideas and Activities for Individualizing Learning

☆ ☆ ☆ ☆ ☆ ☆ ☆ ☆ ☆

Kaplan, Kaplan, Madsen and Taylor are not members of a law firm. They're on the staff of the Inglewood (Calif.) Unified School District who are sharing some ideas about individualization. They present their ideas in an easy-to-take way, beginning with a brief definition of individualized learning and moving immediately to the meat of the matter.

A richly illustrated chapter on environment and organization features techniques for space utilization, storage and movement, and suggests ways of collecting needed materials. Next, learning centers are defined and steps to the creation of one are outlined. There follows an 82-page unit of ideas, drawings and worksheet suggestions for special-purpose learning centers from "alphabetizing" to "television."

A chapter on independent study spells out ways to develop the plan for a single-student project, offers "study starters," ideas for general activities that can be applied to a variety of topics, and helps out in the matters of record keeping and evaluation.

"Planning Classroom Time" shows alternative ways of getting the students "into motion" and includes samples of charts, sheets and other devices for keeping track of and checking up on your individualized individuals.

The book concludes with a 32-page section of worksheets designed for duplication. (These worksheets, drawn from earlier sections of the book, reinforce specific learnings. Your own situation may require modification of many of the worksheets.)

CHANGE FOR CHILDREN is a 200-page, 8-1/2-by-11 paperback. The format is open and easy to use, with clear chapter divisions and content-reference "ears" placed beside page numbers.

The book is realistic, practical, and was written for those teachers who "know where we want to go but don't know how to get there."

Order from: Goodyear Publishing Co., 15113 Sunset Blvd., Pacific Palisades, CA 90272. Grade Level: Teachers of all grades. Cost: $8.95.

## PRACTICAL APPROACHES TO INDIVIDUALIZING INSTRUCTION: Contracts and Other Effective Teaching Strategies

☆ ☆ ☆ ☆ ☆ ☆ ☆ ☆

Whether individualized instruction is in the theory or the practice stage for you, this 254-page text by Rita and Kenneth Dunn will give you a variety of practical strategies for classroom use. Throughout, the authors emphasize the need for clearly stated objectives and well-defined student evaluation, and they give methods for dealing with both.

Contracts, team learning, circles of knowledge, brainstorming sessions and role playing are among the individualizing techniques described. Each approach is designed to promote independent student work at individual rates while encouraging student interaction. Most of the techniques are appropriate for students in early primary through high school.

Particularly useful and descriptive are the chapters on contracts and contract activity packages. Although much has already been written about this type of individualizing, the Dunns have come up with a most definitive description.

The steps for contracting are clearly laid out, and there are complete sample contracts that put their descriptions into practice. The elements common to all contracts are behavioral objectives, media resource alternatives, activity alternatives and reporting alternatives. Add to those an initial teacher diagnosis, a self-test and a final teacher assessment, and you have contract activity packages. Setting up contracts initially calls for no small amount of teacher preparation, but once the program is underway, kids work independently, freeing the teacher to work with individuals or small groups.

The authors don't believe that any one of the strategies they mention is a key to instant individualization but that a combination of strategies will certainly make for a more effective individualized learning environment.

Order from: Parker Publishing Co., Dept. 6611-A1(5), West Nyack, NY 10994. Grade level: Teachers of all grades. Cost: $9.95. Add $.99 on billed orders.

## FABULOUS FREEBEE
## EDC NEWS

From the Education Development Center in Newton, Massachusetts, the innovators of such creative curriculum materials as Elementary Science Study (ESS) and Man: A Course of Study, comes this semi-annual newsletter.

Issues usually describe ongoing EDC projects in social studies, science and math, open education, international education, media and special curriculum areas. There are also miscellaneous "Announcements" which include workshop schedules, book reviews and descriptions of available EDC publications.

Intended as a "continuing conversation with our friends — the teachers, administrators, parents and students who share our intention of making schools a better place for everybody," EDC NEWS also promises to report reader response — ideas and experiences that could benefit others.

For those who are interested in learning about some of the latest educationally sound curriculum developments, this free newsletter makes interesting reading. Write and ask to be placed on the mailing list for EDC NEWS.

Order from: EDC News, 55 Chapel St., Newton, MA 02160. Grade level: Teachers of all grades.

# WORKJOBS

☆ ☆ ☆ ☆ ☆ ☆ ☆ ☆

Ask a student to explain why these activities are called "workjobs" and he'll probably have a hard time finding an answer. After all, what's so joblike about putting a toy airplane with 4 + 3 written on the wings into hangar number 7? Or placing rice, rocks and rulers into a box labeled "R"?

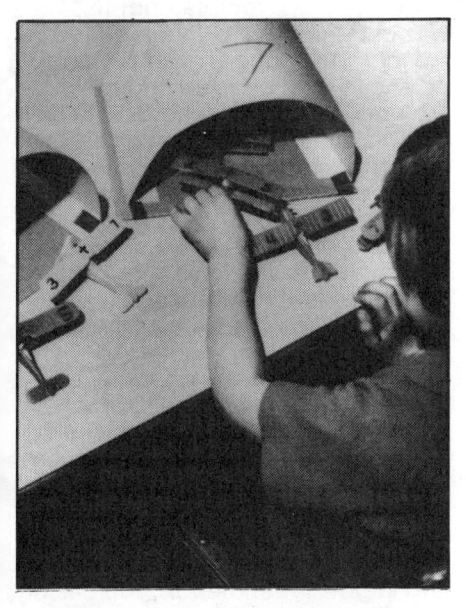

Primary grade teachers trying to turn their classrooms into activity-centered learning environments will find WORKJOBS extremely useful. Not only does the book illustrate (verbally and photographically) some 100 language and math activities, it also gives an excellent set of ground rules for starting, maintaining and keeping records for such a program. Many of the activities are adaptable to the intermediate grades as well. And, just as important, this book can serve as a frame of reference for creating hundreds more activities.

Order from: Addison-Wesley Publishing Co., Innovative Division, 2725 Sand Hill Rd., Menlo Park, CA 94025. Grade level: Teachers of preschool-primary. Cost: $7 plus $.50 postage and handling. Also available: WORKJOBS FOR PARENTS is an adaptation of WORKJOBS for use in the home. Cost: $3.16 plus $.50 postage and handling.

# THE AMAZING 4-IN-1 COOKBOOK

The old-fashioned way to a man's heart and a way to skills reinforcement in four areas are strangely parallel paths. "Goodies" and the recipes that they come from are the vital elements.

Have each student bring in a recipe for a favorite dish — something on the simple side, no puff pastry. Then, once a week, select one of the recipes for students to copy as handwriting practice. That's the first of the four skills. (Be sure to have students allow a wider-than-usual margin at the left in order to have room for staples or fasteners.) A final proofread copy is collected and filed for each student.

During the same week, the recipe contributor and a helper prepare the recipe for everyone to sample. Skill area 2, following directions, becomes important here, and math (skill area 3) comes into play as recipes are doubled or quadrupled to accommodate class-sized appetites.

All the ingredients are provided through cooperative effort, since everyone shares the results. The school kitchen might be available for baking and refrigeration. A small hot plate can be used for direct heating.

After several months, with any luck, all the recipes will have been copied and tasted. At that time, return each student's handwritten recipe collection and prepare for booklet making. Have each student assemble the pages, number them and devise a table of contents. Cover design and construction become an art project, and not so coincidentally, this brings in skill area 4.

The finished 4-in-1 cookbook can become a kitchen-tested gift or a culinary memory book from the school year.

Idea by: Sally Siler, Alice Birney School, Eureka, Calif.

## SUMMER-TO-SEPTEMBER ALBUM

Summer means a change of pace, change of scene, perhaps, and a clearing of the mind. But to guard against having students return in the fall with minds in a state of absolute TABULA RASA, try introducing the "Summer-to-September" souvenir album. Using the albums will help keep kids in touch with school skills while they're also storing away summer thoughts and mementos. (The albums can also serve as first aid for treating the "nothing-to-do" summer syndrome.)

A Summer-to-September album starts out as blank paper (lined, plain, colored and white, plus tracing paper) bound into a cover with paper fasteners. (Note: With paper at a premium, you probably won't be providing all the sheets the albums can use, you might start with a few sheets as "seed" and trust that the album keepers will add pages as needed.)

To stimulate summer thoughts, include a contents starter sheet of suggested page headings or activity topics:

LINED-PAPER SECTION
  A Summer Mystery
  I Explore Outdoors (plants, animals, a rainy day, the beach)
  Summer Help (jobs I liked and those I didn't)
  Just a Little Math Practice (or spelling, or writing, etc.)
  Poems I Wrote (or read — include the poets' names)

PLAIN-PAPER SECTION
  The Way Summer Looks (pictures from magazines, photos)
  Doodles and Designs
  Rubbings
  Summer Drawings by Me
  Letters and Telegrams
  Souvenirs (tickets, movie ads, etc.)
  Unusual News

TRACING-PAPER SECTION
  Try your hand (and pencil) at tracing illustrations, letters and words, or patterns, designs, shapes.

Making covers for the albums can be a special spring art project.

Summer activities will vary widely among children in your class. Children who feel their summers won't be all that exciting should be encouraged to look more carefully and creatively at daily events and common things — and also to use their imaginations to conjure up some fantastic adventures right at home. (Next year's teacher may be surprised to discover what these day-dreamers did on their summer vacations!)

Idea by: Mona Roseland, Merritt Island, Fla.

## INDIVIDUALIZING THROUGH LEARNING STATIONS

☆ ☆ ☆ ☆ ☆ ☆ ☆ ☆

Beginning with the assumptions that (1) you want to individualize, and (2) you're only human, Lorraine Godfrey goes on to offer specific, helpful suggestions about how to implement the learning-stations idea. She stresses at the start the importance of well-defined goals and lesson plans and only then makes suggestions about moving furniture around. She is also convinced that the introduction of learning stations should be made slowly, naturally, and in consultation with the students.

A number of sample grouping plans and evaluation techniques are offered, but if you're one who gets uncomfortable en route between "This is the philosophy" and "These are the dramatic results," you'll especially appreciate chapters two and three. Here, four learning stations — language, art, math and science — are followed through a six-week period. A general overview sets the scene. Specific suggestions fill in the action. Chapter three provides more suggested activities in six subject-matter areas. Each suggestion follows the same format: materials needed, then short, easy directions for children's use.

The book also describes the "ministation," where short-take enrichment activities happen. Students themselves can take the responsibility for much of the setting up and management of such stations. The suggestions for ministation activities range from word puzzles to treasure maps.

At the back of the book you'll find suggested materials, sources of supplies and a bibliography of readings about individualized and learning stations.

Individualizing is not a snap. But it doesn't have to be an unreasonable aim. And ideas that have survived the rigors of the real classroom can be a real help, whether you're an individualizer from away back or a beginner.

Order from: Individualized Books Publishing Co., P.O. Box 591, Menlo Park, CA 94025.
Grade level: Teachers of all grades.
Cost: $4.25 plus $.50 postage and handling. Payment must accompany orders from individuals. School purchase orders will be billed.

# DEAL ME IN!

☆ ☆ ☆ ☆ ☆ ☆ ☆ ☆

"To Jody, Jill and Danny — Shut up and deal!"

Thus Margie Golick dedicates her book to her children. For more than 20 years associated with the Learning Centre of Montreal's Children's Hospital, psychologist Golick has found in the lowly deck of cards a most productive aid to diagnosis and to learning. She would like to see cards in every classroom from kindergarten through high school. She offers suggestions to teachers in "normal" and "special" classrooms, and to parents and school psychologists, about the uses of cards with children of all ages and abilities.

Golick relates the skills used in playing cards to the development of basic learning skills such as sequencing, number concepts, motor and visual skills (how about Concentration for visual memory?), and skills in verbal, social and intellectual areas. A classified listing groups games for the development of specific skills.

The book describes card-playing conventions, provides a glossary of special terms and vocabulary, and offers information about the kinds of cards that are available. There are also suggestions for introducing the deck to children, helping them to become familiar with many fascinating features of the cards. (Do you know which jack has no mustache?)

And then — there are complete rules for more than 80 games, solitaire setups and simple card tricks, from old favorites such as Slapjack and Rummy to such teasers as Tough Beans and Inflation and Oh Hell! (This is not to be confused, notes Golick, with another game named "Oh Hell" by a little boy who, in describing it, told his mother, "They call out numbers, and one person says, 'Bingo!' and everybody else says, 'Oh, hell!' ")

For each game an age range is suggested — beginning with age four — and notation is made of the learning skills that come into play. There are comments about what to expect or watch for during play, and alternative ways to play the games are described.

The book is hardcover, 112 pages, and is illustrated with many photographs, especially helpful in amplifying rules and techniques.

Order from: Jeffrey Norton Publishers, Inc., 145 East 49th St., New York, NY 10017. Grade level: Teachers of all grades. Cost: $6.95 plus $.45 postage and handling. Payment must accompany order.

# SMALL VOICE, BIG VOICE

☆ ☆ ☆ ☆ ☆ ☆ ☆ ☆

The small voice belongs to a youngster named Jed; the big voice belongs to Dick Lourie, the adult member of the duo. Together they sing 12 songs that teachers of primary aged kids will find a joy to use in the classroom.

The songs vary in their content, with some falling into the affective domain ("Scared and Not Scared," "Happy Face") and others oriented toward cognitive skills ("I Like").

The songs can be used in a variety of ways. Besides simply listening, kids can participate in the singing. In some cases, words or phrases are left out so that participants can make up and sing lyrics of their own. In addition, the liner notes, which traditionally accompany all Folkways recordings, suggest many further extensions for the songs.

The voices of Dick and Jed are not the kind traditionally heard on classroom recordings. The singing is very informal and, because of the spontaneous interaction between the two, comes across almost as if they were right in the room putting on a live performance. On occasion, Dick speaks a little too quickly or softly, but his pleasing voice and accomplished playing of either guitar or harpsichord compensate. With Jed's rough voice lending vitality to the performance, all the melodies are pleasing.

Order from: Folkways Records, 43 W. 61 St., New York, NY 10023. Grade level: K – 4. Cost: $6.98 plus $1.50 postage and handling. Payment must accompany order.

## PICK A PUZZLE

Word-maze puzzles — those grids with hidden words — are popular with many students and teachers. The puzzles can be used for review and reinforcement or for pure recreation.

A few notes on puzzle making:

1. Use graph paper that has fairly large squares, or draw your own grid — and run off plenty of copies.
2. Pencil the required words in place on the grid — horizontally, vertically, diagonally. Then letter in the blank spaces to fill out the square.
3. Staple the grid onto a ditto master and mark over (or type in) all letters for the final puzzle.

Puzzles may be built around various subject-matter areas to check recall of facts or vocabulary:

1. Find the 15 reptiles.
2. Find the 13 original states.
3. Find 20 prepositions.
4. Find 10 words that are accented on the second syllable.
5. Find 16 acronyms.
6. Find 10 palindromes. (Look it up.)
7. Find 12 ways of traveling.

When there are clues to be solved, puzzles present a different challenge. With this type of puzzle, suggest that students list words as they find them to make checking easier.

▶ DEFINITIONS — students look for words for which definitions are given.
▶ HOMONYMS — word list gives words such as corps, colonel, aisle; students look for core, kernel, isle.
▶ COMPOUNDS — word list gives part of a compound (book); students find words to make a compound (mark).
▶ ROOTS, PREFIXES, SUFFIXES — word list gives far, under; students look for tele, sub.

Any pair data can be used: animals and their young, singulars and plurals, countries and capitals, natural resources and products.

You might create some seasonally oriented puzzles — ready to slip in when there's an unexpected hiatus in the hectic holiday schedule. Or better yet, let students make up their own holiday puzzles to share.

Idea by: Carolyn Sieber,
West Carrollton Junior High School,
West Carrollton, Ohio.

## CHILDREN ARE PEOPLE

☆ ☆ ☆ ☆ ☆ ☆ ☆ ☆ ☆ ☆

Teachers or schools interested in open classrooms and looking for practical examples should consider this film. Focusing on several classrooms in English infant and junior schools, the film suggests ideas for structuring the classroom, developing student activities and evaluating students.

Throughout, kids work independently on projects they have chosen and developed themselves. Students use a wide variety of manipulative and printed materials. Traditional teacher-centered learning is much less present than in many American elementary schools.

One particularly useful segment shows a group of children taking a field trip and the follow-up activities that develop from it. The kids work either alone or in small groups while the teacher interacts.

Subtitled "A Study of Education in Vertically Grouped Primary Schools," the film provides an overview of open classrooms utilizing vertical grouping — a class organization in which children of several age levels (for instance, 7 – 9's and 9 – 11's) are placed in the same room.

In 43 minutes, the film cannot possibly deal with all phases of open classrooms, but it serves as a useful introduction. And most important, the ideas and activities that are conveyed can be readily applied to single-age, horizontally grouped classes (the way most American schools are set up).

The color film was written and directed in England by Lorna Ridgway, coauthor of FAMILY GROUPING IN THE PRIMARY SCHOOLS. A discussion guide comes with the film.

Order from: Agathon Press, Inc., 150 Fifth Ave., New York, NY 10011. Grade level: Teachers of grades K – 6. Cost: $45, rental; $450, purchase. Add $2 for postage and handling.

## FABULOUS FREEBEE
## AMERICAN QUARTER HORSE Booklet and Posters

Horses, horses, horses! If you have students that are excited by the very sound of the word, you'll be happy to find some free materials for reading and for research offered by an organization with equal equine enthusiasms.

A 32-page booklet called TRAINING RIDING HORSES follows the step-by-step training of foals as carried out by several large ranches. The format — small pictures, each accompanied by a short text — should appeal to some of your less eager readers. The text stresses the importance of gentleness and patience in working with animals, as opposed to the exciting and damaging practices of "bronc busting" that children may associate with western riding.

The American Quarter Horse Association also offers a set of horse posters — some in full color. Check with the AQHA for other horse resources.

Something else to think about: the AQHA handles individual requests from children — a chance for a rewarding letter-writing experience.

Order from: American Quarter Horse Association, Dept. 7, Amarillo, TX 79168. Grade level: 4–junior high.

## LEARNING GAMES
☆ ☆ ☆ ☆ ☆ ☆ ☆ ☆

Problem: five unfilled minutes between homeroom and an assembly — too little time to start a major activity, too much just to sit it out. What to do? How about passing out copies of one of these "learning games"?

The games come in six separate 28-page books of ditto masters. Fairly simple, one-shot activities, the games provide stimulating short-term entertainment along with some skill development in logic, perception, art, math, language, classification, mapping and several other areas.

The games' greatest strengths are in the challenge and the potential for positive reinforcement they provide for kids. Substitutes will appreciate them especially.

As with any materials, a check-through of activities is advised before you have students work independently. For example, a primary level activity that has students combine word parts does not divide all words strictly according to normal syllabication, and that may cause confusion.

The six books carry grade level designations as follows: Book A (K – 1), Books B and C (1 – 2), Book D (2 – 3), Book E (3 – 4), Book F (4 – 6). The books are illustrated with simple line drawings that are generally suited to the age groups noted. In some cases, however, the illustrations may be somewhat immature for older students. All books contain brief lesson notes and also provide answers for many of the activities.

Order from: Milliken Publishing Co., 1100 Research Blvd., St. Louis, MO 63132. Grade level: K – 6. Cost: $3.75 per book. Payment must accompany order.

## SURVIVAL KIT FOR SUBSTITUTES: Activities That Work in Elementary Classrooms
☆ ☆ ☆ ☆ ☆ ☆ ☆ ☆

Substitutes, next time you hear the familiar student cry, "Hey, we gotta sub today!" be ready for 'em. And regular teachers, how about helping assure sub survival in your room?

This 110-page paperback by Vita Pavlich and Eleanor Rosenast, who have been both regular and substitute teachers, describes approximately 150 spur-of-the-moment, high-interest, educationally sound teaching activities that call for few materials not on hand in most schools. Where outside items are required, you can easily tote them along. As an extra help, most chapters conclude with a list of "Materials Not Usually Found In Classrooms."

Most of the activities stand independent of what is going on in class, though some are meant to supplement work that is in progress. None calls for additional research beyond the descriptions given in the book.

The chapters cover the spectrum of curriculum situations most subs face over a period of time. Chapter headings include: "Openers" (how to begin the day), "Language Arts," "For Courageous Substitutes," "Social Studies," "Mathematics," "Art With Limited Materials," "Holidays" and "Rainy Days." Many of the sections are further divided by grade levels and are for use alone or in conjunction with a text.

Though some of the activities will be familiar to experienced teachers, many will find change-of-pace ideas in the book, and substitutes, especially those who have yet to develop their own bag of tricks, will welcome the wealth of doable, no-hassle activities.

Order from: Citation/Scholastic, 906 Sylvan Ave., Englewood Cliffs, NJ 07632. Grade level: Teachers of grades K – 6. Cost: $3.95 (list), $2.97 (school price). Payment must accompany order.

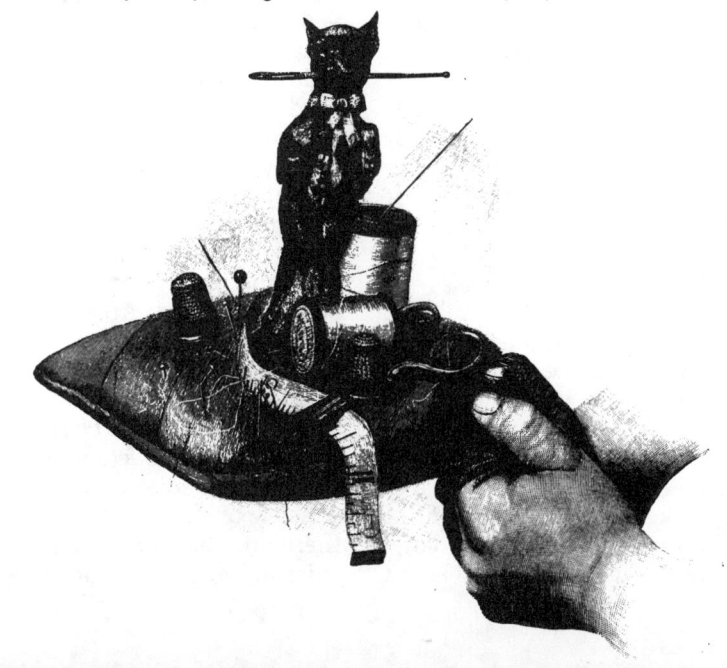

# Self-Instructional Packages
by Odvard Egil Dyrli

Each time we have attended a teachers' conference or teachers' association convention in recent years, it has been clear that "individualization" is the order of the day on the commercial scene. A multitude of competing programs and supplementary materials offer our students alternative pathways, excursions, special investigations, problem breaks, optional exercises, enrichment activities, explorations and various other opportunities to depart from the "usual" course of educational events.

The materials represent a continuum from the tightly closed to the open-ended, from games to worksheets. They come wrapped in the colorful papers of the "right" jargon of key concepts, affective goals, behavioral objectives, and tied with the bright ribbons of captivating brochures, contrived evaluative studies and the customary rosters of "education big-leaguers," who, in more cases than not, served no real functions other than to bless the package. A rose by any other name may smell as sweet. By the same token, inferior and too often well-overpriced materials usually generate clues as to their own state of being. Unwrap those packages!

Once we get by the gift wrapping and ribbons, though, then what? Are there specific indicators of a product's value that can be spotted before the material is thrust on a child? Part of the answer depends, of course, upon the way in which we expect to use the material. Self-instructional materials can, for example, be the primary instructional mode for certain topics, or may be used successfully to introduce, supplement, extend or remediate. It is possible, however, to suggest some basic criteria that will be useful in any critical review, regardless of application.

Our primary focus should be upon finding direct evidence that the program in question is, in fact:

▸ *Inviting for children in format, appearance and use.* Learning need not be drudgery. Would working with this program make *you* feel like any one of a host of animals used in psychology experiments? Or would you laugh sometimes, become truly challenged, and even get caught up in suspense—in short, enjoy yourself? If the materials appear bland to you, why would anyone expect your children to become excited by them? This is a tough test to pass.

▸ *A creative approach to the content.* Cosmetic surgery can cover a multitude of sins. Do you find the same tired old discussions that have appeared in textbooks for a generation? Simply transposing a text to a new format accomplishes little beyond salvaging some money for the company. Try to disregard the *how*, and look and listen carefully to *what* is being presented. An excellent way to do this is to copy some of the script and then reread it without the interference from the "show."

▸ *Well integrated with physical materials.* Children at the elementary school level in particular need to work with concrete objects. In most subject areas, therefore, be very cautious in considering programs that disregard this obvious fact. On the other hand, a number of companies have put together materials kits almost as an afterthought, while others have produced highly specialized items that have limited use in any other context. Programs that utilize inexpensive and easily obtained materials that are already familiar to the child are worth looking for.

▸ *Process-oriented.* Filling kids' heads with terms and facts for that sake alone is no more defensible if done through self-instructional formats than it is through any other approach. This weakness is easy to spot: written materials will include a large number of underlined or italicized words, and the "activities" will emphasize defining terms, writing reports, making lists and completing "fill-in-the-blank" and matching questions.

Ask yourself what *skills* the children will have an opportunity of developing further. If you cannot answer honestly with such processes as "communicating," "measuring," "observing," "inferring" and so forth, it is time to move on. And don't listen to anyone who tells you that children learn such skills by memorizing someone's lists or copying someone's definitions. It simply isn't so.

▸ *Designed to accept alternative solutions and solution strategies.* Programs that press for *the* right answer or *the* right problem-solving strategy continuously, without also giving the student opportunities for developing unique approaches to problems, are unnecessarily limiting. Do all the students have to complete the same experiences in the same sequence, without regard for the differing abilities of each individual?

▸ *Fairly priced for what it is designed to accomplish.* If you and your students could develop materials that would be more efficient, less expensive, more interesting and more enjoyable, what are you waiting for? And, of course, perhaps the same materials that would be purchased can be borrowed from a curriculum center and similar copies made for less money.

If we make a tour of the closets and storage rooms of our schools, we will likely find "panacea prints" and other fossilized evidences of the education dinosaurs from earlier ages. Some of these specimens are in our museums as a result of purchases made too quickly in days when funds were easier to come by. If your school is contemplating the purchase of self-instructional programs, even if the materials seem to meet the basic criteria fairly well, by all means begin on a small and experimental basis. Schools that have signed on the dotted line in haste, sometimes after only a single presentation by a well-coached hawker, have found to their dismay that the call of the masked rider riding off in the distance *wasn't* "Hi Ho Silver!"

Odvard Egil Dyrli is professor of education, University of Connecticut, Storrs.

## A TEACHER'S GUIDE TO COGNITIVE TASKS FOR PRESCHOOL

☆ ☆ ☆ ☆ ☆ ☆ ☆ ☆

Develop cognitive skills in pre-schoolers? It need not be as deadly as it sounds. Despite their academic intent, the cognitive tasks in this 68-page, spiral-bound handbook are just plain fun.

Author Owen W. Cahoon believes that cognitive growth in youngsters can be specifically developed rather than left strictly to chance or to the nebulous world of unfocused enrichment activities. He takes the attitude, from Piaget and others, that such skills are best developed in group settings.

The group tasks are organized by concepts into six different categories — substance, class inclusion, seriation, length, number and weight — and usually call for manipulation of objects. An activity from the "substance" section, for example, asks children to fold a canvas tarp and then to determine if the quantity of tarp has changed. Or from the "length" section, children are instructed to use four-foot lengths of string to measure each other and objects in the room in different ways and then to make comparisons. The activities, which can be expanded or used as they are presented, are concisely described and occasionally accompanied by helpful illustrations. Most activities call for materials that can be made or obtained easily and inexpensively. In some cases, substitute items would be acceptable.

The book includes pre- and post-tests and a score sheet to use in determining levels of cognitive development. The test activities are divided into sections that correspond to the task categories described above.

One point the book fails to emphasize is that not all preschoolers will be mature enough to grasp all of the concepts being developed through the tasks. Teachers should be sensitive to this and not try to push youngsters to accomplish something they are not ready for.

Order from: Brigham Young University Press, Business, 268 UPB, Provo, UT 84602. Grade level: Teachers of preschool – kindergarten. Cost: $2.95. Payment must accompany order.

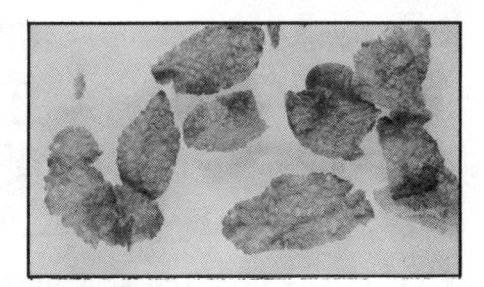

## CEREAL BOX BONANZA

If you've ever found yourself reading cereal boxes (the ones you hide behind in the morning when you're not ready to face the world yet), you may have discovered a long-overlooked teaching aid. Convenient, practical (and biodegradable), the cereal box can be good for lots of things besides keeping cereal in.

Students can help you make a collection of cereal boxes in a short while. (Ask them to bring in samples of the cereals, too, in small plastic containers.) The boxes then become the source of activities in language arts, social studies, science and math.

With young children, try word-matching activities. Copy the names of the cereals on file cards and have children match each label with the correct box. Copy off slogans or characters' names for other matching experiences. Older children can write sentences about the cereals, describing them, noting likenesses and differences in shape, texture and taste. Reluctant readers may find the boxes less formidable than books and may read a box panel without realizing it's "work." They may even recommend favorite boxes to their friends.

The lists of ingredients can lead to investigations in social studies and science. What are the different grains used for cereals? Where are they grown? (Do you suddenly have visions of maps and charts and diagrams?) How do cereals fit into the basic food groups? How important are cereals in a nutritious diet?

Of course, individual cereal preferences will be demonstrated by the boxes that are brought in. (And what is fiercer than the loyalty of the breakfast-food devotee?) Check out the comparative appeal of several cereals by taking a survey and making charts of choices.

The cereal box can be a reader, a social-studies-project box and a math activity starter — and for free!

Idea by: Margery Altman, Brewster School, Durham, Conn.

# LIKE MONEY IN THE BANK

It is a gross understatement to say that sixth grade remedial readers need all the encouragement they can get. The intrinsic rewards of successful learning may be a long time in coming and may need the added strength of an extrinsic reward system for a while.

One kind of reward system deals in a standard medium of exchange which students can earn, collect and "cash in" for more immediately satisfying rewards. Each student receives a paycheck for weekly achievement — so many units for satisfactorily completed work. The paycheck may be banked, with the student receiving a statement of his growing account. Or the check may be converted into paper cash units to be exchanged for "goods" — 25 units for candy, 100 units for a privilege. Students may wish to accumulate units throughout the year for a grand prize. Each student has his own checkbook and may withdraw his total reward credit any time he wants it.

This system, primarily a motivation technique, can also provide practical budgeting experience and give these older students a sense of participating in one phase of the adult world.

It is hoped, of course, that the work patterns stimulated by this form of reward system will eventually develop into greater self-motivation. Success enjoyed more regularly will put the pseudo bank right out of business.

Idea by: Connie Cope,
Stratmoor Hills Elementary School,
Colorado Springs, Colo.

# LEARNING BASIC SKILLS THROUGH MUSIC (Volume 1)

☆ ☆ ☆ ☆ ☆ ☆ ☆ ☆ ☆ ☆ ☆ ☆ ☆ ☆ ☆

Simple, clearly articulated lyrics, strong, catchy rhythms and pleasing, contemporary melodies on this recording appeal to the preschool and primary age set. Part of the Educational Activities, Inc., "Hap Palmer Record Library" — a collection of records designed to teach and reinforce the basic skills for early childhood and special education classes — LEARNING BASIC SKILLS THROUGH MUSIC is composed of ten songs. They develop and reinforce a variety of skills, including counting, color recognition and play-acting.

Children display no reluctance about singing along with the songs or responding to those lyrics that call for active participation. Song lyrics and simple directions, which kids must follow are included in an accompanying teacher's guide.

In a song called "Colors," the lyrics alternately ask reds, blues, greens and yellows to stand up and sit down. The teacher's guide calls for four students, each holding a large, appropriately colored card, to participate while the song is being introduced. The number of participants increases as the kids become familiar with the colors. Teachers are free, of course, to add twists of their own.

Order from: Educational Activities, Inc., Dept. BW, 1937 Grand Ave., Baldwin, NY 11510. Grade level: Preschool–1. Cost: $6.95. Payment must accompany orders less than $15.

# YOU AND ME

☆ ☆ ☆ ☆ ☆ ☆ ☆ ☆ ☆

Most workbooks demand that the student become involved in the curriculum; this one leaves no choice in the matter. In fact, the student is the curriculum.

YOU AND ME, subtitled A BOOK ABOUT THE HUMAN BODY: ITS ACTION, USE, MEASUREMENT AND PLACE IN OUR WORLD, contains 41 "investigations" that use the student and members of the class as the focus of study.

Written by Richard L. Kimball, the book is divided into three sections: "Me in My World," "Parts of My Body" and "Me and My Friends." Each section is further subdivided into investigations around a specific theme. For example, in the section "Me and My World," the student is asked to explore "Me and My Class" by asking, among other things, "How many students are in my class?" "The classroom is how many of my feet long?" and "How does my classroom look from the top?"

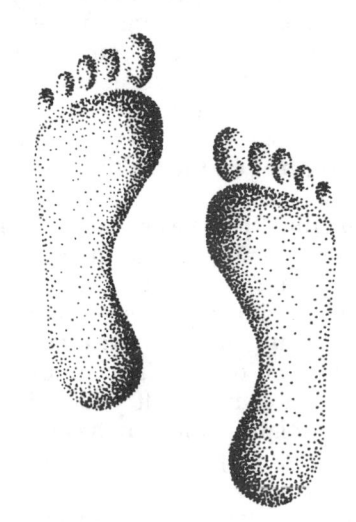

Designed as a workbook with perforated tear-out pages (each page can be thermofaxed and mimeographed), YOU AND ME can — and in the primary grades must — be used as a teacher's guide. Brief notes are included on organizing the investigations, using the book with different grade levels, questioning, evaluating and exhibiting results.

Two cautions: Not all teachers will choose to use one investigation that in a simplistic way tries to deal with reproduction, nor will they all want to mimeograph an investigation that contains an unsophisticated illustration of a black child.

Order from: Educational Science Consultants, P.O. Box 1674, San Leandro, CA 94577.
Grade level: Primary – intermediate.
Cost: $3.50 plus $.35 postage and handling.
Payment must accompany individual orders. School purchase orders will be billed.

## VERI TECH

☆ ☆ ☆ ☆ ☆ ☆ ☆ ☆

"Individualized" and "self-checking" materials often carry another, but unnamed, descriptive: "boring." Veri Tech fits the first two descriptions but fails on the third.

Veri Tech has programs on two levels—Mini Veri Tech for primaries and Senior Veri Tech for intermediate and upper elementary—to reinforce skills in language arts and math in a way that's exciting, absorbing and just plain fun.

Both Veri Tech programs have two parts—a set of problem booklets and a plastic case that looks like a watercolor paint tray and functions as a check-yourself answer key.

The "paint tray" of the Mini Veri Tech case is marked off in squares numbered 1 through 12; any problem in the Mini booklets can be answered by using these numbers. For each of the numbered squares there is a numbered tile, with a colored shape on the back. The tile numbers key in to problem numbers in the booklets. (In the Mini Veri Tech booklets each problem page has 12 problems. The Senior Veri Tech case has 24 squares and 24 numbered tiles that key in to problem numbers in the Senior Veri Tech booklets.)

The procedure for using either Veri Tech program is the same:
▸ Pick a problem page. Take tile 1 and read problem 1:
"A bell can _____."
The number next to the answer, "ring," is number 7. Cover number 7 in the case with tile 1.
▸ When all the squares in the case are covered, close the case, turn it over and open the bottom cover, revealing the pattern side of the tiles. If the pattern matches the corresponding one in the booklet, all answers are correct. Out-of-place tiles mark problems that must be reworked.

Thus far there are 18 problem books available for Mini—3 in prereading (visual discrimination of figures, lines, letters, syllables, words and sentences); 2 in basic language (letters, sounds, endings, picture and word matching, and vocabulary, sentence and story comprehension); 5 in beginning math (perception of figures, shapes, addition and subtraction); 2 in Spanish language; and 6 in French language. Senior now has 24 books—14 in math (including skills in addition, subtraction, multiplication, division, word problems, fractions, decimals, base numeration and metrics); 5 in language (with exercises in vocabulary, sounds, parts of speech, reading comprehension and other topics); and 5 in Spanish language. Exercises are primarily for reinforcement.

Though kids enjoy working randomly on the exercises, Veri Tech is more effectively utilized if teachers familiarize themselves with the workbooks and prescribe specific exercises. This holds especially true in the Senior language books, since the exercises tend to span a wide range of abilities.

In some books the instructions tend to be brief and somewhat vague. The two Senior books in base numeration, for example, should be used only with kids already familiar with the mechanics of Veri Tech and with working in different bases.

Most lower primaries will need constant supervision at first. But once they get the hang of using the materials, kids of all grades find an extra bonus, they can make up patterns and questions of their own—in effect, creating personalized workbooks.

The publishers are planning to add additional workbooks in math and language.

Order from: Educational Teaching Aids, P.O. Box 382, Menlo Park, CA 94025. Grade level: Primary—intermediate. Cost: Mini Veri Tech answer case, $6.90; Senior Veri Tech answer case, $8.50; workbooks for Mini or Senior, $1.75 each. Payment must accompany orders from individuals. School purchase orders will be billed.

## YOU CAN'T MISS IT

If you've ever tried to give verbal directions on how to get here from there, or have gotten lost trying to get there from here, you know about the troubles that gave rise to this idea.

Students can help out-of-towners find your school without the usual problems and confusions. First, you'll need an area map showing streets. Next, have individual students or groups figure out ways to the school from the north, south, east and west. These routes should be discussed and the most convenient route from each direction decided upon.

Now students use the scale of miles to figure mileage for each leg of the routes. Fractions should be changed to decimals to help motorists (and exercise math skills). After this work is completed, have students draw up the verbal directions. Discuss alternative wordings and choose the most accurate, clear and practical one. These directions are typed, copied and distributed to all who might have to direct someone to the school.

Your students will have sharpened some math skills, map skills and communications skills while doing their "good deed." And visitors will appreciate not having to watch for "the fourth—maybe fifth—light after the big supermarket on your right—going north—only it burned down last week. ..."

Idea by: David S. Daniels, Longmeadow Middle Schools, Longmeadow, Mass.

## READING ROUNDUP—'RITHMETIC RODEO

So you're a bit weary of science fairs with their elaborate displays, but you like the enthusiasm these carnivals generate? Why not try a different kind this time around?

A rodeo—arithmetic or reading or what you will—can be planned for a single class, divisional unit or the whole school. The basic plan is to have a number of booths set up to represent rodeo events: bronco riding, steer wrestling, calf roping, etc. Participants make the rounds of the booths performing one brief arithmetic or reading task (oral or written) at each. Points are accumulated and prizes given.

Of course there's more to it than that—planning, primarily. Participants are grouped into three ability levels and assigned coded scorecards to be carried by each contestant during competition. Materials at the booths (prepared by teachers, with student assistance) are divided into ability levels and coded to match the scorecard codes. Include some purely fun activities as well, such as tossing Ping-Pong balls into a boot for extra points or for candy. A chuckwagon refreshment stand adds another festive touch.

Scoring procedures and criteria for prizes—there should be lots of prizes and awards and ribbons—will also need to be worked out. Rodeo titles and terminology may help planners in this task.

Students can carry much of the responsibility for the rodeo themselves—running the booths, ushering younger children around the circuit and arranging for the "atmosphere" (western music, decorations, posters).

And if you're having a really big show, you may want to encourage western dress, have a rodeo king and queen, invite the press and parents, and enjoy the publicity.

The rodeo can be either a simple affair for review and reinforcement, or an extravaganza that clamors to become a tradition. Or it can be a medium-sized happy happening at the end of a busy year.

Idea by: Sister Stephen, S.C., Loyola School, Denver, Colo.

---

**FABULOUS FREEBEE**

### RESOURCES FOR YOUTH

A project of the National Commission on Resources for Youth, this three-times-a-year publication describes educational programs across the country that young people initiate "either by themselves or in cooperation with adults." Though each issue focuses on youths of high school age, there is much here for teachers of all levels.

One issue highlighted over ten ecology projects. Among them was one in Oregon in which students helped discover the causes of pollution in Coos Bay. Another project, the Urban Rat Patrol, resulted in the detection and extermination of rats in a 300-block area of New York City. And in Boulder, Colorado, eight students arranged a large ecology fair that involved members of many different communities.

Write and ask to be placed on the RESOURCES FOR YOUTH mailing list.

Order from: National Commission on Resources for Youth, 36 W. 44th St., New York, NY 10036.
Grade level: Teachers of all grades.

---

## CONCEALED IMAGE PROCESS

☆ ☆ ☆ ☆ ☆ ☆ ☆ ☆

The dream of every ditto grinder across the years has become real and practical. Now, with special transfer sheets that hold concealed images, you can make your own programmed materials or single self-correcting worksheets.

To set yourself up in the concealed image business you will need:
(1) Concealed Image Transfer sheets, (2) Concealed Image Response markers, (3) spirit masters and spirit master copier.

The process is just one step more complex than what you put up with now. Make your ditto master as usual. Remove the carbon sheet and replace it with the Concealed Image Transfer sheet. On the master, write in the answers, or whatever materials you wish to be revealed at a later time. The sheets are then run off like any other ditto sheets.

The student uses the special Concealed Image marker to make his responses. The marker reveals the material you added to your original master. The marker also leaves its own light yellow trace, so the number of attempted answers for multiple choice items will be apparent.

You may also design sheets that allow students to mark answers in pencil and then check by rubbing over the answers with the marker. (This would not be done with the programmed-type materials in which each answer depends on the previous one.)

The applications of the process are most happily myriad. And though you may enjoy discovering them yourself, you might also take a look at the manual. It shows numerous techniques and formats for a variety of subject-matter areas, as well as providing basic directions for the process.

The Concealed Image process puts a whole new light on the lowly, much maligned ditto. It emerges as a self-correcting teaching, review and testing tool in which the only moving part is the hand that holds the marker.

For more information, as well as some free sample worksheets and a marker, you can write to Effective Learning at the address below. You might also want to inquire about demonstration kits.

Order from: Effective Learning Inc., 7 North MacQuesten Parkway, Mount Vernon, NY 10550. Grade level: Teachers of all grades. Cost: $11.50—package of 10 Concealed Image Transfer sheets; $3.70—12 Concealed Image Response markers; $3.75—manual. Payment must accompany individual orders. School puchase orders will be billed.

# FOR PARENTS: SUMMER LEARNING IDEAS
From LEARNING Magazine

**Travel.** If you're planning a trip, getting there can provide half the fun and half the benefit. Travel is a great stimulus for reading. Once your destination is chosen, have your children preview the trip—through library books, automobile-club travel brochures, local chamber-of-commerce pamphlets—noting points of interest along the way as well as at the final destination. Also, planning the route to be followed is excellent map-reading practice.

**It's Planting Time.** Gardening is one of the best ways to teach the virtues of patience and responsibility. A backyard plot or even a window box can become a living science lab. Encourage your children to check the library for such books as EXPERIMENTING WITH SEEDS AND PLANTS by W. Budlong and M. Fleitzer (Putnam) or KIDS GARDENING by Aileen Paul (Doubleday).

**Art.** Art schools often challenge their students to make beautiful things out of ordinary materials. You may be surprised and delighted by the artistic things your children can create from macaroni, buttons, paper-towel rolls, yarn, and who knows what.

**Metrics.** In the next few years, schools are going to be immersing children in the metrics approach to measurement. Get a metric ruler from a local stationery or drafting-materials shop and metric measuring cups from a science or hobby store. Then let your kids do metric measuring of everything from their heights to the amount of juice they drink each day.

**Movie Making.** Many families with movie cameras generally use them only for parties and trips. But a lot of fun and learning can be had by making a family story film. Kids will stretch their imaginations in dreaming up stories and costumes.

**Punch and Judy.** A special project for older children is to hold a story-and-puppet hour for younger children in the neighborhood.

**Cooking.** Preparing meals is a vital survival skill all children should master. It also lets kids play a meaningful role in the family and helps develop many science and math skills —measuring being a prime example. For more fun, find a book called SCIENCE EXPERIMENTS YOU CAN EAT by Vickie Cobb (Lippincott).

**Eating.** Summer evenings provide opportunities for unusual eating experiences. For example, try a late-night dinner-by-candlelight as a way of learning how people used to live in the pre-electric era. It's also not a bad way to stimulate a discussion on the causes and implications of the energy crisis.

**Community Service.** Summer is a time when kids can do social-service work: carry groceries for shut-ins, read to children in hospitals, engage in ecology clean-up drives.

**Weather.** With a good reference book suggested by your librarian, a thermometer, a barometer and a notebook, kids can investigate weather forecasting.

**Television.** The tube is usually a family divider. Adults watch their shows, children theirs. Try to find one program a week that the whole family can view together and later talk about over dinner or a snack. This is a fine way for children to develop critical thinking and conversational skills.

**Behind the Scenes.** Many local institutions—like newspaper plants or the phone company—have tours which reveal the fascinating ways everyday tasks are done. Even visits to an automobile repair shop, a local construction site, the city council meeting or the local court can be exciting, educational experiences.

**Vocational Education.** If possible, arrange for your children to spend all or part of a day with one parent on the job. Or perhaps several working parents in the community can arrange opportunities for their children to visit a variety of work places.

# THE COMPLETE KITE CURRICULUM

### BY MARGARET GREGER

Eighty people lived in the western Nebraska town where I spent my first 17 years. I knew as little about kites as I knew about tigers or roller skates (no zoo, no sidewalks), and I saw my first kite when I was 13 years old. The grocery store changed hands, and the eighth grade son of the new owner brought kite making to Harrisburg with a vengeance. We made kites all that year—at school, at home, individually, and girls against boys. We split orange crates or cut willow canes for spars and covered the kites with brown wrapping paper, using flour-and-water paste. We flew them on saved-up, pieced-together store string or on binder twine. They were clumsy, heavy, gross by any standard I would apply today, but they flew, or died trying.

Our winds were something to reckon with, as Midwestern winds still are. We could stake a kite out and leave it up for three days. Some of the boys made a big kite and took it to the top of Lovers' Leap, a bluff about half a mile south of town. With a strong south wind, they soon had the kite flying over town at about 200 feet, or a little above the crest of the bluff. It would have flown higher if the drag on half a mile of fuzzy binder twine hadn't been so great.

My brother made the best kites. The rest of us were working strictly with diamond shapes and with proportions determined by the available spars. He found a pattern for a three-stick, five-sided model, delicate but stable in handling, in winds that destroyed my kites. To protect his property, he used to hide his reel of string. But once I took a ball of crochet thread and flew his kite by moonlight, country moonlight, uncut by artificial light, with wild clouds using the same wind the kite and I were using, and the kite living and dancing on the end of the fragile thread.

That was the beginning.

Now I take time each spring for a few weeks of teaching kite making and flying in elementary and junior high classrooms. What has developed is a short kite course. We build four or five *different* kites, using various materials and construction methods, and find that kites provide inexpensive and exciting leads into many areas—art, craftsmanship, engineering, math, even history, since the development of kites can be traced in both Oriental and Western experience.

Kites probably originated in China centuries before Christ and from there spread throughout the Pacific. They became elegant and sophisticated toys, for both children and adults, and had religious and ceremonial uses in some cultures. Man-lifting kites were developed, and there were experiments with military applications. By the 15th century, plane-surface kites had been imported to medieval Europe from the Orient. Benjamin Franklin was, of course, America's best-known early kite man. Western kite technology, both military and scientific, had advanced considerably beyond the Franklin level by the time the Wright brothers attached a motor to a box kite and flew it. Alexander Graham Bell constructed multicelled kites. One contained an astonishing 3,393 cells, flew well and landed safely, but was damaged as it was being towed in after landing.

### Kites, Competence and Confidence

But fascinating as the historical detail may be, kite building and kite flying need no further reason for being. They are simply fun, joyous and exciting fun, and therefore self-justifying. Still, the list of side benefits is impressive, beginning with competence and the confidence that competence confers. Mistakes are what we expect to cope with. A spar snaps, we replace it; paper tears, we tape or recover; string breaks, and we may mourn but we also cheer the kite's brief flight in freedom. And then turn to build another. As we adjust bridles and bows to suit the wind-of-the-day, shorten or lengthen tails, tailor for balance, we learn to *observe* how the kite flies, *diagnose* a problem and *prescribe* a remedy. The desperation of "This kite won't fly!" changes to "What shall I do so this kite *will* fly?"

As an example of the kite's curricular flexibility, one of my sixth grade classes put emphasis not only on kite flying but on building for performance and on gathering data for comparing various kites. We made simple wind gauges and instruments to calculate altitude (see Resource List). We studied the physics of flight and the technological uses of early kites. We were delighted to learn that when construction of the suspension bridge at Niagara Falls began, the first line across the gorge was carried by a boy's kite.

We built the Dutch, Eddy and Scott Sled kites—the Dutch kite to satisfy curiosity: "Is this kite really a bumblebee? How will it compare to the Eddy and the Sled?" As a basis for predicting performance and accounting for variations, we calculated the flying rate. This meant finding the area of polygons in square inches and converting to square feet; weighing kites in grams and converting to ounces; and dividing kite weight by kite area. As the spirit of experimentation grew, we scaled kites up to six feet and down to six inches. Ratio, area, weight and the Pythagorean theorem were tools for the task, to be mastered and put to immediate use. Every good day we had kites in the air, with teams assigned to measure wind, calculate altitude, record data.

### Beyond Mere Beauty

"It flies!" An exciting statement in any language. Even veteran kite makers are never blasé as a new kite meets the wind and comes to life for the first time. "It flies. It *really* flies!" Words of achievement—and amazement, too. Words to wipe out earlier failure: "I never had a kite that flew before." "My last kite broke before we got it put together."

A kite *must* fly, and to some of us, all kites are beautiful, but the students in one junior high arts-and-crafts class set out to go beyond mere beauty to the stunning, the dramatic, the humorous. Emphasis in this class was on fine appearance in the hand and in the air.

Students first made the demonstrated kite—a different one each week. Beginning with a proven design facilitated subsequent improvisation. (A successful first kite is important as a standard for comparison for the experiments that follow.) If someone wished to join the group after the basic kites were made, he could get an experienced kite maker to help him. Students were soon back for seconds and thirds, were teaching each other and readily building kites to answer questions. *Dutch kite:* "What will happen if I trim the bottom corners?" (Flies, but not as well; lifting surface reduced.) *Snake kite:* "What if I cut the tail to ribbons?" (Glorious variation; teacher is stunned.) *Eddy kite:* "What if I make tissue-paper windows and glue fringe all around?" (Excellent flier; rather monstrous in appearance.)

The inventiveness of each helped spark the imagination of all. And some brought their dreams to school: "I was flying my Snake after I fell asleep last night, and it had a notched tail like a dragon."

Three of the junior high students later accompanied me to a first grade class, where we helped 36 youngsters make and fly the Dutch kite. My assistants were impressed, having forgotten that the many skills required— measuring, folding, cutting, gluing, tying—were so difficult to master.

### Easy, Cheap and Fun

Classroom kites are easy to build, dependable fliers and made of readily available, inexpensive materials. Cost averages 25 cents per kite. A class period of 45 minutes allows plenty of time for construction, but building the kite is only half the fun; allow time for flying, too. Field kits for Flying Day should contain scissors, Scotch tape, string, crepe-paper streamers for tails, and a supply of notched reels, each wound with 50 feet of crochet thread, a sturdy, inexpensive flying line.

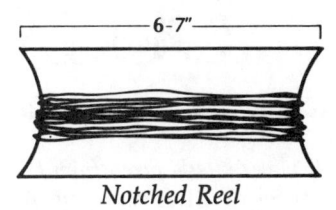

*Notched Reel*

Preparations for your class go like this: Be sure necessary tools are available. Provide for plenty of working space; yard-square kites can't be made on 24-inch desk tops. If the work is going to be done on the floor, move the desks out of the way. If tables are available, move the chairs out of the way. Provide good ventilation. Spread newspapers everywhere so cleanup is easy. Establish a materials center and put up a materials list and step-by-step instructions nearby. Put up a sample kite and lay out other samples in various stages of construction, thereby making the students less dependent on the teacher.

Provide a generous choice of paper and colors. One of the best things about kites is the sense of working with abundance. Plenty of everything, and the wind is free. If you flub the first, start over; there's still time to get it in the air.

I have found it best to spend the first ten minutes of each session making a kite "before your very eyes." As I work, I explain how a kite flies, tell the history of this particular kite, mention what *I* learned in last week's class, and harp on craftsmanship and the accompanying necessity for good tools.

During construction, if I find people struggling with dull scissors, blunt pencils or dented rulers, I make the point that while "a lopsided May basket will still carry flowers, we want these kites to *fly*."

Following the demonstration, students choose their materials and begin work. I circulate, answer questions, and try to ensure against fatal errors. When something of general interest occurs, I raise my voice and tell the whole class about it. When several people reach the point of setting the angle of the bridle, I stop the action and show everyone how. People who finish first help others, work at winding line on the reels so we will all be ready to fly at once, or settle down with one of my kite books.

Here are instructions for and some observations about four tested-and-true classroom models:

# DUTCH KITE

This all-paper kite is taken from the book Adventures With Paper by A. van Breda (Faber and Faber, Ltd., 1955). We use butcher paper, which many schools have in several bright colors. The Dutch kite, incidentally, is a remarkably durable object. Vacationing in Nebraska one summer and overcome by a desire to make use of the midwestern wind, I made a Dutch kite from a grocery bag, attached a strip of newspaper for a tail, and flew it on my brother-in-law's fishing line. When he suggested it would be sporty to try to shoot it down, I said, "Feel free." Nine rifle shots later, the kite was still flying steadily, although with a clipped tail. So we brought it in and found two well-centered hits. Later, my nephews put it up again, used all their ammunition, filled it with holes and finally cut the lower end of the bridle string with a lucky shot. Dutch was still floating at 15 feet when they decided to bring it down and present it to me as a trophy. The gallant kite made a fine exhibit back in my classroom.

The Dutch kite incorporates the basic elements needed for flight—a spine, a crosspiece, a bridle to hold the kite face to the wind, and a tail for stability. It flies easily in light breezes or heavy winds. It can be towed by a bicycle or walked around the park by a two-year-old. It is a tolerant kite, i.e., a less-than-perfect model will still fly.

**Materials for One Dutch Kite:**
Stiff paper (butcher paper), 12 by 16 inches; paper scraps for bridle; light string (crochet thread), 24 inches; toothpick; crepe paper for tail, one inch by four feet.

**Making the Kite:**
1. Fold and crease the paper the long way. Fold and crease again, 3/4 inch from center fold. Open so the folded section forms a ridge up the middle. This will be the front of the kite. (Illustration 1.)
2. Open paper flat. Fold and crease on a line 3 inches from the top (short way). Fold and crease 3/4 inch from this fold. Unfold this crease and cut on heavily marked lines at the top (Illustration 2). Open paper flat, back side up.
3. Brush glue on the top and bottom sections of the long middle fold (between the fold lines) but not on the cross-fold section where the H-shaped slit is. Fold in center, spreading sides out flat, as in Illustration 1, thus gluing the spine of the kite. The cut flaps on the cross fold should slide over each other, one coming out on top of the kite, the other on the back.
4. Glue these flaps down (across the slit) on front and back of kite.
5. On the back, brush glue on the cross-fold area. Bring together to form the cross ridge. Trim corners off top edges. (Illustration 3.)

**Making the Bridle:**
1. Take two scraps of paper, each 2 by 2½ inches, and fold in the middle, across the 2-inch dimension. Fold the other way and snip a small corner off the center fold, making a hole in the center of the paper. Open up. On one piece, cut about 3/4 inch up the middle fold. (Illustration 4.)
2. Tie half a toothpick to each end of the 24-inch string. Poke the sticks through the holes in the small papers, so the sticks ride in the creases and the papers are linked by the string. (Illustration 4.)
3. Over the top joint of the kite spine (parallel to the spine), glue the paper with the slit, which separates to fit over the cross ridge. The other end of the bridle is glued over the center ridge at the bottom of the kite. (Illustration 5.)

A simple way to set the bridle angle on a light kite is to slip a finger through the bridle string, so it forms a right angle with the kite at the juncture of the upright and cross ridges. With the other hand, pinch off a loop in the string, bringing it together about two inches from the top angle. Tie a loop.

**The Tail:**
1. Glue a 4-foot strip of inch-wide crepe paper to the bottom center back of kite. If the wind is strong and the kite flies erratically, add more. If wind is very light and kite will not rise, cut off a little.
2. Tie the flying line through the bridle loop.

**Variations:**
Using the three-to-four ratio, I make this kite in sizes down to 3 by 4 inches (onion-skin paper). Pocket-sized kites will fly if the wind is right and the flier is skillful.

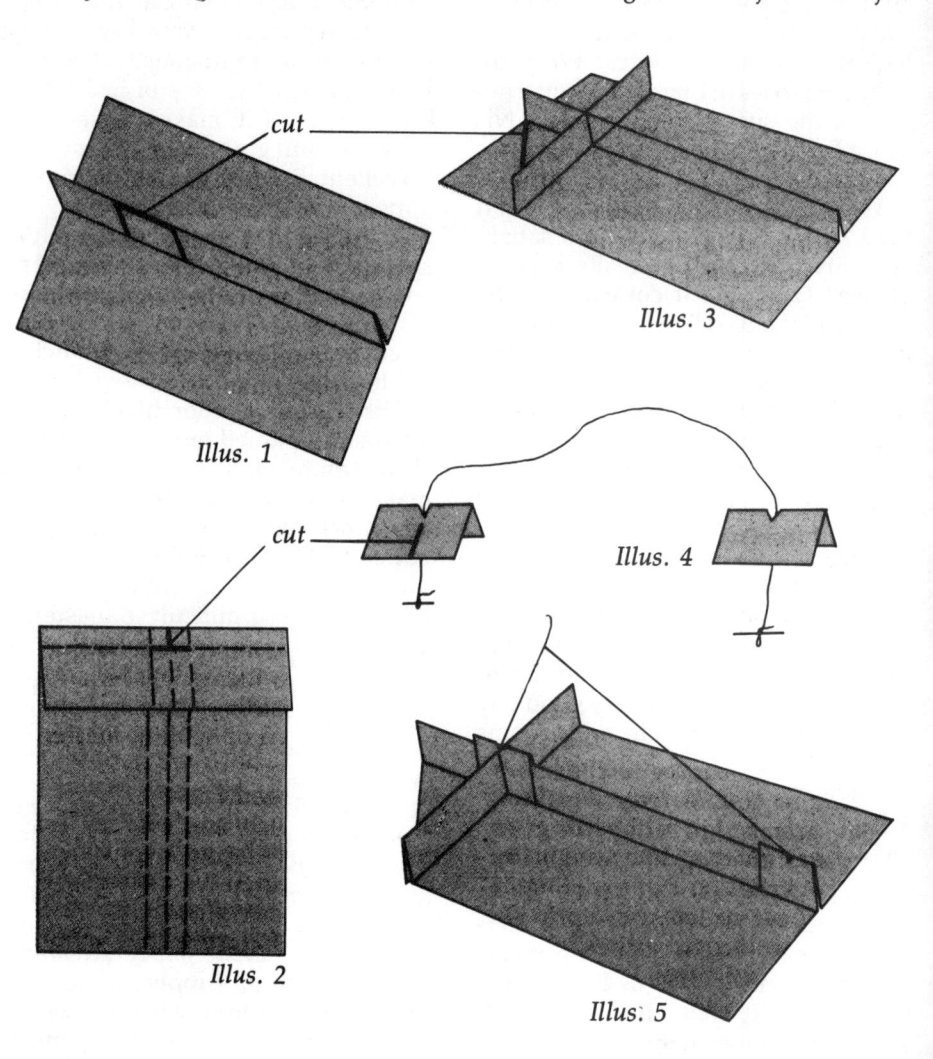

Illus. 1

Illus. 2

Illus. 3

Illus. 4

Illus. 5

POTPOURRI 187

# SNAKE KITE

A classic Oriental kite, the Snake has a 10-foot crepe-paper tail that makes it exciting to fly. A kite for light winds and dry days. Easy to make and tolerant of error. It can be mailed, flat, between two pieces of cardboard, as a greeting or small gift.

Match-stick bamboo reeds taken from window blinds are the best framing material for the Snake. One blind is enough for many kites. Rattan reed sold in craft shops for basket making can be used if the kite is scaled somewhat larger. (Rattan is not as flexible as bamboo, however.) When preparing for class, separate a number of reeds from the blind. Those that are too flimsy to bend into a strong, symmetrical arch should be discarded.

**Materials for One Snake:**
Tissue paper, 10 by 15 inches; crepe paper, 5 inches by 10 feet, cut across the grain (a roll of crepe paper is 10 feet long); match-stick bamboo reed, about 26 inches for arch, and scraps for spine and crosspiece; lightweight string, 60 inches, for bridle tissue scraps.

**Making the Kite:**
1. Illustration 1 is the kite face pattern. Cut patterns for the class from a stack of newspapers.
2. Trace pattern on tissue. Cut out.
3. Measure reed by bending it around curved edge of tissue, about 3/4 inch in from edge, ending about 1½ inches from bottom (straight) edge on each side. Break off correct length.
4. Spread glue on outer one inch of curved edge only. One person holding reed in place around the arch and another folding the glued tissue over it will keep the kite face flat.
5. Mark a vertical line down the middle of the kite. Cut a reed to run down this line from the top of the arch to 1½ inches from the bottom of the kite. Cover with a 2-inch strip of glued tissue.
6. Cut two reeds to fit between the ends of the arch. Cover with glued tissue. (Illustration 2.)
7. Turn kite over. This is the front. Make holes for 60-inch bridle string and tie over reeds as shown in Illustration 3.
8. Glue the tail to the paper flap at the bottom of the kite.

If this is a Flying Day, a good way to find the correct bridle angle is to let the wind do it. Hold bridle string over one finger and the wind will lift the kite to a good flying stance. Tie a loop here. Flying line is tied on through the loop. The bridle may also be set as for the Dutch kite. In a very light breeze, tail may have to be shortened.

**Variations:**
Tail may be cut into four or five streamers, striped with short lengths of crepe paper, tapered, fringed, cut into lace.

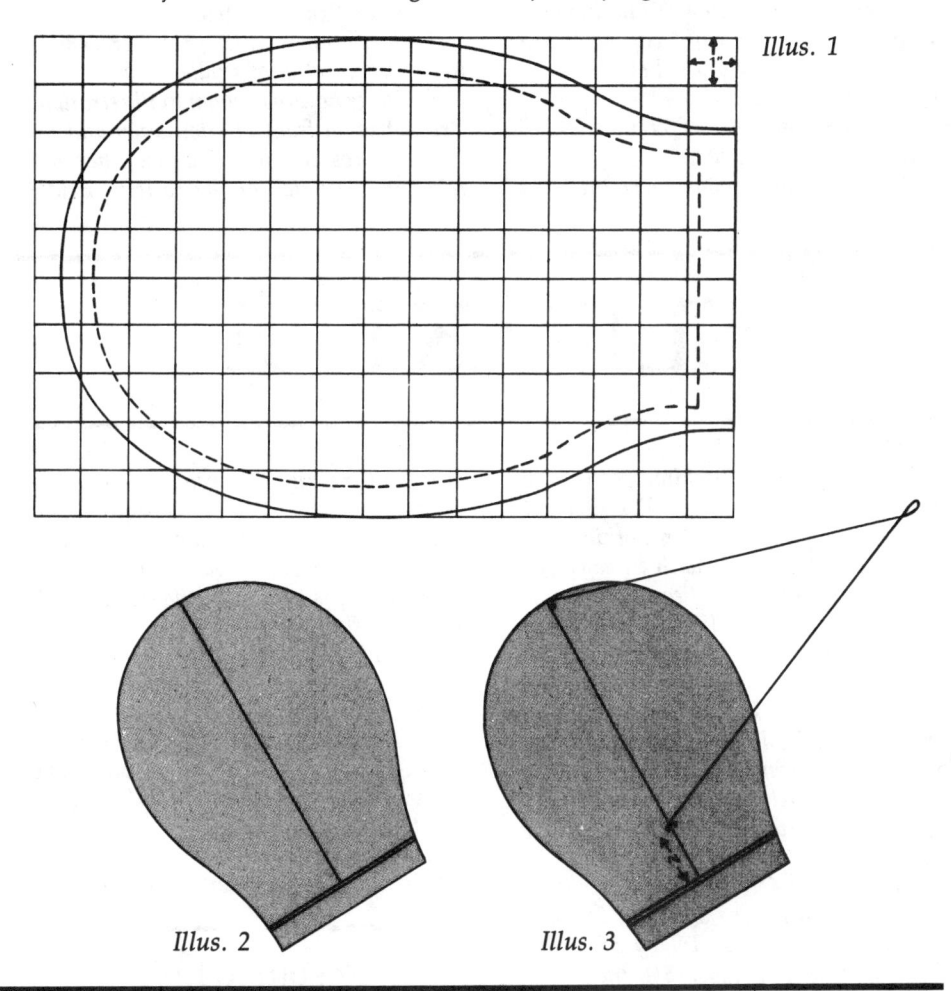

*Illus. 1*

*Illus. 2*  *Illus. 3*

# EDDY KITE

This is a U.S. classic, first patented in this country in 1897 by William Eddy, who more or less reinvented the bowed, tailless kite of Malaya. In our model, the crosspiece is the same length as the vertical spar, and they are joined at a point one fifth of the way down the vertical spar. Properly balanced, bridled and bowed, it flies without a tail and has tremendous lift. Ten- to 15-pound test monofilament fish line is excellent flying line for the heavier kites. However, my classes use the crochet thread reels for all test flights.

A successful Eddy kite must be built with precision. Construction is not difficult but field adjustments are almost always needed. A little experimenting will put every kite into the air. The Eddy kite can be scaled up to very large sizes. We build 24- and 36-inch models, both of which are practical classroom sizes.

I usually arrange with a shop instructor for kite sticks, which should be notched at each end.

Instructions for the Eddy kite are in most kite manuals, but the following method is also suitable for the classroom.

*illus. 1*

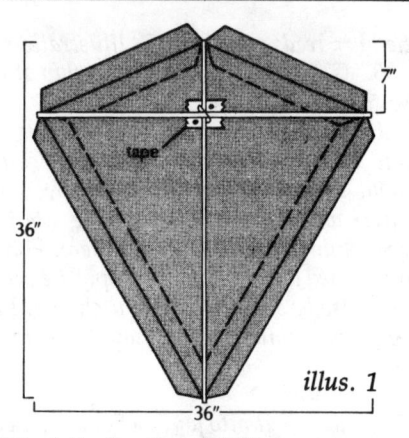

**Materials for One Eddy:**
Two kite sticks, 3/16 by 1/4 by 36 inches; tough string for framing, bridle and bowstring; tough lightweight paper to cover; tape for reinforcing bridle holes.

**Making the Kite:**
1. Mark midpoint of cross stick. Be sure this stick is flexible.
2. Mark 7 inches down on vertical stick.
3. Cross at right angles at marked points. Glue and tie.
4. Tie a loop at the end of the framing string, and slip it through the top notch. Weave and tie through each notch all around the kite, back to the top. Keep sticks at right angles. (Pass out small square cards for the builders to use in checking the angle as construction proceeds.)
5. Lay frame, cross stick down, on paper and trim, allowing a 3/4-inch flap to glue over string. Crease flaps over string and miter corners so stick ends are free and layers of paper don't build up. (Illustration 1.)
6. Glue flap over string.
7. Tape paper under center crosspiece to reinforce holes for bridle.
8. Make holes as shown in illustration. Bridle ties on front of kite, down and up over the crossed sticks. Tie the other end through the notch at the bottom. Bridle string should be 1½ times the vertical length of the kite.
9. Bow the kite—two people make it easy. One person bends the crosspiece like stringing a bow; the other slips a loop over the notch at one end and ties the string through the notch at the other end. Distance from bowstring to center of kite should be about 3 inches. (Illustration 2.)
10. Bridle angle must fit the wind-of-the-day. A light wind calls for more kite surface (higher bridle loop); a strong wind needs a reduced surface. Hold bridle by one finger and see what the wind wants.
11. Well-made Eddy kites fly without a tail, but if some kites cannot be balanced by changes in bow and bridle, a length of tail will give needed stability.

*Illus. 2*

# SLED KITE

This is another U.S. kite, patented by William Allison in 1956. The first successful semi-rigid kite, it is nothing more than a sheet of plastic with three vertical spars. Easy to make, flies in any wind. Needs a strong flying line. I use 15-pound test monofilament fishing line for the 36-inch model. Plastic drop cloths (1 mil) make invisible kites, while trash-can liners can add color. When working space is limited, we make a half-size—18-by-20-inch—model. Bamboo reeds serve as spars for this size, which requires streamer tails.

**Materials for One Sled Kite:**
Sheet of plastic, 1 or 1½ mil, 36 by 40 inches; three dowels, 1/8 by 36 inches; Scotch or plastic tape, 3/4 inch wide; strapping tape, 4 inches; monofilament for bridle, 80 inches of 15-pound test.

**Making the Kite:**
1. Make enough full-size patterns for the class, using a black marking pen, which shows through plastic, for the outlines. (See diagram.)
2. Tape pattern to working surface.
3. Smooth plastic over pattern. Secure with tape.
4. Lay spars in place and cover with tape, pressing firmly to plastic. Do not run tape across vent.
5. Running tape along inside of outer edge, outline kite and vent, overlapping on corners. Cut out. If cut is begun along the outer edge of the tape and the half-open scissors are pushed against the plastic while plastic is held taut, the scissors will slice smoothly along the tape.
6. Fold strapping tape over upper outside corners for reinforcement. Punch eyelets for bridle.
7. Tie monofilament through eyelets, leaving a loop so kite corners can move freely. Tie loop in center of bridle. Flying line ties through loop.

**Variations:**
This is the experimenter's kite. I answer all "Would this work?" questions with "Try it." Kite face can be decorated with indelible markers for a flying carpet, political message or greeting. Various colors can be taped together and colored tape used for outlines.

## Resource List

**Getting Started in Kitemaking** by H. M. Hunt and L. Hunt (Macmillan, 1971). Most useful in kite making. Also tells how to build the "clinograph," which we use to measure altitude, and how to calculate the "flying factor."

**Kite Craft** by Lee Scott Newman and Jay Hartley Newman (Crown Publishers, 1974). Detailed history, plans.

**Kites** by Wyatt Brummitt (Western Publishers, 1971). Tells how the Eddy and Sled kites can be flown in train, several on one line.

**World on a String: The Story of Kites** by Jane Yolen (World Publishers, 1969). History, grades five and up.

**Kite Tales,** a quarterly magazine published by the American Kitefliers Association (P.O. Box 1511, Silver City, NM 88061). An excellent reference for other experimental ideas.

*Margaret Greger is a kite maker and has taught kite making in teachers' workshops.*

## I CAN

☆ ☆ ☆ ☆ ☆ ☆ ☆ ☆ ☆

One of the components of Scholastic's fine library of early childhood and primary filmstrips is the I CAN series, sets 1 and 2. The filmstrips depict, in action sequences, kids in the process of experimenting, role-playing, building, painting, making up stories, taking care of themselves, singing and dancing, and cooking. Rather than teach kids the specifics of any of these, the filmstrips provide them with real models with which to identify, encouraging youngsters to tackle new skills for themselves and to develop competencies of their own.

In stimulating kids to be self-reliant, "Care of Myself" shows one boy doing tasks independently at home and in school—pouring his own cereal and milk, washing up, getting dressed, making his own bed, sharpening his pencil, doing a puzzle and several other everyday tasks. The filmstrip does not paint an unrealistic picture by saying that he can do each of the jobs quickly and easily. Some of the tasks are really difficult for youngsters. So the boy makes it clear that he can pour his milk only when the pitcher is "not too full." And buckling his belt causes more than just a few groans.

The sensitive treatment given these sound filmstrips makes for interesting and exciting viewing. The narrations, done by children in clear, understandable voices, enhance the filmstrips' authenticity. The photography is artistic and always technically excellent. The children in the pictures represent a well-balanced distribution of different ethnic groups. And sex stereotyping seems to have been carefully eliminated.

In addition to developing self-concept, the filmstrips are good starting points for getting kids involved in similar activities in the classroom. An excellent teacher's guide packaged with each set describes how to do many classroom activities related to the filmstrips. The guides also include frame notes, bibliographies of related materials and summaries for each filmstrip. Colorful posters about each filmstrip come with complete sets.

Set 1 comprises "Music and Dance," "Pumpkin Pie," "Something Beautiful" and "Zippety Zip." Set 2 includes "Cardboard City," "Care of Myself," "Living Things" and "Four Stories." All of the filmstrips are also available in a Spanish-English edition.

Order from: Scholastic Book Services, 904 Sylvan Ave., Englewood Cliffs, NJ 07632. Grade level: Preschool – 2. Cost: $59.50 per set, records or cassettes. Add 6 percent for postage and handling.

## BIG ROCK CANDY MOUNTAIN: Resources for Our Education

☆ ☆ ☆ ☆ ☆ ☆ ☆ ☆ ☆

BIG ROCK is literally and figuratively a giant book of excitement. Edited by Samuel Yanes and Cia Holdorf, this hefty publication is a potpourri of, among other things, book reviews, teaching techniques, descriptions of classroom materials, essays and children's writings.

Those browsing through it will discover exciting and innovative ideas. The editors have compiled several lists which describe available resources in specific areas. A filmography of British open education is one good example. In a section entitled "Playground Book" there are detailed instructions and diagrams for building fascinating play areas at school or home. Another section is devoted to education and philosophy from the East, including articles and reviews from Zen to Yoga.

Order from: Ms. Edith Mayer, Dial/Delacorte Press, Box 2000, Pinebrook, NJ 07058. Grade level: Teachers of all grades. Cost: $4 (list); $3.20 (school price). Postage will be added to billed orders.

FINIS.

# PRODUCT INDEX

## ACTIVITY CARDS
CREATIVE ART TASKS CARDS, *Arts & Crafts*, pp. 20–21
DROPS, STREAMS AND CONTAINERS: Science Activity Cards, *Science*, p. 136
GEOBOARD ACTIVITY CARD KIT, *Math*, p. 27
GEOBOARD ACTIVITY CARDS—Primary and Intermediate, *Math*, p. 27
GOOD TIME MATHEMATICS EVENT CARDS, *Math*, p. 28
MIRROR CARDS, *Science*, pp. 130–131
PEOPLE PROJECTS, *Kids Have Feelings, Too*, p. 159
STORY STARTERS, *Language Arts*, p. 87
TANGRAM CARDS, *Math*, p. 42
TANGRAM TASKS, *Math*, p. 42
WRITE ON!, *Language Arts*, p. 111
THE WRITING CENTER KIT, *Language Arts*, p. 103

## ACTIVITY WHEELS
THE NEEDS OF MAN, *Social Studies*, p. 57
READING REEL, *Language Arts*, pp. 106–107
TITLE TWISTER, *Language Arts*, pp. 106–107

## CALCULATING AND MEASURING TOOLS
THE ABA-TEN RULE, *Math*, p. 50
METRIC TAPE, *Math*, p. 25
MULTI-BASE CONVERTER, *Math*, p. 38
PACEMAKER PROTRACTOR, *Math*, p. 34
TRUNDLE WHEEL, *Math*, p. 39

## DUPLICATING MASTERS
AFTERMATH, *Math*, p. 45
LEARNING GAMES, *Potpourri*, p. 177
MAGIC SQUARES, *Math*, p. 26
NEW DIRECTIONS IN CREATIVITY, *Creativity*, p. 55

## FILMS
ANALYZING ADVERTISING, *Social Studies*, p. 58
AFTER THE FIRST, *Kids Have Feelings, Too*, p. 154
THE ANIMALS ARE CRYING, *Science*, pp. 132–133
BUY AND BUY, *Social Studies*, p. 58
CHILDREN ARE PEOPLE, *Potpourri*, pp. 176–177
DAFFODILS, *Language Arts*, p. 93
DECIDING, *Social Studies*, p. 58
FOG, *Language Arts*, p. 97
GREENHOUSE, *Kids Have Feelings, Too*, p. 153
JOHN MUIR: FATHER OF OUR NATIONAL PARKS, *Social Studies*, p. 63
JOSHUA IN A BOX, *Language Arts*, p. 98
KEVIN, *Kids Have Feelings, Too*, p. 158
A KITE STORY, *Language Arts*, p. 83
THE LEGEND OF JOHN HENRY, *Language Arts*, p. 104
THE MANY AMERICAN FILM SERIES, *Social Studies*, p. 59
MAPLE-SUGAR FARMER, *Social Studies*, p. 65
THE MARBLE, *Language Arts*, p. 112
THE MOLE FILM SERIES, *Language Arts*, p. 107
PIGS!, *Science*, p. 118
RIVER, WHERE DO YOU COME FROM? *Science*, p. 135
SEARCHING FOR VALUES, *Kids Have Feelings, Too*, p. 157
THE SELFISH GIANT, *Language Arts*, p. 92
SOCKEYE ODYSSEY, (Fabulous Freebee), *Science*, p. 121
A STORY A STORY, *Language Arts*, p. 107
THE STORY OF SOLO, *Science*, p.124
A STREAM ENVIRONMENT, *Science*, p. 128
WISE AND RESPONSIBLE CONSUMERSHIP, *Social Studies*, p. 58

## FILMSTRIPS
AMERICAN FOLKLORE, *Language Arts*, p. 105
CHARLOTTE'S WEB, *Language Arts*, p. 84
CROSSROADS, *Kids Have Feelings, Too*, p. 155
ECONOMICS FOR PRIMARIES, *Social Studies*, pp. 58 and 68
FIVE CHILDREN, *Social Studies*, p. 69
FIVE FAMILIES, *Social Studies*, p. 69
GETTING ALONG, *Kids Have Feelings, Too*, p. 155
I CAN, *Potpourri*, p. 189
JUST SO STORIES, *Language Arts*, p. 87
LEARNING ABOUT CONSUMER EDUCATION SERIES, *Social Studies*, p. 58
LET THE BUYER BEWARE, *Social Studies*, p. 58
LIFE IN RURAL AMERICA, *Social Studies*, p. 71
LISTENING, LOOKING AND FEELING, *Creativity*, p. 54
MOVING PEOPLE AND THINGS, *Social Studies*, p. 70
PEOPLE WHO ORGANIZE FACTS, *Social Studies*, p. 71
SOUND FILMSTRIP SETS 37 AND 38, *Language Arts*, p. 84
THRESHOLD FILMSTRIPS, *Language Arts*, p. 84
TYPICAL GYPS AND FRAUDS, *Social Studies*, pp. 58 and 66

## GAMES
ARITHMECUBES, *Math*, pp. 50–51
BALDICER, *Social Studies*, p. 64
BLEND AND BUILD 1, *Language Arts*, pp. 90–91
CONNECT, *Potpourri*, p. 165
CONSONANT JUMBLE, *Language Arts*, p. 100
CREATIVE EQUATIONS, *Math*, p. 49
CULTURE CONTACT, *Social Studies*, p. 64
EQUATIONS, *Math*, p. 33
FOO, *Math*, p. 47
GHETTO, *Social Studies*, p. 64
I WIN, *Math*, p. 40
MANCALA, *Math*, pp. 28–29
MARKET, *Social Studies*, p. 64
MATHEMATICS SPINNER KIT, *Math*, p. 33
METRICAT10N, *Math*, p. 25
READ AROUND, *Reading*, p. 8
STARPOWER, *Social Studies*, p. 64
SYSTEM 1, *Social Studies*, p. 64
TUF, *Math*, p. 47

## KIDS' ACTIVITY BOOKS
ADVENTURES WITH A CARDBOARD TUBE: First Science Experiments, *Science*, p. 127
AFTERMATH, *Math*, p. 45
AMERICAN FOLK TOYS: HOW TO MAKE THEM, *Arts & Crafts*, p. 17
A BALL OF CLAY, *Arts & Crafts*, p. 23
BE A FROG, A BIRD, OR A TREE, *Creative Movement & Play*, p. 115
COLOR CRAFTS, *Arts & Crafts*, p. 22
EXAMINING YOUR ENVIRONMENT, *Science*, p. 129
EXPERIMENTING WITH SEEDS AND PLANTS, *Potpourri*, p. 183
GOOD CENTS: EVERY KID'S GUIDE TO MAKING MONEY, *Social Studies*, p. 65
KIDS GARDENING, *Potpourri*, p. 183
MAKING SMALL THINGS LOOK BIGGER, *Science*, p. 127
MATHEMATICS IN THE MAKING, *Math*, pp. 40–41
MODEL CARS AND TRUCKS AND HOW TO BUILD THEM, *Arts & Crafts*, p. 23
OBSERVATION, *Science*, pp. 133–134
SCIENCE EXPERIMENTS YOU CAN EAT, *Science*, pp. 125 and 183
TRASH CAN TOYS AND GAMES, *Arts & Crafts*, p. 17
TURN NOT PALE, BELOVED SNAIL: A Book About Writing Among Other Things, *Language Arts*, p. 96
YELLOW PAGES OF LEARNING RESOURCES, *Social Studies*, p. 61
YOUNG MATH BOOKS, *Math*, pp. 44–45
YOUR CITY HAS BEEN KIDNAPPED, *Social Studies*, p. 60

## KIDS' REFERENCE MATERIALS
CENTER FOR SHORT-LIVED PHENOMENA EVENT REPORTS, *Science*, pp. 131–132
IN OTHER WORDS: An Introductory Thesaurus, *Language Arts*, p. 99
JACKDAWS, *Social Studies*, p. 60

## MEDIA EQUIPMENT
CONCEALED IMAGE PROCESS, *Potpourri*, p. 182

# PRODUCT INDEX

FILMSTRIP REPAIR KIT, *Do-It-Yourself Games & Media*, p. 81
QUICK SLIDE, *Do-It-Yourself Games & Media*, p. 75
THE SNAPSHOOTER, *Do-It-Yourself Games & Media*, p. 81
"U" FILM FILMSTRIP KIT AND SLIDE KIT, *Do-It-Yourself Games & Media*, p. 74

## MICROSCOPE

MICROSCOPE, *Science*, p. 121

## MULTIMEDIA KITS

CONSUMERISM UNIT (Scholastic Dimension Program), *Social Studies*, p. 58
THE IMAGE MAKERS: ADVERTISING IN A CONSUMER SOCIETY, *Social Studies*, p. 58
KOOKIE: THE MOTORCYCLE RACING DOG, *Reading*, p. 13
THE WRITING BUG: A SWARM OF WRITING EXPERIENCES, *Language Arts*, p. 106

## PLANTS AND ANIMALS

THE BUG HOUSE, *Science*, p. 137
BUTTERFLY GARDEN, *Science*, p. 117
HOME-GRO MUSHROOM GARDEN, *Science*, p. 120
PUNCH 'N GRO, (Fabulous Freebee), *Science*, p. 135

## RECORDS

LEARNING BASIC SKILLS THROUGH MUSIC (Volume 1), *Potpourri*, p. 180
SMALL VOICE, BIG VOICE, *Potpourri*, p. 175
TALES OF THE HOPI INDIANS, *Language Arts*, p. 101

## SELF-CHECKING DEVICE

VERI TECH, *Potpourri*, p. 181

## SLIDES

NATIONAL GALLERY OF ART SLIDE SHOWS, (Fabulous Freebee), *Social Studies*, p. 60

## SUPPLEMENTARY READING & ENRICHMENT

ADVENTURES IN THE CITY, *Reading*, p. 13
ALONG THE NIGER RIVER: An African Way of Life, *Social Studies*, p. 61
AMERICAN QUARTER HORSE Booklets and Posters, (Fabulous Freebee), *Potpourri*, p. 177
BODIES, *Science*, p. 121
BREAKTHROUGH BOOKS, *Reading*, p. 10
THE CALIBRATED ALLIGATOR, *Language Arts*, p. 95
CIRCLES, TRIANGLES AND SQUARES, *Math*, p. 46
CITY: A STORY OF ROMAN PLANNING AND CONSTRUCTION, *Arts & Crafts*, p. 20
CITY LEAVES CITY TREES, *Science*, p. 120
CITY ROCKS CITY BLOCKS AND THE MOON, *Science*, p. 118
COUNT AND SEE, *Math*, p. 41
EXPRESSION: BLACK AMERICANS, *Social Studies*, p. 61
THE GIVING TREE, *Kids Have Feelings, Too*, p. 160

ISHI, LAST OF HIS TRIBE, *Social Studies*, p. 60
THE LERNER SCIENCE FICTION LIBRARY, *Language Arts*, p. 95
THE LITTLE CARPENTER, (Fabulous Freebee), *Arts & Crafts*, p. 21
MAKING BABIES: An Open Family Book for Parents and Children Together, *Science*, p. 129
MAN LITERATURE SERIES, *Reading*, pp. 12–13
THE MONSTER BOOKS, *Reading*, p. 7
THE MORE MONSTER BOOKS, *Reading*, p. 7
PAL PAPERBACKS, *Reading*, p. 8
PICTURE BOOK OF THE REVOLUTION'S PRIVATEERS, *Social Studies*, p. 66
PHOTOGRAPHY—HOW IT WORKS BOOKLET, (Fabulous Freebee), *Do-It-Yourself Games & Media*, p. 75
RAILROAD PICTURES AND MAP, (Fabulous Freebee), *Social Studies*, p. 71
SCIENCE FICTION HALL OF FAME, Vol. 1, *Language Arts*, p. 95
THE STAR-SPANGLED BANNER, *Social Studies*, p. 59
TRUCKS AND THINGS YOU'LL WANT TO KNOW ABOUT THEM, (Fabulous Freebee), *Social Studies*, p. 73
THE UPSTAIRS ROOM, *Social Studies*, p. 66
WE ARE BLACK, *Reading*, p. 10
WRAPPED FOR ETERNITY: The Story of the Egyptian Mummy, *Social Studies*, p. 68
ZOO 2000, *Language Arts*, p. 95
ZOOMING IN: Photographic Discoveries Under the Microscope, *Science*, p. 121

## TEACHER RESOURCE MATERIALS

THE ACT OF WILL, *Creative Movement & Play*, p. 116
AN ACTIVITIES HANDBOOK FOR TEACHERS OF YOUNG CHIDREN, *Potpourri*, p. 165
ADVENTURES WITH PAPER, *Potpourri*, p. 186
AHA! I'M A PUPPET, *Language Arts*, p. 87
"All You Will Need to Know About Metric," *Math*, p. 49
ANALOG: SCIENCE FICTION—SCIENCE FACT, *Language Arts*, p. 95
BECOMING SOMEBODY, *Creativity*, pp. 54–55
BIG ROCK CANDY MOUNTAIN: Resources for Our Education, *Potpourri*, p. 189
BUILDING POSITIVE SELF-CONCEPTS, *Kids Have Feelings, Too*, p. 160
THE CAMERA COOKBOOK, *Do-It-Yourself Games & Media*, p. 75
CHANGE FOR CHILDREN: Ideas and Activities for Individualizing Learning, *Potpourri*, p. 168
CHILDREN AS FILM MAKERS, *Do-It-Yourself Games & Media*, p. 78
CLARIFYING VALUES THROUGH SUBJECT MATTER, *Kids Have Feelings, Too*, pp. 157–158
CONSERVATION EDUCATION PUBLICATIONS, (Fabulous Freebee), *Science*, p. 124
CORRUGATED CARTON CRAFTING, *Arts & Crafts*, p. 19
CREATIVE DRAMATICS FOR THE CLASSROOM TEACHER, *Language Arts*, p. 103
DEAL ME IN!, *Potpourri*, p. 175
DEVELOPING CREATIVITY IN CHILDREN, *Creativity*, p. 54
EARLY CHILDHOOD CONSUMER EDUCATION, *Social Studies*, p. 58

ECOLOGY REPRINTS, (Fabulous Freebee), *Science*, p. 132
EDC NEWS, (Fabulous Freebee), *Potpourri*, p. 168
ELEMENTARY LEVEL CONSUMER EDUCATION, *Social Studies*, p. 58
ENRICHED SOCIAL STUDIES TEACHING THROUGH THE USE OF GAMES AND ACTIVITIES, *Social Studies*, p. 66
ENVIRONMENTAL DISCOVERY UNITS, *Science*, p. 134
ESSENCE I AND II, *Science*, p. 133
EXPLORING THE ARTS WITH CHILDREN, *Arts & Crafts*, p. 21
FILMS KIDS LIKE, *Do-It-Yourself Games & Media*, p. 78
FOLK PUPPET PLAYS FOR THE SOCIAL STUDIES, *Social Studies*, p. 67
GETTING STARTED IN KITEMAKING, *Potpourri*, p. 188
A GUIDE TO MOVEMENT EXPLORATION, *Creative Movement & Play*, pp. 114–115
A HANDBOOK OF PERSONAL GROWTH ACTIVITIES FOR CLASSROOM USE, *Kids Have Feelings, Too*, p. 153
HOW 2 GERBILS 20 GOLDFISH 200 GAMES 2,000 BOOKS AND I TAUGHT THEM HOW TO READ, *Reading*, p. 7
AN IDEA BOOK FOR ACTING OUT AND WRITING LANGUAGE, *Language Arts*, p. 105
IMPROVISATION FOR THE THEATER, *Language Arts*, p. 92
INDIVIDUALIZING THROUGH LEARNING STATIONS, *Potpourri*, p. 170
INDUSTRIAL ARTS FOR ELEMENTARY CLASSROOMS, *Arts & Crafts*, p. 18
INEXPENSIVE EQUIPMENT FOR GAMES, PLAY, AND PHYSICAL ACTIVITY, *Creative Movement & Play*, p. 115
IT'S A TANGRAM WORLD, *Math*, p. 42
KITE CRAFT, *Potpourri*, p. 188
KITE TALES, *Potpourri*, p. 188
KITES, *Potpourri*, p. 188
LEARNING TO THINK IN A MATH LAB, *Math*, pp. 38–39
LOCUS, *Language Arts*, p. 95
THE MAGAZINE OF FANTASY AND SCIENCE FICTION, *Language Arts*, p. 95
MATH ACTIVITIES FOR CHILD INVOLVEMENT, *Math*, p. 41
THE MIND BENDERS, *Potpourri*, p. 167
MOVIES WITH A PURPOSE, (Fabulous Freebee), *Do-It-Yourself Games & Media*, p. 78
100 WAYS TO HAVE FUN WITH AN ALLIGATOR & 100 OTHER INVOLVING ART PROJECTS, *Arts & Crafts*, p. 20
OUTDOOR BIOLOGY INSTRUCTIONAL STRATEGIES, *Science*, pp. 126–127
OUTDOOR CLASSROOMS ON SCHOOL SITES, (Fabulous Freebee), *Science*, p. 131
PETS–'N–CARE, *Science*, p. 124
PRACTICAL APPROACHES TO INDIVIDUALIZING INSTRUCTION: Contracts and Other Effective Teaching Strategies, *Potpourri*, p. 168
PRELUDES TO GROWTH: AN EXPERIENTIAL APPROACH, *Kids Have Feelings, Too*, p. 160
PSYCHOSYNTHESIS: A MANUAL OF PRINCIPLES AND TECHNIQUES, *Creative Movement & Play*, p. 116
PUPPET MAKING THROUGH THE GRADES, *Language Arts*, p. 87

## 192 PRODUCT INDEX

PUT YOUR MOTHER ON THE CEILING: CHILDREN'S IMAGINATION GAMES, *Creativity*, p. 55
READING SUCCESS FOR CHILDREN BEGINS AT HOME, *Language Arts*, p. 99
RECYCLE NOTES: Crafts, Activities, Games, *Arts & Crafts*, p. 17
RESOURCES FOR YOUTH, (Fabulous Freebee), *Potpourri*, p. 182
SCIENCE FICTION IN THE CINEMA, *Language Arts*, p. 95
SCIENCE 5/13, *Science*, pp. 136–137
SECONDARY LEVEL CONSUMER EDUCATION, *Social Studies*, p. 58
SF: THE OTHER SIDE OF REALISM, *Language Arts*, p. 95
SIMULATION/GAMING/NEWS, *Social Studies*, p. 67
SLIDES WITH A PURPOSE, (Fabulous Freebee), *Do-It-Yourself Games & Media*, p. 78
STEVEN CANEY'S TOY BOOK, *Arts & Crafts*, p. 23
STRING SCULPTURE, *Math*, p. 31
SUGGESTIONS FOR A MORE CREATIVE TYPE OF TEACHING. SUBJECT: AMERICAN HISTORY, *Social Studies*, p. 57
SURVIVAL KIT FOR SUBSTITUTES: Activities That Work in Elementary Classrooms, *Potpourri*, p. 177
A TEACHER'S GUIDE TO COGNITIVE TASKS FOR PRESCHOOL, *Potpourri*, p. 179
TEACHING MATHEMATICS IN THE ELEMENTARY SCHOOL, *Math*, p. 28
TEACHING SCIENCE WITH GARBAGE, *Science*, p. 118
"Teaching Tools for Consumer Reports," *Social Studies*, p. 58
TWO HUNDRED PLUS ART IDEAS FOR TEACHERS, *Arts & Crafts*, p. 18
"An Updated Representative List of Methods and Educational Programs for Stimulating Creativity" (THE JOURNAL OF CREATIVE BEHAVIOR), *Creativity*, p. 54
THE USER'S GUIDE TO THE PROTECTION OF THE ENVIRONMENT, *Science*, p. 123
VERTEX, *Language Arts*, p. 95
WEBSTER'S INSTANT WORD GUIDE, *Language Arts*, p. 109
WORKJOBS, *Potpourri*, p. 169
WORKJOBS FOR PARENTS, *Potpourri*, p. 169
WORLD ON A STRING: THE STORY OF KITES, *Potpourri*, p. 188
WRITING FOR THE FUN OF IT: An Experience-Based Approach to Composition, *Language Arts*, p. 93
WRITING SUCCESS FOR CHILDREN BEGINS AT HOME, *Language Arts*, p. 99

## WORKBOOKS

AARON ZWIEBACK AND HIS WORLD OF WORDS, *Language Arts*, p. 97
AFTERMATH, *Math*, p. 45
ENHANCE CHANCE, *Math*, p. 27
MAKING IT STRANGE, *Language Arts*, p. 85
METERS, LITERS AND GRAMS, *Math*, p. 25
YOU AND ME, *Potpourri*, p. 180

---

ILLUSTRATIONS BY: *Michel Dattel,* Pages 79 (top), 85 (left); *Brenda Duke,* Pages 39 (left), 117 (bottom); *Nancy Freeman,* Page 183; *Nancy Lawton,* Pages 13 (bottom), 14, 18 (middle left, middle right), 20 (bottom), 25, 26 (bottom), 27 (bottom), 29, 32 (bottom), 33 (left), 39 (right), 41 (top), 42, 45, 46, 50 (right), 53 (middle, right), 62, 64, 67 (both), 69, 75, 81 (right), 87 (top), 90, 91, 99 (bottom), 100, 102, 115 (left), 119, 122, 127 (bottom), 131, 136 (bottom), 153, 159 (top), 160, 165 (top), 168, 170 (bottom), 182 (bottom); *Pat Maloney,* Page 112 (bottom); *Greg Mock,* Page 178; *Tony Naganuma,* Pages 80, 81 (left); *Mike Sanchez,* Page 180 (bottom left); *Christopher Stermer,* Pages 172–173; *Meredith Wilson,* Pages 28 (bottom), 87 (middle); *Dennis Ziemienski,* Pages 9 (top), 11, 12, 13 (middle), 19 (top), 26 (top), 30, 31 (both), 34, 35 (right), 38, 40, 41 (bottom), 43, 44, 47, 48–49, 55, 57, 60, 61, 63, 65 (top), 70, 72 (top), 78, 84 (top), 86, 94, 95 (both), 96, 108, 109 (both), 110, 111 (top), 114, 120 (top), 121 (bottom), 124 (bottom), 126, 128 (top), 132 (bottom), 135 (bottom), 154, 156, 159 (bottom), 169, 176, 181, 189 (top).

ILLUSTRATIONS FROM: *An Activities Handbook for Teachers of Young Children,* Page 165 (bottom); *American Folk Toys: How to Make Them,* Page 17 (top); *American Folklore,* Page 105 (right); *A Ball of Clay,* Page 23 (middle); *Be a Frog, a Bird, or a Tree,* Page 115 (bottom); *Breakthrough Books,* Page 10 (top); *Color Crafts,* Page 22 (middle, bottom); *Creative Equations,* Page 49 (right); *Developing Creativity in Children,* Page 54; *Environmental Discovery Units,* Page 134 (top right); *Geoboard Activity Card Kit,* Page 27 (top); *Good Cents: Every Kid's Guide to Making Money,* Page 65 (bottom); *Good Time Mathematics Event Cards,* Page 28 (top); *Joshua in a Box,* Page 98 (top); *Just So Stories,* Page 87 (bottom); *The Legend of John Henry,* Page 104; *Making It Strange,* Page 85 (top right, bottom); *Mathematics Spinner Kit,* Page 33 (right); *The Mind Benders,* Page 167 (left); *Monster Books,* Page 7 (top); *100 Ways to Have Fun With an Alligator & 100 Other Involving Art Projects,* Page 20 (top); *Picture Book of the Revolution's Privateers,* Page 66; *Recycle Notes,* Page 17 (bottom); *Science Experiments You Can Eat,* Page 125 (top); *The Selfish Giant,* Page 92 (bottom); *Sound Filmstrip Set 38,* Page 84 (bottom); *The Star-Spangled Banner,* Page 59 (top); *A Story A Story,* Page 107 (right); *Two Hundred Plus Art Ideas for Teachers,* Page 18 (top, bottom); *We Are Black,* Page 10 (bottom); *The Writing Center Kit,* Page 103; *You and Me,* Page 180 (right).

PHOTOGRAPHS BY: *George Fry III,* Page 160; *Carol Fulton,* Page 15; *Margaret Greger,* Page 184; *Phiz Mezey,* Pages 88, 89; *Donald Roman,* Pages 76 (top), 77; *Allen Say,* Pages 36, 37; *Ron Shuman,* Pages 161, 163; *Lars Speyer,* Page 22 (top); *Ed Zak,* Page 58.

PHOTOGRAPHS FROM: *The Aba-Ten Rule,* Page 50 (top, middle left); *Adventures in the City,* Page 13 (top); *Crossroads,* Page 155; *Daffodils,* Page 93; *Deal Me In!,* Page 175; *Essence I and II,* Page 133; *Examining Your Environment,* Page 129 (bottom both); *Fog,* Page 97; *Greenhouse,* Page 153; *Kevin,* Page 158; *Making Babies: An Open Family Book for Parents and Children Together,* Page 129 (top); *The Marble,* Page 112 (top); *Pigs!,* Page 118; *Searching for Values,* Page 157; *A Teacher's Guide to Cognitive Tasks for Preschool,* Page 179 (bottom); *Tuf,* Page 47 (top, middle); *Workjobs,* Page 169.